TOWN ORIGINS AND DEVELOPMENT IN EARLY ENGLAND, c.400–950 A.D.

TOWN ORIGINS AND DEVELOPMENT IN EARLY ENGLAND, c.400–950 A.D.

ℭℬ

Daniel G. Russo

Contributions to the Study of World History, Number 58

GREENWOOD PRESS
Westport, Connecticut • London

Library of Congress Cataloging-in-Publication Data

Russo, Daniel G.
    Town origins and development in early England, c.400–950 A.D. /
Daniel G. Russo.
      p. cm.—(Contributions to the study of world history, ISSN
0885–9159 ; no. 58)
    Includes bibliographical references and index.
    ISBN 0–313–30079–8 (alk. paper)
    1. Cities and towns—England—History. I. Title. II. Series.
HT133.R87 1998
307.76′0942′09021—dc20   96–35354

British Library Cataloguing in Publication Data is available.

Library of Congress Catalog Card Number: 96–35354
ISBN: 0–313–30079–8
ISSN: 0885–9159

First published in 1998

Greenwood Press, 88 Post Road West, Westport, CT 06881
An imprint of Greenwood Publishing Group, Inc.

Printed in the United States of America

The paper used in this book complies with the
Permanent Paper Standard issued by the National
Information Standards Organization (Z39.48–1984).

10 9 8 7 6 5 4 3 2 1

Contents

Preface

Medieval English towns have not received the amount of attention given to other components of medieval society, such as the village and manorial life. This imbalance is perhaps understandable, since England remained predominantly rural until recent times. Yet towns attained considerable prominence in medieval England as witnessed, for example, by their involvement in the economic revival of the high middle ages, by their participation in the growth of royal authority and parliaments, and by their role as centers of art and learning. Contrary to the impression conveyed by some accounts, towns did not suddenly appear in England with the Norman Conquest of 1066, nor for that matter with King Alfred's memorable fortification program of the Viking age. Rather, the first manifestations of urbanism in England are to be found in early to mid-Anglo-Saxon times, and it is to this formative period that the main focus of this study is directed. In order to establish a useful context, however, concise examinations of the earlier Romano-British and later Anglo-Saxon town have been provided. Also, much can be gained by viewing early English urban development in a wider European perspective.

A number of controversial issues pertaining to the origins and development of towns in early England have been addressed and, if not fully resolved, at least given greater clarity. Over the years, various branches of scholarship have made significant contributions to the study of medieval English towns. Few, however, have attempted to integrate these disparate works, and fewer still have been concerned directly with the earliest periods. But caution is in order, because the search for the origins of medieval institutions, though enticing, has ended too often in nebulous speculations. Real advances will be made only where conclusions are based firmly upon the available evidence. Some of the most important recent research on early

English towns has come from such fields as archaeology, geography, demography, and place-name study. If treated with care, these research-findings can be of great service to the historian, especially on those occasions when the documentary light dims and other sources of illumination must be sought. This book provides access to such significant but often unfamiliar evidence and offers new insights by judicious synthesis and analysis of the written and archaeological sources. It is intended primarily for students and interested general readers, although more specialized scholars hopefully will find something of value in these pages as well.

I would like to thank the editors of Greenwood Press for their courteous assistance throughout the course of this project. Also, I am especially grateful to Nancy E. Rouquié for her skillful and dedicated work on manuscript preparation, and to Kay M. Warren and John F. Sullivan for their proficient efforts on maps and figures. My thanks go as well to the helpful staff of the Homer Babbidge Library at the University of Connecticut and especially to Robert D. Vrecenak, Interlibrary Loan Librarian, who assiduously obtained numerous obscure reports and studies. My endeavor has been enriched by discussions and correspondence over the years with a number of scholars from this country and abroad. Special thanks are extended to: Susan Reynolds, Barrie Dobson, Edmund King, David Whitehouse, and Michael E. Jones, whose comments at various stages of my work have been both welcome and useful. All contents and conclusions here expressed are, of course, my own. Finally, I would like to convey my appreciation to my mentors and colleagues, in particular: F. A. Cazel, Jr., for his patient ear and careful eye for detail; Lawrence N. Langer, for keeping me in mind of the larger issues; and Allen M. Ward, for his beneficial support and encouragement.

Abbreviations

ASC	*Two of the Saxon Chronicles Parallel [Anglo-Saxon Chronicle]*. Edited by J. Earle and C. Plummer. 2 vols. Oxford: Clarendon Press, 1892-1899
ASE	*Anglo-Saxon England*, by F. M. Stenton. 3d ed. Oxford: Clarendon Press, 1971
B.A.R.	British Archaeological Reports. Oxford, 1974– .
C.B.A.	Council for British Archaeology, Research Reports. London, 1959– .
DB	*Domesday Book*. 4 vols. London: Record Commission, 1783–1816
MGH	*Monumenta Germaniae Historica*. Edited by G. Pertz et al. Hanover, 1826– .
– *AA*	*Auctores Antiquissimi*
– *EE*	*Epistolae*
– *SS*	*Scriptores*
– *SS RG*	*Scriptores Rerum Germanicarum*
– *SS RM*	*Scriptores Rerum Merovingicarum*

RIB   *The Roman Inscriptions of Britain*. Edited by R. G.
                 Collingwood and R. P. Wright. Oxford: Clarendon Press,
                 1965

VCH   *The Victoria History of the Counties of England*. Edited by
                 H. A. Doubleday et al. London, 1900–   .

Town Origins and Development in Early England, c.400–950 A.D.

Chapter 1

Introduction

This study seeks to shed new light on the development of towns in early England from late Roman to late Anglo-Saxon times. It focuses on the early and mid-Anglo-Saxon periods, that is, the fifth to the ninth centuries A.D., wherein the first recognizably urban entities in England emerged. But since towns, like other social institutions neither spring forth overnight nor remain static, it has been necessary to adopt a long-term view and play a Janus role, looking back to the age of Romano-British urbanization and ahead to the burghs of the Viking age and beyond. Such an extended chronological framework both facilitates the identification and analysis of various types of towns and their transformations over time and provides the opportunity to address a series of controversial issues spanning this early stage of English urban history. There are numerous obstacles and pitfalls, however. Indeed, as the distinguished historian F. M. Stenton observed, "No problems in the whole of Anglo-Saxon history are more difficult than those which relate to the origins of the English town."[1] Because the initial stages of English urbanism, like those of many medieval institutions, are but sparsely documented, elucidation requires careful analysis of a range of sources as well as effective conceptual and definitional approaches.

Although it is true that England remained predominantly rural until quite recently, towns were a prominent part of its topography, politics, and society during the Middle Ages. The foundations of the medieval English urban landscape, moreover, were established long before the Norman Conquest. Towns appear in some of the oldest Anglo-Saxon written sources, and this historical record of their early presence, albeit scanty, has been confirmed and illuminated by the recent work of archaeology and related disciplines. In fact, it now appears that by 1066 Anglo-Saxon England had become one of the most highly urbanized areas of northern Europe.[2] And just as the better documented towns of post-Conquest England are known to have been vital components of Norman and Angevin society, so are there grounds to believe that pre-Conquest towns played a central role in the formation and operation of Anglo-Saxon society. Previous research has not neglected this formative phase of English urban development, but much remains to be clarified.

VIEWS OF EARLY ENGLISH TOWN DEVELOPMENT c.1450–1995

The modern study of towns in England before 1066 evolved from various currents of scholarship reaching back over five hundred years. In general, the path has been from physical, topographic description to more source-critical institutional, legal, and socioeconomic studies. Many important contributions were made along the way to the elucidation of various stages in early English town development. Not all of these previous interpretations, including some currently popular ones, have equal claims to validity, however. More importantly, the different types of evidence and methods that have been employed, along with their separate findings, have not received adequate integration. Similarly, previous research has made some progress in refining the crucial issue of urban definition, that is, what can be considered a town and its distinguishing features in this period. Yet these definitions have tended to be overly exclusive and hence not applicable to the entire span of town development under consideration here.

The century that produced the first modern studies of early English towns was a difficult and tumultuous one. Fifteenth-century England appears at first glance as a woeful age of warfare, economic crisis, political and social conflict, and religious turmoil. Though beset with such adversities, the period also generated significant intellectual and literary activity. Especially noteworthy was a heightened interest in England's past stimulated by various factors: a surge of national pride following initial English victories in the last phase of the Hundred Years' War, the emergence of English as the dominant written medium of the realm, political and religious rivalries, and the expansion of education to an influential new middle class largely urban based and status hungry.[3] Legendary tales of the British and English past, composed now in the vernacular, were immensely popular, as, for example, the *Brut* and the *Morte d'Arthur*.[4] Indeed, such works appear to have whetted curiosity about the physical remains and topography supposedly related to this glorious olden time. Thus one finds, in a number of popular chronicles from both clerical and secular hands, the introduction of quasi-historical and topographical descriptions of regions, towns, and churches.[5] Aside from the chronicle insertions, individual studies also were appearing on the past and present topography and physical remains of various counties and towns. The best of these fifteenth-century works, such as those of William Worcester and John Rous, were on the whole commendable regional and town topographies based on personal observations and informants' reports. They were not, however, entirely free from an uncritical blending of fact and fancy.[6]

This thirst for knowledge of England's past, including that of its towns, increased significantly during the following century. Among many contributing factors were the mounting tide of Tudor national patriotism, the stimuli of sectarian controversy, the growing availability of printed books and, moreover, the diffusion of humanism into northern Europe and England from urban Italy.[7] Italian humanists had developed a new scholarship that sought to unravel the past by philological analysis of classical texts and the study of the material remains of classical antiquity.[8] These two kernels of secular humanist scholarship—philology and antiquarianism—found fertile soil in Tudor England, where they were applied to rediscovering the regional and urban past. The topographical-antiquarian impulse had especially fruitful consequences. Although antiquarianism has acquired a rather tarnished image today, it occupied the attention of some of England's finest early scholars, and at its best, it still has much of value to offer.[9] Indeed, one should not overlook the contribution of antiquarianism to the study of English towns even during the Middle Ages.[10]

Although antiquarianism, like humanism, was born of an admiration for the classics, antiquarian study in northern Europe and England quickly expanded its horizons to the pre- and postclassical periods.[11] At the same time, the topographical-antiquarian genre grew to include many more related topics, according to the pattern of ancient chorography.[12] The pioneer modern antiquarian in England was John Leland (c.1503–1552). Having studied at the University of Paris with prominent French and Italian humanists, Leland won the approval of King Henry VIII to undertake a complete chorography of England that would proceed county by county and town by town, employing a full range of topographical, philological, historical, and other material. The ambitious task, however, ultimately proved too large for any one man to accomplish. Leland's extensive manuscript notes (the *Itinerary*), based on a decade of travels and archival study through the realm, were passed on to fellow scholars and became a mine of information for later research.[13]

A younger contemporary of Leland, the jurist William Lambarde (1536–1601), succeeded to the chorographic mantle. His famous *Perambulation of Kent*, completed c.1570, was published at London in 1576.[14] This county study commences with a map of the Anglo-Saxon Heptarchy—the seven pre-Viking age kingdoms—and proceeds to a brief sketch of their locations and ethnic inhabitants.[15] This is followed by a lengthier introductory chapter on the description and history of the shire, which includes

discussions of its etymology, climate and land use, Anglo-Saxon kings of
Kent, early administrative divisions, and lists of towns, markets, religious
establishments, castles, and current nobility and gentry.[16]

In the subsequent main body of the *Perambulation,* Lambarde provides
detailed topographical-historical accounts of each major place in the shire
via circuits within its two dioceses of Canterbury and Rochester. Most
entries are prefaced by etymological analysis (often derived from Leland)
and contain numerous pertinent historical references, along with occasional
oral reports and topographical notes. Lambarde shows particular interest in
the Anglo-Saxon period; indeed, features of the Roman and pre-Roman past
are virtually ignored.[17] This is not entirely surprising, for Lambarde was
associated with those scholars who, under the patronage and direction of
such prominent men as Matthew Parker (Archbishop of Canterbury) and
William Cecil (Lord Treasurer Burghley), were avidly collecting, editing, and
printing all Anglo-Saxon and subsequent medieval manuscripts upon which
they could lay their hands.[18]

Although Lambarde's *Perambulation* was on a more restricted county
scale and included fewer topics than Leland's work, it popularized the genre
of town studies within regions. His greater use of historical documentation,
especially that of the previously neglected Anglo-Saxon and later medieval
periods, is also significant. Lambarde was rewarded for his lifetime archival
work with appointment by Queen Elizabeth I as Master of the Rolls (1597)
and by a renowned, very cordial audience with the queen at Greenwich
Palace only several weeks before his death.[19]

The kind of full-scale chorographic study that Leland envisioned was
finally accomplished by the Oxford-trained classical scholar, William
Camden (1551–1623). Camden began his research with a series of antiquarian travels through the country, with special attention given to Roman routes
and towns listed in the third-century A.D. roadbook, the Antonine Itinerary
(*Itinerarium Antoninianum*). By combining personal observations of Roman
remains, including coinage and inscriptions, with local informants' reports,
archival studies, and the researches of his predecessors such as Leland, he
was able to make reasonable identifications of most major Roman town
sites. These preliminary notes formed the basis of Camden's principal work,
the *Britannia,* first published in Latin in 1586.[20] Camden had been urged for
some years to produce such a sweeping study by his continental humanist
friends such as the geographers Ortelius and Mercator. Moreover, his own
countrymen, including Lambarde, Robert Cotton, and Richard Hakluyt,
provided steady encouragement and a constant stream of topographic-
antiquarian information which Camden often incorporated.[21]

In its first edition, the *Britannia* was essentially a work on the antiquities
of Roman Britain designed to demonstrate to continental scholars that
Britain had indeed been an important part of the Roman Empire and shared

in Europe's Roman heritage.[22] Its form and some topics were similar to those Lambarde had employed, but the scope was kingdom-wide, more information and detail of all kinds were employed, and greater attention was given to the Roman and British past. After a lengthy general ethnographic and historical introduction, Camden takes his readers on a circuit of counties arranged by correspondences with British tribal divisions, passing selectively from town to town with discussions of each site's etymology, topography, notable archaeological remains, and references in historical records.[23]

The *Britannia* was an instant success not only among continental scholars (who dubbed Camden "the British Strabo") but also in England, where it seems to have tapped into the swelling stream of Tudor national patriotism and urban middle-class aspirations.[24] This initial popularity prompted Camden to enlarge the *Britannia* considerably for later editions. His new material included additional relevant historical documentation critically examined and referenced, maps and illustrations, local genealogies of noble families, and much added archaeological and epigraphic evidence of towns and other sites drawn from his continuing travels, archival research and correspondence.[25] Although Camden's treatment of individual towns is not as fulsome, lively, or entertaining as those of Leland and Lambarde, it nonetheless represented an important advance by its application of disciplined order and critical interpretation to a wide body of evidence in a clear, objective, and persuasive style.[26] Indeed, the *Britannia* became an inspirational model and standard for further studies of individual English towns and towns within regions.

During the several decades after Camden's *Britannia* made its appearance, a number of individual town studies were undertaken that employed the new, broader, yet more source-critical chorographic techniques. The most justly celebrated of these works was the *Survey of London* by John Stow (1525–1605), begun c.1590 and published in 1598.[27] Stow was a third-generation native citizen of London, a close friend of Lambarde, Camden, and many other antiquarian luminaries, a lifelong bibliophile, and an indefatigable record searcher. Indeed, he had already established his reputation as an able chronicler several decades before presenting his account of London. Despite the fact that he had no formal university instruction (he was a tailor by trade), Stow acquired adequate linguistic skills in Latin, French, and Old English during the course of his lifelong scholarly pursuits. In addition to his familiarity with the standard classical, medieval, and contemporary histories, he had access to the public records of the realm, monastic and town chronicles, and London's municipal archives.[28] The compelling motives behind the *Survey* were clearly Stow's pride in London and the wish to contribute to the new chorography. In his Preface, dedicated to the Lord Mayor and citizens of London, Stow states that it was after reading Lambarde's *Perambulation* and becoming aware of current work such as Camden's that he had "attempted the discovery of London, my native soil and country."[29]

The *Survay* commences with a brief but sweeping narrative introduction extolling the dignity of London from pre-Roman times to the fourteenth century, replete with pertinent citations from classical and medieval authors.[30] This is followed by detailed descriptions and historical discussions of the town's main topographic features: its waterways, bridges, gates, and towers, along with excurses on popular customs and biographies of London worthies.[31] The subsequent main body of the *Survay* consists of a systematic, orderly perambulation of the town ward by ward. All relevant physical features are described in detail with a skillful combination of personal observation, critical use of historical evidence, and reports of local informants.[32]   Stow concludes his account with appendices, mainly in annalistic form, of the bishops of London since the seventh century, London's mayors from the twelfth century,[33] and the first printed version of William fitz Stephen's important *Descriptio Londoniae* (c.1180).[34]   Also of note is Stow's inclusion of a short treatise (c.1578) by an anonymous London citizen that outlines the town's history, emphasizes its current utility to the realm, and briefly examines town origins and types of towns through etymological and functional analysis.[35]

Stow possessed the rare ability to collect, integrate, and analyze a prodigious array of topographic-historical-antiquarian detail and present it in an orderly, coherent, and entertaining fashion. Taking great pains to verify his facts, he cast a skeptical eye on some of the more fabulous accounts of early British history and refused to be influenced by partisan religious controversy.[36] The *Survay of London* applied the new historical chorography to the investigation of individual English towns. Indeed, by skillfully and engagingly interweaving past and present, this classic study made London truly come alive and is still a delight to read.

Stow's study of London stimulated further work on other English towns in the following decades, yet few of them matched Stow's skill at integrating and analyzing diverse evidence from many periods.[37]   There were several notable exceptions, however. William Somner's *The Antiquities of Canterbury* (1640) was an able chorographic treatise much in the tradition of Stow.[38] Also noteworthy is William Webb's *A Description of the City and County Palatine of Chester* (1656), an admirable wide-ranging topographical-historical work.[39] Additional town studies also were appearing in a flood of new seventeenth-century regional chorographies. Although these works presented some valuable topographical and archaeological evidence on the towns described, most of them were rather mediocre, lifeless accounts, with only limited use and analysis of historical sources.[40] Indeed, on the whole, antiquarian research of the early seventeenth century had become more concerned with pragmatic matters that directly affected local gentry, such as genealogy, heraldry, and land-title searches.[41] It was only after the English Civil War that a new generation of scholars would make more substantial progress toward illuminating the history of individual towns and regions.

As we have seen, the study of English towns began and continued within the context of antiquarian research which focused on such topics as topography, philology, and archaeology. As time went on, the use of historical evidence in such works increased, but only in exceptional cases were the written sources relating to towns subjected to critical, systematic analysis. The great change occurred when antiquarian study became more concerned with explanation than with compilation.

Credit for inaugurating this new age properly belongs to Henry Spelman (1564–1641) whose comparative examinations of charters and feudal law paved the way for modern medieval historical study.[42] Spelman, moreover, served as patron and mentor to a number of promising young English scholars who shared his passion for archival and antiquarian study. The most renowned of them was William Dugdale (1605–1686). Although best known for his editorship of the cooperative project that resulted in the *Monasticon Anglicanum*—that great assemblage of ecclesiastical charters and mine of medieval socioeconomic history[43]—Dugdale also produced an important regional chorography of a new type, *The Antiquities of Warwickshire* (1656). This study, though not devoid of the usual topographic, etymologic, and genealogical fare, is distinguished by its preponderance of written evidence regarding the county and its towns that is not merely collected and transcribed but critically examined in support of clearly presented views.[44] Indeed, in *Warwickshire* and Dugdale's other works, one can observe the process whereby antiquities (and specialized antiquarian methods) became subordinate evidence for historical interpretation.[45] Thereafter the majority of town studies were primarily historical examinations based on and including increasing quantities of documentary evidence.

The two most influential works of this type after Dugdale were Robert Brady's *An Historical Treatise of Cities and Burghs or Boroughs* (1690) and Thomas Madox's *Firma Burgi* (1726). Brady was a careful and exacting historian who repeatedly proclaimed the necessity of proceeding from primary written evidence rather than preconceived theories. His *Treatise* focused mainly on town charter evidence of the Norman and Angevin periods. Brady contended that English towns originated in royal grants for the benefit of trade; hence urban authority and privileges derived from the king, who could alter them at will. This royalist interpretation, though systematically documented and argued, was clearly one-sided. Indeed, Brady's work became a main support for late Stuart policies aimed at undermining the authority of local municipal corporations. Moreover, since the *Treatise* had little to say about the development or condition of towns before 1066, it by no means represented a comprehensive English urban history.[46]

Madox's *Firma Burgi* was essentially a specialized study of the rents rendered to the king or other lords by certain English towns during the thirteenth and fourteenth centuries. It merits recognition as a pioneer monograph on one important aspect of medieval English urban and administrative history.[47] Of particular value was Madox's painstaking and skillful use of public record evidence regarding the towns and his inclusion of numerous pertinent extracts therefrom. Madox, as Royal Historiographer, had already produced the first comprehensive, systematic work on post-Conquest diplomatics, as well as a detailed study on medieval royal financial administration based firmly on primary documents clearly distinguished by type.[48] Although the *Firma Burgi* may be criticized for underrating the sense of historical development,[49] it demonstrated what could be accomplished on a narrow subject by meticulous, objective examination of primary written sources.

The last major contribution to this genre of town studies was H. A. Merewether's and A. J. Stephen's *History of the Boroughs and Municipal Corporations of the United Kingdom* (1835). This ambitious work, much broader in its chronological scheme than that of Brady or Madox, was considered the standard study of this type until nearly the end of the nineteenth century.[50] It contained copious extracts of relevant sources ranging from the Anglo-Saxon laws and *Domesday Book* to town charters and public records. Unfortunately, this material was haphazardly arranged and only superficially examined. Moreover, the work was marred by its overriding purpose of supporting contemporary political programs of municipal reform. Although it contained a wealth of sources and significant detail, partisan generalization outweighed rigorous historical analysis.

In the course of the nineteenth century, town studies, as individual monographs and within regional works, proliferated. Indeed, by the end of the century nearly every English town had its own history in print. Not all these works were of the same quality. Some were quite good, but many exhibited little attention to town records, contained interminable discussions of antiquarian and genealogical material, and offered considerable vague generalizations regarding their town's earliest periods.[51] Yet the local archival research involved in some of the better of these studies generated an important interpretation relating to early English towns which led to further productive debate.

It was Thomas Wright who in 1847 first suggested, on the basis of his research in town archives, that certain institutional features of Anglo-Saxon and later medieval towns were direct continuations of Roman urban customs. For example, he saw the various Anglo-Saxon town officials, or reeves, as linear successors to Roman town magistrates, groups drawn from the highest-ranking town classes.[52] Wright's suggestions were adopted and expanded by historians such as H. C. Coote and C. H. Pearson into a broad "Romanist" theory, which postulated the endurance of many Roman cultural and institutional elements into the Anglo-Saxon age and beyond. Among the range of proposed Roman urban continuations were such features as town self-government, communal defense and guild associations, coin minting, and extramural burial.[53] But as E. A. Freeman and others clearly pointed out, this theory, though quite ingenious, was built more on general, circumstantial analogies than on any firm evidence adduced to support such direct derivations.[54] Nonetheless, the Romanist view retained supporters for some time and also found its way into a number of corollary fields.[55] Indeed, it was to reemerge in an altered form in recent times, as we shall see.

As the nineteenth century advanced, certain important transitions can be observed in the research- literature of early English towns. On the one hand, there were more frequent treatments of town development within general histories of England or of England within medieval Europe. As might be expected, however, most of these analyses were rather brief and superficial. In general, the formative Anglo-Saxon stages were nearly ignored or glossed over, with often contradictory comments. After some lamentations about the documentary poverty of the early Anglo-Saxon period, there would be a swift progression to the Alfredian burghs and later boroughs.[56] More detailed discussions appeared in works with a narrower focus on early medieval England. In these studies, moreover, one can observe the Romanist interpretation of town development in England retreating before the onslaught of a pervasive new Germanist view. Thus Freeman, in the preliminary chapters to his influential study of the Norman Conquest (1867–1879), forcibly contends that the Anglo-Saxons had "utterly swept away" all remnants of Romano-British institutions including the towns. Indeed, this extirpation was actually a very good thing because it enabled the Anglo-Saxon conquerors (who were then in a state of "healthy barbarism") to forge a virile new civilization. The first English towns, Freeman emphasizes, were thus not survivors from Roman times; the English town "is a thing wholly of English growth."[57] This interpretation was carried forward by other prominent English historians of the late nineteenth century, such as J. R. Green and J. H. Ramsay. In these works, the destruction of Romano-British towns by Anglo-Saxon fire and sword was regarded as but one aspect of a fortuitous process whereby Britain became thoroughly Germanized. In effect, the first Anglo-Saxon towns were seen as types of settlements transposed with only slight changes from the coasts and forests of Germany.[58]

Credit for having introduced this Germanist view into the historiography of early England and its towns must be given to a group of specialized Anglo-Saxon scholars of the early nineteenth century. For example, Sharon

Turner, in his wide-ranging study of Anglo-Saxon political, cultural, and legal history (1799–1805), had emphasized the pervasive Germanic nature of Anglo-Saxon institutions.[59] His discussion of Anglo-Saxon towns focused, however, on the fortified places or burghs established by King Alfred and his successors with only occasional allusions to the pre-Alfredian period. Like writers of previous centuries, Turner did not make clear distinctions among various types of Anglo-Saxon towns but spoke collectively and interchangeably of "cities," "towns," "burghs," "fortresses," and "castles." Although his treatment of towns was restricted and ill defined, it sounded the Germanist chord by suggesting, for example, that Anglo-Saxon townspeople retained a considerable measure of the liberties enjoyed by all free members of the early Germanic community.[60] This Germanist view is also conspicuous in the institutional sections of Lappenberg and Thorpe's comprehensive history of Anglo-Saxon England (1845). Indeed, the authors trace the origins of English municipal organization to Anglo-Saxon guild associations, which they claim were descended from the communal sacrificial gatherings of the early Germans.[61]

The scholar who undoubtedly exerted the greatest influence on this Germanist school and its views of early town development in England was the prominent Anglo-Saxonist J. M. Kemble (1807–1857). Best known for his six-volume edition of Anglo-Saxon charters and other documents,[62] Kemble also produced an important institutional treatise, *The Saxons in England* (1849), whose very title conveys much of the author's intentions. Kemble applied to Anglo-Saxon studies the concepts and methods then being employed by German historians in regard to their own early institutions. Based on his formidable knowledge of Anglo-Saxon historical sources as well as Anglo-Saxon and comparative Germanic literary works, Kemble's study found a receptive audience and remains stimulating reading today, although many points of detail did not stand up well to subsequent criticism.

Kemble dealt in an organized and fluent fashion with both the fate of Romano-British towns and the place of the first Anglo-Saxon towns within their social context. Underlying all his remarks was an intense national pride in English institutions and their antecedents.[63] According to Kemble, the towns of Roman Britain were feeble from the start because their leading classes never were treated as equal partners and participants in the fruits of Roman civilization. Mounting oppression by late Roman officials so demoralized British urban nobles that fewer efforts were made to maintain the towns. This urban decline accelerated when the first Anglo-Saxon invaders interrupted the lines of communication as well as the local commerce and industry on which the towns depended. Few Romano-British towns, he contended, actually were taken by force; most simply crumbled through neglect.[64] Indeed, Kemble maintained that the Anglo-Saxons, like the early Germans described by Tacitus, were unfamiliar with towns and wanted to avoid them. On occasion they might forcibly expel the wretched British inhabitants from these deteriorated places of refuge, but only rarely would they take possession.[65]

According to Kemble the first Anglo-Saxon towns of the invasion age had a "totally independent origin" from Roman towns. They were the fortified wooden enclosures of local nobles in a rural context to which freemen flocked for protection, followed by craftsmen and traders. Later, a rural monastery might serve as the focus of a similar early town.[66] In Kemble's view early Anglo-Saxon towns thus were part of the initial settlement organization of Anglo-Saxon England, essentially transposed from the Germanic homelands. Following the established work of German historians, he situated the early Anglo-Saxon town within the basic Germanic settlement unit (*Mark*) as an association of freemen (*Markgenossenschaft*) gathered for protection. In time the town would acquire distinctive economic and legal functions, but it remained in essence a rural community with its constitution based on elements of voluntary association.[67] The problem with Kemble's construction was that it rested too heavily on continental Germanic analogies of much earlier or much later date. The Anglo-Saxon evidence for the *Mark* is rather meager, in fact, and does not support the sweeping suppositions he presented.[68] Nonetheless, Kemble's views had a deep impact not only on the treatment of early town development in general, and more specialized histories, but also on the mounting tide of nineteenth-century constitutional and legal studies dealing with English town origins.

Foremost among English constitutional historians of a great constitutional age was William Stubbs (1825–1901), Regius Professor of Modern History at Oxford and later Bishop of Oxford. In the widely read study of this painstaking scholar, *The Constitutional History of England* (1874–1878), the Germanist theory of early English institutional and town development found expression and some judicious modifications. First, Stubbs essentially reiterated Kemble's version of the fall of Roman Britain: its ruling classes were only superficially Romanized, and they were so disheartened and enervated after the Roman withdrawal that they were unable to offer a manly resistance to Anglo-Saxon invasion. Britain succumbed to fire and sword and its towns generally remained derelict, although a very few may have been continuously occupied. Any influence of Roman urbanism on Anglo-Saxon towns was negligible at best, however.

For Stubbs, the Anglo-Saxon invasion involved large-scale tribal movements and the transposition of Germanic social organization and institutions which were nevertheless altered in the new land.[69] Thus Stubbs agreed with von Maurer and Kemble that the *Mark* was the basic form of sociopolitical organization among the early Germans but denies its existence as such in England. Rather, he argued, it was the Anglo-Saxon township (*tunscipe*) that formed the basis of early English social structure and local administration. According to Stubbs, the Anglo-Saxon township "represented the principle of the *Mark*," the self-governing rural village community, and could be either fully free or dependent on a lord; in either case it possessed its own court and elected officials.[70] Indeed, the Anglo-Saxon burgh was "simply a more strictly organized form of the township" that originated in the fortified house (*tun*) of a powerful man or around a great monastery or at a site favorable for commerce. Later burghs and "large towns" such as London were in effect collections of townships with expanded constitutions resembling those of the larger territorial divisions, the hundreds.[71] Stubbs's work is significant for its authoritative espousal of the Germanist theory of early English town development, albeit in a somewhat less strident, more cautious manner and for the constitutional and legal direction it gave to further research.

Stubbs's comments on early English towns were carried forward to new directions by his distinguished younger contemporary, Frederick W. Maitland (1850–1906), Downing Professor of Law at Cambridge. Maitland's monograph on this subject, *Township and Borough* (1898), followed Stubbs's lead and placed the origin of English towns within the context of the rural township. He pointed, for example, to the enduring agricultural component of medieval English towns such as their intramural fields and commonly worked surrounding lands.[72] Yet he also suggested elsewhere that the town became distinct from the village when it was fortified during the Viking wars and received the special protection of the king's peace. Thus according to Maitland, the ninth-century Anglo-Saxon burgh/borough was a new military town whose institutions and privileges derived from the king. In essence it was a royal fortress manned by a garrison of local noble retainers whose land tenure was encumbent on burghal defense.[73]

Maitland expounded this "garrison theory" more fully in his classic study, *Domesday Book and Beyond* (1897). In this careful and level-headed documentary analysis, Maitland observed that many eleventh-century burghal properties recorded in the Great Survey of 1086 are said to have been attached to outlying rural estates. He regarded this as a vestige of earlier arrangements whereby local nobles maintained dwellings in the burgh to perform their required garrison-duty more easily. On the other hand, he noted that Domesday boroughs display a marked "tenurial heterogeneity," that is, ownership by various classes of people. Maitland contended that this condition arose primarily in the century before *Domesday Book*, when earlier military arrangements had become obsolete and the borough acquired a more commercial character.[74] His description of burghal development concluded with an interesting definition of the late Anglo-Saxon borough as a fortress, a place with a court, and a market center.[75]

Maitland's garrison theory was criticized for its emphasis on the military origin of the borough. Such attacks probably were justified in regard to the early exposition of this theory. But there seems to have been little recognition that Maitland did in fact allow for the operation of other factors, such as commerce in borough development.[76] He must be given due credit for his sense of institutional evolution and his attempts at definition, all accomplished with a firm command of the documentary sources and a sensible, logical style.

The mainly negative response to Maitland's work also was due in part to the subsequent exaggerated application of the garrison theory by his disciple, Adolphus Ballard. In a sweeping and none-too-critical fashion, Ballard asserted that all boroughs that display "composite" holdings arose from the practice of noble landholders stationing their retainers there and that this arrangement lived on in Norman castle-guard.[77] Mary Bateson, one of Maitland's Cambridge colleagues, suggested that tenth- and eleventh-century burgesses, though legal members of their burgh, actually resided on their appurtenant estates. Indeed, she contended that the distinguishing feature of the Anglo-Saxon borough itself was possession of its own court.[78] The American medievalist Morley de Wolf Hemmeon also contributed an important study on the origin and development of burgage tenure, the distinctive, heritable system of town landholding by money rent in return for all services.[79] Such works steadily refined the constitutional and legal aspect of early English town origins and development.

Beginning in the late 1920s, the direction of research shifted toward economic and social lines of inquiry. Many previous writers had noted that Anglo-Saxon towns included markets and some trade, but these economic features were not regarded as central characteristics. In 1930, however, the English scholarly world was jolted by the appearance of an alternative, economic theory of town origins promoted by the American medievalist Carl Stephenson (1886–1954). Stephenson's work in essence applied to the English case the mercantile theory of continental urban origins formulated by one of his mentors, the great Belgian historian Henri Pirenne (1862-1935).

In a series of articles and books published between 1893 and 1927, Pirenne had rejected prevailing views that derived medieval towns and their institutions from free village communities, guilds, or local markets. In his opinion, there were no real towns in Europe until the great revival of international commerce in the late tenth and eleventh centuries. Before this time, old Roman towns were only sparsely settled military, administrative, and ecclesiastical centers economically dependent on and scarcely distinct from the countryside. The revival of long-distance trade, Pirenne argued, was the precondition for the emergence of true towns as centers of large, permanent populations engaged in new commercial pursuits. Wandering merchants sought the protection of old and newly built walled sites (*bourgs*) to pursue their transit trade and soon established themselves in their own fortified quarters (*faubourgs*) beside the walls. These merchants, joined by craftsmen, enjoyed their own law and special status in their new settlements, which in the course of time subsumed the older fortress and gave the medieval town a thoroughly commercial and industrial character.[80] By the years after World War I, Pirenne's mercantile theory of medieval town origins had won general acceptance in French, German, and American historical circles, although English historians remained skeptical.[81]

Stephenson provided the fullest statement of his position in his notable monograph *Borough and Town* (1933).[82] First, he maintained that in the course of the Anglo-Saxon conquest, Roman urbanism, based on thriving commerce and industry, generally expired, as did the Roman distinction between city (*civitas*) and fortified camp (*castrum*). The early Anglo-Saxons may well have quickly occupied some of the major Roman *civitates*, which they treated as fortified sites and hence usually called *ceastra* (later *cestre*); other fortified places they designated burghs (*burga*). Although some former Roman *civitates* became the sites of Anglo-Saxon royal and ecclesiastical residences with mints and markets, such cases were exceptional, and even these places were essentially fortresses and refuges, mere shells, "where true urban life had long since vanished and agriculture dominated all classes."[83]

During the Danish wars, Stephenson continued, the Anglo-Saxons employed as strongholds former Roman *civitates* with old stonework and also newly built forts with wooden defenses. All were generally called burghs. Those tenth-century burghs that became royal administrative centers and permanent strongholds (boroughs), however, were often designated *ports* by virtue of their markets and mints. But they were no more towns or urban, he asserted, than were the earlier *ceastra* (>*cestre*, "chesters"). Their trade was still limited and local and their economy basically agrarian; their inhabitants enjoyed no special laws or courts.[84] He contended that the beginnings of true urban life in England, as on the Continent, are to be found only in the late tenth and eleventh centuries within the milieu of expanding international trade. Indeed, urban genesis involved a radical social transformation, a "new grouping of population induced by commercial revival." Harbingers of such developments began to appear in late Anglo-Saxon times, but the privileged, self-governing borough with its distinctive liberties and mercantile population was a product of the Norman Conquest, though not entirely of the Normans themselves.[85] Stephenson concluded his study with topographical examinations of selected boroughs and described how, as on the Continent, new merchant settlements had grown outside certain older Anglo-Saxon burghs and new Norman castles and had eventually subsumed their old nuclei into a larger walled borough.[86]

Response to Stephenson's work came quickly from the leading English authority on medieval urban history, James Tait (1863–1944). Tait's study, *The Medieval English Borough* (1936), as its title suggests, contested Stephenson's argument for the essentially post-Conquest origin of urban life. Tait contended that urbanism in fact began in England with the seventh-century Anglo-Saxon reoccupation and fortification of old Roman walled towns that had stood deserted for several centuries. These pre-Viking age towns were important royal and ecclesiastical centers with active markets and a commerce that was far more than merely local. Eighth- and ninth-century charters attest to many urban property transactions involving a variety of classes with and without appurtenant rural estates. He noted that the term *port*, frequently used to designate these towns and their commercial character, as well as *wic* for other places of trade, appears long before the Viking wars.[87] Indeed, the Alfredian burghs were not merely fortresses but were often already trading places or places where merchants gathered under protection of the walls. Tenth-century boroughs had only a more intensive commercial character: "Every Anglo-Saxon borough had a market and every borough was a *port*, a place of trade," around which gathered a class of burgess merchants.[88] Moreover, Tait argued, all the essential legal and institutional features of later medieval urban life such as burgage tenure, special law, and courts were already present, albeit in incipient form, well before 1066. Thus it is not just to the eleventh-century extramural mercantile settlements that we must look for the origins of English urban life.[89] In Tait's view the Normans provided a stimulus rather than the creative spark to an established and ongoing current of English urban development.

Tait's work provided valuable counterarguments to a number of previous views on town origins in England, and it properly refocused scholarly attention on the Anglo-Saxon background of the English town. Although long considered to be a conclusive rebuttal of Stephenson (at least among English historians),[90] its own argument was more suggestive than clearly definitive. And in a sense both scholars were emphasizing the formative role of trade and expanding commerce, though at markedly different periods.[91] Moreover, the acrimonious nature of the Stephenson-Tait controversy appears nearly to have exhausted research for decades and long inhibited further testing of their views.

This research vacuum of the 1940s and 1950s was not total, however. A number of significant monographs were produced on the history of individual English towns in the Middle Ages, yet few of them gave more than cursory attention to the Anglo-Saxon phase of their towns' development.[92] When the study of English town origins revived after World War II, it was conducted more often in the broad contexts of world urban history and urban theory.

One such influential work, *The City in History* (1961), was presented by the American cultural historian Lewis Mumford. According to Mumford, the urgent need for protection caused by the Viking invasions of the ninth century resulted in the fortification of many existing settlements. These walled towns (burghs) provided a safe haven for local merchants and markets. This trend fostered the revival of regional economies and urban crafts, which set the stage for urban expansion when international commerce revived in the eleventh century. Pirenne and his followers were wrong, said Mumford, to restrict urban status only to places engaged in long-distance trade and having large mercantile populations such as appeared mainly after the Norman Conquest. Indeed, he asserted that the walled Anglo-Saxon town of the ninth century had created commerce; commerce did not create the town.[93] Mumford's interpretation thus incorporated aspects of the *Mark* theory and Maitland's garrison theory, and it expanded on Tait's argument for earlier Anglo-Saxon market towns. It was a stimulating synthesis in a broad world-historical framework, although many individual points remained undeveloped due to the sweeping nature of the work.

An essentially socioeconomic interpretation of early English town development also was furnished at this time by Soviet Russian historians specializing in medieval English institutional research. In this view, the beginnings of town life in England were to be found not in fortifications, local markets, or long-distance trade but rather in production—in concentrated settlements of specialized craftsmen or artisans. This "artisanal theory" of English urban origins was in effect an application of Marxist economic-historical dialectic, which portrayed European towns originating at the time when craftsmen separated themselves from the prevailing agricultural milieu and settled in their own communities. According to this theory's proponents, such as Yakov Levitsky, that division of labor began in England during the eighth and ninth centuries, when local trade and markets revived and professional merchants appeared. As commerce accelerated over the next century, craftsmen settled in the marketplaces and transformed them into production centers—the first true towns.[94] This interpretation is provocative, but the rigidity of its dialectic allows little room for developmental variations, and its proposed sequence of urban socioeconomic transition is open to question. Although this artisanal theory initially found only minimal support in the West, a somewhat transmuted version has emerged recently.

Another wide-ranging study that considered town origins in England and continental Europe was the American urban sociologist Gideon Sjoberg's, *The Pre-Industrial City* (1960). Sjoberg asserted that the two most significant factors throughout human history in the origin and growth of urban life have been technological advance and sociopolitical control. Towns both sustain and promote the interests of a literate ruling elite; expansion of this urban political control into kingdoms also enlarges that society's economic base and leads to further urbanization. He observed that in western Europe, after Roman urbanism had declined under economic stress, the key figures in establishing towns were kings and bishops. The forts and monasteries that they founded quickly attracted merchants and craftsmen, so that town life blossomed after the tenth century.[95] This emphasis on the critical role played by elites in early town formation and its societal consequences was a constructive contribution, although the basic point had been recognized implicitly in previous studies.

These studies pointed out the limitations of essentially monocausal explanations of English town origins and development that still prevailed among historians after the Stephenson-Tait debate. Indeed, the new, broader perspective owed much to the theoretical work of the renowned German sociologist Max Weber (1864–1920). Weber had argued that all single institutional theories are insufficient to account for urban origins and characteristics. The historical town is a distinct unit or pattern of social relationships, a community distinguished by not one but many institutions. This urban community, he contended, had developed gradually and reached its fully-developed form only in medieval Europe north of the Alps. Weber carefully examined urban theories, including those of Maitland and Pirenne, and then compared and contrasted various types of historical towns in different cultures. Moreover, he showed how town typologies could be established in terms of urban functions, for example, "consumer" and "producer" towns. Weber concluded that a full or mature urban community (such as the medieval town) must be a basically commercial settlement displaying all of the following features: fortification, market, court, oath-bound association, and self-administration.[96]

Weber's concepts and methods were adopted and refined by a number of German medieval urban historians in the decades after World War II. Especially prominent among this group was Edith Ennen. In Ennen's opinion, the history of town development is too varied and complex to be explained by a single causative factor. The most fruitful approach lies in isolating, examining, and comparing different types of towns in various regions of early medieval Europe. Ennen follows Weber in her comparisons of medieval regional town types with the classical town as well as among themselves. In order to discern variations and common patterns, she also applies a Weberian "bundle of criteria" (*Kriterienbundel*) based on functional and institutional features but one less rigid and hence more sensitive to chronological changes.[97] It may be noted that the *Kriterienbundel* approach also was employed to good effect at that time by "prehistorians" to describe the origins of urbanism in the ancient Near East.[98] The Roman town was defined as well in terms of its possession of a certain group of functional and institutional elements.[99]

Somewhat similar methods to those used by Weber and Ennen can be seen in a thoughtful essay by J. H. Mundy that served as an introduction to a popular collection of medieval urban documents, *The Medieval Town* (1958). Mundy also provided an initial general definition of a town: a spatially large and concentrated permanent settlement displaying a variety of functions, such as commerce, government (including defense), and religion. All three criteria need not be present simultaneously to constitute a town. They all depend, however, on good lines of communication, such as transport and trade routes. Indeed, Mundy suggested that towns are simply larger, more demographically concentrated, and more active centers of commerce than villages. Urban specialization in crafts, organized trade, and intellectual pursuits made towns population magnets and promoted a fundamental town-country symbiosis, which, however, always contained the potential for conflict.[100]

Mundy's specific treatment of medieval town development generally follows the mercantile theory of Pirenne with modifications. For example, he argued that towns certainly did exist in northern Europe before the Viking age but they were only small administrative and religious centers in former Roman towns with restricted, local trade. Real urban growth began in the tenth century as a consequence not only of revived international trade but also of other factors, such as the reestablishment of internal peace and the overall expansion of cultivation, which supported higher population levels.[101] Mundy then followed Ennen by comparing medieval northern urbanism as a type with the medieval Mediterranean town and used the features of commerce, administration, and communication as functional variables. Drawing on Pirenne and Ennen, he described how in the "new age of urban history" (tenth through twelfth centuries) the northern "frontier" town arose from a gradual fusion of mercantile settlement with older fortified administrative center. The agglomerative nature of the northern town created a certain sociopolitical dualism and tension between urban burgher and rural noble that did not exist in the Mediterranean town, which had never lost its multifunctional unity inherited from antiquity.[102] Mundy's definitional approach, along with his comparative and typological expositions, were valuable contributions. He may be criticized, however, for lack of supporting detail and perhaps overemphasis on medieval Mediterranean urbanism.

The method of establishing historical town typologies or categories continued and was refined during the 1960s and 1970s. One of its most prominent proponents was the French historian Fernand Braudel. Although Braudel did not discuss the origin and development of the medieval town in any detailed individual monograph, he did provide perceptive overviews of considerable conceptual and methodological value. First, Braudel suggested that all towns have certain fundamental common characteristics, such as town-country connections and geographical communication, which persist in varying degrees over time.[103] Urban functions—political, economic, and social—enable one to distinguish, respectively, administrative, market, and crafts towns, with considerable blendings and variations. Additional town typologies can be made on the basis of historical and topographical development: "open" towns not differentiated from the countryside (the Graeco-Roman town), "closed," self-sufficient towns (medieval), and "subject" towns under state control (early modern).[104] Braudel's work alerted historians to the possibility of discerning underlying patterns of historical town development by examining the forms and functions of towns in their spatial and human contexts. Although his historical town typologies are rather fragile and questionable, they served to introduce this method eloquently to a wide audience and have prompted much further discussion.

Aside from these theoretically oriented studies, great advances were made after World War II toward the elucidation of early English town origins and development by several ancillary fields of historical research. Particularly significant contributions have issued from the relatively new field of medieval urban archaeology. Initial progress was slow, but improvements came rapidly with the inauguration in the 1950s of planned excavation programs conducted, with more rigorous archaeological methods, upon Anglo-Saxon levels of many English towns. This trend gathered momentum in the following two decades, often as "rescue archaeology" on sites threatened by modern urban renewal. By the 1980s a large body of new material evidence regarding the early stages of English towns had become available.[105]

Advances also were made in the closely related field of medieval urban topography. Topographical study of English towns had been an important branch of earlier antiquarian research. In general, this association continued, although historians occasionally incorporated such material for comparative purposes.[106] But as town excavations proceeded in the 1950s and 1960s, interest was renewed in topographical study as a valuable source to chart the evolution of the urban landscape. This revival of urban topographical study in England, which had begun decades earlier on the Continent, culminated in the appearance of the Historic Town Atlas series (1969–).[107]

Other corollary fields that have made significant contributions to the study of early English towns during the postwar decades include place-name study (especially onomastics) and numismatics. Like archaeological research, the findings obtained by these two fields are particularly valuable for the earliest stages of town development, where written evidence is rather sparse. Much valuable specialized research has been conducted under the auspices of the English Place-Name Society. Attention has been given not only to the changing designations of towns but also to internal street, market, and geographical names, which can provide valuable clues to many aspects of early urban development.[108] Numismatic evidence is of obvious importance for dating town occupation as well as for the light it can shed on related matters, such as trade patterns, markets, and administration. Increased excavations on Anglo-Saxon town sites yielded growing quantities of coins useful for many avenues of investigation.[109]

Archaeologists not only have gathered material evidence but also have advanced certain important theories regarding the origins and development of early English towns. The so-called "mercenaries theory," for example, has been particularly prominent. According to this view, developed primarily by Martin Biddle, a number of English towns were occupied continuously from late Roman to early Anglo-Saxon times. Germanic federate troops, including presumably Anglo-Saxons, had been summoned into Britain by late and sub-Roman authorities to help protect their towns from invasion. These mercenaries, however, revolted, assumed control of the towns themselves, and readily received their invading brethren into their midst. This theory, which in a sense represents a modified version of earlier views of continuity, was based on initial archaeological findings within certain towns and comparison of this evidence with continental parallels.[110] Although it does furnish a provocative model for the emergence of Anglo-Saxon towns, the theory has its problems and must be examined more closely in the light of recent evidence. It has had the merit, however, of demonstrating the need to consider the Roman town in Britain and its fate in any discussion of early English town origins and growth. Indeed, in recent years there have been increasing studies of this critical transition period c.400–600, which have incorporated discussions of the towns. These works are valuable archaeological syntheses, though they regrettably have little regard for written evidence.[111]

One currently popular model of early English town origins has been formulated by archaeologists with an economic turn of mind, most notably Richard Hodges. According to this view, the Anglo-Saxon settlements that were set up within some former Roman towns in the sixth and early seventh centuries were small royal and ecclesiastical enclaves not worthy to be called urban places. During the late seventh century, however, cross-Channel and North Sea trade among elites intensified. The kings of emerging Anglo-Saxon realms needed these luxury goods to maintain their gift-giving prestige and create ties of personal allegiance. Thus they established coastal trading places (emporia, *wics*) to gather and redistribute these elite items; in the eighth century, many of these sites also became centers of specialized industrial production. The territorial growth of the kingdom of Wessex under Alfred and his successors both increased the power of its kings and expanded a central royal administration capable of creating a planned network of burghs in response to Danish attack. These places were designed not only as defensive sites but also as market centers, where trade could be controlled. Thus, in Hodges's scheme, the coastal trading site operating within its redistributive economy was replaced by the burgh and a developing market economy. The first English towns were the expanded emporia of the eighth century, with their merchant and artisan population, and the burghs of the ninth and tenth centuries.[112] Hodges's design is interesting, but the dichotomy that it draws between a supposedly redistributive and market economy and the types of town within each system may be rather too sharp and exclusive. Also, the depictions of emporia and burghal development are arguably oversimplified, and his emphasis on royal initiative and control has been challenged.[113]

Medieval urban archaeologists and historians also have demonstrated the value of focusing on town typologies and stages of urban development. Indeed, an urban evolutionary continuum has been proposed that encompasses "pre-urban," "proto-urban," and urban phases. Others have observed that there were many Anglo-Saxon sites lower on the settlement hierarchy than reoccupied Roman towns, emporia, and burghs that functioned as centers of exchange and local administration, such as royal and aristocratic estates and monasteries. It has been noted that these places, whether called proto-urban sites or pre-urban nuclei, constituted important regional central-places with more than agricultural activity.[114]

CONCEPTS, DEFINITIONS, AND METHODS

The recent contributions from various ancillary fields have been valuable, yet they also highlight several unresolved issues. First, there is the matter of definition. Any study that treats the origins and growth of towns owes its readers some statement regarding what is being conceptualized by the key word town. Many attempts have been made in the past to define the early town in England but none of them has proved entirely adequate. For example, the constitutional and legal definitions that rested on evidence from town charters, courts, and parliamentary representation clearly will not do for the early Anglo-Saxon period.[115] Stephenson's mercantile settlement concept is similarly too restrictive.[116] Stenton, following Tait, declared that an Anglo-Saxon town was distinguished by a market, mint, fortifications, tenements, and open fields.[117] This expanded conceptualization was an improvement but still as a whole is applicable only to Anglo-Saxon towns of some maturity.

The use of a more comprehensive "bundle of criteria" would be more satisfactory, provided that we acknowledge no necessity to accept the entire bundle. Biddle and other Anglo-Saxon archaeologists have presented such a list of what they consider to be defining urban features. To hold urban status, they contend, a site must possess more than one of the following

dozen criteria: defenses, planned street-system, market, mint, legal
autonomy, role as central-place, relatively large and dense population,
diversified economic base, plots and houses of "urban" type, social differentiation, complex religious organization, and role as judicial center.[118] This
broader scheme adds topographical, economic, and social characteristics to
the older institutional and legal criteria, and it establishes the flexibility
necessary to examine early stages of urban development.

Recent medieval historians also have recognized the dangers of exclusive
or monocausal definitions. Susan Reynolds has offered one of the best
working definitions of a medieval town: a permanent human settlement with
a significant proportion of its population living off a variety of nonagricultural occupations and forming a social unit more or less distinct from the
surrounding countryside.[119] The first part of this definition needs some
modification because townspeople could indeed be engaged in cultivation
both within and outside their towns. But on the whole, Reynolds's definition,
along with Ennen's and Biddle's less rigid *Kriterienbundel*, will form the
conceptual framework for this study. In addition, the typological method will
be employed to identify and describe the various types of town with their
distinguishing functions as they emerge in Anglo-Saxon England. Thus we
will examine as background the late Roman town in Britain and what
remained of Roman urbanism, the first Anglo-Saxon towns on old Roman
sites as royal and ecclesiastical centers, the emergence of Anglo-Saxon
emporia with their continental ties, and finally the origins and development
of the Anglo-Saxon burgh. The main issues addressed include the question
of settlement or urban continuity from late Roman to early Anglo-Saxon
times, the nature and relationship of Anglo-Saxon towns on former Roman
sites and the emporia or *wics*, and the chronology and function of the
burghs.

Although there has been significant archaeological and related research
on the early English town in recent years, little attempt has yet been made
to integrate these findings with the pertinent written, historical sources. The
need for such a study has been pointed out in more comprehensive
treatments of the medieval English town by Colin Platt and Susan Reynolds.[120] Also, a number of major international congresses on medieval
towns have provided examples of the interdisciplinary approach. It is
especially noteworthy that the early English town has moved from the
European periphery into a general continental context in these important
colloquia studies.[121] Additional examples of what can be accomplished by
the careful integration of written and material evidence include the
collaborative research projects underway at several English towns, although
these campaigns on the whole have not been confined to the pre-Conquest
period.[122] All of these studies have served to emphasize one salient point:
medieval urban history is fundamentally a study in typological and functional

variations, contrasts, and changes rather than uniformity or permanence. A work that places the significant findings and theories of related fields within a more firmly grounded written or historical context offers the best approach to interpret the variations and fluidity that characterize the early stages of urbanism in England.

NOTES

1. Sir Frank M. Stenton, *Anglo-Saxon England* (hereafter *ASE*) (3d ed., Oxford: Clarendon Press, 1971), p. 525. This is essentially a posthumous reprint of the 1947 second edition with updated notes and bibliography supplied by Lady Stenton.

2. At least 10 percent of its population lived in towns, with perhaps one hundred urban places. The most populous late Anglo-Saxon towns such as London and York numbered 5,000–10,000 inhabitants, comparable to or slightly greater than the largest towns of contemporary northern France and Germany but small by the standards of urban Italy. See P. H. Sawyer, *From Roman Britain to Norman England* (London: Methuen, 1976), p. 204; H. C. Darby, *Domesday England* (Cambridge: University Press, 1977), pp. 302–9; M. W. Beresford and H. P. R. Finberg, *English Medieval Boroughs: A Hand List* (Totowa, NJ: Rowman & Littlefield, 1973), pp. 38–40; E. John, "The End of Anglo-Saxon England," in *The Anglo-Saxons*, ed. J. Campbell (London: Penguin, 1982), p. 238.

3. C. L. Kingsford, *English Historical Literature in the Fifteenth Century* (Oxford: Clarendon Press, 1913), pp. 2–8; J. W. Thompson, *A History of Historical Writing* (2 vols., NY: Macmillan, 1942), I, pp. 390–91; H. S. Bennett, *Chaucer and the Fifteenth Century* (Oxford: Clarendon Press, 1947), pp. 98–104, 118–23; J. R. Lander, *Conflict and Stability in Fifteenth-Century England* (London: Hutchinson, 1969) pp. 141–50; A. Gransden, *Historical Writing in England II* (Ithaca: Cornell University Press, 1982), pp. xi–xiv. Growing urban pride and class consciousness can be seen in the expanded production of various town chronicles in English, especially the London Chronicles: C. L. Kingsford, ed., *Chronicles of London* (Oxford: Clarendon Press, 1905), and R. Flenley, ed., *Six Town Chronicles* (Oxford: Clarendon Press, 1911). See further, Kingsford, *English Historical Literature*, pp. 70–112; Thompson, *History of Historical Writing*, I, pp. 418–19, 592–96; Bennett, *Fifteenth Century*, pp. 121–22; Gransden, *Historical Writing II*, pp. 227–48.

The traditional view is that the fifteenth century was a time of overall urban expansion in England. See, e.g., A. S. Green, *Town Life in the Fifteenth Century* (2 vols., London: Macmillan, 1894), I, pp. 1–43; E. M. Carus-Wilson, "Towns and Trade," in *Medieval England*, ed. A. L. Poole (2d ed., 2 vols., Oxford: Clarendon Press, 1958), I, pp. 255–62; A. R. Bridbury, *Economic Growth: England in the Later Middle Ages* (London: Allen & Unwin, 1962), pp. 40–82. But cf. the revisionist opinion: R. B. Dobson, "Urban Decline in Late Medieval England," *Transactions of the Royal Historical Society*, 5th ser., 27 (1977), pp. 1–22. For general assessments of this entire debate, see S. Reynolds, "Decline and Decay in Late Medieval Towns: A Look at Some of the Concepts and Arguments, *Urban History Yearbook* 7 (1980), pp. 76–78; D. M. Palliser, "Urban Decay Revisited," in *Towns and Townspeople in the*

Fifteenth Century, ed. J. Thomson (Gloucester: Alan Sutton, 1988), pp. 1–21; A. Dyer, *Decline and Growth in English Towns 1400–1640* (London: Macmillan, 1991).

4. Kingsford, *English Historical Literature*, pp. 113–39; E. K. Chambers, *English Literature at the Close of the Middle Ages* (Oxford: Clarendon Press, 1945), pp. 185–205; Gransden, *Historical Writing II*, pp. 220–27.

5. Examples include Thomas Elmham's account of St. Augustine's, Canterbury, in his *Speculum Augustinianum* (c.1413) and the Scottish descriptions of John Harding's *Chronicle* (c.1440–63). See Kingsford, *English Historical Literature*, pp. 45–46, 140–49; Gransden, *Historical Writing II*, pp. 283–87, 345–55, and "Antiquarian Studies in Fifteenth-Century England," *Antiquaries Journal* 60 (1980), 75–97.

6. William Worcester's survey of Bristol, included in his *Itinerary* (1478–80), is recognized as the first full topographical description of an English city. Rous's study, *History of the Town of Warwick*, is regrettably now lost, but his *Historia Regum Angliae* (1480–86) contains much topographic and historical material regarding this town and Oxford. See further, T. D. Kendrick, *British Antiquity* (London: Methuen, 1950), pp. 18–33; V. Galbraith, *Historical Research in Medieval England* (London: Constable, 1951), pp. 44–45; Gransden, *Historical Writing II*, pp. 308–41, and "Antiquarian Studies," pp. 84–89.

7. See, for example, F. J. Levy, *Tudor Historical Thought* (San Marino, CA: Huntington Library, 1967), pp. 33–78; Gransden, *Historical Writing II*, pp. 469–74; D. Hay, "England and the Humanities in the Fifteenth Century," in *Itinerarium Italicum*, eds. H. Oberman and T. Brady, Jr. (Leiden: E. J. Brill, 1975), pp. 305–67, esp. 324–67; J. M. Levine, *Humanism and History: Origins of Modern English Historiography* (Ithaca: Cornell University Press, 1987), pp. 45–53.

8. One need only recall the work of Petrarch, Lorenzo Valla, Poggio Bracciolini, Flavio Biondo, and Polydore Vergil in these areas. See Thompson, *History of Historical Writing*, I, pp. 473–509; P. Kristeller, *The Classics and Renaissance Thought* (Cambridge, MA: Harvard University Press, 1955), pp. 3–23; A. Mazzocco, "Petrarcha, Poggio, and Biondo: Humanism's Foremost Interpreters of Roman Ruins," in *Francis Petrarch, Six Centuries Later*, ed. A. Scaglione (Chapel Hill: University of North Carolina Press, 1975), pp. 353–63; E. Cochrane, *History and Historiography in the Italian Renaissance* (Chicago: University of Chicago Press, 1981), pp. 3–40.

9. The antiquary, unlike the historian, primarily collects rather than interprets facts and proceeds within a systematic rather than chronological framework. See A. Momigliano, "Ancient History and the Antiquarian," in Momigliano, *Studies in Historiography* (London: Weidenfeld & Nicholson, 1966), pp. 1–39; Cochrane, *History and Historiography*, pp. 423–44; S. Mendyk, *"Speculum Britanniae": Regional Study, Antiquarianism, and Science in Britain to 1700* (Toronto: University of Toronto Press, 1989), pp. 8–12.

10. For discussions of the principal works from the twelfth through fourteenth centuries, see R. W. Southern, "Aspects of the European Tradition of Historical Writing: 4. The Sense of the Past," *Transactions of the Royal Historical Society*, 5th ser., 23 (1973), pp. 246–56 esp. 253–56; Gransden, *Historical Writing in England I* (Ithaca: Cornell University Press, 1974), pp. 174–75, 255–57, 362–63, 393–94, 376 and II, pp. 50–52; also see, "Realistic Observation in Twelfth-Century England," *Speculum* 47 (1972), 29–51 esp. 44–48. Regional and "national" topography also was employed

by early medieval authors such as Gildas, Bede, and Nennius. See R. W. Hanning, *The Vision of History in Early Britain* (NY: Columbia University Press, 1966), chaps. 2–4; Gransden, *Historical Writing I*, pp. 4–5, 10–12, 23–24.

11. In Germany, the efforts of Konrad Celtis (d.1508) and Beatus Rhenanus (d.1547) toward reconstructing the outlines of ancient Germania are especially noteworthy. See G. Strauss, *Sixteenth-Century Germany: Its Topography and Topographers* (Madison: University of Wisconsin Press, 1959), chaps. 1–4; L. W. Spitz, "The Course of German Humanism," in *Itinerarium Italicum*, pp. 371–436, esp. 401–14.

12. For definitions and discussion of sixteenth-century chorography and its inheritance from Strabo and Ptolemy, see Mendyk, *"Speculum Britanniae,"* pp. 21–24. The expanded topics included social customs, political and natural history, geography, genealogy, and cartography, among others.

13. For Leland's prospectus, presented in 1564, see *The Laboryouse Journey and Serche of Johan Leylande, for Englandes Antiquitees*, ed. J. Bale (London: J. Bale, 1549), esp. Preface. Leland eventually lapsed into insanity, frustrated perhaps by the enormity of his undertaking. The *Itinerary* was first published in 1710 and reedited two centuries later: *The Itinerary of John Leland*, ed. L. Toulmin Smith (5 vols., London: G. Bell, 1907–1910). For Leland's contribution, see Kendrick, *British Antiquity*, pp. 45–64; M. McKisack, *Medieval History in the Tudor Age* (Oxford: Clarendon Press, 1971), pp. 1–11; Levine, *Humanism and History*, pp. 79–82. Leland's wide-ranging interests put one in mind of Braudel's aspects of material life, though Leland was far less organized and methodical.

14. W. Lambarde, *A Perambulation of Kent: Conteining the Description, Hystorie, and Customes of that Shyre* (London: Ralphe Newberie, 1576). This work was intended to be preliminary to a larger, complete historical topography of the British Isles based on his extensive compendium, which remained unpublished until the eighteenth century: *Dictionarium Angliae topographicum et historicum* (London, 1730). Lambarde was also responsible for the first printed collection of Anglo-Saxon law codes (*Archaionomia*, 1568) translated from Old English (O.E.) into Latin with commentary. See further on Lambarde: E. N. Adams, *Old English Scholarship in England from 1566–1800* (New Haven: Yale University Press, 1917), pp. 27–31; W. Dunkel, *William Lambarde, Elizabethan Jurist* (New Brunswick: Rutgers University Press, 1965); McKisack, *Medieval History in the Tudor Age*, pp. 133–37; Southern, "Sense of the Past," pp. 257–61; Mendyk, *"Speculum Britanniae,"* pp. 20–21, 47–49.

15. Lambarde, *Perambulation of Kent*, pp. 1–5. This section concludes with a brief summary of Anglo-Saxon law.

16. Ibid., pp. 6–24. Lambarde states (p. 18) that his purpose is to write a topography, not a history, although "I must now and then use both, since the one cannot fully be performed without interlacing the other."

17. Lambarde incorporates transcriptions and translations of O.E. wills and charters and includes a long excursus on the distinctive early Kentish custom of partible inheritance (*gavelkind*): ibid., pp. 388–415. He also used much evidence from *Domesday Book* and selected medieval charters. None of this material is well referenced, however, and the emphasis is still for the most part on collection rather than interpretation.

18. These labors laid the foundation for modern Anglo-Saxon studies: Adams, *Old English Scholarship*, pp. 11–41; McKisack, *Medieval History in the Tudor Age*, pp. 26–74; R. E. Buckalew, "Nowell, Lambarde, and Leland," in *Anglo-Saxon Scholarship: The First Three Centuries*, eds. C. Berkhout and M. Gatch (Boston: G. K. Hall, 1982), pp. 19–50. A year before the *Perambulation* appeared, Alexander Neville, one of Archbishop Parker's assistants, had published a brief topographical-historical account of the town of Norwich in Latin: *Norvicus*, in Neville, *De furoribus Norfolciensium Ketto duce* (London, 1575). See further: Levy, *Tudor Historical Thought*, pp. 141–42.

19. For a lively account of these honors, see McKisack, *Medieval History in the Tudor Age*, pp. 78–82. As Mendyk properly notes ("*Speculum Britanniae*," p. 49), one can regard Lambarde's *Perambulation* and subsequent regional studies as precursors of the modern *Victoria County Histories* (London, 1900–) (hereafter *VCH*).

20. W. Camden, *Britannia, sive Florentissimorum regnorum, Angliae, Scotiae, Hiberniae, et insularum adiacentium ex intima antiquitate chorographica descriptio* (London: Ralph Newberry, 1586). This was followed by six later editions during Camden's lifetime alone, including an English translation (1610). On Camden, see further: Thompson, *History of Historical Writing*, I, pp. 607–9; F. M. Powicke, "William Camden," *Essays and Studies*, n.s., 1 (1948), pp. 67–84; S. Piggott, "William Camden and the *Britannia*," *Proceedings of the British Academy* 38 (1951), pp. 199–217; Kendrick, *British Antiquity*, pp. 134–56; F. Fussner, *The Historical Revolution: English Historical Writing and Thought 1580–1640* (NY: Columbia University Press, 1962), pp. 230–52; Levy, *Tudor Historical Thought*, pp. 148–59; McKisack, *Medieval History in the Tudor Age*, pp. 150–54; Mendyk, "*Speculum Britanniae*," pp. 49–55.

21. Ortelius in particular prompted him for a work that would, as Camden put it, "restore antiquity to Britain and Britain to its antiquity": *Britannia, or a Chorographical Description of Great Britain and Ireland*, trans. and ed. E. Gibson (2d ed. rev., 2 vols., London: M. Matthews, 1722), I, Preface. See Levy, *Tudor Historical Thought*, pp. 144–49; Mendyk, "*Speculum Britanniae*," p. 51. After Lambarde had read an advance draft of the *Britannia* sent to him by Camden, he immediately deferred to the younger scholar on his own projected large-scale work and later called Camden "the most lightsome Antiquary of this age": *Perambulation of Kent* (2d ed., London: Edmund Bollifant, 1596), p. 9.

22. See further on this point, Piggott, "William Camden and the *Britannia*," pp. 207–8; Levy, *Tudor Historical Thought*, pp. 152–55.

23. Camden's place-name etymologies derived from his linguistic skills in Old English and Welsh. He by no means neglected pre-Roman and Anglo-Saxon material. See further: Piggott, "William Camden and the *Britannia*," pp. 201–5.

24. Camden professes that he undertook his vast project because of "the natural affection I have for my country (by far the strongest affection there is), the glory of the British name, and the persuasions of friends": *Britannia* (1722 ed.), I, Preface. On the widespread Elizabethan thirst for "the discovery of England," see L. B. Wright, *Middle-Class Culture in Elizabethan England* (Chapel Hill: University of North Carolina Press, 1935), pp. 297–338; A. L. Rouse, *The England of Elizabeth* (London: Macmillan, 1951), pp. 31–65; Southern, "Sense of the Past," pp. 262–63; Mendyk, "*Speculum Britanniae*," pp. 12–15. Camden himself, like many of his circle, belonged

to this urban middle class. For further implications, see Fussner, *The Historical Revolution*, pp. 53–59.

25. His frequent source criticisms are usually succinct and sound. On the significance of these textual expansions, see Levy, *Tudor Historical Thought*, pp. 155–59.

26. Powicke, "William Camden," pp. 75–79, 83–84; Kendrick, *British Antiquity*, pp. 108–9, 147–51. Camden's Preface to the *Britannia's* English translation is a magnificent example of the author's level-headed approach and stylistic clarity.

27. J. Stow, *A Survay of London. Contayning the Originall, Antiquity, Increase, Modern Estate, and Description of that Citie* (London: John Wolfe, 1598). A revised and expanded edition in 1603 was used for the standard modern critical edition: C. L. Kingsford, ed., *A Survey of London by John Stow* (2 vols., Oxford: Clarendon Press, 1908). On Stow in general and the *Survay* in particular, see Kingsford, ed., *Survey of London* I, pp. vii–xliii; Thompson, *History of Historical Writing*, I, p. 609; Rowse, *England of Elizabeth*, pp. 191–96; Kendrick, *British Antiquity*, pp. 158–59; Levy, *Tudor Historical Thought*, pp. 186–95; S. Rubinstein, *Historians of London* (Hamden, CT: Archon Books, 1968), pp. 26–72; McKisack, *Medieval History in the Tudor Age*, pp. 82–85, 131–33.

28. For Stow's sources, his continuous antiquarian and archival travels, and book-collecting passion, see Kingsford, ed., *Survey of London*, I, pp. xxx–xxxix; McKisack, *Medieval History in the Tudor Age*, pp. 82–84.

29. Stow, *Survay of London* (1598 ed.), Epistle. He continues: "It is a duty, that I willingly owe to my native mother and country. And an office that of right I hold myself bound in love to bestow upon the body politic and members of the same: what London hath been of ancient time men may here see, as what it is now every man doth behold." (ibid.).

30. Ibid., pp. 1–9. This section follows Camden rather closely.

31. Ibid., pp. 10–82.

32. Ibid., pp. 82–346. This is succeeded by similar chorographic discussions of London's suburbs (pp. 346–69) and then of Westminster (pp. 370–94). The *Survay* provides ample evidence of London's great growth during Stow's lifetime and the author's negative reactions to "urban sprawl." Indeed, the population of London is believed to have quadrupled during the sixteenth century. See further: Rowse, *England of Elizabeth*, pp. 193–204; P. Clark and P. Slack, *English Towns in Transition 1500–1700* (Oxford: Clarendon Press, 1976), Table I, p. 83; J. Schofield, *The Building of London* (London: British Museum Publications, 1984), pp. 131–57.

33. Stow, *Survay of London*, pp. 395–449.

34. Ibid., pp. 473–83.

35. Ibid., pp. 450–69. Stow's own etymologies are usually more succinct than those of Leland, Lambarde, and Camden, though all four authors could be quite fanciful on occasion. Another contemporary attempt to examine English town origins broadly can be found in William Harrison's *Description of England* (1587), which formed part of the introduction to Holinshed's *Chronicles* and was based largely on Leland's work: R. Holinshed, *Chronicles*, eds. J. Hooker, et al. (2d. ed., 3 vols., London, 1587), I, pp. 189–94. See further, G. Edelen, "William Harrison (1535–1593)," *Studies in the Renaissance* 9 (1962), 256–72.

36. For Stow as historian, see McKisack, *Medieval History in the Tudor Age*, pp. 132–33. Stow was repeatedly accused of having Catholic sympathies, however. A search of his library reportedly found much objectionable material, including "popish books printed in the old time, with many such also written in Old English on parchment." No further official action was taken against Stow, due perhaps to his friendship with Archbishop Parker and members of his circle. See Kingsford, ed., *Survey of London*, I, pp. xvi–xx.

37. Some were primarily transcriptions of municipal records with little critical analysis, e.g., John Hooker, *Description of the Citie of Excester* (c.1600), Richard Butcher, *Survey and Antiquitie of the Towne of Stamford* (1646), and Nathaniel Bacon, *Annals of Ipswich* (1654). Others were condensed topographical-historical accounts: William Grey, *Chorographia: Or a Survey of Newcastle-Upon-Tine* (1649) and William Bedwell, *A Brief Description of the Towne of Tottenham* (1631). See further, McKisack, *Medieval History in the Tudor Age*, pp. 128–31; Levy, *Tudor Historical Thought*, pp. 160–63. W. G. Hoskins, *Local History in England* (London: Longmans, 1959), pp. 19–20, aptly described these works as "more or less undigested compilations of material. . . uncooked potatoes and not the finished meal."

38. Somner was a leading figure in seventeenth–century antiquarian and Anglo-Saxon studies. In addition to his Canterbury chorography (which emphasized ecclesiastical antiquities), he compiled the first comprehensive Anglo-Saxon dictionary in print (a much-needed tool at the time), published an English translation of Lambarde's work on Anglo-Saxon laws, and produced an important study on the Roman ports and forts of Kent. See Adams, *Old English Scholarship*, pp. 58–66; Levine, *Humanism and History*, pp. 89–92.

39. Webb, under-sheriff in Cheshire, apparently completed this work c.1620. As might be expected, he had much to say about landholding and administration. See further, Mendyk, *"Speculum Britanniae,"* pp. 86–87.

40. Exceptions include Richard Carew's *Survey of Cornwall* (1602), John Norden's *Description of Hertfordshire* (1598), and, in a wider Camdenian context, John Speed's *Theatre of the Empire of Great Britaine* (1611). See Levy, *Tudor Historical Thought*, pp. 159–62; Mendyk, *"Speculum Britanniae,"* pp. 65–67, 77–81.

41. M. Maclagan, "Genealogy and Heraldry in the Sixteenth and Seventeenth Centuries," in *English Historical Scholarship*, ed. L. Fox (London: Oxford University Press, 1956), pp. 43–48; Mendyk, *"Speculum Britanniae,"* pp. 82–101.

42. Adams, *Old English Scholarship*, pp. 47–57; D. C. Douglas, *English Scholars* (London: Jonathan Cape, 1939), pp. 32–36; H. A. Cronne, "The Study and Use of Charters by English Scholars in the Seventeenth Century: Sir Henry Spelman and Sir William Dugdale," in *English Historical Scholarship*, ed. Fox, pp. 77–87; Fussner, *Historical Revolution*, pp. 101–4.

43. W. Dugdale et al., eds., *Monasticon Anglicanum* (3 vols., London, 1655–73). See further, Douglas, *English Scholars*, pp. 36–45; Adams, *Old English Scholarship*, pp. 68–70; Cronne, "Study and Use of Charters," pp. 88–91.

44. W. Dugdale, *The Antiquities of Warwickshire Illustrated; From Records, Leiger-Books, Manuscripts, Charters, Evidences, Tombes, and Armes* (London: Thomas Warren, 1656), esp. Preface and the accounts of Warwick and Coventry which also were printed separately in the following century. See further, Douglas, *English*

Scholars, pp. 45–47; Hoskins, *Local History*, pp. 17–19, Mendyk, *"Speculum Britanniae,"* pp. 102–10.

45. Fussner, *Historical Revolution*, pp. 114–16. This more source-critical and objective approach is particularly apparent in the work of post-Restoration Anglo-Saxon scholars, who then established their field as a specialized branch of historical inquiry. See Adams, *Old English Scholarship*, pp. 74–84; Douglas, *English Scholars*, Chap. 3, "The Saxon Past."

46. R. Brady, *An Historical Treatise of Cities and Burghs or Boroughs* (London: S. Lowndes, 1690). For these matters and Brady's role in the so-called Norman Controversy, see Douglas, *English Scholars*, pp. 148–74; and, briefly, C. Gross, *A Bibliography of British Municipal History* (NY: Longmans, Green and Co., 1897), pp. xxiii–xxiv. This tendency of early nineteenth-century town research to become embroiled in contemporary political controversy was not confined to England: R. L. Reynolds, "Town Origins," in *Great Problems in European Civilization*, eds. K. Setton and H. Winkler (NY: Prentice–Hall, 1954), pp. 173–174.

47. T. Madox, *Firma Burgi, or an Historical Essay Concerning the Cities, Towns, and Buroughs of England Taken from Records* (London: R. Gosling, 1726). It has been called "the one outstanding work on medieval municipal history before the nineteenth century": Douglas, *English Scholars*, p. 313; also, see Gross, *British Municipal History*, p. xxv.

48. His two previous works referred to were *Formulare Anglicanum* (1702), which surpassed in its rigorous method any earlier study of the kind, including that of Thomas Rymer, Madox's industrious predecessor as Royal Historiographer, and *The History and Antiquities of the Exchequer of the Kings of England* (1711), still considered a defining work. See Douglas, *English Scholars*, pp. 291–315; Fussner, *Historical Revolution*, pp. 82–91, 115–16.

49. J. Tait, "The *Firma Burgi* and the Commune in England," *English Historical Review* 42 (1927), 321.

50. H. A. Merewether and A. J. Stephens, *The History of the Boroughs and Municipal Corporations of the United Kingdom, from the Earliest to the Present Time; With an Examination of Records, Charters and Other Documents, Illustrative of Their Constitution and Powers* (3 vols., London: Stevens & Sons, 1835). The authors were politically active lawyers. See further, Gross, *British Municipal History*, pp. xxv–xxviii.

51. Ibid., pp. xxx–xxxiv; Hoskins, *Local History*, pp. 20–21, with references to some of the better works. The nine individual studies in the series "Historic Towns," edited by E. A. Freeman and W. Hunt (London, 1887–93) are still useful though brief and not always well referenced. See, in addition, Freeman's *English Towns and Districts: A Series of Addresses and Sketches* (London: Macmillan, 1883). This was also the time when many early town archives were first being officially cataloged: *Historical Manuscripts Commission*, Reports, ser. 1–8 (London, 1871–84).

52. T. Wright, "On the Existence of Municipal Privileges under the Anglo-Saxons," *Archaeologia* 32 (1847), 298–311 and *The Celt, the Roman, and the Saxon* (London: A. Hall, Virtue & Co., 1852), Chaps. 4, 16.

53. H. C. Coote, *A Neglected Fact in English History* (London: Bell and Daldy, 1864) and *The Romans of Britain* (London: F. Norgate, 1878), pp. 342–413; C. H. Pearson, *History of England during the Early and Middle Ages* (2 vols., London: Bell and Daldy, 1867), I, pp. 99–103, 264–77. The theory also implied a significant

structural survival of Roman towns during and after the Anglo-Saxon invasions. These "Romanist" interpretations all stemmed essentially from the influential continental studies of F. Savigny, esp. his *Geschichte des römischen Rechts im Mittelalter* (6 vols., 1815–31). See further, R. L. Reynolds, "Town Origins," pp. 178–79.

54. Freeman, "The Alleged Permanence of Roman Civilization in England," *Macmillan's Magazine*, 22 (1870), 211–28 (a devastatingly incisive critique).

55. Such as discussions of the origins of the manor and manorialism in England: F. Seebohm, *The English Village Community* (London: Macmillan, 1883), but cf. P. Vinogradof, *Villeinage in England* (Oxford: Clarendon Press, 1892); G. L. Gomme, *The Village Community: With Special Reference to the Origins and Form of its Survivals in Britain* (London: Walter Scott Ltd., 1896), Chap. 3.

56. See, for example, J. Lingard, *The History of England from the First Invasion by the Romans to the Accession of William and Mary in 1688* (6th ed., 10 vols., London: Charles Dolman, 1855), I, p. 51, where Romano-British towns are said to have been quickly destroyed in initial Anglo-Saxon conquests, and I, pp. 212–14, where most Anglo–Saxon "cities and boroughs" are claimed to have passed successively from Romans to Britons, Anglo-Saxons, and Norsemen; H. Hallam, *View of the State of Europe during the Middle Ages* (4th ed., 3 vols., London; John Murray, 1869–78), III, pp. 19–28, 219–25.

57. E. A. Freeman, *The History of the Norman Conquest of England* (3d ed. rev., 6 vols., Oxford: Clarendon Press, 1877–79), I, pp. 13–21, V, pp. 465–75. "The English wiped out everything Celtic and everything Roman as thoroughly as everything Roman was wiped out of Africa by the Saracen conquerors of Carthage" (I, p. 20).

58. J. R. Green, *History of the English People* (4 vols., NY: Harper & Brothers, 1880), I, pp. 21–24, 28–34, 206–8 and *The Making of England* (London: Macmillan, 1883), pp. 10–45; J. H. Ramsay, *The Foundations of England* (2 vols., London: Swan Sonnenschein, 1898), I, pp. 155, 163, 520; A. Jessopp, "The Origin and Growth of English Towns," in Jessopp, *Studies by a Recluse in Cloister, Town and Country* (3d ed., London: T. Fisher Unwin, 1893), pp. 112–42, esp. 115–30.

59. S. Turner, *The History of the Anglo-Saxons* (2d ed., 2 vols., London: Longman, 1807), II, pp. 159–275. Turner used an array of unprinted sources but not often critically.

60. Ibid., I, pp. 267–68, 335–38, II, 108–9.

61. J. M. Lappenberg, *A History of England under the Anglo-Saxon Kings*, trans. and rev. B. Thorpe (2 vols., London: John Murray, 1845), II, pp. 305–67, esp. 351–54. The authors followed W. E. Wilda, *Das Gildenwesen im Mittelalter* (1831) whose views reappeared in J. T. Smith and L. Brentano's *English Gilds* (London: Trübner, 1870) but were later rejected: Gross, *The Gild Merchant* (Oxford: Clarendon Press, 1890).

62. J. M. Kemble, ed., *Codex Diplomaticus Aevi Saxonici* (6 vols., London: British Historical Society, 1839–1848).

63. Idem, *The Saxons in England: A History of the English Commonwealth Till the Period of the Norman Conquest* (2 vols., London: Longman, 1849), I, Preface, p. vi: "For our customs are founded upon right and justice, and are maintained in a subjection to His will who hath the heart of nations as well as of kings in His rule and governance." In the Introduction to his *Codex Diplomaticus*, I, pp. iii–iv, Kemble

observed that "the appointed work of the Teutons was to reinfuse life and vigor and the sanctity of a high morality into [Roman] institutions perishing through their own corruption. And the Anglo-Saxons were not the least active in fulfilling their part of this great duty." Such Gibbonesque sentiments are not uncommon in the work of Turner and Kemble.

64. Kemble, *Saxons in England*, II, pp. 277–97. "For desolation marches with giant strides, and neglect is a more potent leveller than military engines" (p. 297).

65. Ibid., II, pp. 295–300. Although he allows the possibility that geographical advantages may on occasion have favored Anglo-Saxon settlement around old Roman towns.

66. Ibid., II, pp. 301–4.

67. Ibid., II, pp. 309–18, and I, pp. 35–71, on the *Mark*. Kemble held that the *Mark* constituted both a free community with its cultivated land and a sacral boundary zone delimiting such lands. His references included Grimm's *Deutsche Gränzaltertümer* (1844) and Eichhorn's *Deutsche Staats-und Rechtsgeschichte* (1818–23). The *Mark* theory was elaborated at this time especially by G. L. von Maurer, *Einleitung zur Geschichte der Mark-, Hof-, Dorf-, und Stadtverfassung* (1854), and G. von Below, *Die Entstehung der deutschen Stadtgemeinde* (1889). It was sharply criticized by N. D. Fustel de Coulanges: "Le problème des origines de la propriété foncière," *Revue des Questions Historiques* 45 (1889), 349–439. For analyses of these views, see, H. Pirenne, "L'Origine des constitutions urbaines au moyen âge," *Revue Historique* 53 (1893), 52–83, esp. 70–75; W. Ashley, "The Beginnings of Town Life in the Middle Ages," *Quarterly Journal of Economics* 10 (1896), 359–406; A. Dopsch, *Wirtschaftliche und soziale Grundlagen der europäischen Kulturentwicklung* (2d ed. rev., 2 vols., Vienna: Verlag Von L. W. Seidel & Sohn, 1923–24), I, pp. 8–26; C. Stephenson, *Borough and Town: A Study of Urban Origins in England* (Cambridge, MA: Mediaeval Academy of America, 1933), pp. 4–5 and "The Problem of the Common Man in Early Medieval Europe," *American Historical Review* 51 (1946), 419–38, esp. 420–25; B. Lyon, *A Constitutional and Legal History of Medieval England* (2d ed., NY: Harper & Row, 1980), pp. 69, 74–76.

68. Ramsay, *Foundations of England*, p. 155 n.4; Gross, *British Municipal History*, p. 18; Stephenson, *Borough and Town*, p. 16 n.1: "Nine-tenths of his [Kemble's] account is sheer imagination." This condemnation is overly severe, however.

69. W. Stubbs, *The Constitutional History of England in its Origin and Development* (5th ed., 3 vols., Oxford: Clarendon Press, 1891–95), I, pp. 65–71. For discussions of Stubbs's views on these matters, see C. Petit-Dutaillis, *Studies and Notes Supplementary to Stubbs's Constitutional History*, trans. W. E. Rhodes (Manchester: University Press, 1908), pp. 4, 10, 29–35; Stephenson, *Borough and Town*, p. 16.

70. Stubbs, *Constitutional History* I, pp. 53–58, 88–98. "The historical township is the body of allodial owners who have advanced beyond the stage of land-community [*Markgenossenschaft/Landgemeinde*], retaining many vestiges of that organization; or the body of tenants of a lord who regulates them or allows them to regulate themselves on principles derived from the same" (p. 91). Later, "The township appears in its ecclesiastical form as the parish"; the hundred is a collection or cluster of townships (Ibid.).

71. Ibid., pp. 97–103, where he also firmly rejected the view that Anglo-Saxon or earlier Germanic guilds were the bases for the medieval town's political organization.

72. F. W. Maitland, *Township and Borough* (Cambridge: University Press, 1898), pp. 1–52, including his oft-quoted comment, "Those who would study the early history of our towns. . . have fields and pastures on their hands" (p. 9). Note Stubbs's remark: "The common lands of the *burh* testified to its origin in a state of society in which the *Mark*-system was not yet forgotten." *Constitutional History*, I, p. 100. See further, Stephenson, "Common Man," 427–30.

73. Maitland, "The Origin of the Borough," *English Historical Review* 11 (1896), 13–19. This was essentially an application to England of F. Keutgen's legal study of town origins in Germany, especially the new tenth-century *Burgen* of Henry the Fowler: *Untersuchungen über den Ursprung der deutschen Stadtverfassung* (1894).

74. Maitland, *Domesday Book and Beyond: Three Essays in the Early History of England* (Cambridge: University Press, 1897), pp. 172–98, and 209–19 for borough government, courts, and later differentiation. See further, H. M. Chadwick, *Studies on Anglo-Saxon Institutions* (Cambridge: University Press, 1905), pp. 219–25. Maitland did not think much of the *Mark* theory in this study and also qualified his earlier views on the township: *Domesday Book and Beyond*, pp. 141–50, 346–56.

75. Ibid., p. 195. As Petit-Dutaillis noted, the term "borough" should not be applied to the pre-Alfredian town and might even be discarded altogether because of its modern connotations: *Studies*, p. 71.

76. J. Tait, review of *Domesday Book and Beyond* by F. W. Maitland, *English Historical Review* 12 (1897), 768–77, and later, "The Study of Early Municipal History in England," *Proceedings of the British Academy* 10 (1921–23), 201–3; Petit-Dutaillis, *Studies*, pp. 78–82. For fairer assessments, see H. W. C. Davis, "The English Borough," *Quarterly Review* 208 (1908), 59–61; Stephenson, *Borough and Town*, pp. 17–18, 81–88.

77. A. Ballard, *Domesday Boroughs* (Oxford: Clarendon Press, 1904), esp. pp. 11–40 and "Castle-Guard and Barons' Houses," *English Historical Review* 25 (1910), 712–15. For criticisms, see Petit-Dutaillis, *Studies*, p. 82; Davis, "English Borough," 61; Tait, "Early Municipal History, p. 202; Stephenson, *Borough and Town*, pp. 18, 74, 81–82, 86.

78. M. Bateson, review of *Domesday Boroughs* by A. Ballard, *English Historical Review* 20 (1905), 143–51 and "The Burgesses of Domesday and the Malmesbury Wall," *English Historical Review* 21 (1906), 709–23; Davis, "English Borough," 54–56; cf. Stephenson, *Borough and Town*, pp. 81, 146–49. For an able summary of previous and more recent studies of the late Anglo-Saxon borough, see G. H. Martin, "The Domesday Boroughs," in *Domesday Book Studies*, ed. A. Williams (London: Alecto Historical Editions, 1987). pp. 56–60.

79. M. de Wolf Hemmeon, *Burgage Tenure in Mediaeval England* (Cambridge, MA: Harvard University Press, 1914). Cf. Stephenson, *Borough and Town*, pp. 88–96.

80. H. Pirenne, "L' Origine des constitutions urbaines au moyen âge II," *Revue Historique* 57 (1895), 57–98 and "Villes, marchés et marchands au moyen âge," *Revue Historique* 67 (1898), 59–70, "Les villes Flamandes avant le XIIᵉ siècle," *Annales de l'Est et du Nord* 1 (1905), 9–32 and *Medieval Cities* (Princeton: Princeton University Press, 1925; rev. ed., NY: Doubleday, 1956), French ed.: *Les villes du moyen âge*

(Brussels: M. Lamertin, 1927). Pirenne was much indebted to the works of S. Rietschel, e.g., *Die Civitas auf deutschem Boden* (1894) and *Markt und Stadt in ihren rechtlichen Verhältnis* (1897). See further, Stephenson, *Borough and Town*, pp. 6–13; Lyon, *Henri Pirenne: A Biographical and Intellectual Study*, with Preface by F. L. Ganshof (Ghent: E. Story-Scientia, 1974), pp. 122–25, 162–64, 302–8.

81. G. Seeliger, "Stadtverfassung," in *Reallexikon der Germanischen Altertumskunde*, ed. J. Hoops (4 vols., Strasbourg: K. Trubner, 1911–19), IV, pp. 244–59; A. Coville, "Les villes du moyen âge," *Journal des Savants* 25 (1928), 15–22, 72–80; N. S. B. Gras, *An Introduction to Economic History* (NY: Harper & Bros., 1922), pp. 104–23; G. Unwin, *Studies in Economic History* (London: Macmillan, 1927), pp. 49–70.

82. Stephenson, *Borough and Town: A Study of Urban Origins in England* (Cambridge, MA: Medieval Academy of America, 1933). This monograph represented a revised and modified expression of similar but more extreme views presented in several earlier articles: "The Origin of the English Towns," *American Historical Review* 32 (1926), 10–21 and "The Anglo-Saxon Borough," *English Historical Review* 45 (1930), 177–207.

83. Stephenson, *Borough and Town*, pp. 47–52.

84. Ibid., pp. 52–60, 65–70.

85. Ibid., pp. 70–185.

86. Ibid., pp. 186–205. This topographical approach was then quite novel to medieval English urban research, though it had been a well-established feature of continental studies. Stephenson recognized that medieval urban archaeology still was in its infancy but had much potential value.

87. J. Tait, *The Medieval English Borough: Studies on its Origins and Constitutional History* (Manchester: Manchester University Press, 1936), pp. 5–14. This book has been described as "learned but far from lucid": J. F. Benton, ed., *Town Origins: The Evidence from Medieval England* (Lexington, MA: D. C. Heath & Co., 1968), p. xii. Its extremely compressed and turgid presentation does obscure the author's points. See further: G. H. Martin and S. McIntyre, *A Bibliography of British and Irish Municipal History* (Leicester: University Press, 1972), pp. xxxvi–xxxvii.

88. Tait, *Medieval English Borough*, pp. 15–30, 68–77, 130. Dorothy Whitelock also emphasized the importance of Anglo-Saxon trade and its impact on pre-Conquest town growth: *The Beginnings of English Society* (Harmondsworth: Penguin Books, 1952), pp. 115–29.

89. Tait, *Medieval English Borough*, pp. 42–43, 64–66, 96–108, 132–38; Lyon, *Henri Pirenne*, pp. 434–35.

90. See, for example, R. R. Darlington, "The Early History of English Towns," *History*, 23 (1938), 141–50; *ASE*, pp. 525–38; W. Savage, *The Making of Our Towns* (London: Eyre and Spottiswoode, 1952), pp. 42–49.

91. See Stephenson's reply in his review of *The Medieval English Borough* by J. Tait, *American Historical Review* 43 (1938), 96–99. Also see H. Schledermann, "The Idea of the Town: Typology, Definitions, and Approaches to the Study of the Medieval Town in Northern Europe," *World Archeology* 2 (1970), 116–17; D. M. Nicholas, "Medieval Urban Origins in Northern Continental Europe: State of Research and Some Tentative Conclusions," *Studies in Medieval and Renaissance History* 6 (1969), pp. 109–11. For brief reviews of the debate from Tait's recent

partisans, see H. R. Loyn, "Towns in Late Anglo-Saxon England: The Evidence and Some Possible Lines of Enquiry," in *England Before the Conquest*, eds. P. Clemoes and K. Hughes (Cambridge: University Press, 1971), pp. 115–16: "We are all Taitians now": Martin, "Domesday Book and the Boroughs," in *Domesday Book: A Reassessment*, ed. P. H Sawyer (London: Edward Arnold, 1985), pp. 147–50.

92. J. Hill, *Medieval Lincoln* (Cambridge: University Press, 1948); H. A. Cronne, *The Borough of Warwick in the Middle Ages* (Oxford: C. Batey, 1951); A. Raine, *Medieval York* (London: J. Murray, 1955). See also somewhat earlier, M. D. Lobel, *The Borough of Bury St. Edmunds* (Oxford: Clarendon Press, 1935), and H. Salter, *Medieval Oxford* (Oxford: Clarendon Press, 1936).

93. L. Mumford, *The City in History: Its Origins, Its Transformations, and Its Prospects* (NY: Harcourt, Brace and World, 1961), pp. 248–61. For similar views but with an emphasis on urban geography and topography, see R. E. Dickinson, *The West European City: A Geographical Interpretation* (London: Routledge & Kegan Paul, Ltd., 1951), pp. 251–78.

94. E. Gutnova, Review of *Towns and Urban Handicraft in England in the Tenth to Thirteenth Centuries* [in Russian, 1960] by Y. Levitsky, *Srednie Veka* 20 (1961), 240–46, trans. I. Rudnytsky in *Town Origins*, ed. Benton, pp. 37–41. For a comparable view but in a broader context, see: Y. V. Andreev, "Urbanization as a Phenomenon of Social History," *Oxford Journal of Archaeology* 8 (1989), pp. 167-77.

95. G. Sjoberg, *The Pre-Industrial City: Past and Present* (NY: Free Press, 1960), esp. pp. 56–77. For criticisms and further insights, cf. B. Trigger, "Determinants of Urban Growth in Pre-Industrial Societies," in *Man, Settlement and Urbanism*, ed. P. J. Ucko, et al. (London: Duckworth, 1972), pp. 575–99.

96. M. Weber, "Die Stadt," *Archiv für Sozialwissenschaft und Sozialpolitik*, 47 (1920–21), 621–772 esp. Pt. I: "Begriff und Kategorien der Stadt," 621–45. See further, H. Callies, "Der Stadtbegriff bei Max Weber," in *Vor-und Frühformen der europäischen Stadt im Mittelalter*, ed. H. Jankuhn, et al. (2 vols., Göttingen: Vandenhoeck & Ruprecht, 1973–74), I, pp. 56–60; Schledermann, "Idea of the Town," 117–18; P. Wheatley," The Concept of Urbanism," in *Man, Settlement and Urbanism*, pp. 601–37, esp. 608–12.

97. E. Ennen, *Frühgeschichte der europäischen Stadt* (Bonn: L. Röhrscheid Verlag, 1953; "Les différents types de formation des villes européennes," *Le Moyen Age* 52 (1956), 397–411, and *Die europäische Stadt des Mittelalters* (Göttingen: Vandenhoeck & Ruprecht, 1972), pp. 11–12. She remained very skeptical about urban definitions.

98. V. Gordon Childe, *Man Makes Himself* (NY: Mentor Books, 1951), pp. 114–42, and "Civilization, Cities, and Towns," *Antiquity* 31 (1957), 36–38; L. Wooley, "The Urbanization of Society," *Journal of World History* 4 (1957), 245–50; Wheatley, "Concept of Urbanism," pp. 611–12, and in review: C. L. Redman, *The Rise of Civilization: From Early Farmers to Urban Society in the Ancient Near East* (San Francisco: W. H. Freeman and Co., 1978), chaps. 7, 8.

99. M. Hassal, "Roman Urbanization in Western Europe," in *Man, Settlement, and Urbanism*, pp. 857–61; J. S. Wacher, *The Towns of Roman Britain* (Berkeley: University of California Press, 1974), pp. 13–15, 36.

100. J. H. Mundy, "Medieval Urbanism," in *The Medieval Town*, eds. J. H. Mundy and P. Riesenberg (Princeton: D. Van Nostrand Co., 1958) pp. 9–15.

101. Ibid., pp. 22–31. See also (with caution) the exposition of E. A. Gutkind, who argues that true towns emerged in Anglo-Saxon England only after the ninth-century Viking wars when the economic function of proto-urban sites surpassed their traditional agrarian function: *International History of City Development* (8 vols. NY: Free Press, 1964–72), vol. VI: *Urban Development in Western Europe: The Netherlands and Great Britain* (1971), pp. 152–57, 182–83.

102. Mundy, "Medieval Urbanism," pp. 32–49.

103. See, for example, F. Braudel, *Civilisation matérielle et capitalisme, XVe–XVIII^{e}siècles* (Paris: Librairie Armand Colin, 1967), pp. 369–78. He constantly stressed the human, social dimension of urbanism in history: "The towns are so many electric transformers. They increase tension, accelerate the rhythm of exchange, and ceaselessly stir up men's lives." "Still," he added, "a town is a town wherever it is." See further on this social and attitudinal approach: R. S. Lopez, "The Crossroads within the Wall," in *The Historian and the City*, eds. O. Handlin and J. Burchard (Cambridge, MA: MIT Press, 1963), pp. 27–43, and Gutkind, *History of City Development*, I (1964), "Introduction," pp. 3–51—two very thought-provoking essays.

104. Braudel, *Civilisation matérielle et capitalisme*, pp. 397–400. Braudel seemed to regard European towns primarily as products of the eleventh-century trade and agrarian expansion stimulated by a revived money economy. He took care to observe, however, that this urban growth was not uniform (ibid., pp. 391–94).

105. M. Biddle, "Archaeology and the History of British Towns," *Antiquity* 42 (1968), 109–16 and "The Towns," in *The Archaeology of Anglo-Saxon England*, ed. D. M. Wilson (London: Methuen & Co., 1976), pp. 99–150; T. G. Hassal, "Urban Archaeology in England, 1975," in *European Towns: Their Archaeology and Early History*, ed. M. W. Barley (London: Academic Press, 1977), pp. 3–18. The absence of archaeological evidence from such postwar general works as that of R. L. Reynolds (1954) and J. H. Mundy (1958) is quite glaring, although it does emerge in that of J. F. Benton (1968).

106. Freeman, *Norman Conquest*, IV, pp. 202–4, 209–24 and *English Towns and Districts*; J. R. Green, *Making of England*, pp. 98–107; Stephenson, *Borough and Town*, pp. 22–29, 186–205.

107. *The Atlas of Historic Towns*, eds. M. D. Lobel, et al. (London: Lovel Johns Ltd., 1969—). See further, Martin, "The Town as Palimpsest," in *The Study of Urban History*, ed. H. J. Dyos (NY: St. Martin's Press, 1968), pp. 155–69; M. Biddle and D. Hill, "Late Saxon Planned Towns," *Antiquaries Journal* 51 (1971), 70–85; M. W. Barley, ed., *The Plans and Topography of Medieval Towns in England and Wales*. Council for British Archaeology (hereafter C.B.A.), Research Reports 14 (London, 1976); Lobel, "Some Reflections on the Topographical Development of the Pre-Industrial Town in England," in *Tribute to an Antiquary*, eds. F. Emmison and R. Stephens (London: Leopard's Head Press, 1976), pp. 141–63. For a summation of this topographical research in broad historical perspective, see Gutkind, *City Development*, VI, 158–222. This study and its series represents a good introduction to the topic by regions, though its conclusions are now somewhat outdated and questionable. For a more concise recent example of the topographical approach, see L. Benevolo, *The History of the City*, trans. G. Culverwell (Cambridge, MA: MIT Press, 1980), esp. pp. 203–37, 253–58, covering Rome and the early medieval West,

and now the same author's insightful work, *The European City*, trans. C. Ipsen (Oxford: Blackwell, 1993), esp. pp. 1–22.

108. A. H. Smith, *English Place-Name Elements*, English Place-Name Society, 25–26 (2 vols., Cambridge: University Press, 1956); E. Ekwall, *Oxford Dictionary of English Place-Names* (4th ed., Oxford: Clarendon Press, 1960); M. Gelling, *Signposts to the Past: Place-Names and the History of England* (London: J. M. Dent, 1978); K. Cameron, ed., *Place-Name Evidence for the Anglo-Saxon Invasion and Scandinavian Settlements* (Nottingham: English Place-Name Society, 1977), and "The Significance of English Place-Names," *Proceedings of the British Academy* 62 (1976), pp. 135-55.

109. R. Dolley, ed., *Anglo-Saxon Coins* (London: Methuen, 1961), and "The Coins," in *Archaeology of Anglo-Saxon England*, pp. 349–72; D. M. Metcalf, "The Prosperity of North-Western Europe in the Eighth and Ninth Centuries," *Economic History Review* 20 (1967), 344–57. See also, *Sylloge of Coins of the British Isles* (London: Oxford University Press, 1958–).

110. Biddle, "Archaeology and the Beginnings of English Society," in *England before the Conquest*, pp. 394–96, and "The Towns," in *Archaeology of Anglo-Saxon England*, pp. 103–12. Biddle did not contend that this was the only way in which settlement continuity had occurred. Moreover, he does not regard these early Anglo-Saxon settlements within old Roman towns as urban in nature. See also, S. Frere, "The End of Towns in Roman Britain," in *The Civitas Capitals of Roman Britain*, ed. J. S. Wacher (Leicester: University Press, 1966), pp. 87–100; L. Alcock, *Arthur's Britain: History and Archaeology A.D. 367–634* (Harmondsworth: Penguin Books, 1971), pp. 186–90; D. H. Hill, "Continuity from Roman to Medieval: Britain," in *European Towns*, ed. Barley, pp. 293–302. For modifications, see M. J. Whittock, *The Origins of England 410–600* (Totowa, NJ: Barnes & Noble, 1986), pp. 61–67; P. Dixon, "The Cities Are Not Populated as Once They Were," in *The City in Late Antiquity*, ed. J. Rich (London: Routledge, 1992), pp. 145–60.

111. C. J. Arnold, *Roman Britain to Saxon England* (Bloomington: Indiana University Press, 1984): "This study deliberately avoids the historical evidence" (p. 6). A. S. Esmonde Cleary, *The Ending of Roman Britain* (Savage, MD: Barnes & Noble Books, 1990), does somewhat better but is still very wary: "The fragmentary historical sources have been taken too much at face value" (p. 137). Both agree that Romano-British town life, including meaningful occupation, ended in the early fifth century, prior to the Anglo-Saxon invasions. For Arnold, the causes were gradual economic decline resulting in deterioration of public services, commercial decay, and the flight of wealthy town nobles to rural villas (pp. 21–47). Esmonde Cleary signals out specifically the end of Roman civil and financial administration (411) leading to a quite rapid collapse of town and country life (pp. 144–61). See also: J. Evans, "From the End of Roman Britain to the Celtic West," *Oxford Journal of Archaeology* 9 (1990), pp. 91–103. For the more extreme view that Romano-British towns were in decline from the third century, cf. R. Reece, "Town and Country: The End of Roman Britain," *World Archaeology* 12 (1980), 77–92, and "The End of the City in Roman Britain," in *City in Late Antiquity*, pp. 136–44.

112. R. Hodges, *The Anglo-Saxon Achievement: Archaeology and the Beginnings of English Society* (Ithaca: Cornell University Press, 1989), and in broader context: *Dark Age Economics: The Origins of Towns and Trade A.D. 600–1000* (NY: St. Martin's Press, 1982); also: Hodges and D. Whitehouse, *Mohammed, Charlemagne,*

and the Origins of Europe (Ithaca: Cornell University Press, 1983). Hodges's work is thought-provoking to be sure and apparently quite appealing to a wide social-scientific audience, but its ponderous theoretical emphasis, often abstruse jargon, and penchant for forcing the available evidence into preconceived models, are dubious historical virtues. For a recent, more salutary discussion of early medieval urban development (primarily in ninth and tenth-century Scandinavia and England) see: H. Clarke and B. Ambrosiani, *Towns in the Viking Age* (NY: St. Martin's Press, 1991).

113. J. Haslam,"Introduction" to *Anglo-Saxon Towns in Southern England*, ed. Haslam (Chichester: Phillimore, 1984), p. xiv; G. Astill, "Archaeology, Economics and Early Medieval Europe," *Oxford Journal of Archaeology* 4 (1985), pp. 215-31; C. Dyer, "Recent Developments in Early Medieval Urban History and Archaeology in England," in *Urban Historical Geography: Recent Progress in Britain and Germany*, eds. D. Denecke and G. Shaw (Cambridge: University Press, 1988), pp. 69–80 esp. 74–76; M. Carver, *Arguments in Stone: Archaeological Research and the European Town in the First Millennium* (London: Oxbow Books, 1993), pp. 16–18, 41–62. Hodges's tendency to suggest the operation of modern economic patterns in early medieval society is hazardous. For wider implications, see S. Barnish, "The Transformation of Classical Cities and the Pirenne Debate," *Journal of Roman Archaeology* 2 (1989), 385–400.

114. Biddle, "The Development of the Anglo-Saxon Town," in *Topografia urbana e vita cittadina nell'alto medioevo in occidente* (2 vols., Spoleto: Centro Italiano di Studi Sull'Alto Medioevo, 1974), I, pp. 203–30; Dickinson, *West European City*, pp. 301–32; Nicholas, "Medieval Urban Origins," pp. 57–60, 99–102, 110; Haslam, "Introduction," p. xvi, with criteria for central places; Schledermann, "Idea of the Town," p. 115; D. Hill, "Towns as Structures and Functioning Communities Through Time: The Development of Central Place From 600 to 1066," in *Anglo-Saxon Settlements*, ed. D. Hooke (London: Blackwell, 1988), pp. 197–212; Astill, "Towns and Town Hierarchies in Saxon England, *Oxford Journal of Archaeology* 10 (1991), pp. 95-117, esp. 101-9. For "central place theory" in urban geography and prehistorical study, see Wheatley, "Concept of Urbanism," pp. 614–18; C. Haselgrove, "Central Places in British Iron Age Studies: A Review and Some Problems," in *Central Places, Archaeology and History*, ed. E. Grant (Sheffield: University Press, 1986), pp. 3–12. T. Bekker-Nielsen, *The Geography of Power: Studies in the Urbanization of Roman North-West Europe*. British Archaeological Reports (hereafter B.A.R.), International Series, 477 (Oxford, 1989), pp. 4-8.

115. Stubbs, *Constitutional History*, I, pp. 99–100; Maitland, *Domesday Book and Beyond*, pp. 173, 185–86, 195.

116. Stephenson, *Borough and Town*, pp. 213–14.

117. *ASE*, pp. 527–28; Tait, *Medieval English Borough*, pp. 13, 24–29.

118. Biddle, "The Towns," pp. 99–100; C. Heighway, ed., *The Erosion of History: Archaeology and Planning in Towns* (London: C.B.A. Urban Research Committee, 1972), esp. Pts. 3.8–10. Another prominent medieval archaeologist, M. W. Beresford, still favored the older "lawyer's tests" for urban status: *New Towns of the Middle Ages* (NY: Praeger, 1967), p. 273; Beresford and Finberg, *English Medieval Boroughs*, pp. 25–26. For problems of definition, see further, Dyer, "Early Medieval Urban History and Archaeology," pp. 69–70; Schledermann, "Idea of the Town," 119–21; Nicholas, "Medieval Urban Origins," pp. 58–60; C. Pythian-Adams, "Jolly Cities, Goodly

Towns: The Current Search for England's Urban Roots," *Urban History Yearbook* 1 (1977), pp. 34–39.

119. S. Reynolds, *An Introduction to the History of English Medieval Towns* (Oxford: Clarendon Press, 1977), pp. ix–x. This survey is an essential starting point for further research. It provides not only a masterly political and socioeconomic overview but also evaluates the main theories and trends of medieval urban studies in England and abroad. In addition, see now Clarke and Ambrosiani, *Towns in the Viking Age*, pp. 1-4, 173-178.

120. C. Platt, *The English Medieval Town* (NY: David McKay Co., 1976) esp. pp. 15–37; S. Reynolds, *History of English Medieval Towns*, pp. 1–45, 66–90, 188–96.

121. See, for example, T. Mayer, ed., *Studien zu den Anfängen des europäischen Städtewesens* (Constance: J. Thorbecke, 1958); *La città nell'alto medioevo* (Spoleto: Centro Italiano di Studi sull'alto Medioevo, 1959); H. Jankuhn, et al., eds., *Vor-und Frühformen der europäischen Stadt; Topografia urbana e vita cittadina* (1974); Barley, ed., *European Towns* (1977); R. Hodges and B. Hobley, eds. *The Rebirth of Towns in the West, A.D. 700–1050*, C.B.A. Research Reports 68 (London, 1988); H. Clarke and A. Simms, eds. *The Comparative History of Urban Origins in Non-Roman Europe*, B.A.R., International Series, 255 (2 vols., Oxford, 1985).

122. See esp. Biddle, et al., eds., *Winchester Studies* (Oxford: Clarendon Press, 1976–). Also, R. A. Hall, ed., *Viking Age York and the North*, C.B.A. 27 (London, 1978); J. Bird, et al., eds., *Collectanea Londiniensia: Studies in London Archaeology and History* (London: Middlesex Archaeological Society, 1978).

Chapter 2

Romano-British Towns (c.43–500 A.D.)

One of the most contested issues concerning the early history of English towns has been the so-called "continuity question": Was late Roman urban life or urban settlement maintained long enough and to a sufficient degree to exert a significant influence on Anglo-Saxon town development? For some time, it was widely held that Romano-British towns by the mid-fifth century either had been totally abandoned or had become very sparsely populated, squalid non-urban shells, which succumbed easily to Anglo-Saxon assault or else simply were bypassed and left to fall into ultimate dereliction.[1]   In contrast to this rather bleak picture of decay and discontinuity, certain scholars later argued the case for a rather substantial continuation of Romano-British town settlement and sometimes even town life into and beyond the initial Anglo-Saxon invasion age.[2]

To a large extent, these two dramatically opposing views arose from the nature of the sources employed, combined with overly exclusive methodologies. Thus, for example, the predominantly "fire-and-sword" tone of the documentary evidence alone does lend itself rather well to the idea of catastrophic discontinuity, while archaeological and other nonliterary evidence may more likely speak for certain features of survival and continuity in town life. Historical reality, however, is unlikely to conform to extreme statements. A wider, more comprehensive use of various kinds of evidence, it may be suggested, will lead to a more balanced and plausible interpretation of this and other questions concerning early English town development.

The problem of urban continuity is certainly a critical issue for the initial period of Anglo-Saxon history. One must realize, however, that its roots lie in the context of late Roman Britain. If, for example, we are to consider the various aspects of continuity or discontinuity between Romano-British and early Anglo-Saxon towns, we must first examine Roman town types in Britain and their functions over time. Some key constituent issues that need attention are: the degree of Romano-British urban prosperity, the relationship between town and countryside, the population and administration of the towns, and the changing shape of the Romano-British urban landscape. Indeed, it always must be kept in mind that towns are not static entities. Their various functional and topographical transformations reveal both the trends and the underlying causes of urban growth and decline.

BIRTH AND GROWTH

The introduction of towns and town life based on the Graeco-Roman urban pattern ranks as one of the most significant aspects of the Roman incorporation of Britain. For the Greeks and Romans, civilized life itself meant city and town life. Aristotle had spoken in these terms regarding the city-state (*polis*):

Man is by nature an animal intended to live in a *polis*. He who is without a *polis*, by reason of his own nature and not of some accident, is either a poor sort of being, or a being higher than man: he is like the man of whom Homer wrote in denunciation: "Clanless and lawless and hearthless is he."[3]

Cicero reiterated this view and declared that cities, created by the mutual association of humans, generated the salient elements of civilization:

Without the association of men, cities (*urbes*) could not have been built or peopled; from which [city life], laws and customs were established, then the equitable distribution of private rights and a definite social system. Upon these institutions followed a more humane spirit and consideration for others, so that life was more secure; and by giving and receiving, by the exchange of resources and conveniences, we were in need of nothing.[4]

Various types of towns appeared in Roman Britain. In general, however, Roman towns were meant to be vital population centers serving multiple functions: administration, defense, trade and industry, religion, education, and amusement. They were largely self-governing communities designed with regular street networks and provided with monumental public structures including, most characteristically, the commercial-administrative complex of forum-basilica.[5] It is still rather safe to say that urbanism in this Graeco-Roman sense came to Britain only with the Romans. Although earlier Celtic society did have its hill forts (*oppida*) and lowland enclosures, those generally did not match the functional range, architectural scale, or size of the Roman towns.[6]

The formative period of Roman urbanization in Britain extended from the Claudian Conquest of 43 A.D. through the Antonine age of the late second century. The Roman Empire recognized a great variety of legally defined urban communities, a complex but flexible arrangement that had evolved during imperial expansion. In Britain, four Roman town types were prominent: the *colonia*, the *municipium*, the "*civitas*-capital," and the *vicus*. At the top of the urban hierarchy stood the *colonia*, a town established by imperial charter for Roman citizens, usually army veterans, in newly conquered territory.[7] Four *coloniae* were founded in Roman Britain: Camulodunum (Colchester, 49 A.D.), Lindum (Lincoln, c.93), Glevum (Gloucester, c.97), and later Eboracum (York) which was raised to colonial status in the early third century.[8] Most *coloniae* were established on the sites of former legionary fortresses. Indeed, archaeological excavations have shown that their street networks generally were extensions of the military grid and that major public buildings often were erected over previous legionary structures.[9] Additionally, the *coloniae* as a rule were particularly well embellished with civic architecture. As Tacitus makes clear in regard to Camulodunum, these veteran settlements were meant to be both quasi-military centers and also civilian sites representing the best features of Roman urban life and civilization.[10]

The *municipium*, like the *colonia*, was a chartered town of self-governing Roman citizens. It was not primarily a veteran settlement but rather a town refounded and planned in Roman style on the site of an existing native settlement.[11] The only firmly attested *municipium* in Roman Britain is Verulamium (c.70).[12] It has been suggested that a limited number of additional towns achieved municipal status in the third century, but this is uncertain.[13]

Civitas-capitals were the most numerous of the major Roman town types in Britain and perhaps the most significant. Following it would appear a policy already established in Gaul, the Romans in Britain created urbanized central places as administrative and cultural capitals for the tribal areas (*civitates peregrinae*) they encountered and subdued (Map 2.1). Although the term *civitas* retained its original meaning of the tribal canton as a whole, it increasingly came to refer to the main town itself.[14] Epigraphic evidence attests a dozen such *civitas*-capitals by the second century, and their number appears to have more than doubled by the end of the Roman period.[15]

A *civitas*-capital could have varying origins. In most cases, however, the site began as a Roman military fort at the crossing of an important river or trackway system and very often nearby a native hill fort. Soon civilian trading areas and humble domestic settlements (*canabae*) arose on the outskirts of the fort. When Roman forces moved forward, this settlement complex was developed by Roman civil authorities, using requisitioned military engineers, into a planned urban center with regular streets, administrative, commercial, and religious buildings, and public amenities. Local Romano-British nobles were encouraged to assume residence and administrative duties at these *civitas*-capitals, where they emulated and adopted Roman ways.[16]

Romano-British *civitas*-capitals were self-governing communities of noncitizens. Their constitutions, like those of *coloniae* and *municipia*, were modeled essentially on that of Republican Rome. Administrative responsibility was vested in an elected town council (*ordo, curia*) of one hundred local notables, generally called *decuriones* or *curiales*, who were distinguished by their wealth and social standing. From them, annual magistrates were appointed as executive town officers, such as the *duoviri* in charge of judicial and ceremonial affairs and the *aediles* who supervised public works. The council bore collective responsibility for taxes such as the land tax and poll tax, which were forwarded to the imperial procurator.[17]

In addition to these formal administrative and fiscal duties, decurions also were expected to pay a substantial entrance fee to office and to provide public entertainment or building projects on occasion. Initially, the response was positive, and such burdens always could be offset by local taxes, temple dues, and a widespread patronage system. Diocletian, however, made decurions personally liable for town taxes, and by the early fourth century they were responsible for the expenses of all public works.[18] The holding of town office with its accompanying responsibilities thereafter became increasingly unpopular. As we shall see, however, the negative impact of this factor upon the towns in Britain must not be exaggerated or overgeneralized.

The Romano-British cantonal capitals saw their greatest development in the century following Boudicca's Revolt (60/61 A.D.). During this time, capable Roman governors, most notably Agricola, promoted construction in these towns to make them primary agents of Romanization.[19] This process of acculturation through urbanization is confirmed by archaeological evidence showing a burst of public building activity at this time and also suggesting competition for building munificence among town nobles and perhaps between towns.[20] Cantonal capitals varied in size and population. Most, however, fell within the range of 70 to 140 acres and perhaps 2,000 to 5,000 inhabitants each, though there were a handful of considerably larger sites.[21] At first glance these figures may appear rather small, but they are quite comparable to those of similar towns in Rome's northern provinces.[22] Estimates of overall urban population in early Roman Britain range between 200,000 and 350,000 or about 10 percent of total population—on a par with neighboring provinces of the empire and significantly higher than 1086 urban figures.[23]

The *vicus,* the smallest self-governing urban settlement in Roman Britain, is usually described as a "small town." Some eighty *vici* currently have been identified. They were generally 10 to 20 acres in size, with a few large-scale public buildings but little sign of regular town planning. Many also served as local market and production centers and were fortified after the second century. A *civitas*-capital could comprise one or more *vici* and, indeed, usually held the legal rank of a *vicus.*[24]

In addition to their administrative and social roles, Romano-British towns were designed to be vital centers of trade and industry. In both chartered towns and cantonal capitals, fora and market halls (*macella*) were built and provided with rental stalls for merchants and craftsmen. Privately owned shops often occupied whole blocks of streets as well.[25] Britain and its towns prospered by participation in Roman trade. Foreign merchants are attested at many towns in the first and second centuries, and Tacitus refers to London as teeming with businessmen and merchandise even before the sudden Boudiccan Revolt.[26]

Indeed, Britain quickly became and long remained an important part of the Roman imperial economy. As Romanization and urbanization advanced during the first and second centuries, Romano-British town nobles acquired a healthy appetite for the amenities and luxury goods of Roman civilization. A brisk cross-Channel trade thus was established that conveyed to Romano-British decurions such high-status items as fine pottery, glassware, marble, and choice wines.[27] Britain's main and most valued exports were metals (silver, gold, iron, copper, tin, lead), grain, and woolen cloth, along with hides, slaves and exotic animals.[28] Local and foreign urban commerce may have slackened temporarily amid third-century disruptions caused by imperial usurpations in Britain and Germanic incursions in Gaul and the Rhineland. Yet Romano-British urban economic life does not appear to have been catastrophically affected by the so-called Crisis of the Third Century. Exports of grain, metals, and wool increased, while expanded local production lessened the overall demand for such imports.[29]

Industrial and craft production were located in or adjacent to many Romano-British towns. Metalworking, glass-making, pottery, tile and cloth production, dyeing, tanning, and milling are all attested urban operations. Most of them were done in small, private workshops, but several, such as pottery, tile, and cloth-making, were conducted on a large scale. Again, increased production in the third and early fourth centuries lessened the need for imported items.[30] Archaeological studies also have shown that much of this later industrial growth was centered in the "small towns" of Roman Britain, many of which ranked as *vici,* the smallest self-governing town type.[31] The trend toward self-sufficiency in commerce and industry helped Romano-British towns to acquire in adequate numbers the items needed for Romanized urban life and for agricultural activities in their respective regions. The record of continuing urban prosperity therefore casts doubt on the traditional view, propounded especially by R. G. Collingwood, that Romano-British towns began a slow but irreversible decline in the mid-third century.[32]

A similar picture of generally sustained urban health emerges from an examination of the relationship between Romano-British town and countryside. Although this topic has been studied for some time, it remains very important and deserves reconsideration in the light of recent research. The usual position is that Romano-British towns were essentially "parasitical," draining the countryside of agricultural produce while returning only a minimal amount of goods and services.[33] More recent research suggests that the connection between town and country in Britain was more mutually beneficial and underwent less crippling crises than this picture presents. It also would be well to bear in mind that a sharp town versus country dichotomy may be a more modern phenomenon.

On the one hand, the role of Romano-British towns as regional market and production centers already has been noted. Moreover, there is evidence that many towns at least initially were directly involved in supplying their own food needs. Each chartered *colonia* and *municipium*, for example, was surrounded by an extensive agricultural zone (*territorium*) administered from the town and divided into privately owned plots worked by town inhabitants. In some instances the *territorium* actually lay within the town, and a significant number of such internal farming areas have been excavated.[34] The fact that many early *civitas*-capitals initially exhibit a marked absence of adjacent villas raises the strong possibility that cantonal capitals also controlled and worked surrounding lands.[35]

Indeed, the development of Romano-British villas reveals much concerning the relationship between town and country (Map 2.2.A and B). First, one should recall that the villa in Roman Britain was not an isolated homestead like the Celtic example but rather a working agricultural enterprise with the town as its primary market. This mutual relationship is well demonstrated by the fact that Romano-British villas were sited preponderantly along Roman roads connecting major and minor towns.[36] Furthermore, the greatest periods of villa foundation and improvement coincide exactly with the busiest urban phases in Britain. Thus, during the second century when most *civitas*-capitals were being established, many surrounding small farms developed into more elaborate operations with buildings that reflect both the architectural features and the accompanying master-servant relationship so characteristic of the Mediterranean Roman villa.[37] This suggests that wealthy landowners (i.e., tribal nobles) were opting not only for Romanized town life but also were indulging in the Roman taste for income-producing country estates. Decurions or *curiales* legally were required to reside in their towns, and most at first seem to have done so, leaving villa management to bailiffs (*vilici*).[38]

The truly "golden age" of the Romano-British villa occurred in the late third and early fourth centuries, precisely when, according to Collingwood and others, the towns and general economy of Britain were in serious decline. The evidence on the contrary points to continued prosperity in town and countryside. It used to be held that the early fourth century efflorescence of villa life in Britain represented a general flight to the country by financially hard-pressed town nobles.[39] This view has become rather less tenable, however, since town construction is now known to have continued significantly in this period.[40] Indeed, that close connection between town and country established during the two preceding centuries appears to have been maintained and even intensified, rather than broken.

Around major towns, for example, one can detect an outburst of early fourth-century villa construction, with buildings themselves often assuming quite elaborate proportions.[41] Equally notable is the proliferation of villas around the small towns of fourth-century Britain, which functioned as minor industrial and market centers.[42] This small town-villa relationship can be seen as another version of the same process occurring around chartered towns and cantonal capitals.

The structural defenses of Romano-British towns also serve as indicators of continuing town prosperity. Urban fortification, especially during the early empire, was as much or more a matter of civic pride and competition as it was of military protection.[43] Defensive works were allowed only by successful petition, ultimately to the emperor. Moreover, although the Roman army provided necessary specialists, fortification was the financial responsibility of individual towns.[44] Beginning in the late second century, bank-and-ditch defensive circuits were erected at most Romano-British cantonal capitals and even many small towns. But attempts to connect this phenomenon with any specific threat or, indeed, to identify it as a common program, have been inconclusive.[45] It is worth noting that the establishment of these Romano-British earthworks stands in sharp contrast to the situation in Gaul, where most towns confronted third-century Germanic attacks without fortifications. In addition, second-century British defenses normally enclosed the entire town and occasionally even outlying territory, whereas Gallic town fortifications, when belatedly done, enclosed only small portions of their town area.[46] These initial earthwork urban defenses in Britain were followed by more substantial and costly stone circuits in the mid to late third century. Once again, these new masonry walls do not appear to be associated with any imminent danger. In most cases, they reinforced the earlier earthen ramparts and lay along the same lines without contraction of the enclosed area.[47]

A century later, great projecting stone towers and bastions commonly were added to the walls for artillery installations. This final major sequence of Romano-British town fortification likely was prompted by increased seaborne Germanic raids occurring on both sides of the Channel. The great stone fortresses of the "Saxon Shore," the late Roman defensive system along the eastern coasts (Map 2.1), are perhaps the best-known testaments to the heightened security problems of fourth-century Britain and the northern provinces.[48] Indeed, emperors from Diocletian to Constantine the Great and Valentinian I are known to have generally promoted the strengthening of frontier defenses, including forts and towns, and to have redeployed border troops into the towns.[49] Valentinian's legate in Britain, Count Theodosius (father of Theodosius the Great), specifically is said to have restored both towns and forts in the course of his successful military defense against Saxon raiders and his reestablishment of administrative order in the province (368–370 A.D.).[50] Though this heavy walling more clearly had a primary strategic purpose, it still attests that the towns themselves maintained sufficient resources for the task.

The impressive road system that linked Romano-British towns also was kept in generally good repair into the fourth century. Although this network primarily served military and administrative purposes, it facilitated town trade as well. Moreover, the establishment of official inns (*mansiones*) within towns along the public roads stimulated urban growth, especially that of the small towns.[51] There is also little doubt that the continuing prosperity of Britain and the embellishment of its towns were aided by ongoing imperial concern for the island province, including repeated visitations by such emperors as Hadrian, Septimius Severus, and Constantine the Great.[52] At the very end of the third century, a Roman writer could praise the wealth and resources of Britain, its many trading centers, and lucrative taxes.[53]

Romano-British towns thus appear to have weathered the economic and security crises confronting their region and the empire during the third and early fourth centuries. In the course of three hundred years, they became vital centers of administration, defense, commercial and industrial activities, religion, and social amenities. The town-country nexus remained generally strong and mutually beneficial. There are hence grounds to at least seriously question the long-held view of Romano-British urbanism as superficial or parasitical.[54] After three centuries of general growth and integration, however, the towns of late Roman Britain were subjected to a new series of rapidly mounting pressures, which did result in significant change to both the urban landscape and urban life itself.

CHANGE AND DECLINE

Following the death of Constantine the Great (337), Britain was plunged directly into a decades-long struggle over the imperial succession. Perhaps the most serious episode for the British towns occurred in 350 when Magnentius, a field commander in the Gallic prefecture, which then included Britain, was elevated as Augustus of the West in a palace plot. After some three years of bitter conflict, Constantine's youngest son, Constantius II, finally defeated Magnentius's Gallic and British legions. One of the new emperor's first acts was to dispatch an agent to Britain, Paul "The Chain," in order to purge Magnetius's supporters in the island. This program of reprisal proceeded with notorious severity and seems to have fallen hardest precisely on the wealthy decurions (*curiales*) who were town officials. Summary executions and substantial property confiscations are reported.[55] Magnus Maximus, who soon after usurped imperial authority in the west from his base in Britain and Gaul (383–388), also may have resorted to similar policies.[56]

In addition to these cumulative attacks on their persons and property, Romano-British town nobles were subjected to ever-mounting financial burdens. In Britain as elsewhere within the later empire, imperial rapacity weighed most heavily on members of wealthy, established urban elites. Diocletian had made individual decurions personally responsible for town taxes. Constantine the Great effectively confiscated local urban taxes from tolls, markets, and temples and channeled them directly into central imperial coffers. Constantius II (351–361) then proceeded to appropriate the revenues from urban landholdings throughout the empire. At the same time, a series of imperial laws tied decurions and their descendants to their town offices and town residences.[57]

Moreover, the Diocletianic division of the empire into smaller provinces tended to shift authority away from local town councils to provincial governors and their burgeoning administrative staffs. The urban nobility's authority and the established patterns of urban-rural exchange were further undermined by direct imperial payments in kind to town garrisons and resident imperial officials.[58] Although deprived of much of their traditional wealth, authority, and prestige, decurions were still held responsible for the maintenance of town fabric and services.

There were various ways decurions could escape their heavy financial burdens. They might achieve senatorial rank and spend most of their time on their rural estates. The increasingly sumptuous villas and town houses of early fourth-century Britain probably belonged to prosperous members of this group.[59] Or they might gain exemption by entering the church (while retaining their country estates, of course). This option is perhaps best illustrated by the family history of Saint Patrick (c.390–460), whose father and grandfather were Romano-British decurions who had taken minor Christian orders.[60] Yet even with these and other alternatives, there does not appear to have been any sudden mass exodus of Romano-British decurions from their towns at any time during the fourth century. As elsewhere, there long remained a core group of well-to-do urban *curiales*, though their numbers gradually were diminishing.[51] Still, growing impoverishment and avoidance of urban life, even by a minority of decurions, were bound to have adverse effects on the towns.

Indeed, there are many indications that the mid-fourth century was a watershed in the history of Romano-British towns. Up to this time, urban centers appear to have maintained their essential functions and generally high levels of prosperity. Thereafter, this overall record of urban health begins to show signs of weakening and gradual decline. Much of this slow reversal can be attributed to the worsening financial condition of town nobles and their increasing reluctance or inability to make traditional expenditures on public buildings and services. Archaeological evidence clearly attests to this ominous trend. For example, many of the impressive fora in chartered towns and *civitas*-capitals that once had seen brisk trading activity fell into slow disrepair beginning in the mid-fourth century. Standard urban amenities such as the public baths, water and sewage systems, and burial facilities also deteriorated at this time.[62] The involvement of Britain and Gaul in fourth-century imperial civil wars, along with the renewal of Germanic assaults, further undermined Romano-British urban commerce and industry. For example, both local and foreign urban trade fell in volume as communications were disrupted and transport became more hazardous and costly. Indeed, archaeological evidence indicates that by the close of the fourth century, the ports of London and York had largely silted over.[63] Metalworking and centralized pottery production decreased after c.350 amids the depletion of Britain's gold and silver mines and the devastation wrought upon several major ceramic-producing regions by local warfare and brigandage.[64] There are thus grounds to believe that not only high-ranking decurions but also middle-class merchants and craftsmen began to suffer serious reverses. These latter groups were less likely to enjoy the option of retiring to comfortable country estates in troubled times.

Amid these changes it is not surprising to find evidence of urban settlement contraction and population loss, especially in the larger towns. Recent excavations at London, Winchester, Gloucester, and Cirencester have disclosed significant late Roman deserted areas, and at Verulamium and other towns, suburban expansion also evidently halted.[65] Indeed, such once-occupied areas not infrequently appear to have reverted to agricultural use.[66] These marked alterations to the townscape imply substantial population decline during the late fourth century. Precise figures cannot be determined, but a reduction of between 20 and 30 percent in most Romano-British towns is considered likely.[67]

Urban prosperity in Britain had depended largely on adequate supply and circulation of coinage. Although barter transactions never entirely ceased in the island, Rome's introduction of a uniform money economy was for the most part quite thorough, and its coinage remained the standard for the province's commercial and industrial activities for three centuries. By the later fourth century, however, Britain's coin supply began to dwindle. Britain's primary mint, founded at London in 268, ceased continuous production c.325. Secondary mints at Colchester and Wroxeter had already been closed for several decades.[68] Moreover, regular imports of new gold, silver, and bronze coinages from the Continent, primarily to pay urban military garrisons and officials, fell sharply after 378 and ceased in 402. Older issues continued to circulate, including locally produced small bronzes (*minimissimi*), but by c.430, Britain essentially had lost its money economy.[69] A combination of many factors was responsible for this progressive reduction in coin supply: repeated monetary devaluations in the wake of mounting inflation, disruption of imported cash supplies, commercial slowdown, and successive withdrawals of official, regularly paid urban troops from Britain c.340–409.[70] Decurions responsible for tax collection and town repair, along with urban merchants and craftsmen, were no doubt all adversely affected.

By the close of the fourth century, therefore, the conditions of towns in Britain and the intensity of urban life were much reduced. With their leading social classes beleaguered, their trade and industry diminished, their physical size and public services constricted, Romano-British towns clearly were not what they had been in the second century. Nonetheless, it would be rash and inaccurate to conclude that urbanism had totally collapsed or that the towns had become mere agricultural villages. Recognizably urban activities continued, though on a significantly reduced scale. In general, the town functions of defense and administration appear to have remained most intact. The extensive Theodosian fortification projects in the towns were effective for some time, and there is continuing evidence of both local and imperial officials (though fewer in number) at chartered towns and cantonal capitals into the early fifth century.[71]

A body of written evidence indicates that some of the remaining Romano-British urban upper class still commanded considerable prestige and resources in the early fifth century. For example, between 406 and 409, three prominent men in Britain rose to claim the western imperial throne. The first, Marcus, was a military commander who was quickly replaced by a civilian, Gratian, specifically described as a member of the town nobility. He in turn was deposed by the local general, Constantine, who won recognition as Augustus (Constantine III) from the Emperor Honorius in 409.[72] Indeed, it was at this time that the Britons are said to have become so dissatisfied with Roman authority and Roman military weakness that they rose in revolt, expelled Roman officials, and successfully defended their own towns from barbarian attacks.[73] The leaders of this rebellion most likely were Romano-British decurions still concerned with the safety and well-being of their towns. Honorius evidently was notified of their actions and was also asked for advice, for in the following year (410) the emperor sent a famous rescript or reply-memorandum addressed directly to the *civitas*-capitals of Britain, telling them that for the time being they should indeed now look to their own defense.[74]

The removal of the last Roman civil and military officials may well have benefited Romano-British urban nobles for a time. Freed at last from imperial financial and other burdens, they were left in full command of their towns. Among these individuals were the men who loom so large in the monk Gildas's work, *De excidio Britonum* (c.540), as "tyrants" and "kings" of sub-Roman Britain.[75] According to Gildas, the Roman expulsion of 409 was followed by a period of renewed prosperity and great personal luxury. Before long, however, civil wars among local British "tyrants" brought social disorder, famine, and urban decay. Meanwhile, barbarian attacks and revolts by Germanic mercenaries increased. Eventually, a final appeal to Roman forces in Gaul for help went unanswered (c.446).[76]

As we shall see, however, any improved conditions after 409 such as Gildas alleges were not widespread or very enduring. Nor was there any notable general increase in urban construction and embellishment. Although certain towns did manage to maintain some urban functions well into the fifth century, they certainly cannot be described as bustling urban centers. Similarly, Romano-British villas evidently were in decline during the late fourth century. Very few new villa constructions or major improvements are attested after 400, though many villas continued to be at least partly occupied.[77]

A few towns could still manage fairly well in this "sub-Roman" period. One rather roseate report is contained in Constantius of Lyons' *Life of St. Germanus*, written c.480. In 429, Germanus and his fellow Gallic bishop, Lupus, journeyed to Britain in order to counter the spread of Pelagianism. This anti-Augustinian doctrine appears to have become firmly rooted in Britain and Gaul, primarily among urban nobles.[78] After their arrival, the bishops are said to have held a public debate at an unnamed town (perhaps Verulamium) with local Pelagian notables "conspicuous for riches, brilliant in dress, and surrounded by a fawning multitude," that is, their *clientelae*.[79] The bishop's scriptural eloquence had the upper hand, and Germanus won further crowd approval by restoring the eyesight of the daughter of a man "of tribunician power." They thereafter visited the tomb of St. Alban, evidently nearby.[80] When Germanus again visited Britain ("that most opulent island") nearly twenty years later (c.446) for similar reasons, he met a certain Elafius, described as "the leading man (*primus*) of that region."[81] These are not descriptions of totally impoverished town nobles living among ruins. Although the particular town and its *curiales* may well have been exceptional, these passages furnish at least one example of an urban nobility still prosperous and prestigious enough to put on a good show, and they also demonstrate the presence of a town garrison commander and a cantonal ruler.

Some remarks certainly are in order concerning Gildas's famous account of the fate of towns in Roman Britain. His description has received much attention because it represents the only commentary on this topic in any detail by a near contemporary. Caution must be observed for a number of reasons, however. First, Gildas's overriding providential theme causes him to overdraw his final picture of total destruction as Divine retribution for the sins of his fellow Britons. Also, his polemic style and purpose often lead him into sweeping, broad generalizations. In addition, textual studies now have shown that Gildas's immediate geographical frame of reference was rather sharply limited to western and northern Britain.[82]

Gildas relates that after the Romans' final withdrawal, local British forces in the north could not withstand barbarian attacks, and "our citizens abandoned the towns (*civitates*) and the high wall (Hadrian's Wall)."[83] Nothing is said about urban destruction in the wake of this abandonment or of town conditions elsewhere at this time. There follows an overview of the subsequent fate of the towns, which is placed within the primary context of Anglo-Saxon conquest and settlement in the south. Gildas states that small groups of Saxon mercenaries had been invited into this part of Britain as federate forces by local Romano-British rulers. After their demands for more supplies were not met, these groups, augmented by recent arrivals, rose up against their employers like a fire spreading from sea to sea, "devastating neighboring towns (*civitates*) and fields."[84] Gildas continues and describes how "all the major towns were leveled by the repeated battering of enemy rams" and how, amid toppled towers, walls, and burned buildings, the torn bodies of priests and laymen lay unburied, "covered with a purple crust of congealed blood."[85] He then speaks proudly of the British military recovery and restoration of order under a certain Ambrosius Aurelianus, c.500, and hints that this had benefited the towns. Any urban restoration did not endure, however, as disruptive warfare raged once again among local British rulers: "But the towns of our land are not inhabited even now as they were before; up till the present they are overgrown, deserted, and demolished—external wars may be ceased but not civil wars."[86]

Gildas's famous account is of uneven value. On the one hand, written and, to some extent, archaeological evidence tend to corroborate his general description of federate arrangements and the transition to larger-scale conquests.[87] But his lurid portrayal of town destruction following the Saxon revolt is particularly suspect. As will be shown, there is no firm evidence of widespread, violent destruction from fifth century excavation levels in Romano-British towns. Moreover, the few cases where such violent events are possible did not always have catastrophic results.[88] In this regard one may note that the *Anglo-Saxon Chronicle* specifically speaks of a series of towns in the west that remained in British hands until the late sixth century.[89] Gildas's remark that some British towns were systematically and successfully besieged is also unconfirmed by the archaeological record. Written evidence of such assaults by early Anglo-Saxon or other Germanic peoples against late Roman towns is actually quite rare.[90] Finally, Gildas somewhat contradicts his portrait of town destruction and continued urban ruin by referring elsewhere in his same work to town towers, walls, and gates still standing in impressive condition.[91] Thus, while Gildas's description of town dereliction in his own day may well be broadly valid, his account of earlier urban destruction is exaggerated, over generalized, and inconsistent. Despite Gildas's polemics, Romano-British towns more often succumbed to a less dramatic process of slow abandonment than to "fire and sword," as we shall now see in greater detail.

NOTES

1. J. M. Kemble, *The Saxons in England* (2 vols., London: Longman, 1849), II, pp. 277–302; J. H. Ramsay, *The Foundations of England* (2 vols., London: Swan Sonnenschein, 1898), I, pp. 101–4, 115–17, 137–38, 163; W. E. Lunt, *History of England* (NY: Harper & Brothers, 1928), pp. 31–32; C. Oman, *England Before the Norman Conquest* (8th ed. rev., London: Methuen, 1938), pp. 212A–212D; F. G. Marcham, *A History of England* (rev. ed., NY: Macmillan, 1950), p. 24.

2. S. Frere, "The End of Towns in Roman Britain," in *The Civitas Capitals of Roman Britain*, ed. J. S. Wacher (Leicester: University Press, 1966), pp. 87–100; M. Biddle, "The Development of the Anglo-Saxon Town," in *Topografia urbana e vita cittadina nell'alto medioevo in occidente* (2 vols., Spoleto: Centro Italiano di Studi Sull'Alto Medioevo, 1974), I, pp. 206–12. J. Liversidge, *Britain in the Roman Empire* (NY: Praeger, 1968), pp. 37, 67, 73–75; Biddle, "Development of the Anglo-Saxon Town," pp. 206–12. For a summary of these changing views, see C. J. Arnold, *Roman Britain to Saxon England* (Bloomington: Indiana University Press, 1984), pp. 22–30; R. Reece, "Models of Continuity," *Oxford Journal of Archaeology* 8 (1989), pp. 231-36.

3. Aristotle, *Politics*, i.2.9, trans. E. Barker (Oxford: Clarendon Press, 1946). See further, A. Anderson, "The Culture of the Greek *Polis*: The Unified View of Plato and Aristotle," in *Aspects of Graeco-Roman Urbanism: Essays on the Classical City*, ed. R. Marchese, British Archaeological Reports (hereafter B.A.R.) [Internat. Ser.] 188 (Oxford, 1984), pp. 42–60.

4. Cicero, *De Officiis*, II.iv, ed. W. Miller (London: Heinemann, 1913). Note his inclusion of the economic dimension. See further, L. S. Mazzolani, *The Idea of the*

City in Roman Thought, trans. S. O'Donnell (Bloomington: Indiana University Press, 1970).

5. See, in general, M. Hammond, *The City in the Ancient World* (Cambridge, MA: Harvard University Press, 1972), pp. 226–329; J. Ward-Perkins, *Cities of Ancient Greece and Italy* (NY: Braziller, 1974), pp. 22–36; M. Clavel and P. Lévêque, *Villes et structures urbaines dans l'occident romain* (Paris: Librairie Armand Colin, 1971), esp. pp. 103f. For Britain, see J. S. Wacher, *The Towns of Roman Britain* (Berkeley: University of California Press, 1974), pp. 36–78; H. H. Scullard, *Roman Britain* (NY: Thames & Hudson, 1979), pp. 89–111; S. Frere, *Britannia* (3d ed., London: Routledge & Kegan Paul, 1987), pp. 229–56; P. Salway, *Roman Britain* (Oxford: Clarendon Press, 1981), pp. 573–99; M. Aston and J. Bond, *The Landscape of Towns* (London: J. M. Dent, 1976), pp. 40–57.

6. Frere, *Britannia*, p. 229. E. A. Gutkind, *International History of City Development* (8 vols., NY: Free Press, 1964–72), vol., VI, *Urban Development in Western Europe: The Netherlands and Great Britain* (1971), pp. 128–33, 137. But seen in their own social context, the *oppida* can be considered at least proto-urban: B. Cunliffe, *Iron Age Communities in Britain* (London: Routledge & Kegan Paul, 1974), pp. 40–64; L. R. Laing, *Celtic Britain* (London: Collins, 1979), pp. 55–58; Aston and Bond, *Landscape of Towns*, pp. 35–40.

7. F. Abbott and A. Johnson, *Municipal Administration in the Roman Empire* (Princeton: Princeton University Press, 1926), pp. 4–7; Frere, *Britannia*, pp. 229–30; Wacher, *Towns*, p. 17.

8. Epigraphic evidence attests their status: *Corpus Inscriptionum Latinarum* (hereafter *Corp. Insc. Lat.*) (16 vols., Berlin, 1862–), XIV.3955 (Colchester); XIII.6679 (Lincoln); VI.3346 (Gloucester); VII.248 (York). See further, I. A. Richmond, "The Four *Coloniae* of Roman Britain," *Archaeological Journal* 103 (1946), 57–84; Wacher, *Towns*, pp. 104–77.

9. P. Crummy, "The Origins of Some Major Romano-British Towns," *Britannia* 10 (1982), 125–34; T. F. C. Blagg, "Roman Civil and Military Architecture in the Province of Britain," *World Archaeology* 12 (1980), 27–42. For the early economic role of the Roman army, see P. Garnsey and R. Saller, *The Roman Empire: Economy, Society, and Culture* (Berkeley: University of California Press, 1987), pp. 88–95.

10. Tacitus, *Annales*, xii.32, ed. H. Furneaux (2d ed., 2 vols., Oxford: Clarendon Press, 1896–1907), and *De vita Agricolae*, xiv, xvi, eds. R. Ogilvie and I. A. Richmond (Oxford: Clarendon Press, 1967).

11. Abbott and Johnson, *Municipal Administration*, pp. 8–9; Wacher, *Towns*, p. 18. Municipal communities could hold either full Italian, or more often, intermediate Latin status. After Caracalla's extension of the franchise in 212 these distinctions became less meaningful but were still sought. See J. Reynolds, "Legal and Constitutional Problems," in *Civitas Capitals*, p. 70.

12. Tacitus, *Annales*, xiv.33. See further, Wacher, *Towns*, pp. 202–25; S. Frere, *Verulamium Excavations* (3 vols., Oxford: Oxford University Committee for Archaeology, 1972–84).

13. Salway, *Roman Britain*, p. 575; Frere, *Britannia*, p. 194.

14. Reynolds, "Legal and Constitutional Problems," p. 72; Frere, "Civitas–A Myth?" *Antiquity* 35 (1961), 29–36; Salway, *Roman Britain*, p. 590; S. Johnson, *Later Roman Britain* (London: Collins, 1980), p. 17.

15. R. G. Collingwood and R. P. Wright, *The Roman Inscriptions of Britain*, I (Oxford: Clarendon Press, 1965), Nos. 114, 224, 288, 311, 707, 1672–73, 1843–44, 1962, 2022, 2250. This is confirmed by the "Antonine Itinerary" (ed. O. Cuntz. Berlin: Teubner, 1929) and the "Ravenna Cosmography" (ed. Richmond and O. G. S. Crawford), *Archaeologia* 93 (1949). See further, B. Jones and D. Mattingly, *An Atlas of Roman Britain* (Oxford: Blackwell, 1990), pp. 23–33.

Gildas observed that there had been twenty-eight *civitas*–capitals in late-Roman Britain: *De excidio Britonum*, iii.2, ed. M. Winterbottom (Chichester: Phillimore, 1978) and this number was passed on to Bede, Nennnius, and the medieval chroniclers. See F. Haverfield, *The Roman Occupation of Britain* (rev. ed., Oxford: Clarendon Press, 1924), pp. 289–93. The figure perhaps derives from a misreading of Ptolemy's thirty-eight *civitates* south of the Humber (*Geographia*, ii, ed. C. Müller. Paris, 1883). See further, C. E. Stevens, "Gildas and the *Civitates* of Britain," *English Historical Review* 52 (1937), 193–201; P. Sawyer, *From Roman Britain to Norman England* (London: Methuen, 1976), p. 62.

16. G. Webster, "Fort and Town in Early Roman Britain," in *Civitas Capitals*, pp. 32–42; Frere, *Britannia*, pp. 189–94; Wacher, *Towns*, pp. 30–35; Garnsey and Saller, *Roman Empire*, pp. 12–19, 189–95. For a less optimistic interpretation, cf. M. W. C. Hassall, "The Impact of Mediterranean Urbanism on Indigenous Nucleated Centres," in *Invasion and Response: The Case of Roman Britain*, eds. B. Burnham and H. Johnson, B.A.R. 73 (Oxford, 1979), pp. 241–54; R. F. J. Jones, "A False Start? The Roman Urbanization of Western Europe," *World Archaeology* 19 (1987), 47–57.

17. Wacher, *Towns*, pp. 39–41; Salway, *Roman Britain*, pp. 575–80; Garnsey and Saller, *Roman Empire*, pp. 28–40.

18. A. H. M. Jones, *The Later Roman Empire* (2 vols., Norman: University of Oklahoma Press, 1964), I, pp. 69–70; Hammond, *City in the Ancient World*, pp. 315–17; Abbott and Johnson, *Municipal Administration*, pp. 197–231; Frere, *Britannia*, pp. 198–202.

19. Tacitus, *De vita Agricolae*, xxi. See further, Frere, *Britannia*, pp. 297–300.

20. Wacher, *Towns*, pp. 45–59; Frere, "Civic Pride: A Factor in Roman Town Planning," in *Roman Urban Topography in Britain and the Western Empire*, eds. F. Grew and B. Hobley. Council for British Archaeology Research Report (hereafter C.B.A.) 59 (London, 1985), pp. 34–36; D. F. Mackreth, "Roman Public Buildings," in *Urban Archaeology in Britain*, eds. J. Schofield and R. Leech, C.B.A. 61 (London, 1987), pp. 133–46. For similar processes elsewhere in the Roman provinces, see: Hammond, *City in the Ancient World*, pp. 290–92; Clavel and Lévêque, *Villes et structures urbaines*, pp. 176–85.

21. Frere, *Britannia*, pp. 249, 252–53, 300–302. Cirencester, Wroxeter, Winchester, and Canterbury were the largest *civitas*-capitals (242, 192, 138 and 133 acres, respectively), with individual populations of 5,000 to perhaps 15,000.

22. C. Goudineau, "Les villes de la paix romaine," in *La ville antique*, Vol. 1 of *Histoire de la France urbaine*, ed. G. Duby (5 vols., Paris: Seuil, 1980–85), pp. 259–61, 309–10; E. M. Wightman, *Gallia Belgica* (Berkeley: University of California Press, 1985), p. 98; Frere, *Britannia*, p. 249. Romano-British urban architecture also was on

a scale similar to neighboring areas: Frere, *Britannia*, p. 300; Goudineau, "Les villes," pp. 272–96.

23. Frere, *Britannia*, pp. 301–2; Gutkind, *City Development*, VI, pp. 148–50, and Salway, *Roman Britain*, pp. 542–45 for even higher estimates; H. C. Darby, *Domesday England* (Cambridge: University Press, 1977), pp. 87–91, 364–68 (120,000 total burgesses, 8% of the total population); Goudineau, et al., "Le reseau urbain," in *La ville antique*, pp. 95–98; Wightman, *Gallia Belgica*, pp. 32–33, 98–99.

24. J. Reynolds, "Legal and Constitutional Problems," p. 74; Frere, *Britannia*, p. 197; M. Todd, "The Small Towns of Roman Britain," *Britannia* 1 (1970), 114–30; W. Rodwell and T. Rowley, eds., The *'Small Towns'* of *Roman Britain*, B.A.R. 15 (Oxford, 1975).

25. Wacher, *Towns*, pp. 59–64, surveys the archaeological evidence.

26. *Corp. Insc. Lat.*, XIII, Nos. 634, 7300, 8164, 8793; Tacitus, *Annales*, xiv.33. By the second century London had become the center of Roman civil and financial administration, eclipsing Colchester as provincial capital (Map 2.1). This bureaucratic concentration stimulated the town's economic development, as the port of London became a major hub of Roman imperial commerce. See R. Merrifield, *London: City of the Romans* (Berkeley: University of California Press, 1983), pp. 41–75; Wacher, *Towns*, pp. 79–103.

27. Salway, *Roman Britain*, pp. 629–30, 642–44, 651–53; Jones and Mattingly, *Atlas of Roman Britain*, pp. 196–201.

28. Strabo, *Geography*, iv.5.2, ed. H. Jones (8 vols., London: Heinemann, 1918–33); Tacitus, *De vita Agricolae*, xii. See further, Wacher, *Roman Britain* (London: J. M. Dent, 1978), pp. 92–95; Jones and Mattingly, *Atlas of Roman Britain*, pp. 179–96; Salway, *Roman Britain*, pp. 619–24, 630–41, 655–56. Much of Britain's precious metal went directly to imperial mints or was shipped overseas as bullion.

29. Frere, *Britannia*, pp. 245–46, 282–85. See in general, K. Hopkins, "Economic Growth and Towns in Classical Antiquity," in *Towns in Societies: Essays in Economic History and Historical Sociology*, eds. P. Abrams and E. A. Wrigley (Cambridge: University Press, 1978), pp. 35–77.

30. Wacher, *Towns*, pp. 64–66, and *Roman Britain*, pp. 88–92; Richmond, "Industry in Roman Britain," in *Civitas Capitals*, pp. 76–86; Liversidge, *Britain*, pp. 211–12; Frere, *Britannia*, pp. 251–52, 275–80, 283–92.

31. Salway, *Roman Britain*, pp. 593–96; Frere, *Britannia*, pp. 197, 230–31; Aston and Bond, *Landscape of Towns*, pp. 43–45.

32. R. G. Collingwood and J. N. L. Myres, *Roman Britain and the English Settlements* (2d ed., Oxford: Clarendon Press, 1937), pp. 201–7, 317–19; Gutkind, *City Development*, VI, pp. 146–48, emphasizing a low degree of Romanization in Britain and a hostile rural population.

33. Collingwood and Myres, *Roman Britain and the English Settlements*, pp. 198–207. Gutkind, *City Development*, VI, p. 151, describing Romano-British towns as "parasitic representatives of a hostile culture" and Romano-British urbanism as "second rate," "superimposed," and "superficial." This was essentially an application of Rostovtzeff's wider economic theory to the British case and must be viewed with considerable caution. See further, M. Finley, "The Ancient City: From Fustel de Coulanges to Max Weber and Beyond," in Finley, *Economy and Society* (NY: Viking Press, 1982), pp. 3–23.

34. Salway, *Roman Britain*, pp. 586–87; Wacher, *Towns*, pp. 19–20; M. Finley, *The Ancient Economy* (Berkeley: University of California Press, 1973), pp. 123–30.

35. A. L. F. Rivet, "Social and Economic Aspects," in *The Roman Villa in Britain*, ed. Rivet (London: Routledge & K. Paul, 1969), pp. 180–81. See also W. Rodwell, "Milestones, Civic Territories, and the Antonine Itinerary,'" *Britannia* 6 (1975), 76–101.

36. A. L. F. Rivet, *Town and Country in Roman Britain* (London: Hutchinson University Library, 1958), pp. 72–98, and "Social and Economic Aspects," pp. 199–200; K. Branigan, "Verulamium and the Chiltern Villas," in *Man, Settlement, and Urbanism*, eds. P. Ucko, et al. (London: Duckworth, 1972), pp. 851–55; Jones and Mattingly, *Atlas of Roman Britain*, pp. 240–46.

37. Rivet, "Social and Economic Aspects," pp. 204–6; Frere, *Britannia*, pp. 261–65. For comparisons of urban and rural villa private architecture, see C. V. Walthew, "The Town House and Villa House in Roman Britain," *Britannia* 6 (1975), 189–205; D. Perring, "Domestic Buildings in Romano-British Towns," in *Urban Archaeology in Britain*, eds. Schofield and Leech, pp. 147–55.

38. Salway, *Roman Britain*, pp. 158–60; Wacher, *Roman Britain*, pp. 115–16; C. Taylor, *Village and Farmstead: A History of Rural Settlement in England* (London: G. Philip, 1983), p. 100. The most lavish villa estates, like Fishbourne near Chichester with its impressive gardens, courtyards, and baths, may have served as early examples to local nobles of Roman country life at its best, thus presenting a rural parallel to the purpose of *colonia* foundation. See B. Cunliffe, *Fishbourne: A Roman Palace and its Gardens* (Baltimore: Johns Hopkins Press, 1971).

39. Collingwood and Myres, *Roman Britain*, pp. 215–16.

40. Wacher, *Roman Britain*, pp. 102–3; Frere, *Britannia*, pp. 245–46, 272–73; Liversidge, *Britain*, pp. 73–74; Rivet, *Town and Country*, pp. 94–95.

41. Wacher, *Roman Britain*, pp. 118–22; D. J. Smith, "The Mosaic Pavements," in *Roman Villa*, ed. Rivet, pp. 113–19; S. Johnson, *Later Roman Britain*, pp. 22–26; Jones and Mattingly, *Atlas of Roman Britain*, pp. 220–24, 240.

42. Salway, *Roman Britain*, pp. 595–97, noting the occasional presence of villas within "small towns"; cf. I. Hodder and M. Millet, "Romano-British Villas and Towns: A Systematic Analysis," *World Archaeology* 12 (1980), 69–76.

43. H. Von Petrikovits, "Fortifications in the North-Western Roman Empire from the Third to the Fifth Centuries A.D.," *Journal of Roman Studies* 61 (1971), 189–93, 203–4; C. Wells, *The Roman Empire* (Stamford: Stamford University Press, 1984), pp. 158–64; J. Wacher, *The Coming of Rome* (London: Collins, 1979), pp. 89–91.

44. Von Petrikovits, "Fortifications," 189–93, 203–4; Hammond, *City in the Ancient World*, p. 311; Salway, *Roman Britain*, pp. 279–80, 389–90; S. Johnson, *Late Roman Fortifications* (Totowa, NJ: Barnes & Noble, 1983), pp. 10–12, 20–24; R. Duncan-Jones, "Who Paid for Public Buildings in Roman Cities?" in *Roman Urban Topography*, eds. Grew and Hobley, pp. 28–33.

45. Wacher, *Towns*, pp. 72–75; Frere, *Britannia*, pp. 239–42, and "British Urban Defences in Earthwork," *Britannia* 15 (1984), 63–74; Salway, *Roman Britain*, pp. 261–65. Chartered towns and several cantonal capitals had earlier ramparts. See further, M. Jones and C. Bond, "Urban Defenses," in *Urban Archaeology in Britain*, pp. 81–116.

46. Frere, *Britannia*, p. 240; Wightman, *Gallia Belgica*, pp. 219–33; J. Crickmore, *Romano-British Urban Defenses*, B.A.R. 126 (Oxford, 1984); J. Drinkwater, "Urbanization in the Three Gauls: Some Observations," in *Roman Urban Topography*; D. M. Nicholas, "Medieval Urban Origins in Northern Continental Europe," in *Studies in Medieval and Renaissance History* 6 (1969), pp. 60–62. In Gaul and Germany there is more evidence of town settlement continuity, but not continuity of urban functions (ibid., pp. 88–89).

47. Frere, *Britannia*, pp. 242–45. Town militias apparently were then primarily responsible for manning the walls: Wacher, *Towns*, pp. 77–78.

48. Ibid., pp. 75–78; Frere, *Britannia*, 247–48; S. Johnson, *The Roman Forts of the Saxon Shore* (NY: St. Martin's Press, 1976); D. Baatz, "Town Walls and Defensive Weapons," in *Roman Urban Defences in the West*, eds. J. Maloney and B. Hobley, C.B.A. 57 (London, 1983), pp. 136–40.

49. Zosimus, *Historia nova: The Decline of Rome*, ii.34, trans. J. Buchanan and H. Davis (San Antonio, TX: Trinity University Press, 1967). See further, Salway, *Roman Britain*, pp. 324–31; P. J. Casey, "Imperial Campaigns and Fourth-Century Defences in Britain," in *Roman Urban Defences*, eds. Maloney and Hobley, pp. 121–124.

50. Ammianus Marcellinus, *Res gestae*, xxviii.3.2–3.7, ed. J. Rolfe (3 vols., London: W. Heinemann, 1963). See further, Salway, *Roman Britain*, pp. 380–84, 388–91; Frere, *Britannia*, pp. 339–48; Johnson, *Later Roman Britain*, pp. 122–30. Regular troops were now garrisoned in the towns.

51. Salway, *Roman Britain*, pp. 562–71; Frere, *Britannia*, pp. 291–92.

52. Salway, *Roman Britain*, pp. 185–88, 228–38, and 323–29, discusses the circumstances.

53. *Incerti Panegyricus Constantio Caesari dictus*, viii.11, in *XII Panegyrici Latini*, ed. R.A.B. Mynors (Oxford: Clarendon Press, 1964).

54. Collingwood and Myres, *Roman Britain*, pp. 198–207; Reece, "Town and Country: The End of Roman Britain"; M. G. Fulford, "Town and Country in Roman Britain–A Parasitical Relationship?" in *The Romano-British Countryside*, ed. D. Miles, B.A.R. 103 (Oxford, 1982), pp. 403–19. It may be noted that one of the leading early scholars of Roman Britain, F. Haverfield, did not accept this view of superficial urbanization: *The Romanization of Roman Britain* (4th ed. rev. Oxford: Clarendon Press, 1923), pp. 14-16, 57-64.

55. Ammianus Marcellinus, *Res gest.*, xiv.6–9. See further, Salway, *Roman Britain*, pp. 354–59.

56. Zosimus, *Historia nova*, iv.45–46; Sulpicius Severus, *Dialogi*, iii.11, ed. C. Halm, *Corpus Scriptorum Ecclesiasticorum Latinorum*, I (Bonn, 1866). See further, Salway, *Roman Britain*, pp. 402–5; J. Matthews, *Western Aristocracies and Imperial Court, A.D. 364–425* (Oxford: Clarendon Press, 1975), pp. 173–82; Casey, "Magnus Maximus in Britain: A Reappraisal," in *The End of Roman Britain*, ed. Casey. B.A.R. 71 (Oxford, 1979), pp. 66–79.

57. For details and bibliography on these measures, see Jones, *Later Roman Empire*, I, pp. 732–34; Salway, *Roman Britain*, pp. 576–78.

58. Hammond, *City in the Ancient World*, pp. 314–17; Jones, *Later Roman Empire*, I, pp. 43–46, 623–24; Salway, *Roman Britain*, pp. 371–72.

59. Wacher, *Roman Britain*, pp. 102–3, 118–22; Salway, *Roman Britain*, pp. 266–67, 328–29; Johnson, *Later Roman Britain*, pp. 22–26. Senatorial rank was hereditary from Constantine the Great's time.

60. S. Patricius, *Confessio*, i, ed. A. B. E. Hood (Chichester: Phillimore, 1978). The family estate, where Patrick spent his idle youth, was in northwest Britain, probably near Carlisle (Map 2.1). See C. Thomas, *Christianity in Roman Britain to A.D. 500* (Berkeley: University of California Press, 1981), pp. 307–14; R. P. C. Hanson, *Saint Patrick: His Origins and Career* (Oxford: Oxford University Press, 1968), pp. 113–20. For other ways to avoid urban office, see Jones, *Later Roman Empire*, I, pp. 740–52; F. Millar, "Empire and City, Augustus to Julian: Obligations, Excuses, and Status," *Journal of Roman Studies* 73 (1983), 76–96.

61. Salway, *Roman Britain*, pp. 371–73, 411–12; Frere, *Britannia*, pp. 272–73, 363–64; Jones, *Later Roman Empire*, I, pp. 754–57; Garnsey, "Aspects of the Decline of the Urban Aristocracy in the Empire," in *Aufstieg und Niedergang der römischen Welt*, ed. H. Temporini (Berlin: W. De Gruyter, 1974), pp. 229–52; W. Liebeschütz, "The End of the Ancient City," in *The City in Late Antiquity*, ed. J. Rich (London: Routledge, 1992), pp. 1–49, esp. 6–15. For sensitive sketches of the sociocultural and attitudinal changes experienced by late Roman urban elites, see P. Brown, *The Making of Late Antiquity* (Cambridge, MA: Harvard University Press, 1978), esp. pp. 27–53; H. P. L'Orange, *Art Forms and Civic Life in the Late Roman Empire* (Princeton: Princeton University Press, 1965).

62. Wacher, *Roman Britain*, p. 103; Arnold, *Roman Britain to Saxon England*, pp. 33, 38–39; R. Reece, "Town and Country: The End of Roman Britain," *World Archaeology* 12 (1980), 78–79. For details and discussion, see below, Chaps. 3, 4.

63. Salway, *Roman Britain*, pp. 372–73; Jones and Mattingly, *Atlas of Roman Britain*, pp. 197–98; Arnold, *Roman Britain to Saxon England*, pp. 34, 91–97; Fulford, "Pottery and Britain's Foreign Trade in the Later Roman Period," in *Pottery and Early Commerce*, ed. D. Peacock (London: Academic Press, 1977), pp. 35–84; R. Hingley, "Towns, Trade and Social Organization in Later Roman Britain," *Scottish Archaeological Review* 3 (1984), 87–91. Curial financial difficulties would also have an adverse effect on trade volume. Bulk commodities such as grain and wool, however, continued to be major exports.

64. Salway, *Roman Britain*, p. 645; Frere, *Britannia*, pp. 287–92, 364–65; Jones and Mattingly, *Atlas of Roman Britain*, pp. 209–14; Arnold, *Roman Britain to Saxon England*, pp. 97–100. Production in "small towns" compensated somewhat for these losses. See further, Fulford, "Pottery Production and Trade at the End of Roman Britain: The Case against Continuity," in *End of Roman Britain*, ed. Casey, pp. 120–32.

65. Arnold, *Roman Britain to Saxon England*, pp. 40–41; A. S. Esmonde Cleary, *Extra-Mural Areas of Romano-British Towns*, B.A.R., 169 (Oxford, 1987), pp. 197–200. See below, Chaps. 3, 4 for detailed evidence from individual towns.

66. Arnold, *Roman Britain to Saxon England*, pp. 30–31.

67. Ibid., pp. 122–23; Salway, *Roman Britain*, pp. 545–48; M. E. Jones, "Climate, Nutrition, and Disease: An Hypothesis of Romano-British Population," in *End of Roman Britain*, pp. 231–51.

68. G. Askew, *The Coinage of Roman Britain* (London: B. A. Seaby Ltd., 1951), pp. 55–72; C. H. V. Sutherland, *Roman Coins* (NY: Putnam's, 1974), pp. 252–53,

273; H. Mattingly, *Roman Coins: From the Earliest Times to the Fall of the Western Empire* (2d ed. rev., London: Methuen, 1967), pp. 247–48. The London mint may have been reopened briefly by Magnus Maximus, c.385.

69. Askew, *Coinage*, pp. 73–77; Salway, *Roman Britain*, pp. 424–25, 454; Arnold, *Roman Britain to Saxon England*, pp. 85–91; and esp. J. P. C. Kent, "The End of Roman Britain: Literary and Numismatic Evidence Reviewed," in *End of Roman Britain*, pp. 15–27.

70. For discussions of these issues and others, see Salway, *Roman Britain*, pp. 374–76, 422–23, 660–61; Frere, *Britannia*, pp. 363–64; Johnson, *Saxon Shore*, pp. 99–102, 122–26.

71. Frere, *Britannia*, pp. 342–48, 369; Salway, *Roman Britain*, pp. 746–47; A. R. Birley, *The 'Fasti' of Roman Britain* (Oxford: Clarendon Press, 1981), pp. 319–54, 371–75, 422–23.

72. Zosimus, *Historia nova*, vi.2–3; Orosius, *Historia adversus paganos*, vii.40, ed. C. Zangemeister (Bonn: C. Gerold, 1882) describing Gratian as *municeps eiusdem insulae*. See further, Salway, *Roman Britain*, pp. 426–28; Matthews, *Western Aristocracies*, p. 308. The best study of these British usurpers is still: C. E. Stevens, "Marcus, Gratian, Constantine," *Athenaeum* 35 (1957), 316–47.

73. Zosimus, *Historia nova*, vi.5. The expelled Roman officials would have been those of Constantine III. See further, Salway, *Roman Britain*, pp. 434–36; Frere, *Britannia*, pp. 358–61.

74. Zosimus, *Historia nova*, vi.10; Gildas, *De excidio*, xviii. The cantonal capitals may have formed a provincial council. See further on these matters, Salway, *Roman Britain*, pp. 442–43; Johnson, *Later Roman Britain*, pp. 136–38; E. A. Thompson, "Britain A.D. 406–410," *Britannia* 8 (1977), 303–18, and "Zosimus 6.10.2 and the Letters of Honorius," *Classical Quarterly* 32 (1982), 445–62.

75. Gildas, *De excidio*, xxi–xxiii, xxvii. See also, Procopius, *De bello Vandalico*, i.2, ed. H. B. Dewing (7 vols., London: Heinemann, 1961) and with caution: Nennius, *Historia Brittonum*, lxiii, ed. J. Morris (Chichester: Phillimore 1980). Their rulership was a curious amalgam of older Celtic and more recent Roman traditions: D. N. Dumville, "Sub-Roman Britain: History and Legend," *History* 62 (1977), 173–92; J. H. Ward, "Vortigern and the End of Roman Britain," *Britannia* 3 (1972), 277–89; H. M. Chadwick, "The Foundation of the Early British Kingdoms," in *Studies in Early British History*, ed. N. Chadwick (Cambridge: University Press, 1954), pp. 47–60.

76. Gildas, *De excidio*, xix–xxiii. On these events, see further: Salway, *Roman Britain*, pp. 461–86; Johnson, *Later Roman Britain*, pp. 142–54.

77. Frere, *Britannia*, pp. 365–67; Johnson, *Later Roman Britain*, p. 202; Arnold, *Roman Britain to Saxon England*, pp. 50–52, 58–60.

78. J. N. L. Myres, "Pelagius and the End of Roman Rule in Britain," *Journal of Roman Studies* 50 (1960), 21–36; Liebeschütz, "Pelagian Evidence in the Last Period of Roman Britain," *Latomus* 36 (1967), 436–47; Thomas, *Christianity in Roman Britain*, pp. 53–55; Frere, *Britannia*, pp. 359–62.

79. Constantius, *Vita Germani*, xiv, ed. W. Levison, in *Monumenta Germaniae Historica, Scriptores Rerum Merovingicarum* (hereafter *MGH, SS RM*), VII (Hanover, 1919). See also, Prosper of Aquitaine, *Chronicon*, s.a. 429, ed. T. Mommsen, in *MGH Auctores Antiquissimi* (hereafter *AA*). *Chronica Minora, I* (Berlin, 1892), and

cf. Bede's account: *Historia Ecclesiastica* (hereafter *Hist. Eccl.*), i.17–20, ed. C. Plummer, 2 vols., (Oxford: Clarendon Press, 1896).

80. Constantius, *Vita Germani*, xv-xvi. It was during this visit that Germanus reportedly led a local militia against barbarian raiders in the curious "Alleluia Victory" (ibid., xvii-xviii). See further: Salway, *Roman Britain*, pp. 464–71; Thomas, *Christianity in Roman Britain*, pp. 55–60, and with caution, Thompson, *St. Germanus of Auxerre and the End of Roman Britain* (Woodbridge, Suffolk: Boydell Press, 1984), pp. 15–25.

81. Constantius, *Vita Germani*, xxv–xxvii; cf. Bede, *Historia Ecclesiastica*, i.21. This second visit, probably again to Verulamium, may also have been a response to the "final appeal of the Britons" c.446 (Gildas, *De excidio*, xx): Salway, *Roman Britain*, pp. 479–80; Thomas, *Christianity in Roman Britain*, pp. 333–34; cf. Thompson, *St. Germanus of Auxerre*, pp. 47–70; I. Wood, "The Fall of the Western Empire and the End of Roman Britain," *Britannia* 18 (1987), 251–62.

82. Thompson, "Gildas and the History of Britain," *Britannia* 10 (1979), 203–26; M. Miller, "Bede's Use of Gildas," *English Historical Review* 90 (1975), 241–61; Frere, *Britannia*, pp. 372–74; Johnson, *Later Roman Britain*, pp. 142–45.

83. Gildas, *De excidio*, xix.

84. Ibid., xxii–xxiv.

85. Ibid., xxiv.

86. Ibid., xxvi: "Sed ne nunc quidem, ut antea, civitates patriae inhabitantur; sed desertae dirutaeque hactenus squalent, cessantibus licet externis bellis, sed non civilibus." This is followed by a long invective against specific British rulers (ibid., xxviii–xxxvi).

87. *Chronica Gallica*, s.a. 441/42, ed. Mommsen, in *MGH AA, Chronica Minora*, I, p. 660; *Two of the Saxon Chronicles Parallel* [hereafter *ASC*] s.a. 449 A, eds. J. Earle and C. Plummer (2 vols., Oxford: Clarendon Press, 1892–99) and ibid., 443A, for an often overlooked appeal by the Britons to "the princes of the Angles" on the Continent for aid against other invaders; Bede, *Historia Ecclesiastica*, i.14–15. See further: Salway, *Roman Britain*, pp. 471–74; cf. P. Bartholomew, "Fifth Century Facts," *Britannia* 13 (1982), 261–70. For the archaeological evidence, see J. N. L. Myres, *The English Settlements* (Oxford: Clarendon Press, 1981), pp. 74–143; P. D. C. Brown, *Anglo-Saxon England* (Totowa, NJ: Barnes & Noble, 1978), pp. 18–29; Johnson, *Later Roman Britain*, pp. 159–74; L. Alcock, *Arthur's Britain: History and Archaeology A.D. 367–634* (Harmondsworth: Penguin Books, 1971), pp. 109–15; Arnold, *Roman Britain to Saxon England*, pp. 62–66.

88. See, in general, Frere, "The End of Towns in Roman Britain," in *Civitas-Capitals*, pp. 87–100, and *Britannia*, pp. 368–70; Alcock, *History and Archaeology*, pp. 185–90; Arnold, *Roman Britain to Saxon England*, pp. 41–47.

89. *ASC* 577 E (Gloucester, Cirencester, Bath).

90. For discussions of continental cases, see E. A. Thompson, *The Early Germans* (Oxford: Clarendon Press, 1965), pp. 133–40. The most famous early English example is the successful South Saxon siege of Anderida (Pevensey) in 491 (*ASC* 491 A). This old Saxon Shore fort may have become a late Roman stronghold and administrative center: Myres, *English Settlements*, pp. 135–37. See further, Alcock, *History and Archaeology*, pp. 345–49, and "The Warfare of Saxons and Britons," in

Alcock, *Economy, Society, and Warfare Among the Britons and Saxons* (Cardiff: University of Wales Press, 1987), pp. 225–27.

    91. Gildas, *De excidio*, iii.

For Further Reading

This chapter has been intended to chart the course and pattern of Romano-British town development over four centuries. Many constituent issues and points of detail remain controversial; for these ongoing debates, the following annotated subject bibliographies may also be consulted:

The Iron Age *oppida* of Britain have received considerable attention, with some two dozen sites identified. That many were proto-urban or even urban elite centers with multiple functions at the time of the Roman conquest is now generally considered likely, though their evolution was quite complex: J. R. Collis, *Oppida: Earliest Towns North of the Alps* (Sheffield: University Press, 1984); P. S. Wells, *Farms, Villages, and Cities: Commerce and Urban Origins in Late Prehistoric Europe* (Ithaca: Cornell University Press, 1984); M. Todd and C. Hawkes, "Oppida and the Roman Army: A Review of Recent Evidence," *Oxford Journal of Archaeology* 4 (1985), pp. 187–99; cf. G. Woolf, "Rethinking the *Oppida*," *Oxford Journal of Archaeology* 12 (1993), pp. 223–24.

The extent of Roman urbanization in Britain and its impact on local British elites continues to be hotly debated. One prominent school of research (primarily archaeological) sees Romano-British urban origins deriving from a Roman reinforcement of incipient urban processes directed by local British nobles rather than from an imposed and controlled Roman policy of urbanization. British elites, it is held, did adopt Romanized town life but rather slowly and not as enthusiastically or with such civic display as their continental counterparts. After an apex of activity in the early third century, significant urban change ensued, marked by a decline in commercial and industrial activity, more and larger town houses, and less dense occupation. As the urban economic base decayed, public and private construction faltered, leaving late fourth-century towns as little more than walled meeting places. When financially hard-pressed town nobles finally threw off the Roman yoke, they became rulers of independent realms, but the loss of military and administrative unity led to decisive Anglo-Saxon takeover. Although this scenario contains some valuable points, such as the altered late Roman townscape, much of it suffers from an overdependence on social-scientific "models theory" and arcane statistical analysis (the "New Archaeology"): M. Millet, *The Romanization of Britain: An Essay in Archaeological Interpretation* (Cambridge: University Press, 1990). For a modified approach, see Hingley, "Roman Britain: The Structure of Roman Imperialism and the Consequences of Imperialism on the Development of a Peripheral Province," in *The Romano-British Countryside*, ed. D. Miles, B.A.R. 103 (Oxford, 1982), pp. 17–52; S. D. Trow, "By the Northern Shore of Ocean. Some Observations on Acculturation Process at the Edge of the Roman World," in *The Early Roman Empire in the West*, eds. T. F. C. Blagg and M. Millet (Oxford: Oxbow Books, 1990), pp. 103–18, and Blagg, "Architectural Munificence in Britain: The Evidence of Inscriptions," *Britannia* 21 (1990), 13–32. The most extreme disciple of this revisionist school remains R. Reece, who sees Romano-British towns as having devolved into small administrative villages from at least the late third century: "End of the City in Roman Britain," pp. 136–44. For a more balanced and satisfactory view, which properly notes the strength of Romano-British urbanism into the fourth century, see Wacher, "Cities from the Second to Fourth Centuries," in *Research on Roman Britain 1960–1989*, ed. M. Todd. Britannia Monograph Series 11 (London: Society for the Promotion of Roman Studies, 1989), pp. 75–90.

For analyses of the Roman army's influence on urban foundation in Britain and its later role in the towns, see P. A. Holder, *The Roman Army in Britain* (NY: St. Martin's Press, 1982); C. S. Sommer, *The Military Vici in Roman Britain*, B.A.R. 129 (Oxford, 1984); D. Welsby, *The Roman Military Defense of the British Provinces in Its Later Phases*, B.A.R. 101 (Oxford, 1982); S. T. James, "Britain and the Late Roman Army," in *Military and Civilian in Roman Britain*, eds. T. F. C. Blagg and A. C. King, B.A.R. 136 (Oxford, 1984), pp. 161–86; P. Bartholomew, "Fourth Century Saxons," *Britannia* 15 (1984), 169–85; J. C. Coulston, ed., *Military Equipment and the Identity of Roman Soldiers*, B.A.R. [Internat. Ser.] 394 (Oxford, 1988); V. A. Maxfield, ed., *The Saxon Shore* (Exeter: University Press, 1989); J. Cotterill, "Saxon Raiding and the Role of the Late Roman Coastal Forts of Britain," *Britannia* 24 (1993), 227–39.

For new perspectives on the changing Roman urban economy including particular reference to Romano-British towns, see K. Greene, *The Archaeology of the Roman Economy* (London: Batsford, 1986); Fulford, "The Economy of Roman Britain," in *Research on Roman Britain*, pp. 175–202; A. Wallace-Hadrill, "Elites and Trade in the Roman Town," in *City and Country in the Ancient World*, eds. J. Rich and A. Wallace-Hadrill (London: Routledge, 1991), pp. 241–72; Liebeschütz, "The End of the Ancient City," in *City in Late Antiquity*, ed. Rich, pp. 1–49; W. I. Roberts, *Romano-Saxon Pottery*, B.A.R. 106 (Oxford, 1982).

On the development of "small towns" in Roman Britain, their diverse origins, and their growing importance as local commercial, industrial, and market centers, see: G. D. B. Jones, "Becoming Different without Knowing It: The Role and Development of *Vici*," in *Military and Civilian in Roman Britain*, pp. 75–91; B. C. Burnham, "The Origins of Romano-British Small Towns," *Oxford Journal of Archaeology* 5 (1986), pp. 185–203; R. F. Smith, *Roadside Settlement in Lowland Roman Britain*, B.A.R. 157 (Oxford, 1987); and esp. B. C. Burnham and J. S. Wacher, *The Small Towns of Roman Britain* (Berkeley: University of California Press, 1990).

On Romano-British villas and town-country ties, see: E. W. Black, *The Roman Villas of South-East England*, B.A.R. 171 (Oxford, 1987); K. Branigan and D. Miles, eds., *Villa Economies* (Sheffield: University Press, 1989); M. Millet, "Roman Towns and Their Territories: An Archaeological Perspective," in *City and Country*, eds. Rich and Wallace-Hadrill, pp. 169–89; C. R. Whittaker, "The Consumer City Revisited: The *Vicus* and the City," *Journal of Roman Archaeology* 3 (1990), 110–18.

For interpretations of pertinent late and sub-Roman written sources, see: Thompson, "Ammianus Marcellinus and Britain," *Nottingham Medieval Studies* 34 (1990), 1–15; M. Lapidge and D. N. Dumville, eds., *Gildas: New Approaches* (Woodbridge: Boydell Press, 1984); P. Sims-Williams, "Gildas and the Anglo-Saxons," *Cambridge Medieval Celtic Studies* 6 (1983), 1–30; A. Bammesberger and A. Wollmann, eds., *Britain, 400–600: Language and History*, Anglistische Forschungen 205 (Heidelberg: C. Winter, 1990); S. Muhlberger, "The *Gallic Chronicle* of 452 and Its Authority for British Events," *Britannia* 14 (1983), 23–33; M. E. Jones and P.

Casey, "The *Gallic Chronicle* Restored: A Chronology for the Anglo-Saxon Invasions and the End of Roman Britain," *Britannia* 19 (1988), 367–98.

Finally, for several commendable general works on Roman Britain incorporating recent urban research and interpretations, see T. W. Potter and C. Johns, *Roman Britain* (Berkeley: University of California Press, 1992); B Jones and D. Mattingly, *Atlas of Roman Britain* (Oxford: Blackwell, 1990); R. H. J. Jones, ed., *Britain in the Roman Period: Recent Trends* (Sheffield: Collis Publishing, 1991).

Chapter 3

Romano-British Towns:
Case Studies

Textual evidence of town conditions in Roman Britain is limited, and at times vague and contradictory. Over the past several decades, however, archaeological research has furnished a wealth of findings and interpretations pertinent to all phases of Romano-British towns. A judicious use of this material evidence can help clarify the textual record by providing a much-needed balance of detail. The following discussion of eight individual towns, while admittedly a sampling, looks at representative examples of each major type of Romano-British town in a variety of geographical areas. Verulamium (St. Albans), Silchester, Chichester, Caistor-by-Norwich, Cirencester, Gloucester, Bath, and Wroxeter will be considered. In the course of these examinations, the long-term, larger patterns of urban growth and decline, as well as possible continuities and discontinuities, will come into sharper focus.

First, there is the case of Verulamium, which has been studied intensively in recent years by Sheppard Frere and his archaeological team (Map 2.1, and Fig. 3.1). This important *municipium* on the River Ver appears to have reached the height of its prosperity rather late, c.325 A.D. During the early fourth century, there was major construction of new public buildings, commercial shops, and sumptuous private homes in the town. Verulamium's well-being seems to have been maintained through much of the century, as is attested by the upkeep of most public buildings, repairs made to the urban defense system, and continued construction of courtyard houses.[1]

Several of these town houses show sustained use into the fifth century. One of them, a moderate-sized home in the central part of town between forum and temple (block, or Insula, XIV), was built c.380 with the usual, albeit somewhat modest, Roman amenities. It underwent successive alterations after c.400, including a new hypocaust and mosaic floors, though workmanship was increasingly poor. Occupation appears to have ended here c.435.[2] Another private house, also erected c.380 in the corner of nearby Insula XXVII, was a more substantial two-storied dwelling of twenty-two rooms around a large, central courtyard. It was provided with elaborate amenities, which were expanded c.400 and well maintained until c.430. As the principal excavator has rightly observed, this is the kind of costly town house one can associate with the nobles Germanus had encountered.[3] Yet there are signs of rapidly declining standards after c.430, such as the insertion of a corn-drying oven through one of the tessellated floors. The entire building was torn down soon after (c.435) and replaced by a wooden, barnlike structure whose Roman-style, buttressed walls were bonded with Roman tile fragments. When this building in turn was demolished (c.450), the site was cut by a wooden water-pipe line jointed with heavy iron-collars (c.450–470).[4]

The evidence of these town houses confirms that there were at least some reasonably prosperous Romano-British nobles at Verulamium in the early fifth century, though declining conditions seen after c.430 suggest their increasing impoverishment. The late fifth-century pipeline does indicate an at least partially operative town water system and the presence of craftsmen necessary for its maintenance. But none of this attests to high levels of urban life. Rather, the overall archaeological view of Verulamium at this late date is clearly one of decay and significant loss of its former urban vitality. For example, excavations in the town have failed to find any evidence of dense population, organized trade and industry, or even the presence of a regular money economy after c.400.[5] Verulamium's main theater (Insula XV) was abandoned and had become a rubbish heap by c.395, although the adjacent temple and market hall may have seen limited use for several more decades.[6] Indeed, settlement appears to have shrunken to the central *insulae* as peripheral areas were abandoned slowly from the late fourth century.[7] Also, corn dryers and barns do bring to mind a rural image, though it is probably going too far to regard the topography of late Roman Verulamium as dotted only with farms and ruined public buildings.[8]

The fact that some recognizable late Roman life existed at Verulamium well into the fifth century has led to speculation that the town and its region continued to be a Romano-British enclave, perhaps even through the sixth century. It is true that there is a marked absence of early Anglo-Saxon cemeteries in and around the town, and no clear evidence of either Germanic federate settlement or burning and looting. Also, possible late fourth century repairs to the town walls could well have made Verulamium an effective place of refuge until such time as manpower shortages undermined adequate defense.[9] But there is no firm written or archaeological evidence of any organized British settlement here after c.470. Indeed, there are no signs of flourishing, multifunctional urban life at Verulamium much beyond c.400. Apart from possible transient traffic and the occasional squatter, the town essentially appears to have become abandoned by c.500 at the latest.

This final chapter in Verulamium's history had an interesting sequel worthy of some comment. As the old Roman town had begun to decline, activity increased around the shrine of St. Alban on a hill a half mile beyond Verulamium's east wall. Indeed, the case of Verulamium-St. Albans is one of the best examples from this sub-Roman period of settlement-shift (*Schwerpunktverlagerung*). This general phenomenon, including the special case of shifts to cult centers, has been particularly well studied in recent years by German urban historians.[10] Alban is said to have been a resident of Verulamium who was martyred, probably in the mid-third century, by order of Roman imperial officials in the town.[11] A small Christian church seems to have been built over his martyrial tomb outside the town in late Roman times; the site quickly became, and remained, a renowned center of popular devotion in northern Europe.[12] The proto-urban development of this area was stimulated in the eighth century by the establishment of an Anglo-Saxon royal villa north of the old town and especially by the foundation of St. Albans Abbey late in the same century, apparently over the site of the old *martyrium*. The medieval town of St. Albans grew up just to the north of the Abbey.[13] It must be borne in mind, however, that this development is a better example of religious or cultural continuity than of urban continuity, for Verulamium itself was abandoned and never reoccupied.[14]

Some fifty miles southwest of Verulamium stood the Romano-British town of Calleva (Silchester). Following the Roman conquest, Calleva was developed into an important urban center, a *civitas*-capital of the British Atrebates (Map 2.1, and Fig. 3.2). The town assumed its basic form during the first and second centuries, with a regular street grid and substantial public buildings, including forum and basilica, baths, temples, and also very likely a large, official inn (*mansio*) near the southgate (Insula VIII).[15] A variety of industrial, craft, and merchants' shops are attested, mostly in the central *insulae*; a guild, perhaps of foreign traders, also operated in this town.[16] Private homes ranged from simple wattle-and-daub types to the more elaborate winged and courtyard houses of urban nobles.[17] Calleva also was provided at an unusually early date with earthwork defenses, which were extended and then augmented by a heavy, stone curtain wall in the late third century.[18]

Public and private buildings continued to be constructed and maintained at Calleva during the fourth century, although there is little evidence of any very costly new work after c.350.[19] Indeed, as at Verulamium, significant urban change evidently took place in the course of the fourth century. First, the town basilica was given over in large part to industrial use (iron smithing) c.325–375; a crudely built hypocaust thereafter was inserted into the western corridor.[20] Calleva's amphitheater, lying outside the east curtain wall but within the outer earthwork, had fallen into disrepair by c.350 and its north entrance strewn with rubble.[21]

Finds of late Roman military equipment indicate that official troops likely were stationed in this important cantonal capital.[22] Urban defenses underwent major alterations. For example, previous excavations found that the town's main north and west gates had been fully or partially blocked intentionally, probably toward the close of the fourth century.[23] Recent work has shown that the south gate became increasingly choked with rubble and was disused after 350, while the southeast gate was blocked deliberately around that same time. Moreover, large rubbish heaps were left to accumulate along sections of the town walls late in the fourth century.[24]

Coin finds and structural evidence suggest that the major public buildings at Calleva remained in use until c.400–430, though on a very limited basis and not always for their original official purposes.[25] Scattered finds of imported glassware, pottery, and metal ornaments do attest to a modest level of foreign trade in the early fifth century, but not beyond c.450.[26] Indeed, signs of population decline can be seen beginning c.380 in extramural areas and then within the town itself, after sharp, overall increases earlier in the fourth century.[27] The late fourth-century town may in fact have assumed a more rural aspect, in view of the corn-drying furnaces installed in private dwellings.[28] But as with the case of Verulamium, Calleva has yielded no traces of widespread sack and slaughter in the fifth century.[29] Rather, the sum of evidence indicates that Romano-British Calleva ended its days in a state of dereliction and depopulation accompanied by debased living standards. A number of human bodies found in the latest mid-fifth-century occupation levels had not been properly buried but had been tossed into open pits and wells.[30]

Despite this record of urban collapse, suggestions continue to be made that a sub-Roman Calleva, protected against Anglo-Saxon attack by a series of linear dikes to the north, managed to maintain itself into the mid-sixth century.[31] This view, though somewhat attractive, is largely speculation, and the fact remains that there is no firm written or archaeological evidence that organized Romano-British urban life existed at Calleva beyond c.450 at the latest.[32] The site appears to have been virtually deserted, with no indication of significant settlement-shift.[33]

A rather similar pattern of late fourth-century decline leading to fifth-century near-desertion also can be seen at two Romano-British cantonal capitals situated near the coasts: Noviomagus Regnensium (Chichester) in Sussex and Venta Icenorum (Caistor-by-Norwich) in Norfolk. In both cases, however, several variations are to be noted. Noviomagus was developed under Roman aegis during the first and second centuries as a *civitas*-capital for the Regni, perhaps a southern branch of the Atrebatic people (Map 2.1, and Fig. 3.3). The town appears to have grown around the nucleus of a small Roman fort and was provided with a regular network of graveled streets, major public buildings, and the usual urban amenities.[34] A number of metalworking shops and pottery kilns have been found in excavations north of the proposed central forum-basilica, and a likely fullery operated in the southeastern town quadrant until c.325.[35] Courtyard-type private houses with mosaics and hypocausts are attested, primarily in the western town area. Some were early constructions, but others had been built and enlarged c.275–350 during evidently still-prosperous times.[36] Noviomagus received complete bank-and-ditch defenses toward the end of the second century. A stone circuit was added to these lines perhaps fifty years later, followed by the incorporation of gate towers and projecting bastions c.350. The town area thus enclosed comprised c.100 acres, approximately the same as that of Calleva but half the size of intramural Verulamium.[37]

The available evidence points to urban decline at Noviomagus from the late fourth century or even somewhat earlier. For example, though defenses had been recently upgraded and some industrial activity continued, excavations have shown that a number of town houses, and the public baths in the northwest quadrant, lapsed into a state of disrepair, decay, and gradual abandonment c.375–425.[38] Public services also fell into neglect. Streets were not maintained, and parts of the town sewer system were becoming permanently blocked with building debris and rubbish at this time.[39] One of the town's main cemeteries was found to contain few fourth-century burials, although subsequent excavations have located additional cemeteries in use until the early fifth century.[40] Ceramic and numismatic evidence also indicate that intra- and extramural occupation continued on a very reduced scale into, but probably not beyond, the initial decades of the fifth century.[41] Finally, there are no signs that fifth-century Noviomagus had been sacked or burned. Rather, desertion and decay are indicated by layers of dark or black earth found sealing the last Romano-British occupation levels.[42]

It has been surmised on somewhat circumstantial evidence that the decline of Noviomagus could have been due in part to the abandonment of the nearby Saxon Shore fort at Portchester (c.370) or to a shift in the town's regional administrative authority to Anderida [Pevensey] (Map 2.1).[43] Be that as it may, there is firmer archaeological evidence that, as at Calleva, an official Roman military garrison had been stationed at Noviomagus during its last decades.[44] It is uncertain whether this urban troop included Germanic enlisted forces, though the suggestion has been made.[45] What is clear is that no structural settlement-remains of such a federate presence have been found in or around the town. Moreover, there is also a marked absence of early Anglo-Saxon settlements or cemeteries from Noviomagus and its immediate environs.[46] Indeed, the case for virtual town desertion after c.425 is quite strong. Although Noviomagus's still-standing defenses may have made it a place of temporary refuge,[47] excavations have revealed no evidence of any concentrated Anglo-Saxon occupation on the site until perhaps the eighth century.[48]

Venta Icenorum (Caistor-by-Norwich) was planned and built on a new site near the Norfolk coast as *civitas*-capital of the British Iceni (Map 2.1, and Fig. 3.4). The main period of urban development occurred during the second century when forum-basilica, baths, temples, and water systems all were provided.[49] The Romano-British town appears to have had a high level of industrial and craft activity, including metalworking, pottery production, and possibly woolen cloth manufacture. A glass factory also operated on a fairly large scale north of the forum c.300–360 (Insula IX).[50] Still, Venta was one of the smaller cantonal capitals of Roman Britain. Its late third-century stone walls with bastions enclosed a total area of c.35 acres.[51] Indeed, this town gives the overall impression of both sparse settlement and rather limited financial resources. Private homes generally were quite modest, and a number of *insulae* apparently were never built upon at all.[52] The reasons for this restricted development are unclear but may be related to the series of fires that evidently ravaged parts of the town and to the participation of the Iceni in several early revolts.[53]

Venta does not seem to have experienced serious urban decline during the fourth century. The forum was rebuilt c.325, while the public baths also were used and adequately maintained.[54] Late fourth-century occupation is attested by ceramic finds as well as items of military metalwork indicating the presence of an urban garrison. Also, the town houses excavated at Venta show evidence of continuous occupation through at least the fourth century.[55] Indeed, one of these late-occupied homes yielded some startling material that merits closer attention.

This particular building was a rather substantial private home with several wings and bath-suites, lying just inside the north gate (Insula VII, site 4). First built in the late third century, it remained largely unaltered and occupied until c.400–425 when it appeared to have been destroyed by fire. In this final occupation level were found the skeletal remains of at least thirty-five men, women and children. A layer of charred building debris apparently covered the bones, and some skulls showed signs of having received violent blows. This find has been seen as evidence of a savage end to Venta's urban life—a massacre of Romano-British townspeople by rebellious Germanic federates or raiders such as Gildas described.[56]

There are a number of problems with this interpretation, however. First, no evidence of similar fifth-century destruction has been found elsewhere in the town. Also, the skeletal remains were very fragmentary and showed no signs of burning, and the cranial wounds had not been sword inflicted.[57] Indeed, a strong case recently has been made that these skeletal fragments more likely had been dug up from one of the town's cemetery areas, perhaps in the early fifth century, and used with other material to fill the building's ruined hypocaust.[58] This reinterpretation, whereby the notorious house of slaughter becomes a more mundane (albeit grim) fill-pile, is more in accord with the overall evidence of gradual town decay and desertion rather than sudden destruction.

Excavations over the past two decades also have disclosed several Anglo-Saxon cremation cemeteries just outside Venta. The larger, main area lay some 900 feet beyond the east wall and contained numerous early Anglo-Saxon cremation urns. Its principal excavator initially contended that many of these urns had been made and deposited in the fourth century and a few possibly earlier in view of their stylistic affinities with comparable vessels from northern Germany and southern Scandinavia. This was regarded as evidence for the settlement of early Germanic federates employed to defend late Roman Venta, the same federates who bore the military items found in the town and later arose in bloodthirsty revolt.[59]

Once again, this argument is not very sound. For example, the early dating of some of the Venta cremation urns may well be invalid since the precise chronology of comparative material on which it was based remains far from clear.[60] No conclusive dating evidence was found in association with them and thus none necessarily was deposited before the fifth century. Moreover, it is now recognized that the supposedly "Germanic" or federate fourth-century metalwork items were worn by Roman and provincial civil and military officials as well.[61] In addition, the so-called "Romano-Saxon" fourth-century pottery found at a number of towns, including Venta, is more likely a standard type of late Roman ware and hence also no indicator of specifically Germanic ethnicity.[62] The presence of late Roman federates at Venta and their purported revolt thus are questionable. Indeed, if there had been a period of settlement overlap in the town during the fourth or fifth centuries, one might expect to have found more typically Germanic or Anglo-Saxon artifacts and housing remains such as brooches or "sunken huts" (*Grubenhäuser*)–small, shallow dwellings of wattle-and-daub construction. Such is not the case, however. Rather, the weight of available evidence indicates that the cremation urn-fields came into use at a time when Venta itself already was virtually abandoned, that is, by the mid-fifth century.

What became of Venta's inhabitants is something of a mystery, given the evidence for gradual town desertion rather than final slaughter. The nearby Saxon Shore fort of Gariannorum (Burgh Castle) and the smaller Caister-by-Sea have yielded evidence of late Roman military and civilian occupation up to perhaps the early fifth century but not beyond.[63] More extended settlement sequences ought to have been disclosed had these fortified sites actually received an influx of Romano-British town refugees. Such speculation aside, it is clear that Venta became and long remained a virtually deserted place.[64] Norwich itself, three miles away, emerged as the new town center of this region only in the ninth and tenth centuries, and then in the context of an Anglo-Saxon trading and industrial center, an emporium or *wic*.[65]

The Romano-British towns considered to this point were located mainly in the southeast, the primary area of Romanization in Britain and also the first region to confront the so-called Anglo-Saxon Invasions in the mid to late fifth century. Indeed, according to the traditional historical view, derived ultimately from Gildas, the invasions were massive assaults that quickly and violently extinguished Romano-British urban life. The evidence presented thus far indicates, however, that regardless of the actual scale of the invasions (and this has been hotly debated),[66] Romano-British towns were in a moribund condition on the whole for at least several decades prior to the Anglo-Saxons' arrival. That there are few if any signs of violent fifth-century destruction in the towns need hardly be surprising. In most towns, urban life was at a very low ebb by the early fifth century and soon ceased on its own accord. This Romano-British urban denouement thus took place, properly speaking, in the context of sub-Roman Britain, that shadowy time between the end of late Roman Britain (410) and the beginning of Anglo-Saxon England (c.450). Again, in this twilight period where town conditions are only dimly illumined by the written record, archaeological evidence assumes particular value.

It has often been contended that Romano-British towns further removed from initial Anglo-Saxon attacks were able to maintain their urban conditions for a considerably longer time.[67] To test the validity of this view, one can now consider the later record of a series of Romano-British towns in the west and north: Corinium, Glevum, Aquae Sulis, and Viroconium.

Romano-British Corinium (Cirencester) stood along the River Churn at the base of the Cotswolds in western Britain. The town, growing from a series of Roman forts with associated civilian settlement, was developed quickly as an impressive *civitas*-capital for the British Dubunni (Map 2.1, and Fig. 3.5).[68] Its colonnaded forum and marbled basilica were the largest built in Britain except for those at London. Indeed, Corinium's third-century walls enclosed an urban area of some 240 acres, thereby making this the largest of all Romano-British cantonal capitals and the third largest of all towns in Roman Britain. South of the forum was a commercial district with shop-lined streets (Insula V, site 1), while the adjacent Insula II housed a market hall (*macellum*) with butchers' shops and an associated cattle yard. Excavations also have revealed a number of substantial private town houses with very lavish adornments and amenities, including frescoes, mosaics, multiple hypocausts, and bath suites. Indeed, Corinium was an important center for the production and distribution of luxury goods, in particular, fine mosaics and sculpture. All evidence thus identifies this as a quite prosperous town directed by a highly Romanized, wealthy curial class.

Corinium's prosperity and affluence appear to have been enhanced in the early fourth century when the town became capital of the new Diocletianic province of Britannia Prima and the seat of its governor.[69] For example, numerous late Roman coin finds can be attributed to continuing official payments, as well as sustained economic activity. Forum and basilica clearly remained in regular use through the fourth century, and commercial shops were rebuilt in stone. The town's curtain wall was widened and external bastions added in the mid-fourth century. As at other cantonal capitals, an official late Roman garrison also is attested at Corinium. Moreover, the town's most lavish private homes and its finest mosaics belong to the fourth century.[70]

The archaeological evidence relating to fifth-century Corinium presents a somewhat mixed picture. The forum and its adjacent streets apparently were well used and maintained until c.440.[71] One late cemetery found beyond the west gate also was in regular use from the mid-fourth to the early fifth century.[72] Most earlier town houses evidently remained occupied during this period, and some new constructions are attested. For instance, excavations just inside the east wall (Insula XII) have disclosed two adjoining residential buildings erected in the late fourth century on previously unoccupied ground.[73] One of them was clearly a substantial town house with numerous fine mosaics and baths (XII, 1). The other was also rather well equipped, but its form more closely resembled that of a rural villa (XII, 2). Agricultural and craft implements were indeed found in association with it. Just to the south stood a third large structure, which may have been an aisled barn (XII, 3). The latter two buildings have been interpreted as, respectively, an intramural villa and farm, with the implication that Corinium's latest occupation had become increasingly agrarian and non urban.[74] It has been noted, however, that many Romano-British towns had intramural agricultural features from their earliest days and were still urban. While a number of Corinium's *insulae* evidently were abandoned or given over to agrarian pursuits by the early fifth century, others continued to be used in their traditional ways.[75]

Excavations at Corinium's amphitheater, outside the west gate, yielded perhaps even more significant evidence relevant to the town's final conditions. This large, elliptical public structure was given masonry walls and internal additions during the second century; more radical alterations were made toward the end of the fourth century. At that time, the northeast entrance passage was reduced in width and partially blocked with stones. Moreover, a large, timber building was erected in the arena itself. These

alterations were associated with late Roman domestic pottery and coins so
worn and weathered as to suggest continued use of the site into at least the
early to mid-fifth century. It looks very much as though the town amphitheater had been converted into a fortified retreat, a place more easily
defended by a reduced population than the large town.[76]

Indeed, by the mid-fifth century, only very limited areas of Corinium
appear to have remained inhabited, and town conditions had deteriorated
severely. For instance, in Insula XXIII north of the forum, a stone-built
town house that was occupied and maintained through the fourth century
had become partly engulfed by unswept street silt. Roadside ditches filled
with layers of dark, organic soil and other debris, including several human
corpses.[77] The suggestion that these bodies, and similar examples found at
several other fifth-century towns, were victims of an epidemic or plague that
brought a final and sudden end to urban life in Britain has now been largely
discounted.[78] Nonetheless, derelict buildings, abandoned *insulae*, overgrown
streets, and human bodies rotting in ditches do point to a collapse of
organized urban life.

The overall archaeological evidence indicates that Corinium was virtually
deserted by the late fifth century, at least several decades before any
significant Anglo-Saxon penetration into the region.[79] The first Anglo-Saxon
settlements (c.500–550) appear to have been concentrated a short distance
west of the town.[80] An Anglo-Saxon cemetery with initial burials of the early
sixth century also has been found in this area, at Barton Farm.[81] But there
are no indications of early Anglo-Saxon settlement within the town itself.

The *Anglo-Saxon Chronicle* records that in 577 an advancing West Saxon
army fought the Britons along the lower Severn at Dyrham (Map 3.1), killed
three British kings (Coinmail, Condidan, Farinmail), and took three towns
(*ceastra*):   Gloucester, Cirencester, and Bath.[82]   This annal has been
interpreted by some as indicating (if the phrase-connection and citation-
order are correct) that Cirencester was then the capital of a sub-Roman
kingdom ruled by Condidan, who does bear a Latinized name. The
implication is that the town had continued to be an administrative center
under British rulers such as Gildas described.[83]   On the one hand, there is
artifactual and place name evidence for the survival of a substantial British
population in the Cirencester region.[84]   The *Chronicle* entry also intimates
that the Battle of Dyrham was a memorable conflict against stiff resistance.
Indeed, the battle has been regarded as a critical episode in the West Saxon
advance whereby the British of the southwest were separated from those of
Wales.[85]   Yet the fact remains that there is no archaeological evidence that
Britons actually were settled within the old Roman town or were using it as
a central place of defense or administration in the sixth century. The rather
attractive suggestion has been made that the *ceaster* said to have been taken
in 577 was not the town of Corinium but its amphitheater, which does

appear to have been made into a defended enclosure by the last town inhabitants.[86]

It is not yet possible to determine with precision when Anglo-Saxon reoccupation began in the town. The *Anglo-Saxon Chronicle* relates that King Penda of Mercia apparently defeated a West Saxon army at Cirencester in 628 and that the two sides then reached an agreement.[87] This probably marks the passing of Cirencester and its region to Mercian control whence it formed part of the subkingdom of the Hwicce (Map 3.1) until the Viking age.[88] Recent Cirencester excavations have identified a large, intramural church built with reused Roman stonework, which has been dated on stylistic grounds to the eighth century.[89] Place-name evidence suggests Scandinavian settlement in Cirencester, and the *Anglo-Saxon Chronicle* records that Guthram's host later encamped at the town for a year (878).[90] After the Viking wars, Cirencester evidently came again under the authority of Wessex. Indeed, charter evidence represents it as a royal estate (*villa regia*) and the site of a number of royal assemblies from the early tenth to the early eleventh centuries.[91] There is also some indication that Cirencester at this time was the local administrative center for a surrounding region of seven districts (hundreds).[92] The tenth-century royal estate is presumably the same as that reportedly held by Edward the Confessor in 1066 and which had a "new market" (*novum forum*) by 1086.[93]

To conclude, the sum of evidence thus indicates that Corinium, a highly Romanized and prosperous cantonal capital through the fourth century, underwent gradual decline and loss of urban functions culminating in virtual desertion by c.475. Though this waning occurred somewhat later than at towns farther east, the process and result were the same. After a lapse of settlement, Anglo-Saxon occupation eventually did occur, but it took many centuries for Anglo-Saxon Cirencester to establish even a few of the numerous town functions that Corinium had enjoyed.[94]

Glevum (Gloucester), one of the four known *coloniae* of Roman Britain, stood at a crossing point of the lower Severn some seventeen miles west of Corinium (Map 2.1, and Fig. 3.6).[95] A series of legionary fortresses with civilian settlement areas (*canabae*) initially were established here c.50–75 A.D. After several periods of military construction, the legionary troops were withdrawn permanently, and Glevum officially became a *colonia*—a civilian settlement for retired army veterans (c.97 A.D.). Like other towns of this type, however, its military background left a lasting impression. For example, Glevum's forum-basilica was built on the site of the legionary headquarters, the *principia*, and many homes were modified barracks. The primary residential area lay within what had been the main fortress (43 acres) and utilized its rigidly geometric street grid, including an intravallum road (Fig. 3.7). Indeed, Glevum's third-century stone curtain wall followed the lines of the legionary rampart and thus did not enclose additional residential town areas (c.75 acres) primarily on the west and north sides.

Glevum was not lacking in major public buildings, urban amenities, and substantial town houses: this was after all a *colonia*, a model of Roman urban life at its best. There were colonnaded courtyard-style homes with fine mosaics, an impressive temple, and large public baths. Town industries included ironworking and pottery production, as well as brick and tile manufacture. Excavations also have disclosed timber docks and a large stone quay designed for trade at the town's harbor on the Severn just beyond the west gate. In addition, Glevum possessed a substantial *territorium* of prime agricultural and pastoral lands extending at least several miles on each side of the Severn.

Although Glevum was a successful and prosperous urban place, it never seems to have matched the wealth and cultural attainments of its neighbor and rival town, Corinium. It has been suggested that the inherently conservative natures of Glevum's veterans and their families placed certain constraints on public display and entrepreneurial activities.[96] This is possible but rather speculative, and other explanations are more likely. For example, though there were affluent and civic-minded people in this *colonia*, what was noticeably absent was a leading class of wealthy landholding local nobles assuming town offices such as one encounters regularly at *civitas*-capitals. Also, the size of Glevum's *territorium*, though large, and the resources derived from it were considerably less than that generally available to cantonal capitals.[97]

Significant settlement contraction of extramural areas is evident at Glevum between the late second and fourth centuries. Thus, areas around the first fortress to the north (Kingsholm) and also near the municipal tilery in the northwest suburbs became cemetery grounds (Fig. 3.6).[98] On the other hand, most intramural town houses appear to have been occupied and maintained through the fourth century.[99] Moreover, town defenses were strengthened during the fourth century with the rebuilding of wall sections by the gates and the addition of more bastions.[100] There are further indications of sufficiently organized town authority and ongoing economic activity c.375–400: the forum-basilica was maintained, and finds of late Roman coins and imported pottery are rather abundant.[101]

Despite these signs of continuing urban life, other, perhaps less positive, changes were occurring in late Roman Glevum. First, a number of public buildings lost their original functions and were put to other uses. The public bath north of the forum, for example, apparently was divided into small domestic or industrial compartments and then demolished c.370. On its foundation a timber structure was erected that seems to have been a butcher shop. When this was torn down c.400, the site was leveled and surfaced with fine gravel, perhaps as a marketplace.[102] In this process the town's main east-west street evidently was put out of use, the old west gate blocked, and a new entrance made just to its north. Indeed, extensions of the town walls to the riverside may then have made the western suburb a smaller, fortified enclosure.[103] These late changes that took place at Glevum on the whole do not appear indicative of robust urban health.

By the mid-fifth century, intramural occupation had shrunken to very limited areas around the forum and east-west gates, with only the slightest evidence of any commercial or industrial activity.[104] Parts of the town also may have been subjected to flooding. Moreover, the latest occupation levels commonly are sealed by thick layers of dark earth that represent either organic accumulations or debris heaps.[105] On the other hand, several extramural areas show signs of late activity. For example, at the old Kingsholm fortress site, there was renewed settlement with an associated sub-Roman cemetery and mausoleum. One early fifth-century inhumation here was apparently that of a high-status Briton interred with his military gear.[106] In the northwest suburb also, a large courtyard-type town house was demolished at this time and replaced partly on the same alignments by a timber structure with associated internal burials that may have been a small church.[107]

Although there was thus some limited sub-Roman settlement in and around Glevum after 400, its urban life had reached extremely low levels and expired by c.475. Indeed, written and archaeological evidence points to a rather long gap between the last phase of organized Romano-British life and the first Anglo-Saxon occupation. The entry of the *Anglo-Saxon Chronicle* that implies that the West Saxons captured Gloucester (Gleawanceaster) from its British ruler in 577 is in fact not otherwise substantiated, nor is there evidence of significant early Anglo-Saxon settlement in the area before the seventh century.[108] During that century, Gloucester and its region, like Cirencester, came under the control of Mercia and, more specifically, of the Mercian subkingdom, the Hwicce. An important early charter (674 X 679 A.D.) records that King Aethelred of Mercia granted property at Gloucester (Gleaweceaster) to a certain Osric, his thegn (*minister*) and joint ruler of the Hwicce. Osric then asked and received permission to build a monastery there.[109] This was the "Old Minster" (St. Peter's), at first a community of nuns or possibly a double minster, which is believed to have occupied the northwest corner of the intramural area.[110] Several later works issuing from St. Peter's add some pertinent details concerning this early Anglo-Saxon minster and its town. For example, the monastery's *History* relates that the chapel was a burial site for early Hwiccan royalty such as Osric himself and his sister, Kyneburg, the first abbess, and that eighth-century Mercian kings, including the famous Offa, were lavish benefactors.[111] The now lost *Memorial* of St. Peter's claims that King Wulfhere of Mercia, Aethelred's predecessor and brother, enlarged and beautified Gloucester and began construction of the monastery just before his death (679). Aethelred then continued the initiative and appointed Osric to supervise monastic construction.[112]

The first archaeological evidence of Anglo-Saxon intramural occupation at Gloucester is represented by remains of sunken huts and domestic wooden artifacts found in the upper dark-earth levels and dated to the late seventh and eighth centuries. Succeeding ninth-century levels contained evidence of intensive agrarian and pastoral activity along with leather working but very few signs of trade.[113] These settlements and related activities were not widespread, however, and there must have been considerable vacant intramural space (Fig. 3.7). The Viking army that encamped here in 877 on its way from Exeter was quite able to accommodate itself within the walls.[114] A number of surrounding riverside sites have yielded evidence of Anglo-Saxon settlement from the late seventh century.[115] Two extramural areas are particularly noteworthy for their high-status occupation. At some time, perhaps in the late eighth century, the Kingsholm fortress site became a Mercian royal estate. Its existence is first attested only in 896, in a vernacular charter recording the acts of a major royal assembly held there.[116] Subsequent references to this place and its assemblies include mention of a royal hall or palace, presumably the Gloucester residence of many late Anglo-Saxon kings.[117] Another important early extramural site was the area around the old Roman tilery and its subsequent cemetery, which appears to have been used in the ninth century as a burial ground with associated chapels for the nearby royal estate. It was here that the "New Minster" (St. Oswald's) was erected c.900 by Mercian rulers.[118] Up to this time, early Anglo-Saxon Gloucester exhibited but a few of the elements we have defined as urban features: an intramural minster, royal properties, and low-level industrial activity. During the tenth century, however, Gloucester would experience a period of intensified political, economic, and structural activities, which significantly heightened its urban status.[119]

Some remarks also are in order concerning developments at a third type of Romano-British town in this area of western Britain: Aquae Sulis (Bath). Though no doubt best known for its mineral springs and elaborate bathing facilities, Aquae Sulis was also one of the numerous "small towns" of Roman Britain. The site is located some thirty-five miles southwest of Gloucester, near where the Fosse Way crossed the River Avon. Roman settlement is believed to have begun in the mid-first century with the establishment of a small military fort and associated civilian site just to the north of the springs (Map 2.1, and Fig. 3.8).[120] Toward the close of this century, the springs themselves were developed by the Romans into a large-scale spa and religious center with various components: baths, temple and altar, sacred spring, and possibly a theater (Fig. 3.9). The arcaded Great Bath with its warm and hot rooms occupied the southeast wing of the impressive Temple of Sulis Minerva, deity of the springs. During the second and third centuries, the bathing facilities were greatly expanded with more separate baths, warm rooms, and cold plunges, while the entire bath complex received barrel vaulting. Outside the temple precinct were several other smaller baths (the Hot Bath and Cross Bath) and additional as yet unidentified monumental buildings.[121]

The initial settlement and commercial areas of Aquae Sulis lay immediately to the north, at Walcot and Bathwick (Fig. 3.8).[122] In the late second century, an earthen rampart was built enclosing an area of about 25 acres around the central temple-bath complex.[123] Thereafter, residential houses evidently began to be constructed more frequently within this delimited area (Fig. 3.9). Many of these were substantial masonry homes with mosaics and hypocausts, and several show signs of extended occupation.[124] For example, excavations in the southeast intramural area at Abbeygate Street revealed a rather large third-century masonry house that received elaborate alterations during the fourth century, including central hypocaust heating and lively interior wall painting. It eventually was abandoned (c.375) but then was succeeded by a smaller mortar-built home, erected perhaps as late as c.410. That in turn underwent several occupation phases, including the installation of a large domestic oven. After this amenity fell into disuse, the severed head of a young woman was pushed into the flue. Stratigraphic and ceramic evidence suggests that the building had not been abandoned until the second half of the fifth century.[125] Subsequent excavations slightly to the east of this site disclosed another masonry structure with a very similar sequence of late occupation.[126] Also, just inside the west gate at Citizen House, a large masonry building was found to have received substantial enlargements c.200, followed by partial conversion to an iron workshop. This structure was succeeded in the late fourth century by several smaller wood and masonry buildings. The last of these, a timber building on foundations of reused Roman stone, was constructed in the early fifth century and occupied for perhaps fifty years, after which the site was sealed by layers of dark earth.[127]

Archaeological evidence from residential sites thus indicates that some town life continued at Aquae Sulis into the fifth century, but much reduced in its scale and quality. Evidence of decline and decay is even more dramatic at the two main public buildings: the Great Bath and Temple. From the mid-fourth century, the central hollow in which these edifices lay was subjected to periodic flooding from the Avon and its tributaries which left successive layers of mud and silt.[128] Measures were taken at the Great Bath to counteract this problem by raising floor levels to protect its hypocausts, but by the early fifth century, these efforts were abandoned, the drainage system backed up, and the thermal waters of the Sacred Spring flooded the establishment. The great vault collapsed, and the area reverted to marsh-land.[129] Similar signs of flooding, silt accumulation, and dereliction are evident at the adjoining Temple and its forecourt. Repeated attempts were made to consolidate the waterlogged ground by a series of cobblestone and rubble repavings, which, on numismatic and ceramic evidence, extended to c.430. These sub-Roman rescue activities thereafter ended, and the Temple too gradually tumbled into the swamp.[130] The decay and abandonment of these primary public facilities surely indicates a serious breakdown of civic organization and authority, though other intramural areas did remain thinly occupied for several decades.

The accumulations of dark earth at residential sites and silt over former public buildings at Aquae Sulis point to a rather extended period of virtual desertion after the fifth century. The Sacred Spring itself, however, continued to receive occasional sub-Roman votive offerings.[131] Indeed, its heavy perimeter wall stood largely intact when incorporated into the twelfth-century wall of the King's Bath.[132] Although other Roman town monuments became increasingly derelict on the abandoned site, their remains still must have been impressive. Thus, a strong sense of awe mixed with some lament permeates what most likely is an eye-witness description of Aquae Sulis in the famous early eighth-century Anglo-Saxon poem, *The Ruin*:

> Wondrous this masonry, shattered by Fate;
> Town buildings fell apart, the work of giants decays.
> This building-wall endured, lichened-gray and red-stained,
> One kingdom after another, still-standing under storms;
> Desolate are the buildings and the dome
> With reddened arches sheds its tiles.
> There were stone buildings; a hot spring gushed
> In a wide surge; a wall enclosed all
> Within its bright bosom; there the baths were,
> Hot in the center–that was convenient.
> They then let hot streams pour over gray stone
> Up to the circular pool.[133]

The poet also includes in this somber work a vivid description of perhaps the sub-Roman town's final days: "The dead fell everywhere, pestilence days came; / Death took away all of the sword-brave men."[134] Elsewhere there is some suggestion that the baths continued at least to be used in post-Roman times. The early ninth-century quasi-historical miscellany associated with the Welsh monk Nennius mentions as one of the Wonders of Britain, "The Hot Pool where the Baths of Badon are, in the territory of the Hwicce. It is surrounded by a wall made of brick and stone, and men go to it for bathing at any time, and every man can have the kind of bath he likes. If he wants, it will be a cold bath; if he wants a hot bath, it will be hot."[135]

Although there is circumstantial archaeological evidence of a British presence remaining in the region of Aquae Sulis through the sixth century, no traces of sixth-century British or Anglo-Saxon settlement have been found at the town site itself.[136] As at Gloucester, the first indication of An-glo-Saxon settlement and renewed town functions relates to the establish-ment of an intramural monastery in the late seventh century. A charter of 675 X 676 records that the same Osric, subking of the Hwicce, who later founded the Gloucester minster, granted property just outside Bath (Hat Bathu, "Hot Bath") to support the construction of an intramural convent or perhaps a double minster.[137] It is generally believed that this was St. Peter's, on or very near the site of the late Anglo-Saxon abbey (Fig. 3.9).[138] Mercian kings evidently possessed an estate in Bath at which they are known to have issued charters and held assemblies. This royal presence likely conveyed heightened prestige and additional economic and administrative functions to the town.[139] As in the case of Gloucester, however, the most dramatic urban growth at Bath occurred in the tenth century when the town came under the expanding authority of Wessex.[140]

The final Romano-British town to be considered here is Viroconium (Wroxeter), lying along the upper Severn on the Welsh border. Initial Roman activity involved the establishment of a mid-first century auxiliary fort (20 acres) in the territory of the British Cornovii at a strategic crossing of the Severn (Map 2.1, and Fig. 3.10). This became an important staging ground for Roman military operations along the extended, turbulent frontier. As part of the subsequent Neronian campaign to conquer Wales, a larger legionary fortress (46 acres) was constructed about a half-mile to the north, complete with ramparts, *principia*, barracks blocks, granary, and likely civilian settlements on its north and south sides.[141]

After the withdrawal of legionary troops c.90 A.D., the fortress was developed as a civil *civitas*-capital for the British Cornovii: Viroconium Cornoviorum. The first town constructions at Viroconium were rather modest timber buildings that extended or reused former military struc-tures.[142] In the early second century, however, large-scale urban develop-ment, stimulated perhaps by the emperor Hadrian's initiative, took place.[143] New monumental buildings included an impressive forum-basilica, public baths with smaller basilica, market hall, and temples, all arranged within an expanded regular network of streets and *insulae*. South of the forum was a large commercial and industrial district with merchants' booths and various metalworking shops (Insula VIII); a tilery, pottery kilns, and glassworks each operated on the town's outskirts.[144] Indeed, Viroconium's economic prosperity was based largely on its position as a frontier town with good communications lying amid a very mineral-rich hill country. In addition, much of the town's large northern area appears to have been open space used for communal farming.[145] About a dozen large town houses evidently belonging to affluent decurions have been found, though they were perhaps not quite as lavishly equipped as those at other cantonal capitals. The relative scarcity of surrounding villas and limited extramural settlement suggest that the local elite opted for permanent town residence in this area of unsettled frontier conditions.[146] At the close of the second century Viroconium received earthwork defenses and, in the next century, an expanded stone circuit. The urban area thus enclosed amounted to c.200 acres, making this the second largest *civitas*-capital and the fourth largest of all Romano-British towns.[147]

Viroconium's prosperity evidently endured into the fourth century. Earlier town houses continued to be occupied and maintained, and new ones were constructed. Urban shops and the town market also carried on normal activities.[148] Yet more ominous changes were occurring. For example, the forum-basilica and public baths at the town center were partially demolished and then abandoned c.300–350. The baths-basilica (Insula V), however, continued to be used, perhaps partly as a storehouse, for several more decades.[149] It then was succeeded by a rather remarkable late sequence of timber constructions recently revealed by meticulous excavations.[150] The main building, standing in the center of the basilican area, was a large, residential, wooden hall in Roman style with portico and several projecting wings. On its eastern flank stood a large combination barn-tannery. Along the hall's north side ran a rough stone and gravel street lined with smaller buildings, some with symmetrical facades. One in particular was a colonnaded structure resembling a timber version of a Roman temple. The hall also was fronted by a row of covered shops or booths that partly incorporated the old basilican walls. Numismatic and ceramic evidence dates initial construction of this timber complex to c.395–405, with occupation lasting until perhaps the end of the fifth century. It generally is believed to be the residence and compound of a local sub-Roman ruler such as Gildas described, a petty king of an essentially agrarian realm.[151] Yet it also could represent the last phase of organized Romano-British occupation and town life, confined now to a small area of the old town. In any case, this late town activity at Viroconium was clearly much reduced from previous urban standards. Moreover, outside the baths-basilica compound there is evidence only of increasing squalor and decay. Human bodies were found lying near the forum ruins and inside the disused hypocausts of the public baths.[152]

By the close of the fifth century, when the timber complex evidently had been dismantled, Viroconium was derelict and virtually deserted.[153] Indeed, there are some signs of a settlement-shift by the town's last inhabitants to several nearby refortified hill forts such as Shrewsbury (Scrobbesbyrig), which eventually became the central shire town.[154] Our earliest indication of any Anglo-Saxon presence at Viroconium is the small parish Church of St. Andrew within the southern rampart wall. Its nave, built with Roman stone from the town, is regarded as seventh-century work.[155]   The small village of Wroxeter extending from the old south gate also may have arisen at this time. Anglo-Saxon settlement apparently first spread into the region from the east and intensified after the Battle of Maserfelth [Oswestry] (641), when the Mercian king Penda and his British allies defeated and killed Oswald of Northumbria.[156]   Indeed, the obscure people called the W(r)ocensaetna in the *Tribal Hidage*, an eighth-century Mercian tribute list, are thought to have been former Romano-Britons of Viroconium and early Anglo-Saxon settlers (Map 3.1).[157] Be that as it may, the village and church at Wroxeter were reportedly part of a small estate, R(W)ochechester, held in 1066 by a certain Anglo-Saxon (?) free man, Toret.[158] Most of the old Roman town area had become cultivated Anglo-Saxon open fields; the outlines of its former structures appear distinctly as crop marks from aerial photography.[159] Thus the overall evidence indicates that this major Romano-British cantonal capital of the northwest was essentially abandoned and derelict for over a century before the arrival of Anglo-Saxons into the region.

Certain notable patterns emerge from the preceding examination of selected Romano-British towns. All of these towns, regardless of their type or location, yield evidence of generally sustained prosperity into the mid-fourth century and occasionally slightly longer. By comparison, Roman towns in Gaul and the Rhineland were suffering serious contraction.[160] Significant change then began to occur, marked by a decrease in public and private construction, settlement constriction, selective disuse or alteration of civic structures and services, and economic slowdown. This decline proceeded into the early fifth century, more pronounced at some towns than others. Late Roman urban defense work along with the presence of Roman officials often granted an extended lease of life. The final withdrawal of Roman military and civil authorities, though perhaps initially beneficial to the town elite, only exacerbated long-term urban problems.

By the mid-fifth century, all the examined towns had become but pale reflections of their former selves, with very small populations, increasingly derelict structures and services, and minimal trade. They were nonetheless still towns: some of their traditional urban functions continued, though on a sharply reduced scale. By c.500, however, this faint urban pulse had ceased. Archaeological evidence indicates that the end came to these towns not suddenly or violently but gradually, after a long decline. It serves as a reminder that we must approach the written accounts of town destruction at Anglo-Saxon hands with particular caution. In all these towns, there is firm archaeological evidence of near or total abandonment before the An-glo-Saxon advent. The argument for discontinuity of both Romano-British urbanism and urban settlement in these cases is therefore quite strong. Indeed, concentrated Anglo-Saxon town occupation cannot be demonstrated before the seventh century even when Anglo-Saxon settlement is attested in the area. And on those sites where Anglo-Saxon reoccupation and renewed town life did emerge, it was in a limited ecclesiastical and royal context. In addition to these cases, where upon examination discontinuity looms large, one must now consider a number of important towns that have been set forth perhaps more vociferously as examples of settlement or urban continuity from Roman to Anglo-Saxon times.

NOTES

1. S. Frere, *Verulamium Excavations* (3 vols., Oxford: Oxford University Committee for Archaeology, 1972–84), II (1983), pp. 20–22, 55–58, 212–22; also see J. S. Wacher, *The Towns of Roman Britain* (Berkeley: University of California Press, 1974), pp. 219–20.

2. Frere, *Verulamium Excavations*, II pp. 93–101.

3. Ibid., II, pp. 23, 214–22; S. Frere, "The End of Towns in Roman Britain," in *The Civitas Capitals of Roman Britain*, ed. J. S. Wacher (Leicester: University Press, 1966), p. 97.

4. Frere, *Verulamium Excavations*, II, pp. 223–26.

5. Ibid., III (1984), pp. 3–64.

6. Ibid., II, pp. 20–21. Possible late Roman Christian churches stood within and beyond the east or London gate.

7. Ibid., II, pp. 132–76, 277–87, and Figs. 6, 10; Wacher, *Towns*, p. 220; A. S. Esmonde Cleary, *Extra-Mural Areas of Romano-British Towns*, British Archaeological Reports (hereafter B.A.R.), 169 (Oxford, 1987), pp. 136–40. These findings cast some doubt on the accuracy of Constantius of Lyon's description, if indeed his town was Verulamium.

8. As do R. Reece, "Town and Country: The End of Roman Britain," *World Archaeology* 12 (1980), 88–89; C. J. Arnold, *Roman Britain to Saxon England* (Bloomington: Indiana University Press, 1984), pp. 43, 54; cf. Frere, *Verulamium Excavations*, II, p. 23.

9. J. N. L. Myres, *The English Settlements* (Oxford: Clarendon Press, 1986), pp. 89–91, 129–30; L. Alcock, *Arthur's Britain: History and Archaeology A.D. 367–634* (Harmondsworth: Penguin Books, 1971), p. 188; Frere, *Verulamium Excavations*, II, p. 25. A small Anglo-Saxon cemetery was in use c.600 outside the south gate, but there are no signs of intramural Germanic settlement, apart from some earlier "Romano-Saxon" pottery of dubious interpretive value.

10. Summarized, with bibliography, in E. Ennen, *Die europäische Stadt des Mittelalters* (Göttingen: Vandenhoeck & Ruprecht, 1972), pp. 39–40; H. Planitz, *Die deutsche Stadt im Mittelalter* (Cologne: Böhlau, 1954), p. 25.

11. Gildas, *De excidio Britonum*, x–xi, ed. M. Winterbottom (Chichester: Phillimore, 1978); Bede, *Historia Ecclesiastica* (hereafter *Hist. Eccl.*), i.7, ed. C. Plummer (2 vols., Oxford: Clarendon Press, 1896).

12. Constantius, *Vita Germani*, xvi, ed. W. Levison in *Monumenta Germaniae Historica* (hereafter *MGH*), *Scriptores Rerum Merovingicarum* (hereafter *SS RM*),VII

(Hanover, 1919); Gildas, *De excidio*, x; Venantius Fortunatus, *Carmina*, viii.3, ed. F. Leo in *MGH Auctores Antiquissimi (AA)* IV;1 (Berlin, 1881); Bede, *Hist. Eccl.*, i.7. Many churches dedicated to Alban were founded in early medieval France and Germany. For all of these matters, see the seminal study by W. Levison, "St. Alban and St. Albans," *Antiquity* 15 (1941), 337–59, who argued for the existence of a late fifth-century Gallic *Passio Albani*; see also: W. Page, "Ecclesiastical History Before the Conquest," in *The Victoria History of the Counties of England* (hereafter *VCH*), Hertfordshire, IV (1914), pp. 281–89; C. Thomas, *Christianity in Roman Britain to A.D. 500* (Berkeley: University of California Press, 1981), pp. 48–50.

13. M. Biddle, "The Towns," in *The Archaeology of Anglo-Saxon England*, ed. D. M. Wilson (London: Methuen, 1976), pp. 110–11; Levison, "St. Alban and St. Albans," 350–53; Thomas, *Christianity in Roman Britain*, p. 180; Esmonde Cleary, *Extra-Mural Areas*, pp. 139–40.

14. D. Hill, "Continuity from Roman to Medieval: Britain," in *European Towns: Their Archaeology and Early History*, ed. M. W. Barley (London: Academic Press, 1977), p. 301; cf. Biddle, "Towns," pp. 110–11, who seems to be confusing the two issues.

15. G. C. Boon, *Silchester: The Roman Town of Calleva* (rev. ed., London: David & Charles, 1974), pp. 36–48, 85–159; Wacher, *Towns*, pp. 255–74, and Fig. 60. Calleva, like Verulamium, was on the site of an important older British *oppidum*. See further, M. Fulford, "Calleva Atrebatum: An Interim Report of the Excavation of the *Oppidum*, 1980–86," *Proceedings of the Prehistoric Society* 53 (1987), pp. 271–78.

16. Boon, *Silchester*, pp. 267–93; Wacher, *Towns*, pp. 271–72; S. Frere, *Britannia* (3d ed., London: Routledge & Kegan Paul, 1987), pp. 250–52; P. Salway, *Roman Britain* (Oxford: Clarendon Press, 1981), p. 659; I. Richmond, "Industry in Roman Britain," in *Civitas Capitals*, ed., Wacher, pp. 80–81, and Fig. 16.

17. Boon, *Silchester*, pp. 188–93; Wacher, *Towns*, pp. 272–74. Also like Verulamium, Calleva was never densely built up. Most *insulae* here had large, open spaces, often used for family farms, gardens, or pasturage. Even Calleva's most sumptuously adorned homes were comparatively modest affairs: Boon, *Silchester*, pp. 53–56, 259–61.

18. Ibid., pp. 44–46, 65–66, 100–7; Wacher, *Towns*, pp. 256–61, 264–66. For recent archaeological refinements, see M. G. Fulford, *Silchester: Excavations on the Defences* (Gloucester: Alan Sutton, 1984), pp. 42–73.

19. Boon, *Silchester*, pp. 72–73, 208–21.

20. Fulford, "Excavations on the Sites of the Amphitheatre and Forum-Basilica at Silchester, Hampshire: An Interim Report," *Antiquaries Journal* 65 (1985), 53–55, 59–60, and Fig. 6. The scale and duration of the smithing operation suggest effective central direction. See further, Arnold, *Roman Britain to Saxon England*, pp. 98–100.

21. Fulford, "Amphitheatre and Forum-Basilica," pp. 73, 77, and Fig. 9.

22. Boon, *Silchester*, pp. 66–70. But there is insufficient evidence of Germanic mercenary forces in the late Roman town.

23. Ibid., pp. 68, 106–7.

24. Fulford, *Silchester Excavations*, pp. 74–76, 190–95, 237; Wacher, *Towns*, p. 276.

25. Boon, *Silchester*, p. 72; Fulford, "Amphitheatre and Forum-Basilica," 60, 77, and *Silchester Excavations*, p. 75.

26. Boon, *Silchester*, pp. 73–76.

27. Esmonde Cleary, *Extra-Mural Areas*, pp. 130–31, 197–200; Fulford, *Silchester Excavations*, pp. 288–90. One of the few Christian churches positively identified in any Romano-British town stood near Calleva's forum (Insula IV). This mid fourth-century structure, with apse and side chapels, resembles the Kentish group of early Anglo-Saxon churches. There is no evidence for continuity of worship, however. See: Wacher, *Towns*, pp. 269–71, and Fig. 61; Thomas, *Christianity in Roman Britain*, pp. 169, 214–16, and Figs. 35, 40; B. Cherry, "Ecclesiastical Architecture," in *Archaeology of Anglo-Saxon England*, ed. Wilson, pp. 156, 158; cf. A. C. King, "The Roman Church at Silchester Reconsidered," *Oxford Journal of Archaeology* 2 (1983), pp. 225–38.

28. Boon, *Silchester*, pp. 257–59, describing one certain and several possible examples.

29. Earlier findings that key buildings in the central *insula* ended in flames (ibid., p. 82) have not been confirmed by later investigations.

30. Ibid.

31. B. H. St. J. O'Neill, "The Silchester Region in the Fifth and Sixth Centuries A.D.," *Antiquity* 18 (1944), 113–22; Wacher, *Towns*, pp. 276–77, and Fig. 88; Frere, *Britannia*, pp. 369–70; S. Johnson, *Later Roman Britain* (London: Collins, 1980), pp. 200–201; Myres, *English Settlements*, pp. 156–64. The famous Silchester Ogham (Old Irish)-inscribed tombstone pillar (Insula IX), formerly dated to as late as c.700, now has been assigned to c.450 (if even genuine): Fulford and B. Selwood, "The Silchester Ogham Stone: A Re-Consideration," *Antiquity* 54 (1980), 95–99.

32. Boon, *Silchester*, pp. 75, 82; D. A. Hinton, "Hampshire's Anglo-Saxon Origins," in *The Archaeology of Hampshire*, eds. R. Schadla-Hall and S. Shennan. Hampshire Field Club and Archaeological Society Monographs, 1 (Farnborough: A. E. Fenn, 1981), p. 56.

33. Early Anglo-Saxon settlement is not attested in or immediately around the town, though scattered finds suggest later Anglo-Saxon farming on the site. See: Wacher, *Towns*, p. 276; Myres, *English Settlements*, p. 149; Boon, *Silchester*, p. 76. In 1066 there were two Anglo-Saxon estates held by royal thegns within the old Calleva, then identified as Silcestre: *Domesday Book* (hereafter *DB*), (4 vols., London: Record Commission, 1783–1816), I, 47a, 47b.

34. Wacher, *Towns*, pp. 239–48, 253–54; G. Webster, "Fort and Town in Early Roman Britain," in *Civitas Capitals*, p. 41; A. A. Barrett, "The Career of Tiberius Claudius Cogidubnus," *Britannia* 10 (1979), 227–42; Frere, *Britannia*, pp. 193, 233; A. Down and M. Rule, *Chichester Excavations I* (Chichester: Chichester Civic Society, 1971), pp. 12–17, 53–70; Down, et al., *Chichester Excavations III* (Chichester: Chichester Civic Society, 1978), pp. 145–52; P. Drewett, et al., *The South East to A.D. 1000* (London: Longman, 1988), pp. 184–85, 188–89, 200–201.

35. Wacher, *Towns*, pp. 252–53; Drewett, et al., *South East*, p. 190. A late first-century temple was erected by a guild of craftsmen (smiths?), *collegium fabrorum: The Roman Inscriptions of Britain* (hereafter *RIB*), eds. R. G. Collingwood and R. P. Wright (Oxford: Clarendon Press, 1965), No. 91. See further, Salway, *Roman Britain*, p. 659.

36. Down and Rule, *Chichester Excavations I*, p. 13; Wacher, *Towns*, p. 252; Drewett, et al., *South East*, p. 201.

37. Wacher, *Towns*, pp. 248–52; Frere, *Britannia*, p. 241, 248-249.

38. Down, *Chichester Excavations III*, pp. 45, 81–83, 331–40; Wacher, *Towns*, p. 252; Drewett, et al., *South East*, p. 247. Overall, not many dwellings occupied after 400 have been located.

39. Drewett, et al., *South East*, p. 247; Wacher, *Towns*, p. 247. The extramural amphitheater was overgrown and abandoned at least a century earlier: ibid., p. 248; Esmonde Cleary, *Extra-Mural Areas*, p. 36; Arnold, *Roman Britain to Saxon England*, p. 33.

40. Down and Rule, *Chichester Excavations I*, pp. 53, 67; Down, *Chichester Excavations V* (Chichester: Chichester Civic Society, 1981), pp. 91–95; Esmonde Cleary, *Extra-Mural Areas*, pp. 37–38; Drewett, et al., *South East*, pp. 236–37.

41. Wacher, *Towns*, p. 255; Down, *Chichester Excavations V*, pp. 80–84; Esmonde Cleary, *Extra-Mural Areas*, p. 36; Drewett, et al., *South East*, p. 247.

42. Ibid., pp. 247–48; Arnold, *Roman Britain to Saxon England*, p. 30. See in general, R. Macphail, "Soil and Botanical Studies of the 'Dark Earth,' " in *The Environment of Man*, eds. M. Jones and G. Dimbleby, B.A.R. 87 (Oxford, 1981), pp. 309–31.

43. Wacher, *Towns*, p. 255; Myres, *English Settlements*, p. 135.

44. Wacher, *Towns*, p. 255.

45. D. Hill, "The Origins of the [South] Saxon Towns," in *The South Saxons*, ed. P. Brandon (Chichester: Phillimore, 1978), pp. 174, 178.

46. Ibid., p. 178, and Fig. 11. See further, M. Welch, "Late Romans and Saxons in Sussex," *Britannia* 2 (1971), 232–37; Myres, *English Settlements*, pp. 135–39.

47. The massive, late Roman vaulted west gate and tower was still virtually intact and in use in the eighteenth century: Wacher, *Towns*, p. 251; Hill, "Origins," p. 179.

48. J. Munby, "Saxon Chichester and Its Predecessors," in *Anglo-Saxon Towns in Southern England*, ed. J. Haslam (Chichester: Phillimore, 1984), pp. 322–23; Drewett, et al., *South East*, pp. 307, 335–36. Even the Romano-British town name apparently was totally lost. The Old English (O.E.) designation for the site may be significant: *Cisse ceastre* ("Cisse's fortified place/stronghold"), *Two of the Saxon Chronicles Parallel* hereafter *ASC*, eds. J. Earle and C. Plummer (2 vols. Oxford: Clarendon Press, 1892-96), 894A, thus perhaps involving the reported late fifth-century South Saxon ruler Cissa (*ASC* 477, 491A; Hill, "Origins," p. 178). If indeed there had been a South Saxon takeover of the town c.500, no archaeological evidence of the event has come to light as yet. Chichester's Anglo-Saxon street plan seems to be primarily of late ninth-century date and bears the features of the Alfredian burghal pattern: ibid., pp. 180–82. See also below, Chap. 7.

49. Wacher, *Towns*, pp. 230–34, and Fig. 54; Frere, "The Forum and Baths at Caistor St. Edmund," *Britannia* 2 (1971), 1–26; G. R. Stephens, "Civic Aqueducts in Britain," *Britannia* 16 (1985), 201, 205. A small amphitheater just outside Venta's south gate was discovered in 1977: G. S. Maxwell and D. R. Wilson, "Air Reconaissance in Roman Britain 1977–1984," *Britannia* 18 (1987), 43–44.

50. Wacher, *Towns*, pp. 236–37; Richmond, "Industry in Roman Britain," p. 78, and Fig. 14; Frere, *Britannia*, pp. 251, 291; G. Braithwaite, "Romano-British Face Pots and Head Pots," *Britannia* 15 (1984), 103, 110.

51. But the late second-century earth defenses had enclosed a considerably larger urban area, as at Calleva. See further on this atypical phenomenon: Frere,

Britannia, pp. 240, 249; Wacher, *Towns*, pp. 234–36; J. K. St. Joseph, "The Contribution of Aerial Photography," in *Civitas Capitals*, pp. 23–24 and Pl. III; Esmonde Cleary, *Extra-Mural Areas*, p. 21.

52. Wacher, *Towns*, pp. 236–37. Yet it is surely exaggeration to describe Venta as never being more than a "shantytown": Myres, *English Settlements*, p. 97.

53. Tacitus, *Annales*, xii.32, xiv.31, ed. H. Furneaux (2d ed., 2 vols., Oxford: Clarendon Press, 1896–1907). Boudicca, one recalls, was queen of the Iceni. The town's first-century forum, destroyed by fire c.200–225, was not rebuilt for a century and then only on a reduced scale. For these matters, see Wacher, *Towns*, pp. 227–29, 236, and Fig. 55.

54. Ibid., p. 236; Frere, "Forum and Baths," 22–26. But suburban settlement, which had contracted in the previous century, was not resumed: Esmonde Cleary, *Extra-Mural Areas*, pp. 22–23.

55. Wacher, *Towns*, pp. 236–38; Johnson, *Later Roman Britain*, p. 178; Myres, *English Settlements*, p. 89. No new major town construction is apparent from this chronological horizon, however.

56. Site excavation was conducted by D. Atkinson and reported briefly in *Journal of Roman Studies* 21 (1931), 232–33 but never published in detail. The building stood above the site of an early second-century ceramic industry: Atkinson, "Three Caistor Pottery Kilns," *Journal of Roman Studies* 22 (1932), 33–46, and Fig. 1. It represents the only town dwelling yet found with fifth-century occupancy; dating also was secured by late Roman coin deposits. For the massacre theory applied to this case, see R. G. Collingwood and J. N. L. Myres, *Roman Britain and the English Settlements* (2d ed., Oxford: Clarendon Press, 1937), p. 302; S. Hawkes and G. Dunning, "Soldiers and Settlers in Britain, Fourth to Fifth Century," *Medieval Archaeology* 5 (1961), 25, 31; Frere, "End of Towns," p. 91.

57. Wacher, *Towns*, p. 238; Alcock, *History and Archaeology*, p. 185.

58. M. J. Darling, "The Caistor-by-Norwich Massacre Reconsidered," *Britannia* 18 (1987), 263–72. The author carefully reexamined all extant, nonpublished material, coin finds, and bone analyses.

59. Myres and B. Green, *The Anglo-Saxon Cemeteries of Caistor-by-Norwich and Markshall, Norfolk* (London: Society of Antiquaries, 1973), pp. 12–15, 31–34, 43–71. Also see Biddle, "Towns," pp. 104–5. But cf. Myres's subsequent, more cautious, comments: *English Settlements*, pp. 98–100.

60. J. G. Hurst, "The Pottery," in *Archaeology of Anglo-Saxon England*, pp. 294–99; Johnson, *Later Roman Britain*, pp. 169–71; Arnold, *Roman Britain to Saxon England*, pp. 111–14; Esmonde Cleary, *Extra-Mural Areas*, p. 22.

61. C. Hills, "The Archaeology of Anglo-Saxon England in the Pagan Period: A Review," *Anglo-Saxon England* 7 (1979), pp. 297–308; Johnson, *Later Roman Britain*, pp. 176–77; Arnold, *Roman Britain to Saxon England*, pp. 25–27.

62. J. Gillam, "Romano-Saxon Pottery: An Alternative Interpretation," in *End of Roman Britain*, pp. 103–18; Hills, "Archaeology," pp. 308–9; Johnson, *Later Roman Britain*, pp. 172–74.

63. S. Johnson, *The Roman Forts of the Saxon Shore* (New York: St. Martin's Press, 1976), pp. 18–19, 37–40, 96–99, 150–54. There are indications of Anglo-Saxon settlement within these forts from the later fifth century: P. Rahtz, "Gazetteer of

Anglo-Saxon Domestic Settlement Sites," in *Archaeology of Anglo-Saxon England*, p. 412.

64. In 1086 the site of Venta (called Castrum) comprised a rural estate and small village with church, belonging to Bury St. Edmunds (*DB*, II, 210a). The small parish Church of St. Edmund, located within the southeast intramural area, is presumably the same as that which served the late Anglo-Saxon village community. Its construction date is undetermined (*VCH Norfolk*, I, p. 290).

65. Norwich does not appear to have had any significant Romano-British settlement background. It was an agglomeration of several distinct, small Anglo-Saxon emporia. See J. Campbell, "Norwich," in *Atlas of Historic Towns II*, eds. M. D. Lobel and W. H. Johns (London: Lovell Johns, 1975), pp. 2–4, 25; Biddle, "Towns," pp. 139–40; A. Carter, "The Anglo-Saxon Origins of Norwich: The Problems and Approaches," *Anglo-Saxon England* 7 (1978), pp. 175–203; T. Williamson, *The Origins of Norfolk* (Manchester: University Press, 1993), pp. 79–80.

66. See, e.g., F. M. Stenton, *Anglo-Saxon England* (hereafter *ASE*) (3d ed., Oxford: Clarendon Press, 1971), pp. 17–18, 25–31; D. J. V. Fisher, *The Anglo-Saxon Age* (London: Longman, 1973), pp. 44–54; Myres, *English Settlements*, pp. 107–12, 207–18; Arnold, *Roman Britain to Saxon England*, pp. 6–20, 121–33; J. Campbell, "The Lost Centuries: 400–600," in *The Anglo-Saxons*, ed. Campbell (Harmondsworth: Penguin Books, 1982), pp. 34–37; C. Hills, "The Anglo-Saxon Settlement of England," in *The Northern World*, ed. D. M. Wilson (London: Thames & Hudson, 1980), pp. 71–86; Hodges, "The Anglo-Saxon Migrations," in *The Making of Britain: The Dark Ages*, ed. L. M. Smith (London: Macmillan, 1984), pp. 35–47; C. Taylor, *Village and Farmstead* (London: G. Philip, 1983), pp. 110–12.

67. Frere, "End of Towns," p. 89; Wacher, *Towns*, pp. 420–21; Biddle, "Towns," pp. 110–11.

68. For details on the following survey of Corinium, see Wacher, *Towns*, pp. 289–312; A. D. McWhirr, "Cirencester, 1973–76: Tenth Interim Report," *Antiquaries Journal* 58 (1978), 61–80; *Houses in Roman Cirencester* (Cirencester: Cirencester Excavations Committee, 1986), and "Cirencester: (Corinium Dubunnorum)," in *Fortress into City*, ed. G. Webster, (Totowa, NJ: Barnes & Noble, 1988), pp. 74–90 and Figs. 4.4–4.8. Also see D. J. Smith, "The Mosaic Pavements," in *The Roman Villa in Britain*, ed., Rivet (London: Routledge & Kegan Paul, 1969), pp. 97–102, 114–16; J. M. C. Toynbee, *Art in Roman Britain* (London: Phaidon Press, 1962), pp. 7–8; J. Welsford, *Cirencester* (Gloucester: Alan Sutton, 1987), pp. 1–18.

69. *RIB*, No. 103, commemorating a temple restoration by the provincial governor. See further, Mann, "Administration of Roman Britain," 319; Wacher, *Towns*, pp. 84–86; Salway, *Roman Britain*, pp. 346–47; McWhirr, "Cirencester," p. 83. It may also then have become a bishop's seat: Wacher, *Towns*, p. 311; Thomas, *Christianity in Roman Britain*, pp. 197–201.

70. Wacher, *Towns*, pp. 306–8, 312–13; McWhirr, "Cirencester," pp. 83–85.

71. Wacher, *Towns*, pp. 313, 420.

72. Esmonde Cleary, *Extra-Mural Areas*, pp. 42–44; Welsford, *Cirencester*, p. 15.

73. McWhirr, *Houses in Roman Cirencester*, pp. 70–77; and "Cirencester," p. 85, and Fig. 4.9; Welsford, *Cirencester*, pp. 16–17.

74. McWhirr, "Cirencester," p. 85; Wacher, *Towns*, p. 308; C. Heighway, *Anglo-Saxon Gloucestershire* (Gloucester: Alan Sutton, 1987), p. 5. But cf. Esmonde Cleary, *Extra-Mural Areas*, p. 41.

75. McWhirr, "Tenth Interim Report," 74.

76. Wacher, *Towns*, pp. 299, 313–14; Arnold, *Roman Britain to Saxon England*, p. 37, and Fig. 2.6. The road leading from the west gate to the amphitheater also was upgraded as part of these alterations.

77. Wacher, *Towns*, p. 313; Johnson, *Later Roman Britain*, p. 201.

78. This theory was propounded vigorously by Wacher, e.g., *Towns*, pp. 414–20, and countered rather effectively by M. Todd, *"Famosa Pestis* and Britain in the Fifth Century," *Britannia* 8 (1977), 319–25. Of course, decayed conditions may well have promoted disease and urban flight on a local scale.

79. Wacher, *Towns*, p. 420; Heighway, *Gloucestershire*, p. 145. The area was under threat of attack from west and east since the late fourth century: Johnson, *Later Roman Britain*, pp. 115–17.

80. Welsford, *Cirencester*, p. 21, Map 1, p. 47.

81. Wacher, *Towns*, pp. 308, 315; Esmonde Cleary, *Extra-Mural Areas*, p. 40. Barton Farm was the site of an impressive fourth-century Romano-British villa. Cemetery distribution indicates that Anglo-Saxon penetration had been primarily via the Thames from the east: Alcock, *History and Archaeology*, Map 9, p. 288; Heighway, *Gloucestershire*, pp. 22–30; T. M. Dickinson, "On the Origin and Chronology of the Early Anglo-Saxon Disc Brooch," in *Anglo-Saxon Studies in Archaeology and History I*, eds. S. C. Hawkes, et al., B.A.R. 72 (Oxford, 1979), pp. 53–54.

82. *ASC* 577 E: Gleawanceaster, Cirenceaster, Bathanceaster.

83. Gildas, *De excidio*, xxviii–xxxvi, esp. xxx, for a certain Aurelius Caninus ruling apparently in Gloucestershire. See: *ASE*, p. 4; H. P. R. Finberg, "The Genesis of the Gloucestershire Towns," in *Gloucestershire Studies*, ed. Finberg (Leicester: University Press, 1957), p. 57; Wacher, *Towns*, p. 314; Heighway, *Gloucestershire*, pp. 18–19, 145.

84. Myres, *English Settlements*, pp. 169–72; cf. Heighway, *Gloucestershire*, pp. 32–35.

85. *ASE*, p. 29; Fisher, *Anglo-Saxon Age*, pp. 32–37.

86. Wacher, *Towns*, pp. 313–14; also Welsford, *Cirencester*, p. 21. But cf. Esmonde Cleary, *Extra-Mural Areas*, p. 40. The end of the arena's last occupation phase is not securely dated. A site's possession of a minster and royal property are considered two main distinguishing featues of an early Anglo-Saxon "central place." See Chap. 1, n.114, and also in general: C. L. Redman, ed., *Research and Theory in Current Archaeology* (New York: Wiley, 1973), pp. 15–16; I. Hodder and C. Orton, *Spatial Analysis in Archaeology* (Cambridge: University Press, 1976).

87. *ASC*, 628A.

88. *ASE*, pp. 44–45; Welsford, *Cirencester*, p. 22; Heighway, *Gloucestershire*, pp. 35–40.

89. Welsford, *Cirencester*, pp. 24–25; McWhirr, "Cirencester," p. 87; Cherry, "Ecclesiastical Architecture," pp. 154, 172, and Fig. 4.8. This may have been an early monastic (minster) church: it lay beneath the site of the twelfth-century Abbey of St. Mary's (Insula XXV).

90. *ASC* 879[878]A. On the Scandinavian place-name features, see Welsford, *Cirencester*, p. 23.

91. M. Gibbs, ed., *Early Charters of the Cathedral Church of St. Paul, London*, Camden Third Ser., 58 (London: Royal Historical Society, 1939), No. J10 [935 A.D.]; W. de Gray Birch, ed., *Cartularium Saxonicum* (hereafter *Cart. Sax.*) (4 vols., London: Whiting & Co., 1885–1899), No. 937[956 A.D.]; *Codex Diplomaticus Aevi Saxonici*, ed. J. M. Kemble (6 vols., London: British Historical Society, 1839–48), Nos. 703 [999]: "in villa regia quae Anglica appellatione Cirneceastre dicitur," 1312[990 X 1006]; also, the "Great Assembly" (*mycel gemot*) held at Cirencester by Cnut in 1020: *ASC* 1020E. See further, F. Liebermann, *The National Assembly in the Anglo-Saxon Period* (Halle: M. Niemeyer, 1913), pp. 44–45; Sawyer, "The Royal *Tun* in Pre-Conquest England," in *Ideal and Reality in Frankish and Anglo-Saxon Society*, ed. P. Wormald (London: Blackwell, 1983), pp. 273–99.

92. See H. M. Cam, "Early Groups of Hundreds," in *Historical Essays in Honour of James Tait*, eds. J. G. Edwards, et al. (Manchester: Printed for the Subscribers, 1933), p. 17; Finberg, "Genesis of Gloucestershire Towns," pp. 58–59, suggesting this was a survival of Corinium's jurisdiction; Heighway, *Gloucestershire*, p. 149.

93. *DB*, I, 162b. See further (with caution): Welsford, *Cirencester*, pp. 26–28. The only properties specifically said to be held *in* Cirencester in 1066 were two small freemens' estates (*DB*, I, 162b, 167a).

94. Settlement discontinuity also can be seen in the town plan of medieval Cirencester, which retained very few Romano-British street alignments: Welsford, *Cirencester*, Map 1, p. 47. For the linguistic process whereby "Corinium" may have become "Cirencester," see A. H. Smith, *The Place-Names of Gloucestershire*, English Place-Name Society Publications, 38–41 (4 vols., Cambridge: University Press, 1964–65), I, pp. 60–62.

95. See: M. D. Lobel and J. Tann, "Gloucester," in *Atlas of Historic Towns I*, ed. Lobel (London: Lovell Johns, 1969), pp. 1–4; Wacher, *Towns*, pp. 137–55 and Figs. 32–35, and now: H. Hurst, "Gloucester (Glevum)," in *Fortress into City*, pp. 48–73. Also see C. Green, "Glevum and the Second Legion," *Journal of Roman Studies* 32 (1942), 39–52, and "Glevum and the Second Legion, ii: Evidence of the Pottery, Metal Objects, etc.," *Journal of Roman Studies* 33 (1943), 15–28; Heighway and A. J. Parker, "The Roman Tilery at St. Oswald's Priory," *Britannia* 13 (1982), 25–77; Heighway, "Saxon Gloucester," in *Anglo-Saxon Towns in Southern England*, ed. Haslam, pp. 359–83; Esmonde Cleary, *Extra-Mural Areas*, pp. 78–84.

96. Wacher, *Towns*, p. 155; Salway, *Roman Britain*, pp. 584–86, with some reservations. Certainly the trading potential of Glevum's riverside siting was never fully exploited and economic activity never as brisk after the end of the military phase: Hurst, "Glevum," pp. 62, 66–68.

97. Ibid., pp. 65–69.

98. Ibid., pp. 62–64, and Fig. 3.11; Heighway and Parker, "Roman Tilery," 28–31; Esmonde Cleary, *Extra-Mural Areas*, pp. 80–84. The tilery ceased production c.250. Suburbs immediately to the east and west remained active, however.

99. Wacher, *Towns*, p. 147. But only a few new residential constructions are evident after c.300.

100. Ibid., pp. 147–149.

92   Town Origins and Development in Early England

101. Heighway, "Saxon Gloucester," p. 362; Heighway and P. Garrod, "Excavations at Nos. 1 and 30 Westgate Street, Gloucester," *Britannia* 11 (1980), 88–96, 100–103.

102. Ibid., 78-79. The bath's palaestra (gymnasium) had been converted into an ironworking establishment by the fourth century, while another large, unidentified, public building just to its east also shows signs of contemporaneous industrial use: ibid., 81–84.

103. Heighway, "Saxon Gloucester," p. 361; cf. Esmonde Cleary, *Extra-Mural Areas*, pp. 81–82.

104. Heighway, "Saxon Gloucester," pp. 361–62, and Fig. 117, and *Gloucestershire*, p. 7; Heighway and Garrod, "Westgate Street," 95–96. There is scattered evidence of small-scale smithing operations associated with fifth- and perhaps sixth-century pottery.

105. Wacher, *Towns*, p. 154; Heighway, "Saxon Gloucester," pp. 364–65.

106. Ibid., p. 361; Esmonde Cleary, *Extra-Mural Areas*, p. 83. The initial view that this was the burial of a Germanic mercenary is now generally discounted: Arnold, *Roman Britain to Saxon England*, pp. 26–27. Perhaps it is that of a sub-Roman local chieftain such as Gildas reported.

107. It is thought to be of fifth- or even sixth-century provenance: Heighway, *Gloucestershire*, pp. 126–29. St. Mary de Lode Church, built in the tenth century, was on this site and used the same general alignments. But any actual continuity of religious function here between c.500 and 900 is an unproven assumption: Esmonde Cleary, *Extra-Mural Areas*, p. 84.

108. See Chap. 2, n.89; Heighway, *Gloucestershire*, pp. 22–24.

109. *Cart. Sax.*, No. 60. The grant included the town (*civitas*) and its land (*ager*). This may correspond to the old town and *territorium* of Roman Glevum and the later three districts (hundreds) of Gloucester: Finberg, "Gloucestershire Towns," pp. 55, 59; Heighway, "Saxon Gloucester," pp. 372–75, 381. For the linguistic transformation of Glevum to Gleawanceaster/Gleaweceaster, etc., see Smith, *Place-Names of Gloucestershire*, II, pp. 124–25.

110. Heighway, "Saxon Gloucester," pp. 365–66, and Fig. 117. A later confirmatory charter (872) informs us that the first abbesses had been members of the Hwiccan and Mercian royal families: *Cart. Sax.*, No. 535.

111. W. H. Hart, ed., *Historia et Cartularium Monasterii Sancti Petri Gloucestriae*, Rolls Series, 33 (3 vols., London, 1863–67), I, pp. 4–7. The final version of this work most likely was compiled in the early fifteenth century, incorporating earlier material and traditions, which must be approached with due caution. See C. N. L. Brooke, "St. Peter of Gloucester and St. Cadoc of Llancarfan," in *Celt and Saxon: Studies in the Early British Border*, ed. N. Chadwick (Cambridge: University Press, 1963), pp. 260–77; A. Gransden, *Historical Writing in England II* (Ithaca: Cornell University Press, 1982), p. 391.

112. *Memoriale Ecclesiae Cathedralis Gloucestriae Compendiarium*, in W. Dugdale, ed., *Monasticon Anglicanum* (rev. ed., 6 vols., London: Bohn, 1846), I, p. 563. This document was probably of later provenance than the monastic *History*. See further, Heighway, "Saxon Goucester," p. 366; Lobel and Tann, "Gloucester," p. 2. Wulfhere died in 675 and was succeeded by Aethelred: *ASC* 675 A.

113. Heighway, "Saxon Gloucester," pp. 364–65. This evidence comes primarily from the central area and extends to c.900. See further, Rahtz, "Gazetteer," p. 420.

The view that Anglo-Saxon Gloucester was but a temporarily occupied site until the tenth century is dubious: H. Clarke and B. Ambrosiani, *Towns in the Viking Age* (New York: St. Martin's Press, 1991), pp. 40, 42.

114. Aethelweard, *Chronicon*, s.a. 877, ed. A. Campbell (London: Thomas Nelson, 1962): "They set up their huts (? *ategiae*) in the town (*oppidum*)." The early Anglo-Saxon street pattern retained very few features of the Roman grid: Lobel and Tann, "Gloucester," p. 3; Heighway, "Saxon Gloucester," p. 362.

115. Lobel and Tann, "Gloucester," p. 3; J. Campbell, "Lost Centuries," p. 36, and Fig. 34.

116. *Cart. Sax.*, No. 574. The names of new Anglo-Saxon streets leading to the area also suggest its presence: Lobel and Tann, "Gloucester," p. 3.

117. *Cart. Sax.*, No. 1135[964]; *ASC* 940 D, 1043 D, 1048[1051] E, 1053 D, 1063 D; *Vita Aedwardi Regis*, i.3, ed. F. Barlow (Oxford: Clarendon Press, 1962). Preliminary excavations here did reveal traces of a large timber building: Heighway, "Saxon Gloucester," p. 371.

118. Heighway, "Excavations at Gloucester, Fifth Interim Report: St. Oswald's Priory 1977–78," *Antiquaries Journal* 60 (1980), 207–26, esp. 217–20. St. Oswald's early fabric incorporates Roman stonework.

119. Heighway, "Saxon Gloucester," pp. 377–79; Lobel and Tann, "Gloucester," pp. 3–4. And it was Gloucester rather than Cirencester that gave its name to the shire. The tenth-century town probably was replanned as a Mercian burgh after the Alfredian model: Heighway, "Saxon Gloucester," pp. 366–68, and below, Chap. 7.

120. B. Cunliffe, *Roman Bath*, Reports of the Research Committee of the Society of Antiquaries of London 24 (Oxford: University Press, 1969), pp. 1–3; B. C. Burnham and J. S. Wacher, *The Small Towns of Roman Britain* (Berkeley: University of California Press, 1990), p. 165.

121. Cunliffe, *Roman Bath*, pp. 3–4, 10–38, 95–131, 148–55, and Figs. 26, 31, 72; T. F. C. Blagg, "The Date of the Temple of Sulis Minerva at Bath," *Britannia* 10 (1979), 101–7; Cunliffe and P. Davenport, *The Temple of Sulis Minerva at Bath, I: The Site* (Oxford: University Press, 1985); Cunliffe, "The Excavation of the Roman Spring at Bath, 1979," *Antiquaries Journal* 60 (1980), 187–206, and, *The City of Bath* (New Haven: Yale University Press, 1987), pp. 16–43, and Fig. 24; Burnham and Wacher, *Small Towns*, pp. 168–73. The Celtic deity Sulis was apparently a healing water goddess syncretized with Minerva but is otherwise unknown: Frere, *Britannia*, p. 318; Salway, *Roman Britain*, pp. 687–88.

122. Leatherworking and ironworking, along with pottery production are attested: M. Owen, et al., "Wolcot Street, 1971," in *Excavations in Bath*, 1950–1975, ed. Cunliffe, Committee for Rescue Archaeology in Avon, Gloucestershire, and Somerset; Excavation Reports, 1 (Bath: Lonsdale Universal Printing, 1979), pp. 102–22; Esmonde Cleary, *Extra-Mural Areas*, pp. 11–12. Burnham and Wacher, *Small Towns*, pp. 174–75. Important stoneworking (Bathstone) and pewter industries were located in the environs of Bath, which also may have functioned as a market center for the many rich surrounding villas: Richmond, "Industry," p. 85; Rivet, "Social and Economic Aspects," in *Roman Villa*, pp. 210–14 and Figs. 5.6, 5.7; Cunliffe, *Roman Bath Discovered* (London: Routledge & Kegan Paul, 1971), pp. 83–89.

123. It did not encompass the main early settlement areas: Cunliffe, *Roman Bath*, pp. 166–68, and *Roman Bath Discovered*, pp. 75–78. The stone circuit added to this

rampart is believed to be late third- or early fourth-century work. Because of its primary function as a spa, Bath was not quite the usual Romano-British "small town." For a more typical case, see the discussion of Dorchester-on-Thames in the following chapter.

124. See, in general, Cunliffe, *Roman Bath Discovered*, pp. 71–75. Like other "small towns," Aquae Sulis had no regular street grid, however. J. Patrick Greene, "Bath and Other Small Western Towns," in *The 'Small Towns' of Roman Britain*, eds. W. Rodwell and T. Rowley, B.A.R. 15 (Oxford, 1975), pp. 131–38.

125. Cunliffe, *Roman Bath*, pp. 156–65, and *Roman Bath Discovered*, pp. 71–73.

126. J. Patrick Greene, et al., "Abbey Green, 1971," in *Bath Excavations*, ed. Cunliffe, pp. 72–77, and Fig. 79.

127. Greene, et al., "Citizen House (Westgate Buildings), 1970," in *Bath Excavations*, pp. 4–70, and Fig. 81. Neither Bath nor Cirencester or Gloucester has yielded any examples of the imported Mediterranean pottery that was reaching Ireland, western Britain, and the Severn c.450–650: Alcock, *History and Archaeology*, pp. 187, 201–9; S. Pearce, *The Kingdom of Dumnonia* (Padstow, Cornwall: Lodenek Press, 1978), pp. 37-39. Burnham and Wacher's portrait of continuing Romano-British town life at Bath into the late sixth century is probably a chimera: *Small Towns*, p. 176.

128. Cunliffe, *Roman Bath*, pp. 143–47, and *Roman Bath Discovered*, p. 65. A general rise in sea level appears to have been the underlying cause.

129. Ibid., p. 91; Cunliffe, "Roman Spring at Bath," 201. The process of decay had begun when commercial pottery was still in use. A more massive wall also was built around the spring reservoir in late Roman times.

130. Cunliffe and Davenport, *Temple of Sulis Minerva*, pp. 66–75, 157–60, 184–85; Cunliffe, *Roman Bath Discovered*, pp. 92–94.

131. Cunliffe, "Roman Spring at Bath," 200–201. Among these was a fifth-century enameled penannular brooch. Some of the coins and curse tablets (*defixiones*) also recently found may be late deposits.

132. Ibid., 201–2; Cunliffe, *City of Bath*, pp. 72–74.

133. *The Ruin*, ll.1–2, 9b–11a, 29b–31a, 38–41, 42a–44a, ed. R. F. Leslie, in *Three Old English Elegies*, ed. Leslie (Manchester: University Press, 1961), with historical commentary, pp. 22–28. See further, Cunliffe, "Saxon Bath," in *Anglo-Saxon Towns in Southern England*, ed. Haslam, pp. 349–50.

134. *The Ruin*, ll.25–26. No signs of widespread disease or corpses have yet been found, however. The skull in the flue (see n.125, above) is an isolated and enigmatic case.

135. Nennius, *Historia Brittonum*, lxvii, ed. J. Morris (Chichester: Phillimore, 1980). But there is no archaeological evidence that the baths had been rebuilt or managed as a "going concern," as Campbell suggests: "Lost Centuries," pp. 40–41.

136. Myres argues that the eastern section of Wansdyke just below the town was a British defensive response to the West Saxon campaign of 577: *English Settlements*, pp. 155–56, 168–69. Alcock's contention that the quasi-historical Battle of Mons Badonicus was fought on a hill overlooking Bath c.490–500 is equally speculative, though also somewhat attractive: *History and Archaeology*, pp. 70–71, 359.

137. *Cart. Sax.*, No. 43; also ibid., No. 57 (681 A.D.), for further land grants to this house. See P. Sims-Williams, "Continental Influence at Bath Monastery in the

Seventh Century," *Anglo-Saxon England* 4 (1974), pp. 1–3. The early abbesses and nuns apparently were Frankish.

138. Cunliffe, "Saxon Bath," pp. 347–49, "The Abbey and Its Precinct," in *Excavations in Bath*, pp. 88–93, and *City of Bath*, pp. 49–51; Heighway, *Gloucestershire*, pp. 101–3. During the eighth century it appears to have become an all-male establishment: *Cart. Sax.*, Nos. 327 (757 X 758 A.D.), 241 (781). See Sims-Williams, "Bath Monastery," pp. 8–9.

139. *Cart. Sax.*, Nos. 277 (796): "in the famous estate (*vicus*) called in Saxon *aet Badhum*," 510 (864): "in that famous town (*urbs*) called *calidum balneum*, i.e., *hatum badhum*." Bath also had strategic importance on the frontier between Mercia and Wessex: Cunliffe, "Saxon Bath," p. 349.

140. It was then evidently replanned with a regular street grid characteristic of the late Anglo-Saxon burgh: Ibid., pp. 350, 354–55; Cunliffe, *City of Bath*, pp. 52–63, and Fig. 44. King Edgar was consecrated "in the ancient burgh (*ealdon byrig*) of Acemannes ceastre, also called Bath (Badhan)." *ASC*, 973A.

141. Wacher, *Towns*, pp. 358–59; Webster, *The Cornovii* (London: Duckworth, 1975), pp. 24–40, and "Wroxeter (Viroconium)," in *Fortress into City*, ed. Webster, pp. 120–36 and Figs. 6.2, 6.3.

142. Ibid., pp. 136–40.

143. *RIB*, No. 288 (130 A.D.), an inscription dedicating the new forum to Hadrian. The Emperor, renowned for his civic munificence, had visited Britain and passed through this area in 122. See further, Salway, *Roman Britain*, pp. 185–86; Webster, "Viroconium," pp. 141–42.

144. Wacher, *Towns*, pp. 362–73; Richmond, "Industry," pp. 76, 84; Webster, *Cornovii*, pp. 56–73, 94–97, 102–4; D. R. Wilson, "The Plan of Viroconium Cornoviorum," *Antiquity* 58 (1984), 117–20, 224.

145. Wacher, *Towns*, pp. 360, 372. Viroconium was the western terminus of the great Watling Street route from London and also stood on the main north-south road from Chester [Deva] to Caerleon [Isca] (Map 2.2B). See further, Salway, *Roman Britain*, Map VI; Webster, *Cornovii*, pp. 50–56.

146. Wacher, *Towns*, p. 372; Salway, *Roman Britain*, p. 584; Esmonde Cleary, *Extra-Mural Areas*, pp. 159–60; cf. Webster, *Cornovii*, pp. 79–89.

147. Frere, *Britannia*, p. 249; P. Barker, "Aspects of the Topography of Wroxeter (Viroconium Cornoviorum)," in *Roman Urban Topography in Britain and the Western Empire*, eds. F. Grew and B. Hobley, C.B.A. 59 (London, 1985) pp. 109–14; B. Jones and H. Mattingly, *An Atlas of Roman Britain* (Oxford: Blackwell, 1990), p. 168.

148. Webster, *Cornovii*, pp. 47–48, 107–9; D. R. Wilson, "Plan of Viroconium," 120; Frere, "Roman Britain in 1983," *Britannia* 15 (1984), 291.

149. Wacher, *Towns*, pp. 373–74; Arnold, *Roman Britain to Saxon England*, p. 33.

150. Barker, "The Latest Occupation of the Site of the Baths Basilica at Wroxeter," in *The End of Roman Britain*, ed. P. Casey, B.A.R. 71 (Oxford, 1979), pp. 175–81, and "Topography of Wroxeter," pp. 114–17.

151. Ibid. See further, Webster, *Cornovii*, pp. 115–19; Johnson, *Later Roman Britain*, pp. 207–11; Campbell, "Lost Centuries," p. 40, and Fig. 40; Arnold, *Roman Britain to Saxon England*, pp. 41–43; M. Gelling, "The Early History of Western Mercia," in *The Origins of Anglo-Saxon Kingdoms*, ed. S. Bassett (Leicester: University Press, 1989), pp. 186–87. If such an identification is correct, we may again

be witnessing, in effect, the temporary reemergence of Romano-British and pre-Roman patterns of political authority, with sub-Roman nobles establishing power bases in certain towns as well as *oppida* and old Roman forts.

152. Frere, "End of Towns," pp. 94–95; Wacher, *Towns*, pp. 374, 420. None of the skeletons evidenced marks of violence, nor are there any other certain signs of widespread burning or destruction from the latest occupation levels. One elderly male in the bath hypocaust apparently was clutching a hoard of late Roman coins. Webster contends, however, that these remains were all from burials at a post-Roman cemetery in the old town center: *Cornovii*, pp. 120–21.

153. Barker, "Latest Occupation"; Frere, "Roman Britain in 1985," *Britannia* 17 (1986), 393. An Irish chieftain, however, was buried beside the town rampart c.460–475. His reused Roman tombstone bears an Old Irish inscription in Latin letters rather than Ogham: R. Wright and K. Jackson, "A Late Inscription from Wroxeter," *Antiquaries Journal* 48 (1968), 296–300. See further, Wacher, *Towns*, p. 374; Webster, *Cornovii*, p. 114; Gelling, "Western Mercia," p. 187.

154. (Scrobbesbyrig>Scrobbescir>Shropshire). Wacher, *Towns*, p. 374; Johnson, *Later Roman Britain*, p. 209; Biddle, "Towns," p. 110; Webster, *Cornovii*, pp. 120, 123; Gelling, "Western Mercia," p. 187. For Mercian rulers issuing charters *in civitate Scrobbensis*, see: Cart. Sax., No. 587 (901 A.D.). On the significant phenomenon of sub-Roman hill fort reuse, see Alcock, *History and Archaeology*, pp. 209–29, and "New Perspectives on Post-Roman Forts," in Alcock, *Economy, Society, and Warfare Among the Britons and Saxons* (Cardiff: University of Wales Press, 1987), pp. 154–67; Johnson, *Later Roman Britain*, pp. 202–5; Arnold, *Roman Britain to Saxon England*, pp. 73–80; I. Burrow, "Roman Material from Hillforts," in *End of Roman Britain*, ed. Casey, pp. 212–29.

155. Cherry, "Ecclesiastical Architecture," p. 178; Webster, *Cornovii*, p. 124.

156. *ASC* 641 E. For the archaeological evidence, see K. Pretty, "Defining the Magonsaete," in *Origins of Anglo-Saxon Kingdoms*, ed. Bassett, pp. 174–75.

157. *Cart. Sax.*, No. 297. See further, *ASE*, pp. 41, 44; The British root of this tribal name is related to that of Viroconium and the Wrekin, a nearby hill fort. Nennius knew Viroconium/Wroxeter as Guricon: *Historia Brittonum*, lxvi a. See Webster, *Cornovii*, p. 124; Pretty, "Magonsaete," p. 174.

158. *DB*, I, 254b. In 1086 the estate had passed to the lordship of Roger de Montgomery, earl of Shrewsbury, and was held by Rainald the sheriff, a minor pluralist in Shropshire (Ibid.).

159. J. K. St. Joseph, "Aerial Photography," pp. 22–23 and Pl. 1; M. Aston and J. Bond, *The Landscape of Towns* (London: J. M. Dent, 1976), pp. 53–54.

160. See above, Chap. 2.

For Further Reading

For additional recent studies of town sites discussed in this chapter, see I. M. Stead and V. Rigby, *Verulamium: The King Harry Lane Site* (London: British Museum Publications, 1989); M. G. Fulford, *The Silchester Amphitheatre: Excavations 1979–85*, Britannia Monographs 10 (London: Society for the Promotion of Roman Studies, 1989); Fulford, et al., "A Hoard of Late Roman Rings and Silver Coins from Silchester, Hampshire," *Britannia* 20 (1989), 219–28; R. Bradley, "Roman Salt

Production in Chichester Harbour," *Britannia* 23 (1992), 27–44; J. A. Davies and T. Gregory, "Coinage from a *Civitas*: A Survey of the Roman Coins Found in Norfolk and their Contribution to the Archaeology of the *Civitas Icenorum*," *Britannia* 22 (1991), 65–101; *The Archaeology of Cirencester and District* (Cirencester: Cirencester Excavations Committee, 1989); P. Cracknell, "A Group of Marked Brooches from Gloucester," *Britannia* 21 (1990), 197–206; Blagg, "The Temple at Bath (Aquae Sulis) in the Context of Classical Temples in the West European Provinces," *Journal of Roman Archaeology* 3 (1990), 419–30; J. N. Adams, "British Latin: The Text, Interpretation and Language of the Bath Curse Tablets," *Britannia* 23 (1992), 1–26; R. S. O. Tomlin, "The Twentieth Legion at Wroxeter and Carlisle," *Britannia* 23 (1992), 141–58; and also in general: M. Carver, *Underneath English Towns* (London: Batsford, 1987).

Chapter 4

Early Anglo-Saxon Towns: Continuity or Rebirth? (c.400–650 A.D.)

The examination of selected Romano-British towns in the previous chapter revealed a picture of gradual but steady urban decline beginning in the later fourth century A.D. Manifestations of this devolution include decreasing public and private constructions, disuse or alteration of town services, declining commerce, and marked settlement contraction. Various combined causes for this reversal also were suggested: imperial financial rapacity toward Romano-British town nobles and tightening administrative regimentation, conflicts over the western imperial succession with their repercussions on the towns of Britain, and subsequent economic disruptions. Although this decline began earlier and was more precipitous at some towns than others, it evidently affected all major types of towns in wide areas of Britain.

Town decay and the loss of urban functions, exacerbated by the withdrawal of Roman civil and military authorities, continued into the fifth century. By c.450 the Romano-British towns thus far examined can no longer be regarded as urban places, and by c.475 they were virtually abandoned. The evidence has indicated that these Romano-British towns were already in a state of advanced decay before the Anglo-Saxon invasions. Indeed, there are no signs of that widespread Anglo-Saxon sack and slaughter proclaimed by written sources such as Gildas and many modern writers. Rather, these places stood as empty shells for significant periods until some of them saw limited Anglo-Saxon occupation.

Despite the evidence for this pattern of decline and dereliction, an additional important group of Romano-British towns often have been cited as examples of significant settlement continuity.[1] It has been claimed that these towns–Canterbury, Dorchester-on-Thames, Winchester, London, and York–were never fully abandoned; rather, their first Anglo-Saxon settlement took place within the context of their sub-Roman occupation and its vestigial Roman urban elements. A number of provocative theories have been proposed to explain the mechanisms of this supposed smooth transition from late Roman to early Anglo-Saxon towns. This persistent case for continuity, however, needs reconsideration in terms of its textual foundations and more recent archaeological findings.

Durovernum Cantiacorum (Canterbury) stood at the best local crossing of the River Stour in east coastal Kent (Cantia). Before the Claudian Invasion of 43 A.D., there had been an important Belgic enclosure on this site, which had significant economic and cultural contacts with the larger Roman and Celtic worlds.[2] After a brief period of military occupation, the settlement was redeveloped gradually by the Romans as *civitas*-capital for the Cantiaci, the people of Kent (Map 2.1, and Fig. 4.1).[3] During the second century, Durovernum evidently was provided with a group of lavish public buildings, including a forum-basilica, a pair of public baths, at least one impressive temple, and a large amphitheater. Several of these structures, such as the baths and theater, received costly alterations and enlargements. Private town houses, arranged along the new regular street grid, were generally substantial winged and courtyard-type masonry homes well equipped with hypocausts, bath suites, fine mosaics, and tesselated floors. Industrial operations such as brick, tile, and pottery kilns have been found both within and just outside the town, as has evidence of metalworking and milling. Unlike other cantonal capitals, however, Durovernum has not yet yielded any evidence of second-century earthwork defenses. Rather, its massive stone walls with internal towers appear to have been a new construction of the late third or early fourth century. These roughly polygonal defenses enclosed an area of about 130 acres, making this the fourth largest *civitas*-capital of Roman Britain. Indeed, the near absence of villa estates around Durovernum suggests that local nobles preferred to maintain residences in the town and to enjoy its high levels of urban amenities.

Durovernum's prosperity on the whole seems to have continued into the first half of the fourth century. Most public buildings were well maintained, and external bastions were added to the walls.[4] Toward midcentury, however, there were increasing signs of decay. For example, the town's main bath complex went out of service c.350, and timber buildings were set up within. Along its outer walls were additional wooden structures, perhaps shops or stalls, which encroached on and nearly blocked the street. These appear to have been occupied until c.425. In this same central area, the public sewer system gradually became inoperative and periodically overflowed during this time.[5]

Private town houses excavated in Durovernum attest to a process of selective decay. Many began to fall into disrepair and were abandoned by c.375; a few remained occupied but with poor maintenance and loss of amenities into the early fifth century.[6]   Indeed, archaeological evidence suggests a collapse of civic order at this latter date. For instance, along Stour Street to the west of the amphitheater, a pit burial has been disclosed that contained the remains of a man, a woman, two children, and a dog (a family?), along with associated late Roman pottery of early fifth-century type. Such intramural burials were prohibited by Roman law.[7]   Several substantial coin and treasure hoards found inside and just beyond the walls (Fig. 4.1) also point to social disorder and disruption at this time.[8]   But perhaps the most telling signs of dereliction are the layers of dark earth found sealing the last Romano-British occupation levels on nearly all excavated sites. These soil strata, consisting of accumulated vegetative matter and decayed building debris, suggest virtual abandonment of the town c.425–430.[9]

Excavations in Canterbury over the past forty years have uncovered the remains of some three dozen Anglo-Saxon sunken-huts (*Grubenhäuser*). They are scattered throughout the intramural area but often lie in proximity to Roman buildings, such as the amphitheater and baths, and display a long settlement sequence (Fig. 4.2). The earliest huts were believed at first to date from c.400–450 based on comparisons of their associated pottery with analogous continental ware. Here, it was claimed, was firm evidence at last of town settlement continuity, an overlap between late Roman and early Anglo-Saxon occupation.[10]   The argument went on to proclaim that the occupants of these first *Grubenhäuser* were Anglo-Saxon mercenaries or federates (*foederati/laeti*) called in by late Roman authorities to protect the town, in return for land on which to settle. Later these mercenaries rose in revolt and, together with reinforcements from their continental homeland, took over control of the town. Indeed, such a process was seen as having occurred at a number of fifth-century Romano-British towns. By this transfer of authority, many late Roman towns thus became incipient capitals for emerging Anglo-Saxon kingdoms.[11]

This so-called "mercenaries theory" is rather attractive at first sight and does provide a tidy explanation for the origins of Anglo-Saxon towns and kingdoms. It also appears to accord broadly with the written evidence. Gildas, for example, speaks of the "proud tyrant" ruling in eastern Britain who invited Anglo-Saxon mercenaries, only to see them send for more of their brethren, demand greater payments, and revolt against him.[12]   Bede gives a similar but somewhat more detailed account of these events. In 449, he relates, a band of Anglian mercenaries led by Hengest and Horsa was invited into Kent under treaty arrangements by the sub-Roman ruler Vortigern. These mercenaries and their reinforcements were given grants of land and regular pay, but they became greedy, joined the Pictish enemy, and rebelled.[13] Nennius says that Vortigern at first welcomed Hengest and Horsa's exiled war band, gave them the island of Thanet, and agreed to furnish food and clothing in return for their military service. Hengest then tricked Vortigern into allowing reinforcements. Among these newcomers was Hengest's beautiful daughter, Rowena, with whom Vortigern fell in love at a drunken banquet; the bride-price was the region of Kent, where more of Hengest's people settled.[14] After a series of battles, subterfuges, and negotiations, Vortigern ceded additional districts to Hengest.[15] English tradition recorded in the *Anglo-Saxon Chronicle* relates that Vortigern invited Hengest and Horsa's war band to fight the Picts and gave them unspecified land in the southeast. Hengest summoned reinforcements and fought several battles in Kent against Vortigern, including one at Crayford (457), after which the Britons are said to have abandoned Kent and fled to London in great fear (Map 3.1).[16] All of these accounts, although they do refer to events in Kent, have nothing to say specifically about the fate of any individual town. Rather, they draw highly generalized, folkloric pictures ranging from prolonged negotiations and intermittent warfare to sudden immigration and conquest.

Before returning to the recent archaeological evidence, let us consider other material often cited as proof of settlement continuity at Durovernum/Canterbury. It is true that there were a number of early Anglo-Saxon settlements and cemeteries around the former Roman town, some of which clearly date to the fifth century.[17] But attempts to establish more precise chronologies for them based on stylistic analyses of the associated pottery and urns have been less than successful.[18] Similarly, some early Anglo-Saxon graves near the town have yielded metalwork items such as buckles and brooches that initially were identified as the accoutrement of Germanic mercenaries.[19] More recent study has demonstrated, however, that such artifacts are neither necessarily Germanic nor military and are difficult to date.[20] Moreover, even if these items did firmly attest to the presence of mercenaries, they do not prove that these men were actively defending the walls of the late Roman town if no other evidence of their intramural presence has been found.

Additional arguments for settlement continuity at this town have been based on linguistic and other evidence. For example, it was noted that the Anglo-Saxon name for Canterbury, *Cantwaraburh*, "fortified place of the Kentish people," preserved rather well the Romano-British cantonal name (Cantia), just as did many Frankish towns in Gaul where evidence of settlement continuity is apparently quite strong.[21] Most towns in England retained only garbled forms of their Roman town names compounded with various suffixes, especially *ceaster*. It also has been supposed that the *burh* element shows that the town remained a defended Romano-British enclosure, a place of temporary refuge (*Fluchtsburg*; Old English *heaf-odstede*).[22] The problem with these arguments is that the place-name under consideration was recorded considerably later, in the ninth century.[23] Others have pointed to possible administrative continuity. For example, the Kentish district or lathe called *Burhwalalaeth* ("lathe of the *burh* dwellers") is assumed to be equivalent to the old urban *territorium* of late Roman Durovernum.[24] Again, however, the sources for this terminology do not predate the eighth century.[25] Topographical arguments that have been made for settlement continuity are also weak. Thus, the fact that Canterbury's thirteenth-century walls are on the same lines as the old Roman circuits is a rather specious case for continuous town occupation.[26] Indeed, the medieval town's street plan bears little resemblance to the Roman intramural grid.[27] Other arguments for town settlement continuity point to the high degree of Romanization in Kent, the frequent survival of Romano-British place names, and the late occupation of nearby Saxon Shore forts such as Richborough and Reculver (Map 2.1), which were linked via Watling Street to Durovernum.[28] Such views are for the most part speculative and inferential in regard to the specific fate of this town.

Recent study of the intramural archaeological evidence has considerably strengthened the case for settlement discontinuity at Canterbury. First, nearly all of the Anglo-Saxon sunken huts were found to have cut into layers of thick, dark earth overlying ruined Roman structures or in open spaces between them. This ubiquitous soil layer has been shown convincingly to be natural accumulations from abandoned conditions, not the product of deliberate cultivation.[29] This black earth also built up around the *Gruben-häuser*, and this stratification, along with a careful reexamination of the associated pottery, has enabled a more precise sequence of Anglo-Saxon settlement in Canterbury to be established. Results now indicate that the earliest intramural sunken-huts were built c.450–475 with a subsequent assemblage c.475–550. These two groups comprise eleven of thirty eight huts discovered; the remaining twenty seven belong to the period c.550–700.[30] When the latest Roman occupation is compared with the first Anglo-Saxon settlement on specific sites, one finds everywhere a period of abandonment—a gap ranging from 25 years on some sites to 150 years on others.[31] Although two decades might be considered a rather short span, it is still a significant gap. Moreover, there are no archaeological indications that the last Romano-British occupants of the town had any direct contact with Anglo-Saxons and vice versa. If there had been settlement overlap presumably there would be material evidence of reciprocal cultural influences.[32] Finally, no military items such as might be attributed to mercenaries have been found in the town. None of the late Roman public and private buildings appear to have been burned or sacked; rather, they evidently deteriorated slowly, were abandoned, and covered by the dark earth. Much of the western quadrant of the town became flooded by the Stour, which made a new path through the walls.[33]

The archaeological evidence thus indicates that Durovernum was a virtually abandoned, derelict site when intramural Anglo-Saxon settlement began about 450 A.D. or slightly later. Indeed, on the basis of excavations, Anglo-Saxon Canterbury in its first century (c.450–550) remained quite thinly populated. Of course, the old Roman walls might have made the settlement a defensible enclosure with thus at least one central place function. Yet most excavated *Grubenhäuser* evidently belong to the period c.550–700. This apparent intensification of settlement within Canterbury indeed coincides with the emergence of a unified Anglo-Saxon kingdom of Kent, a "Golden Age" of Kentish prosperity, and the arrival in Kent of the first Christian mission to the English led by St. Augustine of Canterbury.

Written sources suggest, for example, that sixth-century Canterbury was already a place of some political importance. Bede observes that at the time of Augustine's arrival in Kent (597), Canterbury was regarded the "chief seat" (*metropolis*) and "royal capital" (*regia civitas*) of the Kentish king Aethelberht I (c.560–618).[34] He tells us in addition that Aethelberht at that time was not only king of Kent but also exercised an overlordship (*imperium*) over all English provinces south of the Humber.[35] The *Anglo-Saxon Chronicle* later calls this type of king *Bretwalda* ("ruler of Britain" or "wide ruler.")[36] The position probably was won by force of arms and significantly encompassed both Germanic and Roman traditions of rulership.[37] Now there were very practical considerations why early medieval Christian missions normally sought out kings and their courts. First, kings could provide effective protection and a legal place for the Church in a tribal society, to which it was alien.[38] Once a king was converted, his people likely would follow from a combination of reasons: compulsion, the prospect of royal favor, and the traditional Germanic belief that the king was the leading spokesman or representative of the tribal deity.[39] The conversion of a *Bretwalda* such as Aethelberht no doubt offered still wider prospects. It was thus no coincidence that the Roman mission to the English arrived in Kent and was established at Aethelberht's capital, Canterbury, despite the fact that Pope Gregory the Great apparently would have preferred the former Roman provincial capital, London.[40]

The processes involved in the formation of the Anglo-Saxon kingdom of Kent are themselves shrouded in obscurity. Our written sources for this formative period c.450–550 are not very illuminating. As noted, Gildas speaks in broad and polemical terms of an Anglo-Saxon settlement under treaty arrangements in eastern Britain, the revolt of these mercenaries, and their subsequent rampages. Bede generally follows Gildas's outline but supplies the names of Hengest, Horsa, and Vortigern, as well as some ethnographic and genealogical information, all derived presumably from

Kentish oral tradition. Nennius also seems to preserve a core group of early Kentish traditions, which he much embellishes and slants for his British (Welsh) audience. And the list of early battles recorded in the *Anglo-Saxon Chronicle* as having been led by Hengest against Britons in Kent represents at best only vague and garbled memories of actual combats incorporated in ninth-century West Saxon dynastic tradition.[41]

The archaeological record of Anglo-Saxon Kent, its place names, and later traditions indicate that the kingdom likely arose from an amalgamation of at least two originally distinct smaller realms. In the initial decades up to c.500 A.D., Anglo-Saxon settlers, including principally Jutes from Jutland, progressively established a realm that was focused in eastern Kent and directed by warrior kings such as Hengest and his descendants. Jutish-style brooches and pottery found in fifth-century Kentish graves suggest that ties with the homeland were regularly maintained during this invasion period.[42] After c.500, however, there appears to have been a significant influx of Frankish warrior-aristocrats into eastern Kent. This Frankish elite most likely married into the established Jutish royal line in Kent and ushered in a notable period of Kentish prosperity.[43] The great wealth of sixth-century Kentish rulers, as attested by their rich grave-goods (fine glass and bronzeware, gemstone jewelry), was founded on a cross-Channel trade with their Frankish homeland. Indeed, it is likely that by controlling access and distribution of these high-status items, Kentish kings also were able to increase their authority in an age when gift giving created and secured ties of dependence.[44] The Frankish connection of sixth-century Kentish kings involved not only the exchange of prestige goods but also Frankish princesses. For example, Aethelberht before his accession is known to have married Bertha, the daughter of the Merovingian king Charibert. His own father (Irminric), as listed in the Kentish royal genealogy, bears a Frankish name.[45]

The archaeology of eastern Kent with its heavy Frankish cultural overlay is quite different from that of the western region. That the territory west of the River Medway had once been a separate realm is suggested by early Kentish district names and the creation of its own bishopric at Rochester (604).[46] Moreover, in the seventh century we find western Kent with its own subkings, who were usually junior members and subordinate to the main Kentish dynastic line.[47] Exactly when the two areas had been united is unknown, but it may have taken a ruler of Aethelberht's stature and power to accomplish the task.

Sixth- and seventh-century Kentish kings are known to have had a series of royal estates (*villae regales*), which appear to have been centers of administrative districts (lathes). Kings and their households periodically made the rounds of such royal vills, consuming the estate's produce along with the food renders or "farm" (*feorm*) collected there from the district, and attending to matters of local administration and justice.[48] In eastern Kent, there were two early royal estates: at Eastry near Sandwich on the coast, and at Sturry some three miles east of Canterbury along the Stour.[49] There are various indications that another early Kentish royal vill may have been located within Canterbury itself. We have Bede's reference to Canterbury as Aethelberht's chief seat on Augustine's arrival. Bertha's extramural church or chapel could indicate a royal residence within the town. Also, Aethelberht clearly held intramural properties, some of which he bestowed to Augustine's party as residences.[50] So far, no conclusive archaeological evidence of an early Kentish royal hall has been found within Canterbury. A case has been made, however, that one stood within the shell of the old Roman amphitheater whose massive stone walls remained essentially intact until the early twelfth century and must have been the dominant topographical feature of the early Anglo-Saxon site. The new pattern of intramural streets in this southeast sector that emerged with the Anglo-Saxon resettlement converged precisely on the amphitheater (Fig. 4.2).[51] Also, the concentration of *Grubenhäuser* behind the amphitheater may have had some service connection with suggested royal activity there.[52] Such a royal presence in pre-Christian Canterbury would afford a parallel to the tribal capitals (*Volksburgen*) with royal residences of early Merovingian kings that were often established within former Roman towns.[53] The sum of evidence therefore indicates that Anglo-Saxon reoccupation of this former Roman walled town occurred after a period of abandonment and within the contexts of first perhaps royal and then ecclesiastical activity.

Some further remarks are in order concerning the role of the Church in this rebirth. One of the tenets of the continuity theory has been the purported survival of Christianity in the towns of fifth-century Britain. The fact that so many early Anglo-Saxon bishops' sees were set up in former Roman towns, for example, has been seen as evidence of surviving urban religious communities and practices.[54] Yet the choice of such a site may have involved other factors, including politics, geography, or even the ready availability of building material. Although the late Roman episcopate in Britain, as elsewhere in the Empire, was urban based, all indications are that this episcopal superstructure ceased functioning prior to the mid-fifth century in most of Britain as towns gradually declined.[55]

Since Kent was arguably the most heavily Romanized area of Britain, one might expect to find evidence of a strong Christian presence in this canton and at its capital. It would also be reasonable to assume some significant survivals of Christianity, unless we adhere to the unlikely view that the Anglo-Saxon newcomers totally annihilated existing Romano-British populations. Several of Durovernum's extramural cemeteries continued in use into the early fifth century, and at least one contained Anglo-Saxon burials beginning in the late fifth century.[56] Bede tells us that after

Augustine's arrival in Canterbury, King Aethelberht gave him permission to "build and restore churches everywhere."[57] Three specific examples are mentioned that merit attention (Fig. 4.2).

The first case was an intramural church that Augustine was told had been built long ago by Roman Christians. The king apparently granted this to the missionaries as a more fitting residence and helped them repair the structure, which was dedicated as Christ's Church, site of the later Anglo-Saxon and Norman cathedral.[58] There is no suggestion in this instance of continuity of worship from Roman times, nor did the new structure follow the old Roman street alignment.[59] The second of Augustine's ecclesiastical building projects at Canterbury was a new structure outside the east gate, a monastery dedicated to St. Peter and St. Paul—the later St. Augustine's Abbey. Aethelberht proposed the site and endowed it richly.[60] It has been suggested but not proved that the late Roman cemetery here was in use long enough to facilitate this site's becoming the main royal and episcopal burial ground of Kent. Several other Canterbury extramural parish churches overlie Roman burials, but religious continuities there are also unconfirmed.[61]

The third example is St. Martin's Church, which Bede says was built during the Roman occupation and where Aethelberht's Christian queen and her Frankish entourage used to pray. It was apparently in no great need of repair; indeed, Augustine's party at first used it as a place of assembly and worship.[62] It generally has been assumed that this church or royal chapel that Bede described is the predecessor of the current St. Martin's, one-half mile beyond the east gate, and that it was a place of continuous Christian worship since Roman times.[63] Excavations at the present church did in fact disclose the remains of a small, rectangular stone building with reused Roman materials incorporated into the chancel. This original structure has usually been identified as a late fourth- or early fifth-century cemetery church or mausoleum, similar to the one at Stone-by-Faversham, also in eastern Kent.[64] Unfortunately for this argument, there are no late Roman cemeteries in the area of St. Martin's. The late Roman core structure is now better regarded from latest excavations as a domestic suburban building that was fashioned into a church by the addition of a small nave, perhaps during Aethelberht's reign.[65] Assuming that the current St. Martin's was the site to which Bede was referring (and this has legitimately been challenged),[66] there is no archaeological confirmation that the original structure here was necessarily a Christian place of worship in late Roman times or a church in continuous use until the sixth century.

Additional purported evidence of religious continuity at Canterbury is a passage in one of Pope Gregory's correspondences with Augustine. Gregory refers to the shrine and cult of a Romano-British martyr, Sixtus, still maintained in the area of Augustine's authority, and to the elders (*antiquores*) who were asked about their saint's life.[67] These remarks do indicate the existence of a surviving late Roman Christian community in sixth-century Kent, but no more specific location is provided. Since Augustine initially had a wide jurisdiction, the community could have been nearly anywhere in southern England, although the possibility of its presence in or near Augustine's see at Canterbury still cannot be totally excluded.

If there is only slim and questionable evidence of continuous Christian practices at Canterbury from Roman times, there can be no doubt that the reestablishment of Christianity and the foundation of its primary see stimulated the town's growth in the seventh century. As noted, the archaeological evidence indicates intensifying intramural settlement. Bede attests to this increasing density when he describes the great fire, which spread rapidly and threatened to destroy the entire town (619).[68] Also, the likely royal presence in Canterbury would have provided another significant stimulus to growth. Indeed, articles of trade and manufacture are more common on seventh-century sites excavated within Canterbury.[69] The arrival of Archbishop Theodore of Tarsus in 669, followed by the establishment of his famous school here, must also have resulted in a variety of beneficial consequences.[70]

It was during this time that the first Anglo-Saxon coins in England, the gold *thrymsas*, made their appearance from a mint in Canterbury. The history of this early coinage is obscure, but it seems to have been issued by royal as well as ecclesiastical authority to meet the growing requirements of both for specie.[71] Canterbury also appears to have been the principal mint for the Anglo-Saxon silver *sceattas* or proto-pennies (which replaced the *thrymsa* c.675), as well as for the subsequent large silver pennies of King Offa of Mercia and the Wessex kings who controlled the town during the eighth and ninth centuries. It is likely that both the silver *sceattas* and pennies were struck to accommodate increasing cross-Channel commerce and the burgeoning specie demands brought about by royal and ecclesiastical centralization.[72] In terms of our initial definition of urban status, late seventh-century Canterbury was thus a town, with its dual royal and ecclesiastical administrative functions, defenses, commercial and craft activities, mint, and increasingly dense occupation.

During the eighth century, the town's predominant sunken huts were succeeded by more substantial timber structures, often quite tightly packed, and new intramural churches were erected (Fig. 4.2). Charter evidence also shows the presence of an intramural market and a royal reeve.[73] Still, eight-century Canterbury seems to have remained in essence a high-status administrative center rather than primarily a place of long-distance trade or specialized craft production. As we shall see, these economic functions evidently were performed at the time by several associated nearby emporia or *wics*. In the ninth century, however, Canterbury boasted such added urban features as refurbished fortifications, an expanded market for international trade, brisk intramural tenement transactions, a major mint, very dense settlement, and even a guild.[74] Discussion of these eighth and ninth-century transformations, however, intrudes on the period of burghal development. It may merely be noted here that the same royal and ecclesiastical stimuli that gave birth to urban life in early Anglo-Saxon Canterbury continued to promote the town's growth in the following two centuries.

Dorchester-on-Thames is another site where settlement continuity has been claimed. In the late Roman period, Dorchester was not a *civitas*-capital but rather a "small town" or *vicus* (c.14 acres) which likely had grown from minor civilian settlements (*canabae*) attached to an earlier legionary fortress (Map 3.1, and Fig. 4.3). Nonetheless, it was strategically important enough to receive stonework defenses during the third century, and it seems to have had some local administrative and commercial prominence as well.[75] Excavations have shown that town life continued in Dorchester into the early fifth century. Evidence of this sub-Roman occupation includes two-story timber buildings on stone foundations and quantities of Theodosian-period coinage.[76] One of the town's late Roman cemeteries to the north also was found to have been in use in the early fifth century but not beyond.[77]

As at Canterbury and other towns, however, there is evidence of declining standards, structural decay, and settlement contraction at Dorchester after c.400 A.D. Indeed, recent research suggests that the Romano-British town was virtually deserted by c.450.[78] Yet Dorchester often has been cited as one of the towns in which Anglo-Saxon settlement began before Roman occupation ceased.[79] The evidence for this assertion, again, is not conclusive. For example, it is true that *Grubenhäuser* have been found within the town along with early Anglo-Saxon pottery.[80] But neither these structures nor the associated ceramic can be dated more precisely to the early fifth century. A case for settlement continuity here also has been made on the basis of cemetery evidence. In 1874, several important burials were uncovered at Dyke Hills beyond the southwest wall. One was that of a male interred with a continental Germanic spear and an "official" late Roman belt set of early fifth-century type. Nearby was the burial of a female with late Roman buckle and two Germanic brooches. These graves generally have been regarded as those of an Anglo-Saxon mercenary in service to protect the town and his Germanic wife.[81] In reality, however, they need not have been a pair at all, and the male could just as well have been a late Roman officer. Moreover, they obviously cannot prove any settlement overlap in Dorchester itself.[82]

The Dorchester area appears to have been settled by Saxons advancing westward along the Thames and also perhaps overland from the Wash in the mid-fifth century. Concentrated settlement in and around Dorchester did not commence, until the late sixth century.[83] The context for this intensification seems to have been the campaigns of the West Saxon

Bretwalda Ceawlin (560–593) against sub-Roman enclaves in the Chiltern and Severn valleys and also against the kingdom of Kent to the east.[84] Indeed, there are strong indications that Dorchester had become the headquarters of some prominent Anglo-Saxon ruler or leading family at this time. Excavations within the town disclosed Byzantine and early Anglo-Saxon gold coinage, along with gold ornaments and personal jewelry dated c.600–625.[85] Another "princely" or royal site of the early Thames Valley Saxons has been identified at Cuddesdon, some six miles north of Dorchester. The unusually rich finds there were contemporary with those within Dorchester and probably represent a rural *villa regalis* of the same family.[86] It has also been observed correctly that some place in this region, probably Dorchester, was serving as a central, perhaps royally controlled redistribution or production center for early Anglo-Saxon prestige items and raw materials.[87] The sum of the archaeological evidence thus strongly points to Dorchester as an important multifunctional central place of the Thames Valley Saxons and a likely headquarters of their kings by the opening of the seventh century.

Its royal associations apparently lay behind the choice of Dorchester as the first bishop's see of Wessex, just as they had in the case of Canterbury. Bede described, through his Winchester and Canterbury informants,[88] the establishment of this early episcopal seat at Dorchester. It seems that a certain Bishop Birinus had been sent by Pope Honorius I to preach in the more remote inland regions of England, c.633. Arriving first among the West Saxons, and finding them intensely devoted to their native Germanic religion, he decided to begin his missionary work there. Birinus apparently concentrated his attention on the reigning king, Cynegils (611–643), who eventually received baptism (635). Standing as godfather at the ceremony was none other than King Oswald of Northumbria, *Bretwalda* since 633, who thereupon made an alliance with Cynegils and took the West Saxon ruler's daughter as his wife. The two kings then are said to have given the town (*civitas*) of Dorchester (*Dorcic*) to Birinus as his episcopal see.[89]

This important passage raises certain difficulties, however. First, Bede states explicitly that the grant of Dorchester to Birinus was made jointly by Oswald and Cynegils. But since Dorchester was then clearly in West Saxon hands and most likely had been a central place of royal activity for some time, its bestowal must have been primarily the work of Cynegils. Following Stenton's suggestions, Oswald may have confirmed the grant as overlord, being present to arrange his marital alliance.[90] It is also rather hard to imagine that Cynegils gave over the entire town to Birinus. Perhaps certain of the king's town properties were bestowed for the building of suitable churches, which we are told were erected.[91] In any event, the act demonstrates that Dorchester was wholly or partly under royal authority prior to its emergence as an episcopal center.

The question also arises as to why Dorchester was chosen as the first West Saxon episcopal see rather than one of the more southern sites in Hampshire. One explanation is that in the early seventh century there was as yet no unified kingdom of Wessex. Though an occasional ruler, like Ceawlin or Cynegils, might unite the various West Saxon peoples in a temporary confederation, there were apparently real differences and conflicts between the Saxons of the Upper Thames and those of Hampshire. Indeed, there is considerable evidence not only of various independent West Saxon kingdoms but also of multiple rulership or district kingship within each realm at this time.[92] Birinus preached to Cynegils's people, and it may well be that this king had no lasting authority in the southerly regions of the West Saxons. Dorchester likely would have been Cynegils's prime candidate for the siting of an episcopal see by virtue of its probable preexisting function as a royal center. According to our urban definition, by the early seventh century Dorchester, like Canterbury, with its ecclesiastical and royal foci, as well as likely associated craft and commercial activity, had also been reborn as an Anglo-Saxon town.

The case of Winchester may now be considered. Through the diligent archaeological work of Martin Biddle and his colleagues over the past thirty years, the early history of this important Anglo-Saxon town has been brought dramatically to life. In Roman times, Winchester was Venta Belgarum, the administrative, commercial, and cultural center established for the prominent Belgic tribe of southern Britain. The Romano-British *civitas Belgarum* with its capital at Venta, had apparently been formed by the Romans from an amalgamation of neighboring peoples in the late first century A.D. around the nucleus of a small Roman fort just east of a recently abandoned Iron age *oppidum* (Map 2.1 and Fig. 4.4). Excavations have revealed that during the first three centuries of Roman Britain, Venta acquired the range of urban features characteristic of leading *civitas*-capitals: forum-basilica-temple, regular street grid, masonry defensive walls (enclosing c.140 acres), well-built and decorated private homes, and shops for various trades and industries.[93]

During the mid-fourth century, however, a variety of significant change appears to have taken place in the town. First, nearly all existing private houses known from excavations were torn down and replaced, in some cases, by small fenced structures devoted most likely to industrial uses, such as ironworking. But at the same time, distribution-finds of pottery and coinage indicate that occupation was expanding over the entire intramural area. Moreover, urban defenses were strengthened by the addition of bastions and towers to the existing circuit. There also seems to have been increased development of the surrounding urban *territorium*, with richly furnished private homes constructed on all sides of the town.[94] These fourth-century changes on the whole could mark a shift in Winchester's essential functions.

From a primarily administrative and commercial center, the town now seems to have assumed a more defensive and industrial character. In addition to the material remains of metalworking, there is textual evidence that may attest to an important state-run textile factory (*gynaeceum*) in the late Roman town. Winchester's defensive circuit might have been strengthened during this period for the safety of this particular operation or for the protection of the town itself either as a local safehaven or as a collection base for the *annona militaris*—a major late Roman provincial tax in kind (corn) levied to feed the army.[95]

Late Roman Winchester's well-being did not long endure, however. By the close of the fourth century, new public and private construction had virtually ceased, and some streets and town services were no longer well maintained. Two of the latest Roman suburban cemeteries went out of use c.400–420; all organized burial then appears to have been abandoned. By 450 at the latest, Venta's sub-Roman town life evidently had ended.[96] Yet according to some researchers, this town is a prime example of settlement continuity that would have Anglo-Saxon mercenaries arriving in the town from at least the early fifth century, taking control peaceably from sub-Roman authorities before the mid-fifth century, and being buried in extramural cemeteries along with late Roman interments.[97] It is true that there are intrusive burials in several of Venta's late Roman cemeteries, especially Lankhills just beyond the north gate. But studies have shown that only one of these graves is likely to be that of a German buried before 410. At the large pagan cemetery of King's Worthy some two miles north, Anglo-Saxon burials do not begin until the late fifth century. Inside the town, the earliest actual evidence of Anglo-Saxon settlement are some pottery sherds, now regarded as no earlier than c.480, and a late seventh-century burial at Lower Brook Street (Fig. 4.5.A). This means that we are confronted with a likely settlement gap of perhaps fifty years at Winchester.[98]

The first references to Winchester in Anglo-Saxon documents occur in connection with the foundation of its episcopal see toward the middle of the seventh century. Bede notes that the West Saxon king Cenwalh (643-672), second son of the previously mentioned Cynegils, upon returning from a three-year exile in East Anglia (645-648), accepted a certain Agilbert from Francia as his chief bishop and presumably established his see at Winchester. The *Anglo-Saxon Chronicle* confirms this when it records that in 648 Cenwalh ordered the church at Winchester to be built and identifies it as St. Peter's, evidently the Old Minster. Later, Bede says, Cenwalh formally divided his kingdom into two sees (Winchester and no doubt Dorchester), giving the city (*civitas*) of Venta or Wintancaestir to a native Saxon bishop Wini because the king could no longer stand to hear Agilbert's foreign speech.[99] In the early to mid-seventh century, therefore, the site of Winchester, or at least part of it, was under royal West Saxon control and termed a *ceaster (castrum)* "fortified place." Archaeological evidence does indicate limited concentrations of seventh-century intramural occupation in the central and northeast town quadrants (Fig. 4.5.A).[100] Indeed, the presence of an early Anglo-Saxon royal residence adjacent to or within the old Roman forum-basilica complex is considered very likely. It has been plausibly contended that this site, presumably coterminous with Winchester's tenth-century royal palace, was chosen for a royal hall by early West Saxon kings both to utilize existing materials and perhaps to associate their rule with former Roman authority.[101] Moreover, the position of the Old Minster, between the Roman forum and the proposed palace site, suggests its function as a Frankish-style court chapel (*Hofkapelle*) for the early West Saxon dynasty.[102] Cenwalh is also said to have granted to the Old Minster at its foundation the lands surrounding all sides of the town. These could well correspond to the old suburban *territorium* of late Roman Winchester, which had come into royal hands with the town itself perhaps in the previous century.[103] In addition, excavations have shown that late Roman Winchester's main south gate was blocked during the late fifth and sixth centuries, first by a ditch and then by a mortared wall. Traffic from the south thereafter had to enter the town via a more easterly gate (known significantly enough as Kingsgate) leading precisely to the forum and proposed early Anglo-Saxon palace site. These defensive alterations are indeed suggestive of centrally directed, probably royal, supervision.[104]

The Lower Brook Street excavations of 1971, referred to above, disclosed an early Anglo-Saxon residential complex with a seventh-century burial that included an elaborate necklace of gold and garnet pendants and a collar of silver rings. Somewhat later, timber and stone structures were erected on the site and there are indications of gold and boneworking industries.[105] Finds of imported early glassware discovered here and elsewhere within the town may also identify a group of early Anglo-Saxon royal or aristocratic compounds established between the sixth and eighth centuries.[106] The principal excavator has described these sites as "residential enclosures of thegn-status," comparable to the proposed royal hall and, like it, probably occupied intermittently when the king was in town residence.[107]

By the mid-seventh century, therefore, Anglo-Saxon Winchester appears to have become, albeit on a smaller scale, what it was long to remain: the royal and ecclesiastical center or capital of Wessex, housing primarily people of high social rank. Although its population was evidently still sparse and there were large areas of intramural cultivation,[108] Winchester had achieved urban status with its likely royal and ecclesiastical activity as well as incipient industry and trade. Its relationship to the nearby coastal emporium at Hamwic, and its transformations in the Viking age, will be examined in due course.

Roman London (Londinium) appears to have arisen from a Claudian military fort with attached civilian settlement lying at a strategic ford of the middle Thames (Fig. 4.6). It grew quickly and was described as a famous port and trading center teeming with merchants even before the disruptive Boudiccan Revolt (60 A.D.).[109] In addition to its geographical advantages, perhaps the determining feature in London's rapid rise to prominence was the fact that from the outset it was the center of Roman financial administration in Britain, a department that could well have stimulated and directed early commercial development.[110] Amid the more settled times of the late first century, London became the permanent seat of the Roman governor and his civil administration. Both the great governor's palace (*praetorium*) and the impressive forum-basilica complex erected at this time likely attest to the town's rise in official urban status.[111] Thereafter, the administrative presence of Rome continued to ensure London's preeminent rank and its commercial and industrial prosperity.[112] Thus a Roman town with rather humble beginnings developed within a century into a large provincial capital with an international character under the aegis of Roman imperial authority.

Historians and archaeologists have recognized for some time that London evidently underwent a significant transformation in the late second century. Excavations on a variety of sites within the Roman town and its main suburb (Southwark) during the post World War II decades disclosed evidence of what appeared to be sharp urban decline c.175, with many domestic and industrial buildings dismantled, their sites abandoned and then covered by a thick layer of dark earth, which often remained untouched until the ninth century.[113] More recent excavations have provided further refinements of this impression. In general, it now appears that London was experiencing a temporary settlement contraction c.150–225/250, accompanied by a slackening of internal commercial and artisanal activities and a shift toward predominantly defensive and administrative functions. The western zone of the city (west of Walbrook) seems to have been especially affected by these changes. The sequence of coin-finds from this area, for example, breaks abruptly after the mid-second century, and stratigraphic evidence suggests that the northern Walbrook sector was flooded and not reclaimed until c.250. The public baths at Huggin Hill and Cheapside also were intentionally demolished c.200. A significant overall population decline in late second to mid-third-century London is therefore strongly suspected.[114] Indeed, a recent demographic study of Roman London concludes that there had been very substantial losses, perhaps up to two-thirds, in the century c.150–250. This notable decline was followed, however, by slow but steadily increasing urban numbers c.275–375.[115]

What is especially curious is that although London's population evidently was contracting during the late second to mid-third century, significant new public and private construction was underway. London was enclosed for the first time by a great stone wall built around the three landward-facing sides of the town (c.200). Constructed of large ragstones, flints, and mortar, with interval towers and gate houses, it stood twenty-one feet high and eight feet thick, enclosing an area of about 330 acres.[116] In addition, and perhaps somewhat earlier, an impressive new waterfront was provided for Roman London. This project involved the construction of a lengthy timber quay, with wharves and docking facilities, reaching out into the Thames, apparently all along the riverfront. At first sight, this work might suggest that London's port and its merchants were thriving. But excavations have shown that once the quay complex was built, it was never heavily used.[117] Besides these two major public projects, new construction at London also included monumental arches, relief friezes, figured sculpture, and the reconstruction of temple districts, including an imposing Mithraeum. It has been plausibly suggested that these public works and embellishments were initiated by imperial authority as attempts to maintain the strategic importance and appropriate grandeur of London despite its internal decline.[118] Toward the middle of the third century, new, sometimes lavish private homes were built in all town sectors, including Southwark. These large stone residences, strikingly different from their timber-and-wattle predecessors, were likely the homes of wealthy bureaucrats, who then appear to have become the predominant high-status group in London.[119]

Fourth-century London, though evidently not as vibrant a place as it had been in Flavian, Antonine, and Severan times, was still a very important urban center. Under Diocletian's administrative innovations, London apparently became the seat of the *vicarius Britanniarum*, the imperial official charged with supervising and coordinating the governance of all British provinces. London also remained the center of imperial financial administration, it housed the main mint, and it was the seat of an established Christian episcopate.[120] Moreover, it is clear that fourth-century London was regarded by Rome as the strategic base for control and defense of the entire island. When Constantius Chlorus (Constantine the Great's father) was sent to restore imperial authority in Britain after the usurpations there of Carausius and Allectus, command of London had been his first objective (297). Similarly, the general Lupicinus took London as his base on his expedition from the Continent to repulse Pict and Saxon raids (360). And Count Theodosius's renowned campaign that restored the towns and forts of Britain (368–369) operated from London.[121] Indeed, in the fourth century London received the official name *Augusta*, probably as a mark of imperial esteem for its role in the restoration of law and order in the diocese.[122] London's riverside wall, now thought to have been begun in the late third century, was strengthened in the late fourth by the addition of large and costly projecting towers or bastions for the new artillery warfare of that age.[123]　Late fourth-century London also evidently became the command center for the system of forts and fortresses known as the Saxon Shore defenses.[124]

Yet in the course of the fourth century, London appears to have progressively lost the full range and intensity of urban functions it had once enjoyed. Commerce, industry, and local munificence all evidently diminished, as activities related to defense and administration once again increasingly came to the fore. For example, London's basilica and part of the forum were dismantled and not rebuilt c.300, coin production at the London mint halted c.324 and ceased permanently c.388, the great Mithraeum was ruinous by c.350, and there is no firm evidence of an active British episcopate at London after 359.[125]　By the end of the fourth century, moreover, portions of the large riverside quay were rotted, disused, and silted over.[126]　Indeed, coin and ceramic finds suggest that London's population had become concentrated in the eastern sector, especially at the waterfront, while much of the town area west of Walbrook was slowly abandoned during the century.[127]　Along the Thames from Old London Bridge east to the Tower, excavations have disclosed a small number of substantial late Roman residences which continued to be well maintained and occasionally enlarged until the close of the fourth century. Several hoards of late Roman silver ingots, such as were used as donatives to militias, have been found with coins in the vicinity of the Tower and may well indicate a late or even sub-Roman official and/or military presence in this area. The late fourth-century construction of a second, inner river wall here also suggests that the Tower precinct had been made into a defended enclosure perhaps in use into the early fifth century.[128]

For some time it was assumed that London had survived as a Romano-British enclave in the early Anglo-Saxon period, sheltering its inhabitants behind its walls, controlling a wide band of its old urban *territorium*, and stoutly maintaining itself as a political and military force during the fifth and sixth centuries. London thus would represent a prime example of uninterrupted urban settlement continuity, with its sub-Roman authorities carrying on for centuries until presumably melding smoothly into the new Anglo-Saxon political landscape of the late sixth and seventh centuries.[129] The available evidence, however, does not support this view. In regard to the historical or written record, there is only one reference to fifth-century London: the already cited entry of the *Anglo-Saxon Chronicle*, which relates that after a British force was soundly defeated at Crayford (Kent) by the West Saxons, the Britons abandoned Kent and fled to London in panic (457).[130]　All this annal actually tells us is that London was not yet in Anglo-Saxon hands at the time and that it was used on at least one memorable occasion as a defensive retreat by a perhaps considerable number of refugees. The site could just as well have been an empty shell as a still-thriving Romano-British enclave. If London Bridge was still serviceable in the mid-fifth century, as this annal may imply, it was almost certainly out of use by the close of that century, according to archaeological evidence.[131]

Excavations near the eastern waterfront at Billingsgate along Lower Thames Street have disclosed remains of a substantial late Roman winged courtyard-type house with hypocaust and elaborate attached bath suite. Coin finds and amphorae indicate that this complex was still in use during the early decades of the fifth century.[132] By that time, however, its central heating system was inoperative, and the bath suite evidently was used only for storage. Indeed, occupation had become confined to a few rooms with individual small furnaces. By c.430 the buildings were finally abandoned and lay derelict for some time until visited by a passing band of Anglo-Saxons, one of whom (a woman?) lost a fine disc brooch of early to mid-fifth-century provenance among the collapsed roof tiles of the bath. The great Antonine Governor's Palace (*praetorium*) just to the west also then seems to have been in decayed condition, though still partially occupied, into the early fifth century.[133] The evidence thus indicates that these late Roman buildings succumbed to decay and desertion rather than any enemy attack; indeed, there are no indications of Anglo-Saxon sack and slaughter in fifth-century London. Other than some scattered sub-Roman pottery of uncertain date, this is virtually all the material evidence we possess for London's last Romano-British occupation.[134] If any sub-Roman Londoners were left to welcome the retreating Kentishmen after Crayford, they were living in squalid conditions on an essentially nonurban site. Unless some dramatic finds emerge, there is at present no firm evidence to support the case for settlement or urban continuity at London from late Roman to early Anglo-Saxon times.[135]

There is, in fact, very little indication of any permanent Anglo-Saxon presence within London before the late sixth or early seventh century. The few earliest archaeological finds suggest a limited domestic settlement with the means to acquire rather exotic items, such as wheelturned imported pottery from Gaul and the Rhineland, an elaborate cruciform brooch, and glass beakers.[136] Outside London, nearly a dozen Anglo-Saxon settlements have been identified, some of which may be as early as c.425, but their relationship to the town itself, if any, is uncertain.[137] Intramural Anglo-Saxon occupation is attested by local pottery and also sunken huts, most of which, however, are of ninth century or later date; the oldest *Grubenhaus* yet found has been ascribed to c.650. The concentration of early finds in the western zone of the town is significant, however, as this was evidently the area first abandoned by the late Roman population and thus perhaps most suitable for initial Anglo-Saxon settlement.[138]

The Anglo-Saxon settlement of London appears to have been a high-status initial occupation, much as in the cases of Canterbury and Winchester

(Fig. 4.7). According to Bede, London's first minster, St. Paul's, was erected within the town in 604 by order of the Kentish *Bretwalda*, Aethelberht.[139] As seen in a number of other cases, this grant implies a significant degree of pre-existing Anglo-Saxon royal involvement with this former Roman site, an involvement not necessarily limited to Kentish kings. Bede remarks in the passage cited that St. Paul's was intended to serve the East Saxons, whose "chief seat" (*metropolis*) was London. Aethelberht's actions in Essex demonstrated and perhaps solidified his overlordship by extending his authority over a site that may already have been an East Saxon royal center. The finds of Frankish luxury items at London also could reflect Aethelberht's commercial and marital connections with the Merovingians. As will be seen in greater detail, seventh-century London also possessed a major mint for the production of early Anglo-Saxon gold coins. London's population in the early seventh century, small as it may well have been, evidently had a mind of its own. We are told, for instance, that despite the efforts of Bishop Mellitus, his initial Christian mission was run out of town in 616 by the pagan Londoners, who "preferred their own idolatrous priests."[140]

Most early Anglo-Saxon finds in London have been located not only in the minster area but also in and around the old Roman fort of Cripplegate, which occupied the northwest quadrant of the walls (Fig. 4.7). The eastern area of the fort and land just beyond its wall formed the medieval tenement of Aldermanbury, "the fortified place of the alderman," and contained one of the earliest aristocratic enclosures (*hagas*, "haws") in Anglo-Saxon London.[141]   Moreover, according to later medieval tradition, the Aldermanbury area near the fort's east wall was the site of London's Anglo-Saxon royal palace.[142] The law code of King Hlothere of Kent (c.685) specifically mentions a Kentish royal hall (*sele*) and royal reeve in London, and there are various later references to London's Anglo-Saxon royal palace.[143]

Archaeological search for this royal site focused initially on the Cripplegate fort's eastern gate house whose assumed position shares the same street frontage as the tenement. Indeed, the altered post-Roman alignment of Addle Street at its eastern end does suggest that the gate house served some important purpose in early Anglo-Saxon times.[144] It is also possible that the recently found intramural Roman amphitheater, just outside Cripplegate, may have housed an early royal residence. Again, new Anglo-Saxon street topography suggests that this former public structure remained standing and had some significant function, if not as the site of a royal hall, then perhaps as the traditional gathering place of the London folkmoot.[145] The major Anglo-Saxon north-south street through this western zone entered at Aldergate and passed by the main route to Aldermanbury on its way to St. Paul's where it connected with Watling Street.[146] Thus, written, archaeological, and topographic evidence point to the presence and location of two main settlement foci in very early Anglo-Saxon London: the minster of St. Paul's and a probable royal palace with aristocratic compounds in the Cripplegate-Aldermanbury area. Although intramural occupation may have been increasing only slightly around these nuclei, early to mid seventh-century London exhibits sufficient urban functional features (i.e., ecclesiastical and royal administration, defense, coin production, elite trade) to then regard it as a town.

The last case of possible continuity to be considered here is York (Eboracum), the most prominent Roman town of northern Britain. Founded as a Roman legionary fort near the confluence of the Rivers Ouse and Foss in the late first century A.D., its accompanying civilian settlement grew rapidly into a major port and capital of the expansive northern province, Britannia Inferior, early in the third century (Fig. 4.8). At about this time, the town was promoted to the highest rank of *colonia* and underwent major architectural renewal.[147] During the third century, this civilian York on the west bank of the Ouse boasted highly elaborate public and private buildings, including an imperial palace, multiple temples and baths, and richly furnished houses.[148] The town's commercial and industrial vitality is particularly well attested by epigraphic and archaeological evidence.[149]

Late Roman York was the strategic hub of Britain's northern defense. The walls of its military fortress were repeatedly strengthened during the second and third centuries, and the *colonia* itself (c.70 acres) was enclosed by another stone circuit.[150] Early in the fourth century, York became capital of the new Diocletianic province Britannia Secunda as well as the headquarters for the Dux Britanniarum commanding all northern defenses. Great multangular projecting towers were then added to the fortress's southwest wall, overlooking the adjoining town. These massive stoneworks, still largely intact, may well have been intended primarily to impress visitors with the military, administrative, and economic importance of late Roman York.[151]

Archaeological evidence indicates that urban life continued at York during the fourth century, although conditions were slowly declining. For example, in the southeast area of the *colonia* at Bishophill, a substantial private house with attached hypocaust was found to have been completely rebuilt in standard Roman style after 350 A.D. This structure remained occupied for a considerable time, but the baths eventually were dispensed with and the additional rooms turned over to domestic industries.[152] Suburban cemeteries were also in continuous use until the late fourth century. Thereafter, however, stone sarcophagi (including those of town decurions) were crudely reused and dismembered skeletons cast about.[153] Another telling sign of declining standards is the blockage and disuse of part of the sewage system in the late fourth century.[154] Within the fortress, the hall of the legionary headquarters building (*principia*) was also rebuilt on a smaller scale and occupied late in the fourth century. Its painted walls and inlaid floors display traditional Roman technique but debased workmanship. As seen within the town, several of its rooms also were given over to home crafts.[155] The legionary bath house across from the *principia* was partly demolished c.370 and thereafter crudely reconstructed perhaps as a domestic residence.[156] There is thus evidence that York remained occupied in the late fourth and early fifth centuries but was progressively losing its full complement of urban functions and high living standards.

One factor contributing to the apparent urban decline in late Roman York may have been an intensification of periodic winter flooding by the rivers Ouse and Foss. These natural events have been attributed to a general rise in sea level that caused the backing up of rivers and streams along the Humber estuary.[157] Evidence of such flooding has been observed at several late Roman sites, yet effective countermeasures were apparently not taken. Indeed, deposit layers of riverine sand and silt sometimes three feet deep could indicate annual inundations up to the 35-foot contour at York.[158] Although such flooding would not have directly affected the *colonia* or fortress, both on higher ground, it probably undermined riverine defenses and certainly had a disastrous impact on the shipping facilities so vital to York's economy. Indeed, one excavation disclosed the remains of a late Roman wharf and a massive loading crane buried under a thick bank of river silt.[159] The primary Roman bridge connecting town and fortress also is believed to have become derelict in the late fourth century, and the naval port of Brough-on-Humber farther downstream was abandoned soon after 360 for perhaps similar environmental reasons.[160] Reclamation of these flooded areas at York began only in the seventh century and was not fully completed until the tenth century.[161]

It is not yet clear exactly how long Roman York remained occupied. The final withdrawal of its legion and administrative bureaucracy, periodic flooding, and decay of harbor facilities must have had serious social and economic impacts on a town that was already showing signs of settlement contraction. Find spots of occupation c.400 indicate that population had been reduced to areas within the *colonia* primarily in ribbon fashion along its main north-south street.[162] There is no firm evidence to contradict the impression that Roman York was virtually deserted by c.425. Indeed, it appears to have ceased functioning as an urban center at, or very soon after, the Roman departure (409/410).

Nonetheless, York has been cited often as a major example of settlement continuity from late Roman to Anglo-Saxon times, and it is thus necessary to reconsider the pertinent evidence and arguments. York is surrounded by several large Anglo-Saxon cremation cemeteries or urn fields (the Mount, Heworth) that, according to some opinions, were in use during the early fifth century at the same time as nearby late Roman burials (Fig. 4.9). The argument, again, is that these urn fields are the interments of Anglo-Saxon mercenaries initially brought in for the defense of York and that these federates or their immediate descendants took over control of the sub-Roman town in the fifth century.[163] But the early dating of some of the pertinent pottery is open to serious question, and the cemeteries themselves do not continue into the sixth century. Moreover, there is no archaeological evidence of any substantial Anglo-Saxon domestic occupation within the town or fortress before perhaps the late seventh century.[164]

Another argument for settlement continuity at York represents the opposite side of the coin: that the town remained a British stronghold until the late sixth century, when it finally passed into Anglo-Saxon (Anglian) hands. Welsh literary sources seem to support this scenario and may even refer to several sub-Roman rulers of York.[165] This later material, however, is at best garbled and its historicity rather dubious. Advocates of the continuity view also were encouraged by results of excavations at York's *principia*, which surprisingly revealed that part of the stone complex evidently had been maintained until the ninth century. This discovery prompted the suggestion that the principial complex had been the center of sub-Roman town authority and then the site of an Anglian royal palace after the supposed peaceful transfer of control.[166] Such a view is attractive but as yet unsubstantiated. The attested maintenance may have been intermittent and need not indicate continuous occupation from late Roman times; indeed, the structure could have been first refurbished as part of a limited seventh-century Anglo-Saxon resettlement.[167] As we shall see, there probably was an Anglo-Saxon royal presence in York but this was not likely to have been as early as the fifth century. Similarly, the famous "Anglian Tower" on the fortress's west wall, which may well be pre-Viking age work, need not predate the ninth century. In addition, although repairs apparently were made to the fortress's walls after the tower was refurbished but before York fell to the Vikings (867), these Anglian defensive works have not been more narrowly dated.[168]

York first appears in Anglo-Saxon written records in connection with the foundation of an early seventh-century minster by royal command. In 627 King Edwin of Northumbria, his noble retainers, and many "humbler folk" reportedly were baptized at York by the missionary bishop Paulinus in a timber church that Edwin evidently had just built for the occasion (St. Peter's). The king then established Paulinus's episcopal see in the town and ordered a "more noble basilica of stone" erected to replace the wooden church on the same site.[169] Once again, the king's activities suggest that York was already a royal center of some importance. The precise location of Paulinus' St. Peter's is uncertain, but there is general agreement that it stood within the old fortress area, perhaps in the courtyard of the *principia*

(Fig. 4.9).[170] If part of the former legionary headquarters was an established Anglian royal palace and residence, the adjacent St. Peter's may have been a *Hofkapelle*, as has been suggested at Winchester and London. York Minster, built atop a section of the large principial complex, certainly became the primary royal and episcopal burial ground of Northumbria in the seventh and eighth centuries.[171] Also, the eighth-century *Anonymous Life of Gregory the Great* does mention a "hall" (*aula*) and "public square" (*platea populi*) presumably in York in connection with a miracle story involving King Edwin and Paulinus.[172] Unfortunately, there is only slight and scattered archaeological evidence of pre-Viking age occupation within the fortress, although the new Anglian street pattern, which cut across Roman *insulae* and roads, suggests at least frequent passage. In the *colonia*, however, there are more widespread signs of domestic settlement, including perhaps pottery production. Indeed, the cluster of churches around Bishophill (Fig. 4.9) may have served a growing intramural population from the seventh century.[173] Moreover, it is now believed that a group of early Anglo-Saxon gold *thrymsas* were minted in York, perhaps as early as the 640s.[174] By the mid seventh century York, with its ecclesiastical and likely royal foci, defenses, mint, and developing economic activity, can be said to have achieved urban status. After what appears on existing evidence to have been an extended period of virtual desertion following the Roman departure from Britain, York was reborn as an Anglo-Saxon town with the potential to again become the leading urban center of northern England.

The examination of selected, representative towns in this and the preceding chapter has shown that the evidence for urban continuity or even town settlement continuity from late Roman to early Anglo-Saxon times is negligible. Rather, Romano-British towns underwent a gradual decline with progressive loss of urban functions after the mid-fourth century that culminated in periods of virtual abandonment, in most cases well before Anglo-Saxon newcomers appeared in their respective regions. Indeed, Romano-British urbanism, even in its reduced late and sub-Roman forms, evidently did not endure many decades beyond 400 A.D. Thus the record of both urban life and urban settlement from late Roman Britain to early Anglo-Saxon England is one more of discontinuity than continuity. The evidence would indicate that after lapses of intramural settlement ranging from several decades to over a century, these former Roman towns were reoccupied by the Anglo-Saxons first as royal and then also as ecclesiastical centers. It has been contended that by the early to mid seventh century, these sites possessed sufficient attributes and functions for them to be regarded as towns. They were distinctive places of nonagricultural royal and ecclesiastical administration, with defensive walls occasionally refurbished, incipient trade and production, sometimes a mint and multiple churches, and growing permanent populations. Soon, however, they were not to stand alone as the only type of town in the emerging Anglo-Saxon urban landscape.

NOTES

1. For example: S. Frere, "The End of Towns in Roman Britain," in *The Civitas Capitals of Roman Britain*, ed. J. S. Wacher (Leicester: University Press, 1966), pp. 87–100, and *Britannia* (3d ed., London: Routledge & Kegan Paul, 1987), pp. 368–70; J. S. Wacher, *The Towns of Roman Britain* (Berkeley: University of California Press, 1974), pp. 418–22; S. Johnson, *Later Roman Britain* (London: Collins, 1980), pp. 191–93; M. Aston and J. Bond, *Landscape of Towns* (London: J. M. Dent, 1976), pp. 52–53; M. Biddle, "The Development of the Anglo-Saxon Town," in *Topografia urbana e vita cittadina nell'alto medioevo in occidente* (2 vols., Spoleto: Centro Italiano di Studi Sull'Alto Medioevo, 1974), I, pp. 206–12; L. Alcock, *Arthur's Britain: History and Archaeology A.D. 367–634* (Harmondsworth: Penguin Books, 1971), pp. 181–92; J. N. L. Myres, *The English Settlements* (Oxford: Clarendon Press, 1981), pp. 122–25, 167–68.

2. For the pre-Claudian background, see B. Cunliffe, *Iron Age Communities in Britain* (London: Routledge & Kegan Paul, 1974), pp. 75–84, 148–50; R. Jessop, *South-East England* (NY: Praeger, 1970), pp. 140–44; A. Detsicas, *The Cantiaci* (Gloucester: Alan Sutton, 1983); P. Arthur, "Roman Amphorae from Canterbury," *Britannia* 17 (1986), 239–58; D. Nash, "The Basis of Contact between Britain and Gaul in the Late Pre-Roman Iron Age," in *Cross-Channel Trade between Gaul and Britain in the Pre-Roman Iron Age*, eds. S. Macready and F. Thompson (London: Society of Antiquaries of London, 1984), pp. 92–107 esp. 102–5.

3. On Canterbury in the Roman period, see in general, S. Frere, *Roman Canterbury: The City of Durovernum* (Canterbury: J. A. Jennings, 1962); Wacher, *Towns*, pp. 26, 178–95, 420. For summaries of recent archaeological work: Blagg, "Roman Kent," in *Archaeology in Kent to A.D. 1500*, ed. P. Leach. Council for British Archaeology (hereafter C.B.A.) Research Report 48 (London, 1982), pp. 51–60; P. Bennett, "The Topography of Roman Canterbury: A Brief Reassessment," *Archaeologia Cantiana* 100 (1984), 47–56; A. S. Esmonde Cleary, *Extra-Mural Areas of Romano-British Towns*, British Archaeological Reports (hereafter B.A.R.) 169 (Oxford, 1987), pp. 25–27; C. J. Arnold, *Roman Britain to Saxon England* (Bloomington: Indiana University Press, 1984), pp. 38–39, 43–45; D. A. Brooks, "The Case for Continuity in Fifth-Century Canterbury Re-Examined," *Oxford Journal of Archaeology* 7 (1988), pp. 99–114; S. Frere, et al., "Roman Britain in 1989," *Britannia* 21 (1990), 360–62, and Fig. 26; M. Todd, "The Early Cities," in *Research on Roman Britain 1960–89*, ed. Todd. Britannia Monograph Series 2 (London: Society for the Promotion of Roman Studies, 1989), pp. 84–85. For greater detail, see esp. the serial publications of the Canterbury Archaeological Trust edited by S. Frere, et al., e.g.: *Excavations on the Roman and Medieval Defences of Canterbury* (1982), and *Canterbury Excavations: Intra- and Extra-Mural Sites* (1987).

4. Wacher, *Towns*, pp. 184, 189, and "Cities from the Second to Fourth Centuries," in *Research on Roman Britain 1960–89*, p. 96. But the town walls when

erected did not enclose peripheral settlement and industrial areas, which became burial grounds by the close of the fourth century: Esmonde Cleary, *Extra-Mural Areas*, pp. 26–27.

5. K. Blockley and M. Day, "Marlowe Car Park Excavations," *Archaeologia Cantiana* 95 (1979), 267–70; Arnold, *Roman Britain to Saxon England*, p. 39; D. A. Brooks, "Fifth-Century Canterbury," pp. 103–4.

6. Wacher, *Towns*, p. 192; D. A. Brooks, "Fifth-Century Canterbury," p. 101; cf. B. Jones and D. Mattingly, *An Atlas of Roman Britain* (Oxford: Blackwell, 1990), p. 311.

7. P. Bennett, "68–69a Stour Sreet," *Archaeologia Cantiana* 96 (1980), 406–10; Arnold, *Roman Britain to Saxon England*, p. 39, and Fig. 2.7; D. A. Brooks, "Fifth-Century Canterbury," p. 103.

8. Ibid., p. 101; C. M. Johns and T. W. Potter, "The Canterbury Late Roman Treasure," *Antiquaries Journal* 55 (1985), 313–52. This particular hoard, containing fine silver domestic utensils, coins, ingots, and some gold jewelry, had been buried hastily against the town's outer west wall near the London gate c.420, perhaps by wealthy members or officials of a Christian group.

9. Arnold, *Roman Britain to Saxon England*, p. 30; D. A. Brooks, "Fifth-Century Canterbury," pp. 100, 104, 109–13.

10. See esp. Frere, "End of Towns," pp. 91–93. Also see S. Hawkes, "Early Anglo-Saxon Kent," *Antiquaries Journal* 126 (1970), 186–92; Alcock, *History and Archaeology*, pp. 188–89; Jessop, *South-East England*, p. 179; Wacher, *Towns*, pp. 193–95.

11. M. Biddle, "The Towns," in *Archaeology of Anglo-Saxon England*, ed. D. M. Wilson (London: Methuen, 1976), pp. 103–10.

12. Gildas, *De excidio Britonum*, xxiii–xxiv, ed. M. Winterbottom (Chichester: Phillimore, 1978).

13. Bede, *Historia Ecclesiastica* (hereafter *Hist. Eccl.*) i.15, ed. C. Plummer (2 vols., Oxford: Clarendon Press, 1896). The reinforcements included Jutes who were to comprise the largest new population group of Kent. See further: J. M. Wallace-Hadrill, *Bede's "Ecclesiastical History of the English People": A Historical Commentary* (Oxford: Clarendon Press, 1988), pp. 20–24; Myres, *English Settlements*, pp. 112–17.

14. Nennius, *Historia Brittonum* (hereafter *Hist. Brit.*) xxxi, xxxvi–xxxvii, ed. J. Morris (Chichester: Phillimore, 1980). This romantic tale, not totally implausible, may reflect the ethnic admixture of early Anglo-Saxon Kent. Nennius also claims that the grant was made without the knowledge or consent of the local sub-Roman ruler of Kent subject to Vortigern's overlordship (ibid., xxxvii).

15. Ibid., xliii–xlvi. Morris called these sections "The Kentish Chronicle" and argued that they dated no later than the sixth century (ibid., p. 4). For the possible incorporation of such early Kentish annals into the ninth-century *Anglo-Saxon Chronicle*, see Myres, *English Settlements*, p. 10. For criticisms of Nennius's accuracy and other reservations cf. D. M. Dumville, "Sub-Roman Britain: History and Legend," *History* 62 (1977), 173–92.

16. *Two of the Saxon Chronicles Parallel* (hereafter *ASC*), eds. J. Earle and C. Plummer (2 vols., Oxford: Clarendon Press, 1892–1899), s.a. 449, 455A, 457E (Crayford). See further on the textual evidence concerning early Kent: N. Brooks, "The Creation and Early Structure of the Kingdom of Kent," in *The Origins of Anglo-*

Saxon Kingdoms, ed. S. Bassett (Leicester: University Press, 1989), pp. 55–74 esp. 58–64. But for further words of caution regarding the historicity of this early textual material, see: P. Sims-Williams, "The Settlement of England in Bede and the *Chronicle*," *Anglo-Saxon England* 12 (1983), pp. 1–41.

17. Myres, *English Settlements*, pp. 123–24; P. Drewett, et al., *The South-East to A.D. 1000* (London: Longman, 1988), Fig. 7.2; S. Hawkes, "Anglo-Saxon Kent c.425–725," in *Archaeology in Kent to A.D. 1500*, ed. Leach, pp. 64–78.

18. Johnson, *Later Roman Britain*, pp. 169–71; M. Welch, *Discovering Anglo-Saxon England* (University Park: Pennsylvania State University Press, 1993), pp. 71–87, 99–100.

19. Frere, "End of Towns," pp. 91–93; Biddle, "Towns," pp. 104–5.

20. C. Hills, "The Archaeology of Anglo-Saxon England in the Pagan Period: A Review," *Anglo-Saxon England* 8 (1979), pp. 297–308; Arnold, *Roman Britain to Saxon England*, pp. 25–27; Welch, *Discovering Anglo-Saxon England*, pp. 100–103.

21. Myres, *English Settlements*, p. 31; E. Ennen, *Die europäische Stadt des Mittelalters* (Göttingen: Vandenhoeck & Ruprecht, 1972), pp. 34–45; A. Verhulst, "Les origines urbaines dans le Nord-Ouest de l'Europe," *Francia* 14 (1989), pp. 61–64.

22. Biddle, "Development of the Anglo-Saxon Town," p. 206; D. Hill, "Continuity from Roman to Medieval:Britain," in *European Towns: Their Archaeology and Early History*, ed. M. W. Barley (London: Academic Press, 1977), pp. 298–99.

23. *ASC* s.a. 754 [756]A.

24. Myres, *English Settlements*, p. 125.

25. *Cartularium Saxonicum* (hereafter *Cart. Sax.*), ed. W. de Gray Birch (4 vols., London: Whiting & Co., 1885–99), No. 248 (786 A.D.).

26. Biddle, "Towns," pp. 106–7.

27. T. Tatton-Brown, "The Towns of Kent," in *Anglo-Saxon Towns in Southern England*, ed. J. Haslam (Chichester: Phillimore, 1984), p. 9.

28. Myres, *English Settlements*, pp. 122–26.

29. D. A. Brooks, "Fifth-Century Canterbury," pp. 104, 109–13.

30. Ibid., p. 104, 106.

31. Ibid., p. 107.

32. Ibid., p. 108.

33. Drewett, et al., *South-East*, pp. 254–55.

34. Bede, *Hist. Eccl.*, i.25–26. For what it may be worth, the ninth-century Old English translation of Bede's work uses the terms *ealdorbyrig* ("chief seat"), and *cynelecan byrig* ("royal capital") and refers to Canterbury as both *byrig* and *ceaster*: *The Old English version of Bede's "Ecclesiastical History of the English Church and People*," i.25–26, trans. T. Miller (London: Early English Text Society, 1890).

35. Bede., *Hist. Eccl.*, i.25, ii.3,5.

36. *ASC* s.a. 827 [829]A.

37. On the *Bretwalda* problem, see: F. M. Stenton, *Anglo-Saxon England* (hereafter *ASE*) (3d ed., Oxford: Clarendon Press, 1971), pp. 34–35; E. John, *Orbis Britanniae and Other Studies* (Leicester: University Press, 1966), pp. 6–21; H. Vollrath-Reichelt, *Königsgedanke und Königtum bei den Angelsachsen*, Kölner Historische Abhandlungen 19 (Cologne: Böhlau, 1971), pp. 199–21; P. Wormald, "Bede, the *Bretwaldas*, and the Origins of the *Gens Anglorum*," in *Ideal and Reality*

in Frankish and Anglo-Saxon Society, ed. Wormald (Oxford: Clarendon Press, 1983), pp. 99–129.

38. As demonstrated by the Anglo-Saxon law codes or dooms, the first of which was issued by Aethelberht in Kent c.603: *Laws of Aethelberht*, in F. Attenborough, ed., *Laws of the Earliest English Kings* (Cambridge: University Press, 1922), pp. 4–17. See further, J. M. Wallace-Hadrill, *Early Germanic Kingship in England and on the Continent* (Oxford: Clarendon Press, 1971), pp. 32–44.

39. Ibid., pp. 8–16. For a discussion of the early Anglo-Saxon king's role in religion, see W. A. Chaney, *The Cult of Kingship in Anglo-Saxon England* (Berkeley: University of California Press, 1970), pp. 7–42, and on the specifically Germanic component, see D. G. Russo, "Sacral Kingship in Early Medieval Europe: The Germanic Tradition" (M.A. thesis, University of New Hampshire, 1978), pp. 194–202, 249–57; also, H. A. Myers and H. Wolfram, *Medieval Kingship* (Chicago: Nelson-Hall, 1982), pp. 2–6.

40. Bede, *Hist. Eccl.*, i.29. See further, M. Deanesly, *The Pre-Conquest Church in England* (NY: Oxford University Press, 1961), pp. 41–42, 50; R. A. Markus, "Gregory the Great and a Papal Missionary Strategy," in *Studies in Church History* 6 (1970), pp. 29-38; H. Mayr-Harting, *The Coming of Christianity to England* (NY: Schocken Books, 1972), pp. 57-65; N. Brooks, *The Early History of the Church of Canterbury* (Leicester: University Press, 1984), pp. 9–11.

41. See on these matters: N. Brooks, "Kingdom of Kent," pp. 58–64.

42. Myres, *English Settlements*, pp. 114–16; Drewett, et al., *South-East*, p. 257.

43. Ibid., pp. 258, 278–79.

44. R. Hodges, *The Anglo-Saxon Achievement: Archaeology and the Beginnings of English Society* (Ithaca: Cornell University Press, 1989), pp.69–78; Drewett, et al., *South-East*, pp. 278–80.

45. Bede, *Hist. Eccl.*, i.25. See, Dumville, "The Anglian Collection of Royal Geneaologies and Regnal Lists," *Anglo-Saxon England* 5 (1976), pp. 23–50, and N. Brooks, "Kingdom of Kent," pp. 64–67.

46. Ibid., pp. 68–69.

47. B. Yorke, "Joint Kingship in Kent c.570–785," *Archaeologia Cantiana* 99 (1983), 1–20.

48. *ASE*, pp. 287–88.

49. Tatton-Brown, "Towns of Kent," p. 5, Map 1; N. Brooks, "Kingdom of Kent, pp 69–74.

50. Bede, *Hist. Eccl.*, i.25, 26.

51. N. Brooks, *Church of Canterbury*, pp. 24–25; Biddle, "Towns," p. 110.

52. Tatton-Brown, "Towns of Kent," p. 5.

53. H. Büttner, "Studien zum frühmittelalterlichen Städtewesen in Frankreich," in *Anfängen des europäischen Stadtewesens*, ed. T. Mayer (Constance: J. Thorbecke, 1958), pp. 151–89, esp. pp. 152–55; C. Brühl, *Fodrum, Gistrum, Servitium Regis*, Kölner Historische Abhandlungen 14 (Cologne: Böhlau, 1968), pp. 9–17; Ennen, *Stadt des Mittelalters*, pp. 38–39, 43–45. The early Merovingians were quite accustomed to towns, where they often had their residences and burial places; later Frankish kings preferred their rural estates, leaving town administration to count and bishop: Büttner, "Studien," pp. 154–57; H. Planitz, *Die deutsche Stadt im Mittelalter* (Cologne: Böhlau, 1954), pp. 35–37. For *Fluchtsburg/Volksburg* terminology, see: ibid.,

pp. 39, 48–50; E. A. Gutkind, *International History of City Development* (8 vols., New York: Free Press, 1964–72), vol. I, *Urban Development in Central Europe* (1964), pp. 452–54.

54. Biddle, "Development of the Anglo-Saxon Town," pp. 209–10; Hill, "Continuity from Roman to Medieval," p. 300.

55. The condition of the British Church during the fifth and sixth centuries is a controversial topic. In the fourth century, each of the perhaps two dozen *civitates* appears to have had its own bishop, with four urban metropolitans (London, York, Lincoln, and Cirencester) corresponding to the fourfold provincial division of that time: C. Thomas, *Christianity in Roman Britain to A.D. 500* (Berkeley: University of California Press, 1981), pp. 197–201; J. Mann, "The Administration of Roman Britain," *Antiquity* 35 (1961), 316–20. British bishops attended the Councils of Arles (314) and Ariminum (359): A. Haddan and W. Stubbs, eds., *Councils and Ecclesiastical Documents Relating to Britain and Ireland* (3 vols., Oxford: Clarendon Press, 1869–71), I, pp. 7–10. Some of the last references to an organized British episcopate occur during the Pelagian controversy (c.420–450), with indications of continuing Gallic Church contacts: Ibid., pp. 12–16. See further, Thomas, *Christianity*, pp. 56–59; R. P. C. Hanson, *St. Patrick: His Origins and Career* (Oxford: University Press, 1968), Chap. 2, "The British Church in the Fifth Century," esp. pp. 40–41.

56. Esmonde Cleary, *Extra-Mural Areas*, p. 26; Drewett, et al., *South-East*, pp. 254, 272.

57. Bede, *Hist. Eccl.*, i.26.

58. Ibid., i.26, 33. Kentish kings continued to bestow royal property in this northeast town quadrant to the Church. See further, N. Brooks, *Church of Canterbury*, pp. 37–59, and "The Ecclesiastical Topography of Early Medieval Canterbury," in *European Towns*, ed. Barley, p. 490.

59. Ibid. A small secular compound (perhaps houses for church servants) occupied continuously from the early sixth to ninth centuries, has been found in this area: S. Young, et al., "Medieval Britain and Ireland in 1985," *Medieval Archaeology* 30 (1986), 154-56.

60. Bede, *Hist. Eccl.*, i.33.

61. Tatton-Brown, "Towns of Kent," pp. 9–10, N. Brooks, *Church of Canterbury*, pp. 32–36.

62. Bede, *Hist. Eccl.*, i.26.

63. N. Brooks, "Ecclesiastical Topography," pp. 491–92.

64. F. Jenkins, "St. Martin's Church at Canterbury: A Survey of the Earliest Structural Features," *Medieval Archaeology* 9 (1965), 11–15; N. Brooks, *Church of Canterbury*, p. 17.

65. Esmonde Cleary, *Extra-Mural Areas*, pp. 26–27.

66. Thomas, *Christianity*, pp. 170–74; but cf. Wallace-Hadrill, *Commentary*, pp. 36–37.

67. M. Deanesly and P. Grosjean, "The Canterbury Edition of the Answers of Pope Gregory I to Augustine," *Journal of Ecclesiastical History* 10 (1959), 28–29. See further, N. Brooks, *Church of Canterbury*, p. 20.

68. Bede, *Hist. Eccl.*, ii.7. See Tatton-Brown, "Towns of Kent," p. 5; Drewett, et al., *South-East*, p. 305.

69. Ibid. P. Grierson, "The Canterbury (St. Martin's) Hoard of Frankish and Anglo-Saxon Coin Ornaments," *British Numismatic Journal* 27 (1952–54), 39–51; N. Brooks, *Church of Canterbury*, p. 23. See further, C. J. Arnold, *Archaeology of the Early Anglo-Saxon Kingdoms* (Bloomington: Indiana University Press, 1989), pp. 56–70.

70. Bede, *Hist. Eccl.*, iv.1–2. See further, Brooks, *Church of Canterbury*, pp. 71–76; Mayr-Harting, *Coming of Christianity*, pp. 121-22, 196-98, and 206-9.

71. Such as payments at royal and church courts. The early Anglo-Saxon gold coinage was struck c.604–670: C. H. V. Sutherland, *English Coinage 600–1900* (London: Batsford, 1973), pp. 3–4; M. Dolley, "The Coins," in *Archaeology of Anglo-Saxon England*, p. 351. The *thrymsa* was apparently modeled upon, and named after, the late Roman and Merovingian *tremissis* (one-third of the Constantinian *solidus*). It was also used occasionally as ornamental jewelry.

72. Sutherland, *English Coinage*, pp. 5–23; Dolley, "The Coins," pp. 352–56. There were lesser mints in the southeast at London and Rochester. For a good brief summary, see D. M. Metcalf, "Anglo-Saxon Coins I: Seventh to Ninth Centuries," in *The Anglo-Saxons*, ed. J. Campbell (London: Penguin, 1982), pp. 62–63.

73. *Cart. Sax.*, Nos. 192 and 319. See, N. Brooks, *Church of Canterbury*, p. 51; Tatton-Brown, "Towns of Kent," pp. 7, 9. A memorable conflagration at Canterbury in 754 is said, probably with exaggeration, to have burnt down the town: *ASC*, 754A.

74. *Cart. Sax.*, Nos. 248, 426 and 515. For further discussion and details of Mercian and West Saxon Canterbury, see Chap. 7, below.

75. D. B. Harden, "Romano-British Remains: Dorchester-on-Thames," in *The Victoria History of the Counties of England* (hereafter *VCH*), *Oxfordshire* (London, 1939), pp. 288–96; Frere, *Britannia*, pp. 114–15, 195, 252; T. Rowley, "The Roman Towns of Oxfordshire: Alchester and Dorchester-on-Thames," in *The "Small Towns" of Roman Britain*, eds. W. Rodwell and T. Rowley, B.A.R. 15 (Oxford, 1975), pp. 115–18; J. Cook and T. Rowley, *Dorchester through the Ages* (Oxford: Clarendon Press, 1985), Chap. 1; B. Burnham and J. Wacher, *The Small Towns of Roman Britain* (Berkeley: University of California Press, 1990), pp. 117–22. Dorchester-on-Thames may be the "Tamese" of the Ravenna Cosmography (ibid., p. 117). It was evidently the local headquarters of a minor imperial official, the *beneficarius consularis*, probably in charge of military supplies: *RIB*, No. 235.

76. Frere, "End of Towns," pp. 93–94; L. Alcock, "Roman Britons and Pagan Saxons: An Archaeological Appraisal," *Welsh History Review* 3 (1966–67), 228–49, rpt. with additions in Alcock, *Economy, Society, and Warfare among the Britons and Saxons* (Cardiff: University of Wales Press, 1987), pp. 267–81 esp. pp. 271–72; K. R. Davis, *Britons and Saxons: The Chiltern Region 400–700* (Chichester: Phillimore, 1982), p. 22; Burnham and Wacher, *Small Towns*, p. 121.

77. Esmonde Cleary, *Extra-Mural Areas*, p. 73; R. A. Chambers, "The Late- and Sub-Roman Cemetery at Queenford Farm, Dorchester-on-Thames, Oxon.," *Oxoniensia* 52 (1988), 35–69.

78. T. Rowley, "Early Saxon Settlements in Dorchester-on-Thames," in *Anglo-Saxon Settlement and Landscape*, ed. Rowley. B.A.R. 6 (Oxford, 1974), pp. 42–56; G. Astill, "The Towns of Berkshire," in *Anglo-Saxon Towns*, p. 56; Arnold, *Roman Britain to Saxon England*, p. 66; D. A. Brooks, "A Review of the Evidence for Continuity in British Towns in the 5th and 6th Centuries," *Oxford Journal of*

Archaeology 5 (1986), p. 89. One substantial town house built c.250 was converted to industrial use by c.325 and stood derelict toward the end of the fourth century: Burnham and Wacher, *Small Towns*, pp. 117, 119.

79. Frere, "End of Towns," p. 94; Biddle, "Towns," p. 104; Alcock, *Britons and Saxons*, p. 272; Myres, *English Settlements*, pp. 167–68; Burnham and Wacher, *Small Towns*, p. 122.

80. Frere, "End of Towns," p. 94;   P. Rahtz, "Gazetteer of Anglo-Saxon Domestic Settlement Sites," in *Archaeology of Anglo-Saxon England*, p. 417. The huts lay primarily in the south- and northwest intramural areas.

81. J. P. Kirk and E. T. Leeds, "Three Early Saxon Graves from Dorchester, Oxon," *Oxoniensia* 17–18 (1954), 63–76; Frere, "End of Towns," p. 93.

82. Esmonde Cleary, *Extra-Mural Areas*, pp. 73–74; D. A. Brooks, "Evidence for Continuity," p. 98. If the timber building, dated c.425–50, which succeeded a rectangular late Roman masonry structure inside the south gate can be shown to be Anglo-Saxon and not sub-Roman, a stronger case can be made for settlement continuity here: Ibid.; Burnham and Wacher, *Small Towns*, pp. 121–22.

83. Myres, *English Settlements*, pp. 162–67; T. M. Dickinson, "The Present State of Anglo-Saxon Cemetery Studies," in *Anglo-Saxon Cemeteries 1979*, eds. P. Rahtz, et al., B.A.R. 82 (Oxford, 1980), pp. 23–26 and Figs. 1.2–1.4 (distribution maps); Davis, *Chiltern Region*, pp. 62–65.

84. *ASC*, s.a. 568, 571, 577, 584, 592A. For a careful analysis of the very complex and often contradictory written evidence, see: D. P. Kirby, "Problems of Early West Saxon History," *English Historical Review* 80 (1965), 10–29 esp. 20–25. Also: *ASE*, 27–30; D. J. V. Fischer, *The Anglo-Saxon Age* (London: Longman, 1973), pp. 32–37; B. Yorke, *Kings and Kingdoms of Early Anglo-Saxon England* (London: Seaby, 1990), pp. 128–56; B. Cunliffe, *Wessex to A.D. 1000* (London: Longmans, 1993), pp. 276–79. Economic motives for Ceawlin's aggression have been suggested. See with caution, Arnold, "Wealth and Social Structure: A Matter of Life and Death," in *Anglo-Saxon Cemeteries*, eds. Rahtz, et al., pp. 84–90.

85. Dickinson, *Cuddesdon and Dorchester-on-Thames: Two Early Saxon "Princely" Sites in Wessex*, B.A.R. 1 (Oxford, 1974), pp. 25–30.

86. Ibid., pp. 10–24, suggesting that the family was that of Ceawlin. The rich central burial was surrounded by an unusual ring of secondary graves, perhaps sacrificial in nature.

87. Arnold, "Wealth and Social Structure," pp. 91, 96, 117–23, 138–39, noting also that there may have been an early mint for the gold *thrymsa* in or near Dorchester c.640; Astill, "Towns of Berkshire," pp. 56–57.

88. Bede, *Hist. Eccl.*, Preface. See Wallace-Hadrill, *Commentary*, pp. 97–98.

89. Bede, *Hist. Eccl.*, iii.7, and *ASC* 635A, which calls Birinus bishop of Dorchester. Cynegil's eldest son and grandson were baptized at Dorchester (ibid., 636, 639A). For the career of Birinus, possibly a Frank, see: Deanesley, *Pre-Conquest Church*, pp. 78–81; and *ASE*, pp. 117–18, where it is rightly observed that Birinus's work of evangelization was only partially successful. The town name Dorcic is most likely British and derived from **derk* ("bright/splendid"): Harden, "Romano-British Remains," p. 289 n.1. See further, G. Copley, *Archaeology and Place-Names in the Fifth and Sixth Centuries*, B.A.R. 147 (Oxford, 1986), pp. 31–32.

90. *ASE*, p. 82. But cf. Wormald, "The *Bretwaldas*," pp. 111–12; Wallace-Hadrill, *Commentary*, pp. 98, 231.

91. Bede, *Hist. Eccl.*, iii.7.

92. Kirby, "Problems of Early West Saxon History," 27–28; *ASE*, pp. 66–67; B. Yorke, "The Jutes of Hampshire and Wight and the Origins of Wessex," in *Origins of Anglo-Saxon Kingdoms*, ed. Bassett, pp. 84–96.

93. Biddle, "Winchester: The Development of an Early Capital," in *Vor- und Frühformen der europäischen Stadt im Mittelalter*, eds. H. Jankuhn, et al. (2 vols., Göttingen: Vandenhoeck & Ruprecht, 1973–74), I, pp. 229–31; Wacher, *Towns*, pp. 277–86. Venta Belgarum will hereafter be called Winchester to avoid confusion with Venta Icenorum (Caistor-by-Norwich).

94. Biddle, "The Study of Winchester: Archaeology and History in a British Town, 1961–1983," *Proceedings of the British Academy* 69 (1983), pp. 111–13; Wacher, *Towns*, pp. 286–88. See further, Cleary, *Extra-Mural Areas*, pp. 151–52.

95. *Notitia Dignitatum Occ.*, xi.60, cited by Biddle, "Study of Winchester," pp. 113–15; Frere, *Britannia*, pp. 188, 290–91. See further, Cunliffe, *Wessex to A.D. 1000*, pp. 244–45, 257, 270.

96. Biddle, "Early Capital," pp. 134–36; Wacher, *Towns*, p. 288; Arnold, *Roman Britain to Saxon England*, pp. 39–40; Esmonde Cleary, *Extra-Mural Areas*, p. 156; D. A. Brooks, "Evidence of Continuity," p. 89.

97. Biddle, "Early Capital," pp. 232–34; Myres, *English Settlements*, pp. 150–51; Cunliffe, *Wessex to A.D. 1000*, pp. 279–80, 286, 289 who carefully add that this would not be a case of continuity of urban life or urbanism.

98. D. A. Brooks, "Evidence of Continuity," pp. 91–92, 96–98; D. A. Hinton, "The Towns of Hampshire," in *Anglo-Saxon Towns*, pp. 161–62; G. N. Clarke, *The Roman Cemetery at Lankhills* (Oxford: Oxford University Press, 1979); R. Baldwin, "Intrusive Burial Groups in the Late Roman Cemetery at Lankhills, Winchester–A Reassessment of the Evidence," *Oxford Journal of Archaeology* 4 (1985), pp. 93-104. Even Biddle has acknowledged that there is no firm evidence of substantial Anglo-Saxon intramural settlement before the mid-seventh century: "Early Capital,"p. 236.

99. Bede, *Hist. Eccl.*, iii.7; *ASC* 643A, 648F. Wini was installed in 660 and Agilbert returned to Francia to become bishop of Paris (ibid., 660A). For excavations at St. Peter's, see Biddle, "Early Capital," p. 242 and Fig. 7.

100. Ibid.

101. Ibid., pp. 239–40; Biddle, "Study of Winchester," pp. 116–17. For written reference to the tenth-century *palatium*, see Wulfstan, *Narratio Metrica de Sancto Swithuno*, i.13, l.1393, ed. A. Campbell (Zurich: Thesaurus Mundi, 1950). But for a contrary view of Winchester's status as an early royal center, cf. Yorke, "Origins of Wessex," in *Origins of Anglo-Saxon Kingdoms*, p. 96.

102. Biddle, "Early Capital," p. 239. For the Frankish analogies, see: Brühl, *Fodrum, Gistum, Servitium Regis*, pp. 20, 25.

103. *Cart. Sax.*, ed. Birch, No. 620. This is the Chilcombe estate, extending 4.5 kilometers in diameter around the town. See Biddle, "Early Capital," p. 241, and Fig. 1.

104. Ibid., p. 240.

105. Ibid., pp. 242–43, and Fig. 5; Myres, *English Settlements*, p. 151, n.1.

106. The great majority were from Lower Brook Street; other locations were beneath Wolvesey Palace, the Assize Courts, and the Cathedral: Biddle, "Study of Winchester," p. 118. The eastern length of High Street may have served as a town market or trading area for some time before its first designation as *ceapstraet*, c. 900: *Cart. Sax.*, No. 630.

107. Biddle, "Study of Winchester," p. 118. An area of seventh-century industrial(?) activity and settlement, perhaps associated with the ecclesiastical-aristocratic compounds, has also been disclosed west of the Lower Brook Street site: Hinton, et al., "The Winchester Reliquary," *Medieval Archaeology* 25 (1981), 45–77.

108. As on the Wolvesey Palace site (southeast sector): Biddle, "Early Capital," pp. 245–46.

109. Tacitus, *Annales*, xiv.33, ed. H. Furneaux (2d ed., 2 vols., Oxford: Clarendon Press, 1896–1907), and see R. Merrifield, *London: City of the Romans* (Berkeley: University of California Press, 1983), pp. 41–52. London was the road hub of southeast Britain and the distribution center for Roman goods imported into the island (Map 2.2.B).

110. Merrifield, *London*, pp. 57–60. The basic entrepreneurial spirit of the London townspeople also has been seen as decisive: Wacher, *Towns*, pp. 80–82.

111. Merrifield, *London*, pp. 68–75, suggesting rapid promotions from *vicus* to *municipium* and then *colonia*: Frere, *Britannia*, p. 193.

112. Merrifield, *London*, pp. 90–106. In 1988, archaeologists discovered an impressive Roman amphitheater in London's northwest zone almost directly beneath the thirteenth-century guildhall. Its construction has been dated provisionally to the early second century: Merrifield, "Roman London," in *Atlas of Historic Towns III: The City of London*, ed. M. Lobel (Oxford: University Press, 1989), p. 19.

113. Summarized in Merrifield, *London*, pp. 140–41, and "Roman London," pp. 14–15. See further, W. F. Grimes, *The Excavation of Roman and Medieval London* (NY: Praeger, 1968); B. Yule, "The Dark Earth and Late Roman London," *Antiquity* 64 (1990), 620–628.

114. Merrifield, *London*, pp. 141–48.

115. P. Marsden and B. West, "Population Change in Roman London," *Britannia* 23 (1992), 133–40. Various causes for this depopulation have been suggested, ranging from fires, to epidemics, to banditry. Perhaps one should focus more upon increasing Romano-British economic self-sufficiency and its effects on a long-distance trading port such as London: Merrifield, *London*, pp. 144–48, 195–97.

116. Thus making London the largest walled town in Roman Britain: Ibid., pp. 154–67. The eleven-acre Cripplegate fort also was built at this time within the northwest corner of the walls.

117. The earlier quay was still in good condition: Ibid., pp. 194–97; T. Brigham, "The Late Roman Waterfront in London," *Britannia* 21 (1990), 158–59.

118. Merrifield, *London*, pp. 167–83.

119. Ibid., pp. 183–94.

120. Frere, *Britannia*, pp. 198–201; Merrifield, *London*, pp. 205, 210, 264, referring to the tradition that the medieval church of St. Peter Cornhill, built above the old Roman basilica, was on or near the site of Roman London's earliest and most important Christian church. See Stow's comments: *A Survey of London* (London: John Wolfe, 1598), pp. 151-52.

121. For these events, which were several times commemorated by special *Adventus* or *Restitutio* gold coins, see: Frere, *Britannia*, Pl. 32; Merrifield, *London*, pp. 200, 209–10, 213–16.

122. Ammianus Marcellinus, *Res gestae*, xxviii.8.7, ed. J. Rolfe (3 vols., London: W. Heinemann, 1963). It may have been bestowed as early as 305: Frere, *Britannia*, pp. 198–99; cf. Merrifield, *London*, pp. 214–15, who observes that the old name Londinium remained in general use. By this time, London had become the capital of the entire British diocese.

123. Brigham, "Waterfront," 134–41; Merrifield, "Roman London," pp. 16–17; Johnson, *Later Roman Britain*, pp. 120–32. This late work generally is attributed to Count Theodosius with a final defensive strengthening by Stilicho during his campaign in Britain (396–98).

124. Frere, *Britannia*, pp. 344–45; Merrifield, *London*, p. 216. For this system, see Map 2.1.

125. Merrifield, *London*, pp. 206, 212–13.

126. Brigham, "Waterfront," 106–11.

127. Merrifield, *London*, pp. 246–47. The Southwark suburb was virtually deserted by 400: Esmonde Cleary, *Extra-Mural Areas*, pp. 199–200. Burials in the large Romano-British cemetery outside London's east wall evidently do not extend beyond the early fifth century: B. Barber, et al., "Recent Excavations of a Cemetery of Londinium," *Britannia* 21 (1990), 1–12.

128. Merrifield, *London*, pp. 224–26, 239–55, and Fig. 33. The Tower coinage included issues of Theodosius I, Arcadius, and Honorius (388–402). The old imperial treasury still may have been housed there.

129. The continuity position was presented forcefully by Sir Mortimer Wheeler: R. E. M. Wheeler, "The Topography of Saxon London," *Antiquity* 8 (1934), 290–302, and *London and the Saxons*, Museum Catalogues, 6 (London: Museum of London, 1935). See also Frere, "End of Towns," p. 87; Biddle, "Towns," pp. 106, 109, and "A City in Transition: 400–800," in *Atlas of Historic Towns: London*, ed. Lobel (1989), pp. 20–29, esp. 21–22, who advocates settlement continuity but not urban continuity at London. For the earlier view, which saw quite an extended period of virtual abandonment at London before Anglo-Saxon occupation began c.600, see: W. Page, *London: Its Origins and Early Development* (Boston: Houghton Mifflin, 1923), pp. 29–32; C. Oman, *England before the Norman Conquest* (8th ed. rev., London: Methuen, 1938), pp. 212A–212D; cf. *ASE*, pp. 55–58, for a cautious intermediate position.

130. *ASC* 457A. See above, n.16. Neither Gildas nor the *Vita S. Germani* makes any mention of London.

131. Tatton-Brown, "The Topography of Anglo-Saxon London," *Antiquity* 60 (1986), 22; A. Vince, *Saxon London: An Archaeological Investigation* (London: Seaby, 1990), pp. 8–9.

132. Merrifield, *London*, pp. 247–55 and Figs. 37, 38, who favors the suggestion that the complex may have been an official inn (*mansio*). The presence of imported, eastern Mediterranean amphorae speaks for more than local trade, perhaps in exchange for slaves captured in Gaul or Germany and held in London. See further, Vince, *Saxon London*, pp. 7–8; Merrifield, "Roman London," p. 18. Storage buildings found at Pudding Lane (Fig. 4.7) on the east side of Old London Bridge also were

in partial use into the early fifth century: N. Bateman and G. Milne, "A Roman Harbour in London," *Britannia* 14 (1983), 219–24.

133. Merrifield, *London*, pp. 72–77, 250. For this public building's construction and plan, see Wacher, *Towns*, pp. 91–94, and Fig. 25.

134. Merrifield, *London*, p. 255; Vince, *Saxon London*, pp. 7–12, who does not envisage any significant Romano-British settlement in London after c.400.

135. Merrifield, "Roman London," p. 19; D. A. Brooks, "Evidence of Continuity," pp. 88–90; Vince, *Saxon London*, pp. 8, 12. For a host of arguments for settlement continuity, most of them attractive but all rather speculative, along with perhaps an overly strident attack against the use of negative evidence, see Biddle, "City in Transition."

136. Merrifield, *London*, pp. 256–57; Vince, "The Economic Basis of Anglo-Saxon London," in *The Rebirth of Towns in the West*, eds. R. Hodges and B. Hobley, C.B.A. 68 (London, 1988), pp. 84, 90, and *Saxon London*, pp. 11–12, with Figs. 5 and 6.

137. T. Dyson and J. Schofield, "Saxon London," in *Anglo-Saxon Towns in Southern England*, pp. 286–87, and Fig. 96. It has been speculated that many of these settlements were initially communities of Anglo-Saxon mercenaries hired by sub-Roman authorities in London to help protect the town: Myres, *English Settlements*, pp. 129–32; Biddle, "City in Transition," pp. 21–22; K. Bailey, "The Middle Saxons," in *Origins of Anglo-Saxon Kingdoms*, pp. 112–13. The large late Roman cemetery extending east of Aldgate has now yielded several early fifth-century Anglo-Saxon burials: Barber et al., "Cemetery of Londinium," 8, 11.

138. Merrifield, *London*, pp. 255–56; Dyson and Schofield, "Saxon London," pp. 300–301.

139. Bede, *Hist. Eccl.*, ii.3, and see also *ASC* 604E. The site of the first Anglo-Saxon St. Paul's is thought to lie immediately south of the medieval cathedral in the western town zone: Vince, *Saxon London*, pp. 61–62. For the proliferation of seventh-century churches in London, especially west of Walbrook along Watling Street, see Tatton-Brown, "Topography," 23. Note again that Pope Gregory I had instructed Augustine in 601 to establish his primatial see at London: Bede, *Hist. Eccl.*, i.29.

140. Ibid., ii.6. Of course, these irate Londoners could have been a royal war band rather than a general town mob. This passage contains one of the few references in the literature to an organized priesthood among the pre-Christian Anglo-Saxons or other early Germanic peoples. See Chaney, *Cult of Kingship*, pp. 62–63; also Russo, "Sacral Kingship," pp. 102–3, 146–47, 153–54 for additional Germanic instances. Upon Aethelberht's death (616), his son Eadbald immediately returned to the old religion and was followed zealously by the three joint kings of the East Saxons, who evidently also held a personal grudge against Mellitus. Even after Eadbald was converted by Bishop Laurentius of Canterbury, he still did not have enough personal authority to restore the Christian faith to London: Bede, *Hist. Eccl.*, ii.5–6. For the coinage see Chap. 5, below.

141. That is, "Basingahaga." Another high-status holding, "Staeningahaga," stood just outside the fort's south gate: Dyson and Schofield, "Saxon London," pp. 306–7; Vince, *Saxon London*, p. 55, and Fig. 29; Biddle, "City in Transition," p. 23, noting that *haga*, like *burh*, denotes an enclosure.

142. Mathew Paris, *Gesta Abbatum Monasterii Sancti Albani*, ed. H. Riley, Rolls Series 28 (3 vols., London, 1867–69), I, p. 55. The church of St. Alban Woodstreet within Cripplegate is mentioned here as being adjacent to King Offa's palace and having served as his court chapel (*Hofkapelle*). In another tradition, Aldermanbury is said to have been the site of Aethelberht's palace: *Historical Manuscripts Commission*, 9th Report (London, 1883), p. 44a.

143. *Laws of Hlothere and Eadric*, xvi, in *Laws*, ed. Attenborough; *Cart. Sax.*, ed. Birch, Nos. 117, 335; *Codex Diplomaticus Aevi Saxonici*, ed. J. M. Kemble (6 vols., London: British Historical Society, 1839–48), Nos. 351, 702, 733, 1258; Florence of Worcester, *Chronicon*, s.a. 1017, ed. Thorpe (2 vols., London: English Historical Society, 1848–49), I, p. 182.

144. Dyson and Schofield, "Saxon London," pp. 307–8; Vince, *Saxon London*, pp. 54–57.

145. See n.112, above; Tatton-Brown, "Topography," 23; Biddle, "City in Transition," pp. 23–24; Vince, *Saxon London*, p. 56.

146. Tatton-Brown, "Topography," 22–24, and Fig. 2.1.

147. Frere, *Britannia*, pp. 171, 184; Wacher, *Towns*, pp. 156, 161. See further, H. G. Ramm, "Romano-British York," in *VCH Yorkshire, City of York* (London, 1961), pp. 2–3; L. P. Wenham, "The Beginnings of Roman York," in *Soldier and Civilian in Roman Yorkshire*, ed. R. M. Butler (Leicester: University Press, 1971), pp. 45–53.

148. Wacher, *Towns*, pp. 156–66.

149. See the inscribed altar stones of wealthy York merchants who traded with Gaul: *The Roman Inscriptions of Britain*, eds. R. G. Collingwood and R. P. Wright (Oxford: Clarendon Press, 1965), Nos. 653, 678, 687. Major export industries included jet carving and linen production: Wacher, *Towns*, pp. 168–70. See further for York's industries, Jones and Mattingly, *Atlas*, pp. 217–19.

150. B. R. Hartley, "Roman York and the Northern Military Command to the Third Century A.D.," *Soldier and Civilian*, ed. Butler, pp. 55–69.

151. Wacher, *Towns*, p. 161; Frere, *Britannia*, pp. 198–99, 334–35; Butler, "The Defenses of the Fourth-Century Fortress at York," in *Soldier and Civilian*, ed. Butler, pp. 97–106; D. J. Breeze, *The Northern Frontiers of Roman Britain* (NY: St. Martin's Press, 1982), pp. 155–56; J. Campbell, "The End of Roman Britain," in *Anglo-Saxons*, ed. Campbell, p. 14, Pl. 11. York was also the main Christian episcopal see of late Roman northern Britain: Ramm, "Romano-British York," p. 2; Frere, *Britannia*, pp. 321–22; Wacher, *Towns*, p. 165.

152. H. G. Ramm, "The End of Roman York," in *Soldier and Civilian*, p. 187. For additional evidence of late Roman reduced settlement in the *colonia*, see S. Frere, et al., "Roman Britain in 1987: York," *Britannia* 19 (1988), 439-40, and "Roman Britain in 1989: York," *Britannia* 21 (1990), 325–27.

153. Ramm, "End of Roman York," pp. 187–89; Wacher, *Towns*, p. 174; Esmonde Cleary, *Extra-Mural Areas*, p. 164.

154. Arnold, *Roman Britain to Saxon England*, pp. 38–39; D. A. Brooks, "Evidence for Continuity," p. 83.

155. Ramm, "End of Roman York," pp. 185–87. See further, nn. 166–67, below.

156. Ramm, "End of Roman York," p. 186. But the York legion, Legio VI Victrix (created by Julius Caesar and stationed in York from the early second century), remained until the final Roman withdrawal from Britain: A. R. Birley, "VI Victrix

in Britain," in *Soldier and Civilian*, ed. Butler, pp. 81–96. The legionary barracks within the fortress do seem to have remained in use until the early fifth century: Ramm, "End of Roman York," pp. 186-87.

157. Ibid., pp. 181–83; S. Eyre and G. Jones, eds., *Geography As Human Ecology* (NY: St. Martin's Press, 1966), pp. 106–7.

158. Ramm, "End of Roman York," p. 183 and Fig. 28; cf. R. A. Hall, "York 700–1050," in *Rebirth of Towns*, pp. 125–26 for some cautionary remarks on this purported flooding.

159. Ramm, "End of Roman York," p. 181 (Hungate on the Ouse, southeast of the fortress). Repeated fourth-century raids by Picts and Scots also had serious effects on the urban and rural economy of northern Britain: Frere, *Britannia*, pp. 336–56; N. Higham, *The Northern Counties to A.D. 1000* (London: Longman, 1986), pp. 236–41.

160. Ramm, "End of Roman York," p. 183; Wacher, *Towns*, p. 176. For the walled fort at Brough, see, Ibid., pp. 393–97; R. Goodburn, et al., "Roman Britain in 1978: Brough-on-Humber,"*Britannia* 10 (1979), 287; B. Whitwell, "Late Roman Settlement on the Humber and Anglian Beginnings," in *Recent Research on Roman Yorkshire*, eds. J. Price, et al., B.A.R. 193 (Oxford, 1988), pp. 50–51.

161. Ramm, "End of Roman York," pp. 183–85.

162. Ibid., p. 180, and Fig. 28; M. Faull, "Roman and Anglian Settlement Patterns in Yorkshire," *Northern History* 9 (1974), 2; D. A. Brooks, "Evidence for Continuity," 89.

163. Biddle, "Towns," pp. 105–6, 110; Myres, *English Settlements*, pp. 103, 187–89, 195–96; P. Hunter Blair, *An Introduction to Anglo-Saxon England* (2d ed. Cambridge: University Press, 1977), p. 43, and *Northumbria in the Days of Bede* (NY: St. Martin's Press, 1976), pp. 26–29; Hill, "Continuity from Roman to Medieval," p. 301; Ramm, "Romano-British York," p. 3; Fisher, *Anglo-Saxon Age*, p. 15.

164. D. A. Brooks, "Evidence for Continuity," pp. 85, 95; Ramm, "End of Roman York," p. 191; Hall, "York," p. 126, noting that the Anglo-Saxon cemeteries could have served extra-mural rural settlements. See also in general, R. Cramp, "Northumbria: The Archaeological Evidence," in *Power and Politics in Early Medieval Britain and Ireland*, eds. S. Driscoll and M. Nieke (Edinburgh: University Press, 1988), pp. 69–78.

165. *Annales Cambriae*, s.a. 573, 580, ed. J. Morris (London: Phillimore, 1980); cf. Nennius, *Hist. Britt.*, lxvi a, ed. Morris. See further, Faull, "Settlement Patterns," 23–24; Hall, "York," p. 125; Whitewell, "Settlement on the Humber," pp. 69–72; Higham, *Northern Counties*, pp. 259–62; Dumville, "The Origins of Northumbria: Some Aspects of the British Background," in *Origins of Anglo-Saxon Kingdoms*, pp. 213–22, esp. 214–17.

166. Biddle, "Towns," p. 110; J. Campbell, "The Lost Centuries: 400–600," in *Anglo-Saxons*, ed. Campbell, p. 39, Pl. 38; Rahtz, "Gazetteer," p. 452; Ramm, "End of Roman York," pp. 185–86.

167. D. A. Brooks, "Evidence for Continuity," pp. 85–86; Hall, "York," p. 126.

168. P. V. Addyman, "Anglo-Scandinavian York," in *The Anglo-Saxons*, ed. Campbell, p. 166; Ramm, "End of Roman York," pp. 184–85. For the "Anglian Tower," see: Johnson, *Later Roman Britain*, p. 192, Pl. 50.

169. Bede, *Hist. Eccl.* ii.14; ASC 626, 626E. At the time, Edwin, king of Northumbrian Deira, had also been *Bretwalda* for nearly a decade (ASC 617E). Before his baptism, he had conquered the upland British kingdom of Elmet west of the Vale of York (Map 3.1): Bede, *Hist. Eccl.* ii.9; Nennius, *Hist. Britt.*, lxiii. According to Northumbrian tradition, Edwin's dynasty had begun to rule in Deira during the mid- to late fifth century: ibid., lxi; Dumville, "Anglian Collection of Royal Genealogies." See further, M. Miller, "The Dates of Deira," *Anglo-Saxon England* 8 (1979), pp. 35–61; Dumville, "Origins of Northumbria."

170. Addyman, "York and Canterbury as Ecclesiastical Centres," in *European Towns*, pp. 500–501. It did not lie exactly on the medieval minster site, as formerly assumed.

171. Ibid. The episcopal precinct apparently occupied all or most of the fortress's western area by a royal grant of 685: *Historia de Sancto Cuthberto*, v, ed. T. Arnold, in *Symeonis Monachi Opera*, Rolls Ser., 75 (2 vols., London, 1885), I.

172. *The Earliest Life of Gregory the Great*, xv, ed. B. Colgrave (Lawrence: University of Kansas Press, 1968). But for recent doubts about the passage's historicity and its identification with York, see C. Daniell, "York and the Whitby Author's *Anonymous Life of Gregory the Great*," *Northern History* 29 (1993), 197–99.

173. Hall, "York," pp. 126–28; Addyman, "Ecclesiastical Centres," pp. 502-503.

174. Sutherland, *English Coinage*, Pl. 2; P. Grierson and M. Blackburn, *Medieval European Coinage I: The Early Middle Ages* (Cambridge: University Press, 1986), p. 643; Hall, "York," p. 128. See Chaps. 5 and 7 for further discussion of Anglo-Saxon and Viking age York, London, and their commercial-industrial foci.

Chapter 5

The Age of Anglo-Saxon
Emporia (c.600–850 A.D.)

During the seventh and eighth centuries, a new and important type of urban place appeared in Anglo-Saxon England. These sites, variously called "emporia," "*wics*," or "gateway communities," are now becoming recognized by historians and archaeologists as having played significant roles both in the economic growth and the political consolidation of pre-Alfredian England.[1] Indeed, many of these newly founded centers of trade and industry evidently were involved not only in local economic activity but also participated in overseas trade via a network of similar new towns in northwest Europe. Examples of these emporia in Anglo-Saxon England are Hamwic in Wessex, Ipswich in East Anglia, Fordwich and Sandwich in Kent, along with Aldwych on the Strand next to London and Eorforwic outside York (Map 5.1).

Among this group of new Anglo-Saxon towns, Hamwic has been receiving particularly intensive archaeological attention (Fig. 5.1.A).[2] The site, covering some 40 to 70 acres, lay on low ground near the mouth of the River Itchen, about one-quarter mile northeast of medieval Southampton and one mile downstream from the old Roman fortress of Clausentum (Bitterne). Hamwic's location thus provided ready access to both the Channel via the Solent and interior Wessex via the Itchen and the old Roman road from Clausentum to Winchester and beyond.[3]

A series of distinct developmental stages can be identified at Hamwic. Evidence of the earliest settlement phase (c.690) is rather slight, but includes several dispersed timber frame structures, two inhumation cemeteries with one or more associated churches, several Anglo-Saxon *sceattas* or proto-pennies of the initial series, and sherds of grass-tempered pottery.[4] No previous British or Roman occupation on the site is attested. The period from c.700 to 750 evidently saw intensified activity at Hamwic. A regular street grid divided the town into fenced "blocks" (*insulae*), each containing numerous tightly packed buildings of varying timber styles. Behind the larger buildings stood smaller structures identified as workshops, as well as refuse pits and timber-lined wells. Indeed, these pits and wells have yielded valuable evidence of substantial industrial and commercial activity and have allowed a more precise chronology by the coin deposits found there. Among the industrial operations attested at Hamwic are iron smelting and smithing, bronze, lead, and silverworking, textile production, and pottery making. Items indicating cross-Channel trade are also abundant, including imported pottery and luxury glassware from northern France and Germany.[5] This industrial and commercial vitality, coupled with dense permanent occupation, is very noteworthy; indeed, such a concentration of urban features had not been seen in Britain since the fourth century.

Hamwic's interconnecting roads were metaled with flints and appear to have been frequently resurfaced. The uniformity of these operations along with the regular street network itself and the maintenance of property alignments all suggest some central planning and direction.[6] Botanical and faunal studies indicate that Hamwic's inhabitants were quite well fed. Barley, wheat, and corn were the main cereal crops, grown most likely on the arable fields immediately adjoining the town. Beef cattle and unusually large sheep were also apparently brought into the town on the hoof in large numbers for slaughter.[7] Estimates of Hamwic's population range from 4,000 to 9,000, making it larger than any other contemporary Wessex site.[8] In sum, Hamwic appears as a thriving, well-provisioned and regulated, bustling town community of traders and artisans. There are indications, however, that this apparent prosperity declined after the mid-eighth century. The reasons for this constriction are complex and will need further examination, but by the closing decades of the eighth century, a population and settlement shift seems to have been underway from Hamwic southward to the site of medieval Southampton and perhaps also inland to Winchester.[9]

The Hamwic coinage provides a valuable key to the town's development.[10] The main coin-deposit phase belongs to the first half of the eighth century and includes a wide variety of so-called secondary *sceattas* from southern, central, and eastern England. Indeed, the quantity of this coinage well identifies this period as the zenith of Hamwic's prosperity. Moreover, it now appears that two types of sceattas were issued directly from a mint located in the town. In fact, all of Wessex's coinage prior to the ninth century is currently believed to have been minted in Hamwic.[11] Following a brief hiatus during the late eighth century, a series of Offa of Mercia's silver pennies circulated at Hamwic until c.825. After this, coin finds drop dramatically, which likely indicates the town's final economic decline.

In addition to these recent archaeological disclosures, written evidence also attests to the important role Hamwic played as a port and trading center from the early eighth century. For example, in 721 St. Willibald and his companions reportedly took ship for the Continent at Hamblemouth "nearby that trading place (*mercimonium*) which is called Hamwih."[12] Moreover, Hamwic appears to have given its name to the shire of Hampshire (Hamtunscir) at this time.[13] That it should have been Hamwic and not Winchester is significant, since Anglo-Saxon shires generally took the name of their leading town.[14] The remembrance, a century later, of a particularly destructive fire in Hamwic (764) also points to a substantial settlement density during the mid- to late eighth century.[15] Furthermore, Wessex charters of the ninth and tenth centuries indicate that there was a royal vill at Hamtun, where the king and his following were sometimes present.[16] Although the town appears to have declined in the ninth century, it was still sufficiently prominent to be the target of repeated Viking attacks. In 840, Wulfheard, ealdorman of Wessex, defeated a Danish fleet of thirty-three ships off Hamwic,[17] but two years later the town and its inhabitants were ravaged by the Danes.[18] This event no doubt hastened the contraction and settlement-shift previously suggested. Still, prior to the Viking raids Hamwic clearly was a town, with planned streets, churches, mint, dense and permanent settlement, and notable commercial and industrial functions.

The etymology of Hamwic's name is also instructive. In Anglo-Saxon written sources, the town is primarily referred to as Hamwic or Hamtun.[19] *Ham* appears to have been an early Anglo-Saxon generic term for a civilian, domestic settlement. On the other hand, *wic* apparently designated a place known for its commercial or industrial activity. It evidently derived from Latin *vicus* ("small town"), which had these same primary functions in Roman Britain.[20] Hamwic's name thus aptly reflects its role as a trading and production settlement, which is seen in the historical and archaeological evidence. Another significant feature that archaeology has revealed about this important group of Anglo-Saxon *wic*-towns is their apparent lack of defenses or fortifications. In this respect they stand quite apart from former Roman walled towns, which generally were named by the early Anglo-Saxons with *castrum* derivatives (e.g., -caster, -ceaster, -chester).[21] At Hamwic, no evidence of defensive works has been found, and what this lack implies will need to be examined. For the moment, however, it may merely be noted that Hamwic's name-form well represents its function as one of a significant group of newly founded towns distinctively engaged in trade and industry.

The period of Hamwic's foundation and main development coincides with Winchester's rise to prominence as the royal and ecclesiastical capital of Wessex. As has been seen, however, seventh and eighth-century Winchester was not primarily a commercial and industrial center, although imported luxury items and local domestic wares have been found there. Its urban features were limited to its defenses, ecclesiastical and probably royal compounds, and associated low-level economic activity. It thus appears not unlikely that Hamwic had been deliberately founded to supply the demand for imported luxuries and craft products created by the growth of Wessex's inland capital at Winchester. The two towns are indeed a complementary pair: the one (Winchester) a royal, ecclesiastical, inward-looking administrative site, and the other (Hamwic) an active, outward-looking, commercial and industrial "boom town," with intensive economic activity, regular street plan, large settled population, churches,and mint.[22] Both were connected by road and waterway. For its part, Hamwic's growth seems also to have furthered Winchester's development. For example, the impressive expansion of Winchester's southern and western suburbs in the eighth and ninth centuries has been attributed to the stimulus of trade from Hamwic.[23]

This suggested interrelationship between Hamwic and Winchester becomes clearer with an examination of the record of the two towns during the ninth century. Whatever its cause, Hamwic's decline rather strikingly corresponded with Winchester's growth as an Alfredian burgh. At the close of the ninth century, Winchester had a newly imposed street system, a relatively large and diversified population with distinct tenements, refurbished defenses, an active town market, and at least one mint (Fig. 4.5.B).[24] Hamwic, on the other hand, had been largely abandoned as a site of permanent settlement. A shift of Hamwic's merchants and craftsmen to the inland capital may well account at least in part for Alfredian Winchester's intensified urban functions and character.[25] A similar emigration to nearby Southampton on the Test could also have promoted this town's development as a major international port of the tenth century.[26] It may also be observed that unlike Hamwic, both Winchester and Southampton were fortified in the late ninth century.[27] Despite its eventual displacement, Hamwic had nonetheless clearly played a significant role as the main entrepôt and production center of pre-Alfredian Wessex.

Several features in Hamwic's topography have been noted that suggest it was a deliberately planned town, founded and structured at one moment in the late seventh century. Indeed, the very size of the site and its managed development point to a royal establishment. If so, the most likely architect would be King Ine, whose long reign (688–726) ushered in a noteworthy period of peace and prosperity for Wessex. Ine was recognized during most of his life as the leading king in southern England, an influential supporter and organizer of the West Saxon Church, and a notable law giver.[28] His famous law code attests to significant trading activities in the realm, primarily, though not exclusively, along the south coast.[29] Although Hamwic is not specifically named, early eighth-century charters from Kent and Mercia imply that contemporary kings derived considerable profit from tolls collected on trade at their own "*wic*-towns."[30] Indeed, the royal interests at such trading centers could be maintained by a special "king's *wic*-reeve."[31]

Finally, a brief entry in the *Anglo-Saxon Chronicle* implies that Ine may also have established towns in those regions that he had annexed to Wessex. This annal, for 722, speaks tantalizingly of the destruction of Taunton (Somerset) "which Ine had built."[32]

Some suggestions can be made concerning how Hamwic was able to be established. First, we learn from Ine's Code that this king had exacted certain services and rents from every freeman in his realm. In addition to the obligation of army (*fyrd*) service, everyone holding ten hides or more of land was required to render substantial food rents in kind (*fostre*, and later *feorm*) to the king.[33] Most of these supplies went to support the royal household, but a recent quantitative analysis has demonstrated that such provisions would generate more than adequate reserves to supply the population of such an emporium as Hamwic.[34] It is also possible that Hamwic had been built by corvée work. Certain eighth-century charters do speak of labor obligations imposed by kings on holders of bookland (land granted by charter) for construction of public works and royal vills.[35] Such services were distinct from the universal threefold obligations of *fyrd* service, the building of fortresses, and the construction of bridges. This could imply that the West Saxon nobility was also involved in Hamwic's creation, a process that may be a precursor of the aristocratic management of separate *insulae* in late Anglo-Saxon towns.[36] Whether Hamwic is regarded, then, as a profitable extension of the royal household or as a collection of noble holdings under royal aegis, the town and its commercial and industrial workers no doubt prospered as a result of Ine's long reign. Indeed, though the sources are mute, some integrating administrative machinery must have been put in place, since Hamwic continued to flourish long after Ine's abdication (726) and the subsequent political turmoil in Wessex.[37] It has also been plausibly suggested that Ine saw in Hamwic's foundation not only economic advantages but also a means to increase his prestige and secure dynastic authority from potential rivals.[38]

Hamwic's lack of fortifications has already been observed. There is no historical or archaeological evidence that the town was attacked prior to the Viking assault of 840, although Wessex had its share of both interstate warfare and Viking raids before the ninth century.[39] Some kind of effective protection must have been extended to Hamwic, which, after all, was a very exposed coastal site. Had the town been a royal establishment, however, the king would logically have been responsible for its defense and well-being. This security may have been provided from the *villa regalis*, which stood somewhere in or close by Hamwic. If not in the town, a likely location would have been within the nearby Roman fortress of Clausentum, where recent excavations have revealed sporadic Anglo-Saxon occupation from the late fifth to the late ninth centuries.[40]

Some final comments are in order regarding Hamwic's regular street pattern. This feature, remarkable at first sight for its early date, seems to have been a characteristic of many *wics* established in both England and along the North Sea coast during the seventh and eighth centuries.[41] It is clearly not the street pattern of Anglo-Saxon rural settlement or of early Anglo-Saxon reoccupation in many former Roman towns.[42] Rather, this regular internal street arrangement most closely resembles a skeletonized version of the Graeco-Roman urban plan.[43] As we shall see, prototypes for Hamwic's street grid may have existed in Kent and several new towns on the North Sea coast. It is also possible, however, that Ine and other contemporary rulers derived the concept from those Roman cultural influences then flooding into Anglo-Saxon England with the Christian missionary tide.[44] Anglo-Saxon law codes and charters are well-known written products of this ideological influx. In the architectural sphere, apart from a host of monastic basilicas built within various former Roman towns, one can mention the Mediterranean-type amphitheater erected within the seventh-century Northumbrian royal compound at Yeavering and the Roman-style watermill with vertical wheel built in the late seventh century on the West Saxon royal manor at Old Windsor.[45] Whatever may have been the inspiration, it is not too far-fetched to regard Hamwic's regular street pattern as predecessor to the better-known geometric street grid later established within Alfredian burghs—both those newly-founded and those rebuilt.[46]

Another Anglo-Saxon emporium, apparently older than Hamwic and displaying a somewhat different developmental pattern, was located at Ipswich in East Anglia (Fig. 5.1.B).[47] Systematic excavations begun in 1974 revealed evidence of a major trading and production settlement established c.625 on low-lying ground at the sheltered head of the River Orwell estuary. Like Hamwic, Ipswich was a large, initially unfortified site (125 acres), set up on previously vacant land and equipped in its core area with a regular street network.[48] As at Hamwic, dating has been made possible by examination of stratified pits and wells, imported and local pottery, cemetery finds, and coin deposits. Unlike Hamwic, however, Ipswich was continuously occupied from early Anglo-Saxon times up to and beyond the Norman Conquest, when it was a thriving borough town.[49] This continuous occupation has hindered excavations at Ipswich, where only 2 percent of the total site has yet been examined. Nonetheless, work to date has yielded important results.

Ipswich's initial occupation period (early seventh century) is marked by several inhumation burials with simple grave goods and also scattered finds of imported Frankish pottery.[50] A large Anglian cemetery containing burials dated c.575–625 lay just two miles to the east at Hadleigh Road.[51] On the immediate fringes of the settlement were farms and arable fields under cultivation at this time, and along the riverfront simple post-and-wattle revetments for off-loading light vessels probably belong to this early phase.[52]

An analysis of the imported ceramics at Ipswich suggests that initial trade was conducted primarily with the Merovingian Rhineland and Frisia. Wares from northern Francia are far less numerous than at Hamwic, for example. Finds of later-style vessels indicate that Ipswich maintained its Rhenish commerce into the early ninth century.[53] By far the most widespread pottery type at the site is that known in archaeological circles as Ipswich ware. This stout, well-fired, gray domestic pottery spans the period 650–850 and has been found in large quantities throughout East Anglia, as well as aristocratic sites as far away as Kent and Yorkshire.[54] Recent excavations now confirm that Ipswich was the major production center for this elite ware. The industry appears to have been concentrated specifically in the northeast quadrant of the town, where the discovery of several kilns and extensive waste deposits suggests prolonged and controlled mass production.[55] Other industries attested at Ipswich include weaving along with iron, bone, and leatherworking. These operations were evenly distributed over the site and were apparently conducted on a smaller scale than the ceramic industry.[56] Notably absent are any signs of gold, silver, gem working, or glass production such as were seen at Hamwic. Precious metals may have been either less available or were put to other uses. Also, evidence of industrial buildings is more meager, though excavation in Ipswich has not been as extensive as at the West Saxon emporium.

Numismatic findings provide a further index of Ipswich's development. Concentrations of secondary *sceattas* indicate, for example, that the town reached its peak of economic activity in the mid-eighth century.[57] The most prevalent coinage is of a type whose distribution is largely confined to East Anglia and may have been minted in Ipswich itself.[58] Like contemporary Hamwic coinage, it is a runic-style issue, although after c.760 there appear coins in the name of the obscure East Anglian king Beonna, modeled on the reformed Carolingian silver penny.[59] The scarcity of subsequent coin-finds suggests an economic decline after East Anglia, and apparently Ipswich, passed grudgingly under Mercian suzereignty during the later eighth century. Still, an Ipswich mint, striking primarily for Mercian kings but also for an occasional bold local ruler, is believed to have operated until the Viking conquest of East Anglia in 869.[60] Indeed, the increased evidence of Anglo-Viking coinage c.875–920 found in Ipswich intimates that the Danes brought renewed prosperity to the settlement.[61] Several other early East Anglian emporia have recently been identified near Ipswich.[62] Though participants in East Anglian trade c.650–750, they appear to have played a smaller, less continuous role than Ipswich, which, on the basis of recent archaeological excavations, was the primary commercial and industrial center for the East Anglian realm by the eighth century.

In fact, were it not for the archaeological work underway at Ipswich, we would have little clue of the site's importance before 1066. The historical record of Anglo-Saxon Ipswich is scanty and of late date. For example, the town is first mentioned in connection with the second great Viking invasion of England late in the tenth century. In 992, the Norse leader Olaf Tryggvason (Old English: Anlaf) harried the countryside of Ipswich (Gipeswic) prior to his renowned victory at Maldon.[63] Twenty years later, Thurkil's Danish host landed at Ipswich and plundered East Anglia for three months before moving on to burn the towns of Thetford and Cambridge.[64]

The beginnings of Anglo-Saxon Ipswich can be further clarified by observing the sixth- and seventh-century historical context of East Anglia in which it emerged. Anglian royal genealogies suggest that a certain family led by one Wuffa had established an hereditary kingship over the East Angles during the mid-sixth century.[65] Bede supports this general chronology by noting that Wuffa, after whom East Anglian kings were called the Wuffing-as, was the grandfather of King Raedwald (c.599–624), the East Anglian *Bretwalda*. He also observes that the Wuffingas had a royal vill at Rendle-sham, in the Sandlings district of southeast Suffolk some seven miles east of Ipswich (Map 3.1).[66] The Wuffingas were clearly a family with which to be reckoned. Indeed, prior to the consolidation of Mercia under King Penda in the early seventh century, East Anglia appears to have been the most powerful realm in southern England.[67]

Archaeological and place-name studies confirm the documentary evidence that fifth-century Anglian settlement around the Wash was dense and quite early. Recent systematic field research in southeast Suffolk points to an intensification of rural settlement c.475–550 and the consolidation of small hamlets under the authority of a single aristocratic family.[68] A number of specific rich burials in East Anglia can likely be assigned to the Wuffingas. The fifth- and sixth-century cemeteries at Spong Hill (Norfolk) and Snape (Suffolk), for example, both contained spatially separated graves of high-status individuals.[69] The most renowned among these early East Anglian sites is Sutton Hoo (Map 3.1), located in the Sandlings district close by Ipswich. Excavation of the famous Mound 1 boat grave yielded outstandingly rich grave goods and symbolic items that reasonably identify this site as a royal East Anglian cenotaph, erected perhaps to Raedwald.[70] Its wealth alone attests to the considerable resources available to seventh-century East Anglian kings and the wide range of their commercial and cultural contacts. Merovingian gold coins, eastern Mediterranean ("Coptic") utensils, and ceremonial accoutrements of likely Swedish origins are the most prominent examples.[71]

One has to wonder how such prestige objects had entered East Anglian territory. A likely answer would be through the nearby emporium at Ipswich, whose origins are closely contemporary with Raedwald's reign. Although it would be overly hazardous to single out Raedwald as Ipswich's founder, or to attribute modern economic motives to either this or other contemporary rulers, the evidence certainly suggests that Ipswich began and prospered under the commercial and political tutelage of the Wuffingas, who maintained a royal seat not far away. As an entrepôt created primarily to supply the needs of the East Anglian kings, it would parallel the likely royal foundation of Hamwic in Wessex.[72] Additional material evidence tends to support this conclusion. For example, the *sceatta* coinage found at Ipswich appears to be a product of the trade route extending from the Rhineland to southern Sweden, whose main English participants were the East Angles. The ceramic evidence linking East Anglia to this Rhenish-North Sea route has already been noted. Indeed, if the Wuffingas were a clan of Swedish (Vendel) warlords, as is often suggested, these trading connections become more comprehensible as continuing ties with the homeland.[73] Furthermore, elite Ipswich ware has been found at Sutton Hoo, and a sherd of this pottery recently uncovered in Ipswich bears a curious face-mask imprint remarkably like the face on the Sutton Hoo royal whetstone scepter.[74]

Ipswich therefore can be recognized as a major trading and production-distribution center for the early East Anglian kingdom. Like Hamwic in Wessex, it represents an important new form of specialized urban settlement, which significantly appeared in conjunction with the creation of firm royal dynastic control in various Anglo-Saxon kingdoms. Indeed, the establishment and direction of these coastal centers of trade and production appear to have generated both state-building wealth and interstate aggression.[75] The previously observed designs of landlocked Mercia on Ipswich during the eighth century are but one example of this process.

Certain differences can be recognized, however, between the early emporia of Wessex and East Anglia. For example, Hamwic appears to have been the only coastal emporia in Wessex, whereas several emporia are evident in early East Anglia prior to the ascendancy of Ipswich. Attempts have thus been made to devise a developmental typology of these sites. One prominent scheme, energetically propounded by Richard Hodges, depicts the earliest Anglo-Saxon emporia as temporary coastal or riverine trading settlements ("Type A"), which then expanded to include areas of warehouse facilities for periodic commerce. Only later, during the eighth century, were planned street networks and industrial workshops provided, as the emporia came under central, probably royal, direction and acquired full urban status ("Type B").[76]

Although this model is thought provoking, there is equally good, and perhaps better, evidence that Hamwic and Ipswich were planned, permanent settlements under royal aegis from their earliest days. Indeed, royal involvement with certain emporia may have given them precedence over similar competing sites, though there is no necessity to equate this involvement with deliberate monopolistic policy. Nor is there a need to wait until the mid-eighth century to designate these sites as urban. Finally, as noted in chapter one, the Hodges model suggests a deceptive linear, deterministic development. The Anglo-Saxon emporia clearly underwent changes in topography and function, but each case must be carefully considered on the merits of its own evidence before conclusions and comparisons can be drawn.

The early kingdom of Kent also seems to have been served by a number of emporia from the late sixth through the eighth centuries. These include Fordwich, Sarre, Sandwich, and Dover. Kentish trade with the Merovingian Franks evidently increased dramatically during the reign of King Aethelberht (c.560–618). Luxury items in particular made their way into Kent in quantities that well attest to this kingdom's outstanding wealth. It was also at this time that Aethelberht made the old Roman town of Canterbury his political and ecclesiastical capital, a decision followed by intensified Anglo-Saxon settlement within the walls. Still, Canterbury apparently remained primarily an administrative and ceremonial rather than a commercial and industrial town during the seventh and eighth centuries.[77]

The bulk of Kentish prestige goods now appears to have entered the realm via a group of emporia deliberately founded to facilitate elite cross-Channel trade. Among these, Fordwich, some three miles east of Canterbury, was the most prominent (Fig. 5.2.A). Just outside Canterbury's eastern wall stood St. Augustine's Abbey and, slightly beyond, St. Martin's Church.[78] An extent of gravel land then stretched eastward to the mouth of the Stour, terminating at Fordwich. Preliminary excavations of this entire area, belonging to Canterbury's jurisdiction in Anglo-Saxon times, suggest the presence of an early emporium or *wic* serving the Kentish capital. Concentrations of Ipswich ware as well as primary- and secondary-series *sceattas* indicate a significant level of commercial activity on this new site from at least the seventh century.[79] Fordwich itself first appears in the historical record in 675 (Fordewicum) in a charter of King Hlothere of Kent, whose law code also mentions a Kentish *wic*-reeve.[80] Later Kentish royal charters of 747 and 761 granted to the monasteries at Reculver and Minster (Thanet) freedom from shipping tolls formerly exacted by the Kentish kings at Fordwich.[81] These references suggest a significant and profitable amount of trade initially under royal control. It may also be observed that the early Kentish royal vill at Sturry, which lay just across the Stour from Fordwich, could have provided protection for the unfortified emporium.[82]

Another early Kentish emporium has been identified at Sarre beside the Wantsum Channel on the Isle of Thanet. In 1863, a large Anglo-Saxon cemetery of sixth- and seventh-century date was uncovered here. The nearly three hundred excavated graves yielded evidence of a prosperous community with varied occupations. Most of the burials were of males accompanied by full weaponry, but several also included sets of balances, along with Frankish and Byzantine *tremisses*. Other signs of commercial activity at Sarre were imported pottery, glassware, bronze "Coptic" bowls, jeweled brooches, and Middle Eastern cowrie shell ornaments. Finds of metalworking crucibles and carpentry tools suggest further industrial activity.[83] Although still a matter of some debate, the Sarre burials can perhaps be interpreted as representing a mixed community of traders and militia assigned to guard the emporium.[84]

Sarre may also have had some commercial relation to the early religious houses of eastern Kent. For example, large quantities of primary *sceattas* from the late seventh century have been found at Reculver some five miles north of Sarre.[85] This site, which had been an important Saxon Shore fort (Regulbium), was reportedly given by King Egbert of Kent to his priest, Bass, for the establishment of a monastery (669).[86] As we have seen, Reculver was one of the houses directly involved in trade at Kentish emporia during the eighth century. St. Peter's Minster on Thanet is also specifically said to have been granted toll remission at Sarre (Serrae/Seorre).[87] Such evidence could indicate that Sarre functioned primarily as a monastic emporium by the eighth century. The role of the Kentish Church as an active economic institutions to some extent in competition with royal economic programs should not be underestimated.[88]

Two additional early Kentish emporia must be considered. Sandwich, situated at the eastern mouth of the Wantsum Channel, appears to have been an important port from at least the mid-seventh century (Fig. 5.2.B). St. Wilfrid, for example, is said to have disembarked at Sandwich (Sandwic) in 664 after returning from his episcopal consecration on the Continent.[89] During the fifth and sixth centuries, this area was the major access way into southeast England. Both Hengist and Horsa, and St. Augustine's party, reportedly had entered Kent via the eastern Wantsum.[90] The late Roman fort at Richborough (Rutupiae), some two miles north of Sandwich, had guarded this important passage. Indeed, the probable silting of the bay at Richborough by the seventh century may have led to the establishment of a new haven at Sandwich.[91]

The site had an excellent natural harbor, protected by an extensive offshore shingle bank. In addition to its ease of access to the sea, Sandwich was connected by trackways to the seventh-century royal vill at Eastry two miles inland, and thence to the rich agricultural areas of eastern Kent.[92] Although much of Sandwich's earliest occupation levels have now been encroached upon by the sea, there are indications that here, as at Fordwich, a regular street grid was in place by the eighth century.[93] Furthermore, as in the case of Sarre and Reculver, Sandwich may have had early commercial ties to the small religious community established at Richborough within the old Saxon Shore fort.[94] Along with Hamwic and Ipswich, Sandwich was a target for the Viking assaults, and its harbor saw several major naval engagements.[95]   But unlike Hamwic, the settlement survived these setbacks and became an important port and borough of late Anglo-Saxon England.[96]

More concerted archaeological work has been underway on Anglo-Saxon occupation levels at Dover. In the fourth century, Dover (Dubris) was a major Roman harbor and naval base equipped with a massive Saxon Shore fortress and lighthouse. Progressive silting, however, seems to have relocated the port site toward the south, in the area known significantly as the Wyke in medieval times.[97]   Recent excavations have revealed evidence of initial early Anglo-Saxon settlement, including sunken huts dated to the sixth century, within the fort at Dover, and traces of a rectilinear street grid have been found in the proposed adjacent emporium area.[98]   Just outside the fort's walls, several fifth- to seventh-century Anglo-Saxon cemeteries have been disclosed. One of these (Buckland, late fifth century) contained a majority of burials well furnished with armaments, much like the Sarre cemetery but a century earlier. Finds of Frankish glass beakers at Buckland also suggest very early Kentish trading activity in the Dover area.[99]   That Anglo-Saxon Dover (Dofras) was an important port of the early Kentish realm is attested by a (toll?) charter (696 X 716 A.D.) of King Wihtred.[100] At about this time, the same king is believed to have founded Dover's first minster (St. Martin's) within the old walled fortress.[101]   In addition to its trading activities, Dover has also been identified as a likely production center for the elaborate seventh-century Kentish disc brooches.[102]

Further evidence relating to Anglo-Saxon Dover is still somewhat fragmentary. It has been suggested that the decay of the Roman fort's east wall left an inlet, which provided a suitable trading or emporium area. This site, in turn, later became the medieval marketplace.[103]   Archaeologists have found a number of fairly substantial buildings, some containing loom weights, at Dover, but these structures cannot be dated more closely than c.850–1066.[104] At any rate, the establishment of a royal mint here c.930 is usually regarded as evidence of a sizable trading community established for some time.[105]   The *Anglo-Saxon Chronicle*, in a very lively entry for 1048, confirms the presence of a significant body of townsmen who were quite willing and able to defend themselves. Certainly by 1066 Dover ranked as an important borough and major port of a group of southern towns holding special fiscal privileges. In return for providing the king with annual ship service, the townsmen of Dover enjoyed freedom from tolls throughout England and the profits of justice in their own court.[106]

Among the more exciting discoveries of recent medieval urban archaeology has been the disclosure of early Anglo-Saxon emporia outside the major towns of London and York. As we have seen in our previous look at London, there is virtually no evidence for any continuity of settlement within the walled site from late and sub-Roman times to the late sixth or early seventh century. Instead, London appears to represent a case of Anglo-

Saxon reoccupation on a former Roman site that had been largely abandoned for perhaps over a century after c.450 A.D. When Anglo-Saxon intramural settlement did occur, moreover, it evidently was primarily a high-status royal and ecclesiastical reoccupation, much as in the cases of Canterbury and Winchester.[107]

The dearth of archaeological evidence for commercial activity stands in sharp contrast to the rather abundant historical testimony of active trade at London c.650–850. For example, a late seventh-century charter of Frithuwold, subking of Surrey, first mentions "the port of London, where ships tie up."[108] At this time London apparently had come under effective control of the Mercians, who may have been deliberately seeking an active trading outlet.[109] As noted previously, the seventh-century kings of Kent also maintained a royal hall at London, supervised by a *wic*-reeve, where Kentish merchants could obtain warranties for their purchases.

The details of this early trade are not entirely clear, though there are strong indications that slaves were major exports. Bede, for example, mentions an incident (679) where an Anglo-Saxon prisoner was sold at London as a slave to a Frisian.[110] The interkingdom warfare that marked the early Anglo-Saxon period no doubt had generated a brisk market in English slaves, as Gregory the Great's memorable remarks on Angles and angels must remind us.[111] Many early Anglo-Saxon *sceattas* minted at London (and copies) have been found in Frisia, and Frisian traders were actively engaged from their own emporia in North Sea commerce, including slave trading, as middlemen between eastern and western Europe. Other items of trade through early Anglo-Saxon London likely included textiles and salt for Frankish pottery, glassware, wine, and quernstones.[112] The Kentish interests in London and their Frankish connections may well account for this particular high-status trade.

There are indications that the scale of London's commerce, and its control by Mercia, was increasing in the early eighth century. King Aethelbald, for example, was in a position to confer minor toll exemptions at London on a variety of religious houses in eastern England, including Minster-on-Thanet (733), Rochester (734), and Worcester (743 X 745 A.D.). In these charters, London is described as a port (*portus, hydh*).[113] Aethelbald's action would indicate the presence of Mercian officials comparable to the Kentish *wic*-reeve; the Worcester charter specifically mentions tax collectors at the port. A slightly later charter of King Offa (790) demonstrates that this powerful Mercian king had received lucrative dues "in gold, silver, and other renders" at the port (*portus*) in addition to shipping tolls.[114] Also, Willibald, in his *Life of St. Boniface* (written 754–768), refers to London as Lundenwich and mentions its market.[115] Indeed, Bede himself, early in the second book of his *History* (chap. 3), calls

London in his time "a trading center (*emporium*) for many nations who visit it by land and sea."

The fact that these pre-Alfredian sources refer to London as a port or emporium (*wic*) rather than a fortified burgh is significant. Before considering the implications of this, however, attention must be given to early Anglo-Saxon London's coinage. The first coins to be issued in Britain since the fourth century were the Anglo-Saxon gold "thirds," or *thrymsas*. Some of this early coinage apparently was struck at Canterbury, but others clearly issued from a mint in London. Among these, the largest number bear a central cross surrounded by the mint name "Londiniu(m)," with an obverse-facing bust that could be either royal or priestly. Another type has profile busts and inscriptions "Londinium," and a third variety, perhaps the earliest, bears the name "Londenus" and an obverse legend, "Auduarld Reges" (most likely Eadbald of Kent, 616–640, Aethelberht's son). The full series of London *thrymsas* is believed to date c.625–675.[116] Kentish involvement in London's commerce has already been observed from legal sources of the 680s; the numismatic evidence would take this activity back at least a half-century. Considering the Kentish kings' critical role in the rebirth of London as a royal and episcopal center, they may well have been instrumental in the creation of this coinage.

The London mint (or mints) expanded its operation to the production of the silver "proto-pennies," or *sceattas*, which replaced gold coinage c.675 in response to Frankish initiative. Certain early *sceattas* (c.670–710) are generally held to be of London provenance, though they bear no specific identifications. Their distribution, like the London *thrymsas*, is confined primarily to east Kent and the Thames Valley, with outliers in East Anglia and the Midlands.[117] An important series of later *sceattas* (c.730–760), however, does bear the mint-mark "(De) Lundonia" around a profile bust with reverse of a standing figure with a diadem holding one or two large crosses. This coinage enjoyed a wide circulation in the Thames Valley, eastern and central England, East Anglia, and Frisia.[118] It will be noted that these issues coincide with the period of intensified Mercian-directed trade at London. Indeed, the plausible suggestion has been made that King Aethelbald was responsible for this coinage, which marked his control over the town.[119] In any case, London was by all indications one of the most prolific mints in England from the mid-seventh century. Since Anglo-Saxon gold and, especially, silver coins were intended primarily as instruments of cross-Channel commerce, the appearance of these London issues presupposes the establishment of substantial trade there.[120]

This body of evidence for significant commerce at London during the seventh and eighth centuries contrasts strongly with the paucity of archaeological evidence for intramural settlement. Recent investigations have begun to resolve this apparent contradiction, however. In 1985, excavations at

Jubilee Hall, Covent Garden, revealed the first signs of what appears to be a major seventh to ninth-century Anglo-Saxon emporium lying outside, not within, the walls of Roman London (Fig. 5.3.A). Since then, some twenty more adjacent sites have yielded evidence of an important pre-Alfredian trading area extending from the River Fleet to Westminster, with a central concentration just north of the Strand in the area traditionally known as Aldwych ("the old *wic*").[121] This core zone encompassed about 150 acres, though the full settlement may have been up to twice this size. Among the finds that indicate trading activities were large quantities of seventh- and eighth-century pottery from the Rhineland and northern France, Ipswich ware, Rhenish quernstones, and *sceattas* dated c.700–740. Of particular interest has been the discovery of an extensive timber-and-wattle embankment filled with reused Roman stone and tiles, aligned along the Strand foreshore to form a level causeway where vessels could be directly beached, and exchange conducted. Outward-jutting revetments were added successively to this embankment which in places was at least fifty feet wide.

The construction of this significant feature has been dated by dendro-chronological analysis to c.670–690. A single inhumation burial at the Jubilee Hall site bears a carbon-14 date of c.630–675, and another undated grave some 350 yards west appears to be of the same age or slightly older. A number of domestic buildings, and perhaps warehouses, have been found in the area, along with timber-lined wells and rubbish pits. The outlines of a regular street grid have been tentatively identified, and traces of gravel metaling have been uncovered along the Strand, apparently the settlement's main road. Indeed, several nearby gravel quarries worked in this period could indicate communal resurfacing projects under central direction.

Additional material evidence attests to such industrial activities as iron, copper, and bone working. Textile production may also have been signifi-cant, judging from the large numbers of loom weights, spindlewhorls, and residual dyed items uncovered. On the whole, however, these operations appear to have involved household production or perhaps very small workshops rather than the controlled craft specialization and mass production witnessed at Hamwic and Ipswich. Faunal and floral analyses further indicate a substantial population enjoying a balanced diet of barley, wheat, and ground corn, supplemented by meat (beef, pork, mutton) and a surprisingly wide variety of fish, fruit, and nuts.

All of these findings strongly point to Aldwych along the Strand as a permanent settlement of trade and production, the busy emporium evidenced by the documentary and numismatic sources. The likelihood thus arises that there were two distinct early Anglo-Saxon town sites at London. One was the former Roman walled town, thinly reoccupied near the beginning of the seventh century as a royal and ecclesiastical seat of authority but not, it would seem, primarily as a commercial center. The other, Lundenwic, was an extramural trading site, a more densely populated, active center of local and international trade—the emporium known to Bede and Willibald, Frithuwold and Offa.[122] A more precise chronology for the creation of Lundenwic is difficult to determine, but the London coinage and Ipswich ware would suggest a settlement well in place by c.630–650.[123] The settlement presumably was established by East Saxon rulers and then prospered under successive Kentish and Mercian overlords who were clearly interested in controlling commerce at London during the seventh and eighth centuries. This proposed duality of administrative-ceremonial center and commercial-production site is similar to the relationship proposed between Canterbury and Fordwich, or Winchester and Hamwic, though the interrelated London sites were in much closer proximity.[124]

The second important recent discovery concerning London is that the old walled town apparently absorbed its *wic* rather rapidly during the late ninth century. There is mounting archaeological evidence that London's intramural area was deliberately replanned and repopulated in Alfredian times, specifically after its memorable recapture by King Alfred from the Danes (886).[125] Indeed, historical and archaeological evidence combine to indicate that immediately after 886, London was being brought into Alfred's comprehensive system of town strongholds (burghs), intended both to protect the surrounding countryside and to promote trade.

Two West Saxon royal documents are of particular interest in this regard. A charter of King Alfred and the Mercian earldorman Aethelred (889) granted an old stone enclosure (*curtis*) within London to Bishop Waerferth of Worcester for use as a market and also refers to a "trading shore" (*ripa em(p)toralis*) where commerce was liable to royal dues.[126] Thus we are apparently presented with references to a new intramural marketplace, and a maritime trading site, which could be either the extramural *wic* or a new Thames-side intramural port. The latter possibility is made more likely by a second document (898/899), which reports the conferral of two adjacent plots of land with mooring rights at *Aetheredes hyd(th)[port]*, later identified as Queenhithe. It mentions a series of evidently new streets bounding them (Fig. 4.7).[127] The inference is that rectilinear town blocks (*insulae*) were being created, each holding commercial privileges.[128] Recent excavations have confirmed that intramural reoccupation did take place at that time in this southwestern part of the town along a newly established street grid. A series of primarily north-south lanes, some with surface metaling, was set up from St. Paul's to the riverfront.[129] Also dating from this period is a larger network of new intramural roads in the eastern area, extending from Watling Street south to Billingsgate and centered around a new, eastern street market [Eastceap] (Fig. 4.7).[130] Many of these new roads in both areas bear significant commercial names (Fish Street, Bread Street, Milk Street). Moreover, comparison of domestic occupation sites shows a very dramatic population shift from the extramural *wic* into these new areas late in the ninth century. This intramural population seems initially to have been less involved with long-distance, overseas trade than the previous *wic* inhabitants had been, although the times were certainly more troubled.[131]

Along with the creation of these new streets and markets in the old Roman town, work was also underway on the more pressing matter of defense. The historical sources imply that London had to be taken by siege from the Danes in 886 and that considerable repairs were needed.[132] The old Roman walls, especially in the Cripplegate area, which may have been a royal enclosure, were apparently strengthened at this time. More dramatically, the very long street running directly inside the walls on three sides of the town is thought to have been built as part of these Alfredian defensive measures (Fig. 4.7).[133] In addition, late ninth-century fortification of the Southwark suburb and possibly of London Bridge may belong to an Alfredian system of double burghs linked by bridges.[134] The last documentary reference to Lundenwic occurs in 857, and there is no evidence of significant continued settlement there beyond the end of the century.[135] It seems reasonable to conclude that former Roman London was reborn as both a defensive and a commercial center during the turbulent late ninth century, in part, at least, by subsuming the population and function of its extramural *wic*. The town's traditional royal and ecclesiastical roles were likely strengthened by this development.

A somewhat similar pattern can now be identified at York. In the preceding chapter, we examined the evidence for settlement continuity at Eboracum from late Roman to early Anglo-Saxon times (c.400–600) and the results were largely negative. During the early seventh century, however, certain limited areas within the extensive walled circuit evidently were being resettled. Again, as at London, Canterbury, and Winchester, this earliest Anglo-Saxon occupation appears to have been a royal and ecclesiastical affair. For example, we have seen that in 627, King Edwin of Northumbria received baptism in a church (St. Peter's) he had just ordered built for Bishop Paulinus at York and then ordered the construction of a more elaborate stone basilica. This cathedral is believed to have stood near the site of York Minster, within the old Roman fortress area in the town's northwest zone.[136] Within the old civilian settlement area (*colonia*) south of the walled fortress, a series of small churches also were erected in the seventh century around Bishophill, perhaps forming a satellite ecclesiastical compound. Intramural royal activity may be indicated by repairs made to the western wall of the legendary fortress, itself a putative royal enclosure. Furthermore, within the fortress area, new streets seem to have been installed that led more directly between the old gates and often disregarded former Roman *insulae*.[137] Apart from these few signs of limited royal and ecclesiastical activity, there is no evidence of any truly large-scale domestic occupation or intensive commercial-industrial operations within either the fortress or the *colonia* areas of York before the ninth century.[138]

On the other hand, numismatic and historical evidence attests significant commercial life at York from the early seventh century. For example, a series of *thrymsas* dated to the 640s are now believed to have been struck from a mint in York.[139] Primary and secondary *sceattas* bearing the names of various Northumbrian kings of the late seventh to late eighth centuries are also regarded as York royal issues, and a parallel series of *sceattas* was struck by the archbishops of York from 734.[140] Again, written evidence attests that Frisian merchants were active at York during the eighth century and perhaps had established a resident trading colony. They were reportedly driven out in 773, after one of their members accidentally killed a Northumbrian noble.[141] Moreover, York's eighth-century commercial life also may be inferred from Bede's terminology, Eorforwic (c.730), as well as Alcuin's use of *emporium* for York (c.790).[142]

Recent excavations have at last disclosed where the trade site implied by this numismatic and documentary evidence had been located. It now appears that, as at London, early Anglo-Saxon York's emporium was extramural, lying by the eastern side of the old *colonia* area around the confluence of the Rivers Ouse and Foss (Fig. 5.3B). Initial excavations at Fishergate Street on the banks of the Foss revealed a complex of post-built structures, with numerous pits and a surfaced road, arranged in regular zones. A small hoard of *sceattas*, including some "London" types of c.730, along with early eighth-century Anglian metalwork and pottery, were also found. Overseas trade is evidenced by imported Frankish pottery and quernstones, and industrial activity by metalworking crucibles and loom weights. This recently discovered site was in all probability the Eorforwic of seventh- and eighth-century sources. Its size has not yet been determined, but it likely encompassed both riverbanks, perhaps up to the southern *colonia* bridge at Skeldergate and east to Walmgate.[143]

There are indications that areas of former Roman occupation at Eboracum/York began to be resettled slowly in the course of the eighth century, beginning perhaps with the old *colonia* district. Here, domestic artefacts of the late eighth to early ninth centuries are fairly widespread, with heaviest concentrations in the Micklegate area and also Tanner Row (Fig. 4.9).[144] A somewhat later but more substantial focus of renewed industrial and commercial activity has been identified just to the east of the *colonia* across the River Ouse. Excavations at Coppergate revealed that this area was being redeveloped as an important industrial district at the time of or just before the Viking conquest of York in 866.[145] Significant evidence was found of metal, leather, wood, and bone working, textile production, and dyeing. Indeed, the site had been divided into regular industrial and domestic tenements, each producing a variety of crafts over time.[146] Yet this planned area, unlike the early *wic* to the south, by Fishergate, was primarily an Anglo-Scandinavian development (Old Norse:Jorvik) and evidently also enjoyed the Vikings' far-flung commercial contacts. Imported items emanating from Ireland to Norway, Byzantium, and the Red Sea, found here in tenth-century occupation levels, attest to the Viking reopening of Far Eastern trade networks via the Baltic and great Russian riverways.[147]

As at London, commercial and industrial activities at York, initially centered in an extramural emporium, appear to have been relocated during the late ninth century within and up against the former Roman walled site. These areas remained foci of Anglo-Scandinavian settlement and, along with suburban expansions to the east and west, were enclosed by extended defensive walls (Fig. 4.9).[148] It is not without significance that the Anglo-Saxon annals begin to refer to York as a *ceaster*, a (re)fortified site, in the late ninth century, though it had evidently acquired a range of urban functions beyond that of defense.[149]

Anglo-Saxon London and York therefore share a broadly similar pattern of development. In both cases, limited high-status resettlement first took place c.575-650 within former Roman walled areas. Extramural unfortified trading and production centers (*wics*) then were established, which prospered during the following two centuries of relative peace and security. With the advent of Viking attacks, however, the *wics'* populations of merchants and craftsmen found it expedient to relocate within nearby walled areas. By the demographic and functional incorporation of their *wics*, ninth-century London and York became major commercial as well as defensive and administrative centers. York seems to have slightly preceded London in this final transformation, just as its emporium could perhaps also claim an initially greater industrial and long-distance trading role.

The recent discoveries of seventh-to-ninth-century *wics* close by London and York have greatly clarified the heretofore rather obscure early histories of these two prominent Anglo-Saxon towns. Indeed, Lundenwic-Lundenburh and Eorforwic-Eoforwicceaster now appear to fall into a recognizable pattern of emporium-capital represented in southeast England, for example, by Hamwic-Winchester and Fordwich-Canterbury. The Anglo-Saxon *wic* itself, with its primary commercial and industrial functions, represented a major new type of town on the developing English urban landscape. Whether founded by kings, nobles, or churchmen, it stimulated economic growth and furthered the process of political stabilization. Although many emporia did not survive the turbulence of the Viking age, they often bequeathed their important functions to the royal and ecclesiastical towns that had preceded them.

NOTES

1. See, in general, G. H. Martin, "New Beginnings in North-West Europe," in *European Towns: Their Archaeology and Early History*, ed. M. W. Barley (London: Academic Press, 1977), pp. 405–15; R. Hodges, "Ports of Trade in Early Medieval Europe," *Norwegian Archaeological Review* 11 (1978), 97–117, "The Evolution of Gateway Communities: Their Socio-Economic Implications," in *Ranking, Resource and Exchange*, eds. C. Renfrew and S. Shennan (Cambridge: University Press, 1982), pp. 117–23, and *Dark-Age Economics: The Origins of Towns and Trade A.D. 600–1000* (NY: St. Martin's Press, 1982), pp. 47–86; C. J. Arnold, *An Archaeology of the Early Anglo-Saxon Kingdoms* (London: Routledge, 1988), pp. 194–202.

2. P. Addyman, "Saxon Southampton: A Town and International Port of the Eighth to the Tenth Century," in *Vor-und Frühformen der europäischen Stadt im Mittelalter*, eds. H. Jankuhn, et al. (2 vols., Göttingen: Vandenhoeck & Ruprecht, 1973–74), I, pp. 218–28; M. Biddle, "The Towns," in *The Archaeology of Anglo-Saxon England*, ed. D. M. Wilson (London: Methuen, 1976), pp. 112–15; J. Cherry and R. Hodges, "The Dating of Hamwih: Saxon Southampton Reconsidered," *Antiquaries Journal* 58 (1978), 299–309; and more recently, P. Holdsworth, "Saxon Southampton," in *Anglo-Saxon Towns in Southern England*, ed. J. Haslam (Chichester: Phillimore, 1984), pp. 331–43; M. Brisbane, "Hamwic (Saxon Southampton): An Eighth-Century Port and Production Centre," in *The Rebirth of Towns in the West*, eds. R. Hodges and B. Hobley, Council for British Archaeology (hereafter C.B.A.) Research Reports 68 (London, 1988), pp. 101–108; R. Hodges, *The Anglo-Saxon Achievement: Archaeology and the Beginnings of English Society* (Ithaca: Cornell University Press, 1989), pp. 80–92.

3. Addyman, "Saxon Southampton," pp. 219–21, and Fig. 1. The shallow-keeled vessels of the time could be beached directly at the port.

4. Ibid., pp. 223–24; Holdsworth, "Saxon Southampton," p. 335. The sites of three identifiable churches at Hamwic were later taken by industrial shops, although another church, St. Mary's, may have remained in continuous use. See further, Hodges, *Anglo-Saxon Achievement*, p. 83; Brisbane, "Hamwic," p. 104. Males outnumbered females two to one in the Hamwic burials, which points to the commercial-industrial nature of the settlement (Ibid.).

5. Addyman, "Saxon Southampton," pp. 226–27; Hodges, *Dark-Age Economics*, pp. 117–26. Additional industries have now been confirmed: wool processing, along with gold, glass, leather, and wood working. See Brisbane, "Hamwic," p. 104.

6. Hodges, *Anglo-Saxon Achievement*, pp. 80, 86; Brisbane, "Hamwic," pp. 104–5, and Fig. 61 for a reconstruction showing the regular network of three north-south streets and six (to fourteen?) interconnecting east-west streets.

7. Holdsworth, "Saxon Southampton," pp. 335, 341; Hodges, *Anglo-Saxon Achievement*, pp. 84–85; J. Steane, *The Archaeology of Medieval England and Wales* (Athens, GA: University of Georgia Press, 1984), pp. 259–60. Recent study suggests, however, that Hamwic's fields were not worked as intensively as one might expect: Brisbane, "Hamwic," p. 107.

8. Hodges, *Anglo-Saxon Achievement*, pp. 83, 86; Biddle, "The Study of Winchester: Archaeology and History in a British Town, 1961–1983," *Proceedings of the British Academy* 69 (1983), p. 123.

9. Addyman, "Saxon Southampton," pp. 227–28; Holdsworth, "Saxon Southampton," pp. 336–37. The important Six Dials excavation site on the northern fringe of Hamwic shows a similar development pattern: an early phase marked only by a small timber building along a rough east-west road; a second period with three road remetalings and at least fourteen timber structures built for industrial uses, and a final phase where the roadway deteriorated to a narrow path without resurfacing, although property alignments were usually maintained (ibid., p. 336). Still, the site and street system appear to have been originally planned and imposed at one time: Brisbane, "Hamwic," p. 103; and see n. 28, below.

10. Cherry and Hodges, "Dating of Hamwih"; Hodges, *Dark-Age Economics*, pp. 44–45; P. Grierson and M. Blackburn, *Medieval European Coinage I: The Early Middle Ages* (Cambridge: University Press, 1986), pp. 168–71. Over two hundred coins, including one major hoard, have been found.

11. Addyman, "Saxon Southampton," p. 226; M. Dolley, "The Coins," in *Archaeology of Anglo-Saxon England*, p. 352; Grierson and Blackburn, *Medieval European Coinage*, pp. 294–95. The circulation of Hamwic *sceattas* exclusively within the town also suggests a controlled economy: Brisbane, "Hamwic," p. 106; Hodges, *Anglo-Saxon Achievement*, p. 88.

12. *Vita Willibaldi Episcopi Eichstetensis*, iii, ed. O. Holder-Egger, in *Monumenta Germaniae Historica* (hereafter *MGH*), *Scriptores Rerum Merovingicarum* (hereafter *SS RM*), XV; 1 (Hanover, 1887). One variant text has Hamwich.

13. *Two of the Saxon Chronicles Parallel* (hereafter *ASC*), eds. J. Earle and C. Plummer (2 vols., Oxford: Clarendon Press, 1892–99), s.a. 755[757]A.

14. See F. M. Stenton, *Anglo-Saxon England* (hereafter *ASE*) (3d ed., Oxford: Clarendon Press, 1971), pp. 336–37; Holdsworth, "Saxon Southampton," p. 335.

15. Simeon of Durham, *Historia Regum*, s.a. 764, in *Symeonis Monachi Opera Omnia*, ed. T. Arnold, Rolls Series 75 (2 vols., London, 1882–85), II. This northern chronicle is believed to be of late eighth- to tenth-century date: see *ASE*, pp. 693–94.

16. *Cartularium Saxonicum* (hereafter *Cart. Sax.*), ed. W. de Gray Birch (4 vols., London: Whiting & Co., 1885–99), Nos. 389, 431, 596, 598, 601. This *villa regalis* may not have stood within Hamwic, however.

17. *ASC* 837 [840]A. Wulfheard is also described as *praefectus* (reeve) and had received a grant of twenty-two hides on the River Meon (S. Hants.) from King Egbert in 824: *Cart. Sax.*, No. 377. In the next year he took part as *ealdorman* in the West Saxon conquest of Kent (*ASC* 823 [825]A), and he is probably identical with the Wulfhard *dux* who attests a number of Egbert's charters, 826–838 A.D.: *Cart. Sax.*, Nos. 392, 395, 411, 418.

18. Nithard, *Histoire des fils de Louis le Pieux*, iv. 3, ed. P. Lauer (2d ed. Paris: Société d'Edition Les Belles Lettres, 1964); *ASC* 839[842]A.

19. As in the charters n. 16, above. See further, Biddle, "Towns," p. 114.

20. Ibid., p. 115; J. N. L. Myres, *The English Settlements* (Oxford: Clarendon Press, 1981), pp. 33–35. In seventh-century Kentish law, *ham* and *tun* are equivalent terms for domestic houses: *Laws of Aethelberht*, iii, xvii, ed. F. A. Attenborough, in Attenborough, *The Laws of the Earliest English Kings* (Cambridge: University Press, 1922). See A. H. Smith, *English Place-Name Elements* (2 vols., Cambridge: University Press, 1956), s.v. *ham* (I, pp. 226–31) and *tun* (II, pp. 188–98). For further discussion of variant Old English meanings of *wic*, see: J. Bosworth, T. Toller and A. Campbell,

An Anglo-Saxon Dictionary (2 vols., Oxford: University Press, 1898–1972), s.v. *wic*; Smith, *English Place-Name Elements*, II, pp. 257–64; E. Ekwall, *Old English* Wic *in Place-Names* (Uppsala: Lundequistska Bokhandeln, 1964); M. Gelling, "English Place-Names Derived From the Compound *Wicham*," in *Place-Name Evidence for the Anglo-Saxon Invasion and Scandinavian Settlements*, ed. K. Cameron (Nottingham: English Place-Name Society, 1977), pp. 8–26. Recall also the view that the term *Viking* (*vikingr*) was a Scandinavian loan word from *wic*, *vicus* designating "*wic* dwellers" or traders: J. Brøndsted, *The Vikings*, trans. K. Skov (Harmondsworth: Penguin Books, 1965), pp. 37–38; cf. H. Planitz, *Die deutsche Stadt im Mittelalter* (Cologne: Böhlau, 1954), pp. 54–55. A full listing and analysis of all *wic* place-names in Anglo-Saxon England with special attention to chronology and topography would no doubt be illuminating.

21. Biddle, "Towns," pp. 104, 114; Smith, *English Place-Name Elements*, s.v. *ceaster*, I, pp. 85–87.

22. Biddle, "Towns," p. 114; Holdsworth, "Saxon Southampton," pp. 335–36. The industrial aspect of Hamwic has been emphasized in the most recent studies: Brisbane, "Hamwic," p. 106.

23. Biddle, "Study of Winchester," pp. 123-24.

24. For these later developments, see ibid., pp. 119–26, where it is observed that most of Winchester's intramural area was occupied by the late ninth century. On the Alfredian burghs: also see Chap. 7, below.

25. Biddle, "Study of Winchester," pp. 123–24; Holdsworth, "Saxon Southampton," p. 337. Such population-shifts and transfers of urban functions have been met before and will be encountered again both in regard to England and the Continent. They bear some similarity to Pirenne's scheme of *faubourg/bourg* incorporation, which he believed occurred only with the tenth- and eleventh-century revival of international trade: H. Pirenne, *Medieval Cities* (rev. ed. NY: Doubleday, 1956), pp. 101–9.

26. Addyman, "Saxon Southampton," pp. 227–28; C. Platt, *Medieval Southampton* (London: Routledge, 1973), pp. 6–11.

27. Biddle, "Study of Winchester," pp. 199–20; Holdworth, "Saxon Southampton," pp. 340–42.

28. For a survey of his career, see *ASE*, pp. 71–73. On Ine's role as the founder of Hamwic, see H. R. Loyn, *Anglo-Saxon England and the Norman Conquest* (NY: St. Martin's Press, 1962), p. 138; Holdsworth, "Saxon Southampton," p. 335; Hodges, *Anglo-Saxon Achievement*, pp. 85–92, noting that the precondition for Hamwic's foundation was the conquest of the Solent coast of Hampshire and the Isle of Wight by Ine's father, Caedwalla, in 686 (*ASC*, 686A).

29. *Laws of Ine*, xxv; ed. Attenborough. See further, Sawyer, "Kings and Merchants," in *Early Medieval Kingship*, eds. P. Sawyer and I. Wood (Leeds: University Press, 1977), pp. 150–51, who contends very plausibly that traders were under Anglo-Saxon royal protection.

30. *Cart. Sax.*, Nos. 149, 150, 152, 171, 173, 177, 188, 189. See further, Sawyer, "Kings and Merchants," pp. 143–44, 153.

31. *Laws of Hlothhere and Eadric*, xvi (London), ed. Attenborough, in Attenborough, *Laws*. When the first band of Danish Vikings landed in Wessex, the king's reeve rode to meet them, probably thinking they were foreign merchants, but

was promptly killed for his efforts: *ASC* 787 [789]A; Aethelweard, *Chronicon*, iii.1, ed. A. Campbell (London: Thomas Nelson, 1962).

32. *ASC* 722A. But this place may have been the *villa regalis* known from the tenth century. There is no archaeological evidence of concentrated Anglo-Saxon settlement at Taunton (Map 7.3) before the ninth century: M. Aston, "The Towns of Somerset," in *Anglo-Saxon Towns in Southern England*, ed. Haslam, pp. 189–92. To compound the mystery, the reported destroyer of Taunton in the *Chronicle* entry was none other than Ine's wife, Queen Aethelburh (a curious name in itself).

33. *Laws of Ine*, li, lxx. The hide in Wessex was generally 40 acres; elsewhere, and perhaps more normally it was 120 acres. See further Chap. 7, below. On the early Anglo-Saxon royal *feorm*, *ASE*, pp. 287–89.

34. Hodges, *Dark-Age Economics*, pp. 136–39.

35. *Cart. Sax.*, Nos. 321, 341, 416. See further, N. Brooks, "The Development of Military Obligations in Eighth and Ninth-Century England," in *England before the Conquest*, eds. P. Clemoes and K. Hughes (Cambridge: University Press, 1971) pp. 69–84, esp. pp. 69–72; Hodges, *Anglo-Saxon Achievement*, pp. 88–89, and Chap. 7, below.

36. Biddle, "Towns," pp. 132–33.

37. *ASC* 725–784A. See *ASE*, pp. 202–30; J. M. Wallace-Hadrill, *Early Germanic Kingship in England and on the Continent* (Oxford: Clarendon Press, 1971), pp. 89–90; Hodges, *Anglo-Saxon Achievement*, pp. 91–92.

38. See with caution: Hodges, "Gateway Communities," p. 122; Arnold, "Stress as a Stimulus for Socio-Economic Change: Anglo-Saxon England in the Seventh Century," in *Ranking, Resource and Exchange*, pp. 124-31.

39. ASC 755, 778, 784, 787A. A ditch has been found surrounding the earliest settlement at Hamwic, but it was a boundary not a defensive line: Brisbane, "Hamwic," pp. 102–3.

40. D. A. Hinton, "The Towns of Hampshire," in *Anglo-Saxon Towns in Southern England*, pp. 160–61, but cf. Holdsworth, "Saxon Southampton," pp. 334–35. The relationship between royal vill and coastal trading place is shown in Aethelweard's version of the incident, see n. 31, above, where the king's reeve rode directly from the *villa regalis* at (near?) Dorchester (Dorset) to the *port* (Portland) in order to meet the Danes.

41. Hodges, "Gateway Communities," p. 120. See also, Chap. 6, below, for continental cases.

42. P. Rahtz, "Buildings and Rural Settlement," in *Archaeology of Anglo-Saxon England*, ed. Wilson, pp. 58–61; Biddle, "Towns," pp. 107–9.

43. Hodges, *Anglo-Saxon Achievement*, p. 86.

44. Ibid., p. 192; Arnold, *Archaeology of the Early Anglo-Saxon Kingdoms*, p. 200.

45. Hodges, *Anglo-Saxon Achievement*, p. 86; Rahtz, "Buildings," pp. 65–68.

46. M. Biddle and D. Hill, "Late Saxon Planned Towns," *Antiquaries Journal* 51 (1971), 70–85; Biddle, "Towns," pp. 130–31, and also Chap. 7, below, for the burghs of Wessex.

47. See, in general, K. Wade, "Ipswich," in *Rebirth of Towns*, pp. 93–100; also, Hodges, *Anglo-Saxon Achievement*, pp. 97–101.

48. Wade, "Ipswich," pp. 93–94. The largest late Roman town in the vicinity was Combretovium (Coddenham), a small walled site eleven miles to the north; see R. Dunnett, *The Trinovantes* (London: Duckworth, 1975), pp. 43, 89.

49. Thus *Domesday Book* (hereafter *DB*) records 538 burgesses in the borough of Ipswich (Gepeswiz) in 1066 holding 40 acres and rendering £15 to the king. By 1086 the town seems to have been greatly impoverished: 110 burgesses rendered dues and another 100 "poor burgesses" paid only 1 penny each, with 328 waste burgages reported: *DB*, II, 290a. This would give Ipswich a pre-Conquest population of 2,000–4,000 and a sixth-place rank among all forty-six recorded boroughs by population: C. Stephenson, *Borough and Town* (Cambridge, MA: Mediaeval Academy of America, 1933), pp. 153, 221; H. C. Darby, *Domesday England* (Cambridge: University Press, 1977), pp. 295–98, 308; Ipswich's defenses are tenth-century work, possibly Viking: Wade, "Ipswich," p. 97.

50. Wade, "Ipswich," p. 93 (north side of the Orwell).

51. This major pagan burial, rather haphazardly excavated in 1907, yielded numerous Anglian long brooches as well as several significant Kentish disc-brooches and glass bowls of the early seventh century: R. A. Smith, "Anglo-Saxon Remains," in *The Victoria History of the Counties of England* (hereafter *VCH*), *Suffolk*, I (1911), pp. 330–33; D. B. Harden, "Glass Vessels in Britain and Ireland, A.D. 400–1000," in *Dark Age Britain*, ed. Harden (London: Methuen, 1956), pp. 162–65.

52. Wade, "Ipswich," pp. 93–95, 97, who estimates that land within the later borough boundaries could easily have produced enough agricultural surplus to feed a town population of 2,000. The lack of permanent structures and large-scale, regular street grids in the earliest occupation phase may suggest that Ipswich initially had been a temporary trade and production site: H. Clarke, "Seasonally-Occupied Settlements and Anglo-Saxon Towns," in *Trade and Exchange in Prehistory*, eds. B. Hardh, et al. (Lund: Bloms Boktryckeri, 1988), pp. 247–54, esp. 249, 252.

53. Wade, "Ipswich," p. 96; Hodges, *Dark-Age Economics*, pp. 36–37.

54. J. Hurst, "The Pottery," in *Archaeology of Anglo-Saxon England*, ed. Wilson, pp. 299–303; Wade, "Ipswich," pp. 95–96 and distribution map, Fig. 54. Ipswich ware was wheel thrown and kiln fired. This much improved technique suggests Frankish contacts and greater local production control: Hodges, *Anglo-Saxon Achievement*, p. 141. For Ipswich ware as elite export items, see further, T. Williamson, "Settlement Chronology and Regional Landscapes: The Evidence from the Claylands of East Anglia and Essex," in *Anglo-Saxon Settlements*, ed. D. Hooke (London: Blackwell, 1988), p. 160.

55. Wade, "Ipswich," p. 95; Hodges, *Dark-Age Economics*, pp. 146–47.

56. Wade, "Ipswich," p. 95.

57. Ibid., p. 97, and Fig. 56 for "histogram" of coin finds.

58. Grierson and Blackburn, *Medieval European Coinage*, pp. 166–69, 180 and Plate 32 for examples.

59. Ibid., pp. 182, 277–78; Hodges, *Anglo-Saxon Achievement*, p. 74. This is the first known Anglo-Saxon silver coinage in southern England to bear a king's name.

60. Grierson and Blackburn, *Medieval European Coinage*, pp. 273, 281, 286, 293–94; Dolley, "Coins," pp. 352–55.

61. Wade, "Ipswich," p. 97: Grierson and Blackburn, *Medieval European Coinage*, pp. 318–20.

62. E.g., Barham and Burrow Hill, where concentrations of primary and secondary *sceattas* and evidence of dense settlement have been uncovered. See Hodges, *Anglo-Saxon Achievement*, pp. 98–99; Grierson and Blackburn, *Medieval European Coinage*, pp. 165–68; M. Carver, "Kingship and Material Culture in Early Anglo-Saxon East Anglia," in *The Origins of Anglo-Saxon Kingdoms*, ed. S. Bassett, (Leicester: University Press, 1989), p. 146.

63. *ASC* 991E. The designation Gipeswic likely derives from the River Gipping, which flows on the western side of the town into the Orwell.

64. Ibid., 1010E.

65. D. Dumville, "The Anglian Collection of Royal Genealogies and Regnal Lists," *Anglo-Saxon England* 5 (1976), pp. 23–50.

66. Bede, *Historia Ecclesiastica* (hereafter *Hist. Eccl.*), ii.15, iii.22, ed. C. Plummer (2 vols., Oxford: Clarendon Press, 1896). See further, R. Bruce-Mitford, "Saxon Rendlesham," in Bruce-Mitford, *Aspects of Anglo-Saxon Archaeology* (NY: Harper & Row, 1974), pp. 73–113.

67. *ASE*, 52–53.

68. Myres, *English Settlements*, pp. 96–115; Carver, "Kingship and Material Culture," pp. 144–58. For references to the early settlement of East Anglia see Bede, *Hist. Eccl.*, i.15; *ASC*, 449, 547A.

69. Bruce-Mitford, "The Snape Boat-Grave," in Bruce-Mitford, *Aspects of Anglo-Saxon Archaeology*, pp. 114–41; J. Campbell, "The Lost Centuries: 400-600," in *The Anglo-Saxons*, eds. Campbell et al. (Harmondsworth: Penguin Books, 1982), Figs. 30 and 34.

70. Carver, "Kingship and Material Culture," pp. 149-50; Bruce-Mitford, "Who Was He?" in *The Sutton Hoo Ship-Burial*, ed. Bruce-Mitford (3 vols., London: British Museum Publications, 1975–83), I, pp. 683–717; P. D. C. Brown, *Anglo-Saxon England* (Totowa, NJ: Barnes & Noble, 1978), pp. 60–61; Arnold, *Archaeology of the Early Anglo-Saxon Kingdoms*, pp. 190–91. The current Sutton Hoo research campaign (1983–) has uncovered a second boat grave (Mound 2), a nearby high-status infant burial, and evidence of ritual human sacrifice. The Sutton Hoo complex continued as an elite burial ground into the mid-eighth century and overlay a prehistoric site with earthworks likely still visible in the seventh century: Carver, "Kingship and Material Culture," p. 150.

71. Bruce-Mitford and M. Luscombe, "Complete Inventory of Finds," in *Sutton Hoo Ship-Burial*, I, pp. 436–57; Bruce-Mitford, "The Sutton Hoo-Ship Burial: Comments on General Interpretation," in Bruce-Mitford, *Aspects of Anglo-Saxon Archaeology*, pp. 1–72.

72. Biddle, "The Development of the Anglo-Saxon Town," in *Topografia urbana e vita cittadina nell'alto medievo in occidente* (2 vols., Spoleto: Centro Italiano di Studi Sull'Alto Medievo, 1974), I, pp. 215–16; P. H. Sawyer, *From Roman Britain to Norman England* (London: Methuen, 1976), pp. 223–24; Hodges, "Gateway Communities," p. 120; Carver, "Kingship and Material Culture," p. 152. There is presumed to have been a royal vill on the northern fringe of the town, near the area traditionally known as the Thingstead: Hodges, *Dark-Age Economics*, pp. 72–73. The recent discovery of a large seventh to ninth-century cemetery with some rich grave goods in the center of the *wic* supports the view of royal foundation: H. Clarke and B. Ambrosiani, *Towns in the Viking Age* (NY: St. Martin's Press, 1991), pp. 20–22.

73. Hodges, *Dark-Age Economics*, pp. 36–37; Arnold, *Archaeology of the Early Anglo-Saxon Kingdoms*, p. 71. For the Vendel origins of the East Anglian royal family, see Bruce-Mitford, "General Interpretation," pp. 35–60; but cf. I. Wood, "The Franks and Sutton Hoo," in *People and Places in Northern Europe, 500–1600*, eds. Wood and N. Lund (Woodbridge: Boydell Press, 1991), pp. 1–14.

74. Bruce-Mitford and Luscombe, "Complete Inventory," p. 456; Hodges, *Dark-Age Economics*, p. 147.

75. See with caution: Hodges, *Anglo-Saxon Achievement*, pp. 55-58; Arnold, *Archaeology of the Early Anglo-Saxon Kingdoms*, pp. 69–71, and "Stress as a Stimulus for Socio-Economic Change"; cf. J. Callmer, "Three Fundamental Perspectives for the Study of Trade and Exchange in Northern Europe in the Second Half of the First Millennium A.D.," in *Trade and Exchange in Prehistory*, eds. B. Hardh, et al., pp. 261–70.

76. Hodges, *Dark-Age Economics*, pp. 50–52, and "Gateway Communities." Also, the suggestions that Ipswich at least initially was more self-sufficient in its agricultural supply and less specialized in craft production than Hamwic are possible but as yet unproven: Wade, "Ipswich," pp. 97-99; Clarke and Ambrosiani, *Towns in the Viking Age*, pp. 35-36.

77. See Tatton-Brown, "The Anglo-Saxon Towns of Kent," in *Anglo-Saxon Settlements*, ed. Hooke, pp. 214–15. For early Frankish/Kentish trade connections, see also Chaps. 4 and 6.

78. Ibid., p. 215, and Fig. 10.2, also noting that this church lay in the medieval manor known as Wyke.

79. Ibid.; Wade, "Ipswich," p. 97; Tatton-Brown, "Anglo-Saxon Towns of Kent," pp. 215-17. More extensive excavations need to be undertaken at all Kentish emporia.

80. *Cart. Sax.*, No. 36; *Laws of Hlothhere and Eadric*, xvi, ed. Attenborough.

81. *Cart. Sax.*, Nos. 173, 189. See further, Sawyer, *Roman Britain to Norman England*, pp. 87–88, who speculates that early Anglo-Saxon royal toll rights were inherited from late Roman official prerogatives.

82. T. Tatton-Brown, "Towns of Kent," in *Anglo-Saxon Towns in Southern England*, p. 30; N. Brooks, "The Creation and Early Structure of the Kingdom of Kent," in *Origins of Anglo-Saxon Kingdoms*, p. 71. For grants of royal lands at Sturry to the Church (679–690), see *Cart. Sax.*, Nos. 35, 41, 45.

83. Smith, "Anglo-Saxon Remains," in *VCH* Kent, I (1908), pp. 358–361, discussed the finds. See further, Arnold, *Archaeology of the Early Anglo-Saxon Kingdoms*, pp. 20, 63–64, 85, 170.

84. Ibid., p. 170; Hodges, *Dark-Age Economics*, p. 36; Drewett, et al., *South-East*, p. 280.

85. Grierson and Blackburn, *Medieval European Coinage*, pp. 508, 512, 516; Hodges, *Dark-Age Economics*, p. 69.

86. *ASC* 669A, and see also the grant of property by the East Anglian king Sigebert (founder of Bury St. Edmunds and later victim of Penda) close by Burgh Castle to the Irish pilgrim Fursey for a monastery c.633: Bede, *Hist. Eccl.*, iii.18-19. For this process of transferring former Roman forts from early Anglo-Saxon kings to the Church, see further, S. Johnson, *Later Roman Britain* (London: Collins, 1980), pp. 192–94.

87. *Cart. Sax.*, No. 189.

88. Hodges, *Anglo-Saxon Achievement*, pp. 92–93, and "Emporia, Monasteries, and the Economic Foundation of Medieval Europe," in *Medieval Archaeology*, ed. C. L. Redman (Binghamton, NY: State University of New York Press, 1989), pp. 57–72; N. Brooks, *The Early History of the Church of Canterbury* (Leicester: University Press, 1984), pp. 129–36.

89. Eddius Stephanus, *Vita S. Wilfridi*, xiii, ed. B. Colgrave (Cambridge: University Press, 1927).

90. *ASC* 449A; Bede, *Hist. Eccl.*, i.25. See further, Tatton-Brown, "Towns of Kent," pp. 17–18.

91. Ibid., "Towns of Kent," p. 17.

92. Tatton-Brown, "Anglo-Saxon Towns of Kent, p. 217; N. Brooks, "Kingdom of Kent," p. 70, and Fig. 4.2.

93. Tatton-Brown, "Towns of Kent," pp. 17–21.

94. The evidence is mainly numismatic: Hodges, *Anglo-Saxon Achievement*, pp. 92–93; Grierson and Blackburn, *Medieval European Coinage*, p. 520.

95. See, for example *ASC* 851A, 993A, and later, 1006, 1013E.

96. There was a serious jurisdictional quarrel over Sandwich between Christ Church and St. Augustine's, Canterbury, in the early part of the eleventh century, which finally was resolved in Christ Church's favor: *Codex Diplomaticus Aevi Saxonici*, ed. J. Kemble (London: British Historical Society, 1839–48), No. 758. During the controversy we learn that Sandwich traditionally claimed to enjoy all revenues at the mouth of the Wantsum Channel (ibid., No. 737). In 1066, Sandwich ranked above Canterbury in population and was one of the few boroughs with a substantial increase (25 percent) by 1086: *DB*, I, 3a. Fordwich was one of the smallest pre-Conquest boroughs and was diminished even more in 1086 (ibid., I, 12b.). See further, Stephenson, *Borough and Town*, p. 221; Darby, *Domesday England*, pp. 299–300, 308.

97. Tatton-Brown, "Anglo-Saxon Towns of Kent," pp. 220–21, and Fig. 10.5.

98. Ibid.

99. Ibid., p. 220; Hodges, *Anglo-Saxon Achievement*, pp. 28, 32; M. Welch, *Discovering Anglo-Saxon England* (University Park, PA: Pennsylvania State University Press, 1993), pp. 76–79.

100. *Cart. Sax.*, No. 91.

101. Tatton-Brown, "Towns of Kent," p. 23.

102. Arnold, *Archaeology of the Early Anglo-Saxon Kingdoms*, p. 86.

103. Tatton-Brown, "Towns of Kent," p. 23, and Fig. 8.

104. Rahtz, "Gazetteer of Anglo-Saxon Domestic Settlement Sites," in *Archaeology of Anglo-Saxon England*, p. 417.

105. Tatton-Brown, "Towns of Kent," p. 22; D. Hill, *An Atlas of Anglo-Saxon England* (Toronto: University of Toronto Press, 1981), pp. 127–28, 130–31.

106. *ASC* 1048 [1051]E, *DB*, I, 1a. See further for these Anglo-Saxon rights of the later Cinque Ports: *ASE*, pp. 431–32; Stephenson, *Borough and Town*, pp. 117–19, 156–58; Darby, *Domesday England*, pp. 300, 365.

107. See Chap. 4, above.

108. *Cart. Sax.*, No. 34 (672 X 674 A.D.). The casual way in which this London trade is spoken of suggests it was no new development at the time.

109. T. Dyson and J. Schofield, "Saxon London," in *Anglo-Saxon Towns in Southern England*, p. 292; Hodges, *Anglo-Saxon Achievement*, p. 57. King Wulfhere could expel the bishop of London for his own man c.670: Bede, *Hist. Eccl.*, iii.7, ed. Plummer. See *further, ASE*, pp. 57–58.

110. Bede, *Hist. Eccl.*, iv. 22.

111. Gregory had noticed some young boys being sold as slaves in Rome's marketplace and asked for the name of the people from which such fair-haired, handsome youths had come. When told they were called Angles (Angli) from Britain, he supposedly exclaimed how appropriate that was, because they had an angelic (*angelica*) appearance: ibid., ii.1. The incident occurred before he became pope in 590 and may have stimulated his designs toward the conversion of England. See also: *The Earliest Life of Gregory the Great*, ix, ed. B. Colgrave (Lawrence: University of Kansas Press, 1968), and *Gregorii I Papae Registrum Epistolarum*, vi.10, ix.222, eds. P. Ewald and L. Hartmann, in *MGH Epistolae (EE)*, I-II (2d ed. Berlin, 1957). Later, the Anglo-Saxon missionary Bishop Boniface (d.754) would claim that English prostitutes and pimps were to be found in nearly all the towns of western Europe: *S. Bonifatii et Lulli Epistolae*, lxxviii; ed. E. Dümmler, in *MGH EE* III. See further, D. Pelteret, "Slave-Raiding and Slave-Trading in Early England," *Anglo-Saxon England* 9 (1981), pp. 99–114.

112. Hodges, *Dark-Age Economics*, Chap. 6, esp. pp. 117–29; A. Vince, "The Economic Basis of Anglo-Saxon London," in *Rebirth of Towns in the West*, eds. Hodges and Hobley, pp. 85, 90, and *Saxon London: An Archaeological Investigation* (London: Seaby, 1990), pp. 93–102; Levison, *England and the Continent in the Eighth Century* (Oxford: Clarendon Press, 1946), pp. 7–10, 50–51.

113. *Cart. Sax.*, Nos. 149, 152, 171; cf. No. 335 (811 A.D.) for London as a *wic*.

114. Ibid., No. 259. In this interesting and significant charter, Offa confirms a grant by two brothers (bearing Frankish names) of all their land "in the port which is called London" to St. Denis near Paris.

115. Willibald, *Vita S. Bonifatii*, iv, ed. Levison, *MGH SS RG*, XLVIII (Hanover, 1905).

116. C. H. V. Sutherland, *English Coinage 600–1900* (London: Batsford, 1973), pp. 3–4 and Pls. 1–2; Grierson and Blackburn, *Medieval European Coinage*, pp. 161–62.

117. Ibid., pp. 164–68, 174–78; Vince, "Economic Basis," pp. 86–87, and Fig. 44.

118. Ibid., and Fig. 45; Grierson and Blackburn, *Medieval European Coinage*, pp. 172–73, 178–81; Sutherland, *English Coinage*, pp. 6–7 and Pl. 2; Biddle, "City in Transition: 400–800," in *Atlas of Historic Towns III: City of London*, ed. M. Lobel (London: Lovell Johns, 1989), pp. 24–25, 27, who suggests that the early London coinage was produced in the *wic* and formally issued from the walled town. Many contemporary Frisian *sceattas* have also been found in these same areas of England: Hodges, *Anglo-Saxon Achievement*, p. 78, and Fig. 22; Grierson and Blackburn, *Medieval European Coinage*, pp. 149–54.

119. Ibid., p. 186.

120. Sutherland, *English Coinage*, p. 7; Hodges, *Anglo-Saxon Achievement*, pp. 76–78; Vince, *Saxon London*, pp. 109–13. Anglo-Saxon England, like Roman Britain, appears to have had adequate silver deposits (Bede, *Hist. Eccl.*, i. 1.). See Hill, *Atlas of Anglo-Saxon England*, p. 107, and Fig. 191. Gold was a much rarer commodity, obtained often from Frankish coins and ornaments.

121. For the following archaeological evidence, see R. Cowie and R. Whytehead, "Lundenwic: The Archaeological Evidence for Middle Saxon London," *Antiquity* 63 (1989), 706–18 and Figs. 1, 2; B. Hobley, "Lundenwic and Lundenburh: Two Cities Re-Discovered," in *Rebirth of Towns*, pp. 69–82; Biddle, "City in Transition," pp. 26–29; Vince, *Saxon London*, pp. 13–25.

122. B. Hobley, "Lundenwic and Lundenburh," p. 73, aptly describes pre-Alfredian Lundenburh as a "small, kremlin-like reservation for kings and priests" and Lundenwic as "an international open trading centre." See further, Cowie and Whytehead, "Lundenwic," 706–7; T. Tatton-Brown, "The Topography of Anglo-Saxon London," *Antiquity* 60 (1986), 25; Myres, *English Settlements*, pp. 133–34; K. Bailey, "The Middle Saxons," in *Origins of Anglo-Saxon Kingdoms*, p. 110; Vince, *Saxon London*, p. 13; cf. Biddle, "City in Transition," p. 27. Significant population density may be confirmed by the references to repeated fires that ravaged late eighth-century London, probably the *wic*: Simeon of Durham, *Historia Regum*, s.a. 764, 798.

123. Cowie and Whytehead, "Lundenwic," 709; Vince, *Saxon London*, p. 17; Biddle, "City in Transition," p. 28. The earliest occupation site (c.575?) appears to have been restricted to a quite small area on the central Strand.

124. Biddle, "Towns," pp. 114–15; Tatton-Brown, "Topography," 24. But cf. Hodges, *Anglo-Saxon Achievement*, pp. 95–97, who argues that Lundenwic cannot be compared to a full-scale trading and industrial emporium ("Type B") like Hamwic, at least not before Offa (757–796).

125. *ASC* 886 [885]A. The event apparently was celebrated by the issuance of a new, heavy-standard coinage bearing a portrait bust with the legend "Aelfred Rex" and a "Lundonia" monogram on the reverse: Grierson and Blackburn, *Medieval European Coinage*, pp. 313–14 and Pl. 59. See further, Vince, *Saxon London*, p. 22.

126. *Cart. Sax.*, No. 561. See Hobley, "Lundenwic and Lundenburh," pp. 73, 77–78; Dyson and Schofield, "Saxon London," p. 296. The enclosure was called *Hwaetmundes stan* and extended from the public street (*strata publica*) to the town wall.

127. *Cart. Sax.*, No. 577. The recipients were Waerferth and Archbishop Plegmund of Canterbury. These grants were made as a result of discussions held at Chelsea (*Celchylth*) among Alfred, Aethelred, Plegmund, and Waerferth concerning the rebuilding (*instauracio*) of London (Ibid.). Waerferth's property probably was the same as that mentioned in 889. See the comments by Vince, *Saxon London*, pp. 20–22.

128. Dyson and Schofield, "Saxon London," pp. 296–97; Vince, "Economic Basis," p. 83.

129. Hobley, "Lundenwic and Lundenburh," pp. 76–77; Tatton-Brown, "Topography," 25, and Fig. 2.2, suggesting that this area was resettled somewhat earlier, just after the first Viking attacks on London (842, 851).

130. Ibid., 25–26, and Fig. 2.3; Biddle and Hill, "Late Saxon Planned Towns," 83; Vince, *Saxon London*, Fig. 65a. This provision of settlement areas and markets shows that Alfred had more in mind than a purely defensive site. See C. N. L. Brooke and G. Keir, *London 800–1216* (Berkeley: University of California Press, 1975), pp. 60–62.

131. Vince, "Economic Basis," pp. 90–92 and Figs. 41, 42. See also Chap. 7, below, for burghal developments.

132. *ASC* 886A; *Cart. Sax.*, No. 577; Asser, *De rebus gestis Aelfredi [Life of King Alfred]*, lxxxiii, ed. W. H. Stephenson (Oxford: Clarendon Press, 1904). Alfred's taking of London was a major symbolic as well as strategic coup, that immediately led to his recognition as the leader of united English resistance. The fact that he handed over the town to a Mercian nobleman (Aethelred) seems to have been a calculated token gesture, although several early place-names in London may well preserve memories of Aethelred's presence (*Aetheredes hyd*, Aldermanbury). See further, *ASE*, pp. 258–60; Dyson and Schofield, "Saxon London," pp. 296–97, 307; cf. Brooke and Keir, *London*, p. 20, who contend that London remained a Mercian "frontier city" until Edward the Elder united Mercia with Wessex.

133. Tatton-Brown, "Topography," 26, and Fig. 2.3; Dyson and Schofield, "Saxon London," pp. 306–7.

134. Ibid. p. 299; Hobley, "Lundenwic and Lundenburh," p. 79; cf. Biddle, "Towns," p. 136.

135. *Cart. Sax.*, No. 494. For the demise of Lundenwic, attributed primarily to its lack of defenses, see Cowie and Whytehead, "Lundenwic," pp. 709, 716; Vince, *Saxon London*, pp. 22–25. In late Anglo-Saxon times, the old central *wic* area was redeveloped as a large, triangular market on the extensive ecclesiastical estate of Westminster: Tatton-Brown, "Topography," 27.

136. Bede, *Hist. Eccl.*, ii.14; *ASC*, 627E, and Chap. 4, above. Also: Addyman, "York and Canterbury as Ecclesiastical Centres," in *European Towns*, ed. Barley, pp. 500–501; R. A. Hall, "York 700–1050," in *Rebirth of Towns in the West*, p. 126. Old Roman fortifications and public buildings were still an imposing part of York's topography in the eighth century. For the deep impression they left on Alcuin (a hometown boy), see his *Versus De Patribus Regibus et Sanctis Eboracensis Ecclesiae*, ll.18–45, ed. Dümmler, *MGH Poetae*, I: 1 (Berlin, 1881).

137. Hall, "York," p. 126. For Northumbrian kings of the late seventh and eighth centuries evidently resident at York: Bede, *Hist. Eccl.*, iv. 28 (685); *ASC* 774E. Royal officials or reeves (*praefecti, praepositi*) were in charge of various Northumbrian towns such as Carlisle and Dunbar (Map 7.3) in the late seventh century: *Vita S. Cuthberti Auctore Anonymo*. vii. ed. B. Colgrave (Cambridge: University Press, 1940); Eddius Stephanus, *Vita S. Wilfridi*, xxxvi–xxxvii, ed. Colgrave (Cambridge: University Press, 1927). Note also that the Northumbrian king and queen are said to have made official perambulations "per civitates et castellas vicosque" (ibid., xxxix).

138. Hall, "York," pp. 127–28; D. A. Brooks, "A Review of the Evidence for Continuity in British Towns in the 5th and 6th Centuries," *Oxford Journal of Archaeology* 5 (1986), pp. 85, 90. For possible sites of the Anglian royal palace and monastery, see Hall, "Sources for Pre-Conquest York," in *People and Places in Northern Europe, 500–1600*, pp. 86–87.

139. Grierson and Blackburn, *Medieval European Coinage*, p. 643; Sutherland, *English Coinage*, p. 5 and Pl. 2; Hall, "York," p. 128.

140. Grierson and Blackburn, *Medieval European Coinage*, pp. 166, 169, 182, 273, 296–97; Sutherland, *English Coinage*, p. 7 and Pl. 2. Addyman, "Ecclesiastical Centres," pp. 502–3, rightly observes that the powerful eighth-century Church of York must have provided a major economic stimulus to the town's growth.

141. Altfrid, *Vita S. Liudgeri*, xi–xii, ed. G. Pertz, in *MGH SS*, II (Hanover, 1829); see also Alcuin, *Epistolae*, xvi, ed. Dümmler, in *MGH EE*, IV (Berlin, 1895). On

Frisian trade in general see further, Hodges, *Dark-Age Economics*, pp. 88–91, 124–27, and Chap. 6, below.

142. Bede, *Hist. Eccl.*, ii.14; Alcuin, *Versus*, l.24.

143. Hall, "York," pp. 128–29, and "The Making of Domesday York," in *Anglo-Saxon Settlements*, ed. Hooke, pp. 238–39 and Pl. 36; Hodges, *Anglo-Saxon Achievement*, pp. 102–3.

144. Hall, "York," pp. 126, 129–30. Structural evidence dates primarily from the late ninth century, with a few eighth-century finds that may indicate Frisian settlement: D. Bullough, "Social and Economic Structure and Topography in the Early Medieval City," in *Topografia urbana*, I, p. 378 and Pl.6. Several memorable conflagrations occurred at mid eighth-century York: *ASC* 741E; Simeon of Durham, *Historia Regum*, s.a. 764.

145. For the few, laconic references to York's fall, see *ASC* 866A; Asser, *Life of King Alfred*, xxvi. The pertinent Scandinavian and Anglo-Norman sources have been analyzed by A. P. Smyth, *Scandinavian Kings in the British Isles 850–80* (Oxford: University Press, 1977), Chap. XIII: "The Great Army and the Capture of York," pp. 178–88.

146. Hall, "York," p. 130, and "Making of Domesday York," pp. 240, 242. These properties are believed to be the same as the eleventh-century *mansiones*; the entire production-settlement zone was in place c.900–930 (ibid.). For the regular layout and details of tanning and copper-working operations, see Bullough, "Social and Economic Structure," p. 391 and Pls. 17, 18; J. Radley, "Economic Aspects of Anglo-Danish York," *Medieval Archaeology* 15 (1971), 37–57.

147. Hall, "Making of Domesday York," p. 241; H. E. Davidson, *The Viking Road to Byzantium* (London: Allen & Unwin, 1976), esp. Pts. 1, 2. Much more research needs to be done on ninth- and tenth-century Viking-fortified towns in England and abroad. Suffice it to say that they, like the burghs of Wessex and Mercia, appear to have been both defensive and commercial-industrial centers. See further, Biddle, "Development of the Anglo-Saxon Town," pp. 217–27; J. Brøndsted, *Vikings*, pp. 149–66; Hall, "The Five Boroughs of the Danelaw: A Review of Present Knowledge," *Anglo-Saxon England* 18 (1989), pp. 149–206; Clarke and Ambrosiani, *Towns in the Viking Age*, pp. 92–102.

148. Hall, "York," pp. 129–30, and "Pre-Conquest York," pp. 88–91; Biddle, "Development of the Anglo-Saxon Town," p. 220; H. Turner, *Town Defenses in England and Wales, 900–1500* (Hamden, CT: Archon Books, 1971), p. 21. The redirection of the *colonia*'s main north-south street toward the Coppergate area may well attest to the shift of commercial-industrial center in Viking times: Clarke and Ambrosiani, *Towns in the Viking Age*, pp. 94-95. The palace of the Danish earls of York is believed to have been sited within the strengthened Roman fortress area: Biddle, "Towns," p. 121; Smyth, *Scandinavian Kings*, pp. 183–84; Hall, "Pre-Conquest York," pp. 91–92. Asser implies that Anglian York was not well fortified in 866/867: *Life of King Alfred*, xxvii.

149. Eoforwicceaster: *ASC* 867[866]A, 918C, 923E.

Chapter 6

Continental Emporia and Their English Connections (c.600–900 A.D.)

The Anglo-Saxon emporia or *wics*, that appeared in the seventh and eighth centuries, were not a uniquely English urban development. On the contrary, they represent an insular expression of a new network of early medieval commercial and production sites established along the coasts of northern Europe (Map 5.1). In many cases, early Anglo-Saxon emporia had direct or indirect contacts with these continental *wics*. By considering these early English sites in a wider context, we can discern more clearly the underlying economic and political factors involved in their creation and their overall significance to English urban development.[1]

From the Claudian Conquest through the fourth century, Britain had stood at the northern end of Roman trade routes linking northwest Europe to the Mediterranean world. As we have seen, Romano-British towns, especially the cantonal capitals and larger municipalities, prospered as active participants in this far-flung commerce. The principal Roman overland route to Britain and the North Sea region passed from northern Italy over the Alps, then it bifurcated into two Gallic routes: one leading north from Provence to the Channel coast, and the other passing through the Rhineland to Frisia.[2] These long-distance trade routes were effectively cut, however, by fifth-century Germanic tribal movements that breached the *limes* of northern Germany and Gaul.[3] This rupture hastened the demise of Romano-British urban life which was already in decline.

After a hiatus of perhaps a half-century, the transalpine trade route was revived early in the sixth century amid the concurrent state-building efforts of Clovis in Gaul and Theodoric in Italy (Map 6.1.A). At the height of

Justinian's reign, Mediterranean luxury goods again were passing in small but significant quantities into northern Gaul, the Rhineland, Frisia, southern England, and Scandinavia.[4] This renewed long-distance trade, however, now appears to have been focused on political and ecclesiastical elites, either at newly occupied old Roman towns (e.g., in England) or surviving within greatly contracted town circuits (as in Gaul).[5] Indeed, it is most likely that in the essentially barter economy of sixth-century northern Europe, such exotic luxury goods served primarily as gift exchanges among elites seeking advantageous alliances.[6] In Francia, Syrian, Jewish, and Byzantine Greek merchants, often under royal protection, were evidently the main conveyors of this high-status, long-distance commerce. In England, we should probably look to Frisian traders as primary middlemen.[7]

The revival of the older Roman trade route into northern Europe proved to be short-lived. Archaeological studies have demonstrated that after c.560, the flow of Mediterranean luxury exports to the north slowed appreciably. It is currently believed that the widespread Mediterranean recession, brought about largely by Justinian's military overextensions, was the principal (though not the only) factor behind this commercial curtailment.[8] By the close of the sixth century, quite a different pattern of trade had emerged in northern Europe. Most significantly, long-distance commerce had become a more regional, Frankish affair, with its main route passing up the Rhone to the Parisian basin and then forking down the Rhine to Frisia (Map 6.1.B). The foci of this new network appear to have been the nascent royal courts, respectively, of Neustria and Austrasia, which often had town settings.[9]

It was during this critical period, c.550–625, that Merovingian kings appear to have embarked on a policy to promote and regularize this small-scale North Sea trade for their economic advantage. The volume of Frankish luxury exports to southern England and Scandinavia, attested to by finds of high-status grave goods, increased during the later sixth century. The St. Martin's (Canterbury) coin hoard (c.580) and the Faversham (Kent) hoard (c.590), with their quantities of Merovingian gold *tremisses*, reflect this heightened interchange between Francia and southern England.[10] Indeed, Merovingian rulers seem to have formalized their new policy through marital alliances, such as the betrothal of the Neustrian princess Bertha to King Aethelberht of Kent. Somewhat later, the Merovingian king Dagobert I was instrumental in founding the fair at St. Denis outside his Neustrian capital of Paris. This initiative represented a significant centralization of both local and cross-Channel trade then being conducted by Frankish and Frisian merchants.[11] Although it may well be an exaggeration to speak of a sixth-century Merovingian North Sea "empire" that encompassed southern England,[12] it does now seem clear that these early Frankish rulers were deliberately expanding their economic horizons.

An integral part of this new policy was the establishment of major emporia along the Channel and North Sea coasts. The earliest of these Merovingian trading sites appears to have been Quentovic, founded on the Channel coast south of Boulogne, perhaps in the final decades of the sixth century (Map 5.1).[13] Although excavations are incomplete, Quentovic was apparently an unfortified settlement of Frankish, Saxon, and Frisian merchants involved primarily in luxury trade with southern England. An important Frankish mint was located here from the early seventh century that struck large quantities of gold *tremisses* and, later, silver deniers until the late ninth century.[14] Archaeological and numismatic evidence confirms the close commercial ties between Quentovic and the early *wics* of Kent and Hampshire. Indeed, the foundations of Sarre and Fordwich outside Canterbury, and Hamwic below Winchester, are very likely to be seen as Anglo-Saxon responses to the growing cross-Channel trade emanating from Quentovic and northern Francia.[15]

Documentary sources indicate that Quentovic was a major, and perhaps the primary, port for travelers to and from southern England during the seventh and eighth centuries. Such prominent figures as bishops Theodore of Tarsus, Wilfrid, and Boniface, for example, can all be seen here in the course of their continental journeys.[16] Moreover, Quentovic ranked as a leading Frankish toll port, where resident royal officials collected duties and directed merchant activities. Among other evidence, the commercial correspondence between Charlemagne and Offa underscores the importance of this emporium in cross-Channel trade.[17] But like the unfortified Anglo-Saxon *wics*, Quentovic presented a very attractive target for Viking raiders during the ninth century. The settlement was plundered in 842 in an attack that also fell on Hamwic.[18] Although Quentovic continued to house a royal mint into the tenth century, most of its commercial population apparently departed for more defensible centers nearby (such as Wissant), the site having been abandoned by the eleventh century.[19]

The second major continental emporium conducting trade with early Anglo-Saxon England was located near the mouth of the Rhine at Dorestad [Wijk-bij-Duurstede] (Map 5.1). Long-term archaeological excavations have disclosed a complex commercial, industrial, and agricultural settlement occupied from the early seventh through the ninth centuries (Fig. 6.1.A).[20] The core area, north of the medieval town, included some sixty fenced, boat-shaped homesteads with attached byres. Immediately along the river lay the unfortified emporium zone with more tightly packed houses and rows of aligned, rectangular tenements. An elaborate series of wharves with causeways extended out from these merchants' quarters into the river. Such jetties and causeways were also encountered at Ipswich and Lundenwic.

The Dorestad excavations have revealed evidence of intensive commercial and industrial activity. For example, large quantities of imported pottery, quernstones, glassware, and jewelry, most of Middle Rhineland provenance, have been found. Industrial operations attested include metal, bone, wood, and leather working, cloth making, tanning, and shipbuilding. These industries appear to have been widely distributed over the settlement area rather than concentrated in distinct districts. Indeed, the *wic* at Dorestad was quite large, perhaps 100 to 200 acres, and the entire settlement area, including an extensive agricultural zone, may have encompassed up to 600 acres. It is currently believed that the emporium housed from 1,000 to 2,000 people at its height. These figures for Dorestad may be compared with population estimates from 1,000 to perhaps 5,000 for contemporary Anglo-Saxon *wics*, which also ranged in size generally between 100 and 150 acres.

Dorestad has been shown to have been the principal trading partner of Anglo-Saxon emporia in eastern England, especially Ipswich. From the late seventh to ninth centuries, in fact, Dorestad ranked as the primary port of trade between the Austrasian Rhineland and the North Sea littoral (Map 6.1.C).[21] Moreover, all indications point to Dorestad as the main base of Frisian traders under Frankish hegemony. In the early seventh century, a Merovingian royal mint striking a variety of Frankish gold *tremisses* and local imitations evidently was established here.[22] At this initial stage, Dorestad appears to have been a settlement of Frisian farmer-traders engaged in limited seasonal commerce. During the seventh century it seems to have prospered as Frisian commercial influence and Frankish royal authority expanded.[23] Dorestad, like Quentovic, first appears in the historical record late in the seventh century as a leading port for Anglo-Saxon travelers to the Continent. Thus, Wilfred, on his way to Rome in 678, reportedly wintered over at Dorestad under the protection of the Frisian king Aldgisl.[24] Archaeological evidence suggests that Dorestad was elevated into a major Frankish emporium after Pepin of Herstal's temporary annexation of Frisia (689).[25] Thereafter, Dorestad became a primary base for Anglo-Saxon missions to northern Germany. Both Willibrord and Boniface began their continental evangelizations from this site (692, 716 A.D.).[26]

These increasing cross-Channel missionary activities were but reflections of Dorestad's mounting commercial prominence. Indeed, Charles Martel's firm incorporation of Dorestad within Frankish hegemony (c.719) seems to have stimulated the settlement's development greatly. Numismatic evidence, for example, clearly demonstrates that Dorestad reached its peak period of prosperity c.730–830.[27] Under Charlemagne and Louis the Pious, Dorestad was a major port of the Frankish Empire, a tightly controlled emporium where merchants from many lands congregated under the protection and direction of palace officials.[28] Alcuin, writing in the 780s, confirms the close commercial links between Dorestad and England, well attested by recent excavations at Anglo-Saxon emporia.[29] Dorestad's specialized economic functions, large settled population, mint, and important Frankish imperial role all distinguish it as an urban place.

But Dorestad, like many Anglo-Saxon *wics*, did not survive the tumults of the ninth century. On the one hand, there are signs of an early ninth-century economic decline at the site (Map 6.1.D). It has been suggested that this slowdown, also attested at several Anglo-Saxon emporia, was brought about by the shifting of Frankish trade networks from the lower Rhine-North Sea to interior Germany and the Baltic. In addition, the weakening of royal authority in the dynastic quarrels among the sons of Louis the Pious during the 830s may have been another factor undermining Dorestad's prosperity. [30] The decisive final blow, however, clearly was delivered by the Vikings, who sacked the unfortified river site six times between 835 and 863. Although there may be some exaggeration in the report that their last raid left the site depopulated, especially when one considers the otherwise close cooperation between Frisians, Saxons, and Vikings, it is nonetheless true that Dorestad thereafter virtually disappears from the written record.[31] With the Viking onslaughts, this once-vibrant emporium, like Hamwic, Ipswich, and Lundenwic, seems to have been abandoned progressively for better-defended, walled sites nearby, in this case, probably Tiel and Utrecht.[32]

Quentovic and Dorestad were the forerunners of many other trading and production centers founded during the eighth and ninth centuries along the coastal regions of northern and eastern Europe. In particular, archaeologists have identified and studied an important series of more easterly emporia ranging from northern Germany to southern Scandinavia and the Baltic. This group includes, to name but a few sites, the following: Bardowic, Domburg, Hamburg, Haithabu (Hedeby), Ribe, Kaupang, Helgö, Reric, Birka, and Wollin (Map 6.2).[33] All of these emporia, despite their geographic and ethnic diversity, ultimately owed their origin and growth to the reorientation of Frankish trade networks toward the Baltic late in the eighth century. This new Baltic trade, which supplied the West with Islamic silver, was opened first by the Swedish Vikings and then the Varangian Rus.[34] Among those sites that have yielded the best material evidence, Haithabu on the Frankish-Danish border, Kaupang in southern Norway, and Helgö and Birka in east-central Sweden can be taken as representative examples.

Haithabu stood on low-lying ground near the mouth of the River Schlei in southern Denmark. Largely due to this favorable location at the base of the Jutish peninsula, it became during the ninth century the main emporium linking North Sea and Baltic trade (Map 6.3).[35] Modern excavations have shown that Haithabu began as a small site (the South Settlement) encompassing some forty sunken huts with associated burial ground c.750 (Fig. 6.1.B). Artifacts and grave goods suggest that its initial inhabitants were Frisian and Saxon farmer-traders already engaged, albeit on a small scale, in both Frankish North Sea trade and local industrial production.[36] By c.825, however, this core area and two similar satellite settlements to the north appear to have been consolidated into a larger, permanent 60-acre emporium, which displays substantial evidence of intensive long-distance trade, craft production, and a planned topographical structure.

Haithabu's commercial activities are attested, for example, by finds of Rhenish glassware and quernstones, Rhenish and Slavic pottery, Anglo-Saxon jewelry, and Scandinavian soapstone, amber, furs, and hides. Its industries comprised a full range of metalworking (including sword production), weaving, glassmaking and leatherworking.[37] A regular network of streets, flanked by substantial timber-framed dwellings with workshops, led to the waterfront and a 500-foot harbor jetty. The Haithabu buildings were constructed in a wide variety of styles, while their fenced tenement boundaries and alignments generally remained fixed over time.[38] Dendrochronology places the establishment of these first central *wic* buildings in the period c.810–830, with supplemental construction to c.880.[39] At the height of its prosperity (c.850–950), Haithabu is estimated to have had between one and two thousand inhabitants, the majority of whom, judging from grave excavations, were males.[40] As with other *wics*, Haithabu initially was unfortified, though a low earthen bank did serve to delimit the trade and craft area itself.[41] A mint also was established at Haithabu in the early ninth century that struck silver coinage imitating Frankish (Dorestad), Frisian, and Anglo-Saxon issues.[42] But unlike many other emporia, Haithabu appears to have prospered during the Viking period, perhaps because of its imposing semicircular rampart constructed early in the tenth century.[43] Still, the site shows signs of having suffered massive destruction by fire in the mid-eleventh century, followed by gradual abandonment.[44]

Written sources provide further clarity to this archaeological portrayal of Haithabu's development. Although the first eighth-century settlements are unrecorded, there are fairly numerous historical references to the main, central emporium and its emergence in the milieu of Carolingian political and economic expansion into northern Germany. Thus, when Charlemagne unleashed his Frankish forces on the Saxons in 772, the nearby Danes became alarmed and supported their neighbors' cause by harboring Saxon fugitives.[45] The treaty arranged some ten years later between Charles and the Danish king Sigifrid may have temporarily stabilized relations but also appears to have fostered the further spread of Carolingian economic interests to the northeast.[46] In 808, the new Danish king, Godfred, properly fearing Frankish imperial ambitions, broke the accord and sacked the Saxon or Slavic emporium called Reric (possibly Old Lübeck), then in alliance with the Franks (Map 6.2). Godfred thereupon reportedly transferred the merchants of this place to a new emporium he had just set up on the Schlei, evidently Haithabu.[47]

This foundation or, more likely, consolidation of earlier small *wics*, is in accord with the dendrochronological dating and early planned layout of the site. The critical role of Anglo-Saxon and Merovingian kings in the establishment of emporia for their realms already has been observed. Haithabu also appears prominently in the *Life* of St. Anskar, who visited the site on his mission to the Danes (826). In this biography, composed by his disciple Rimbert c.865–870, Haithabu is described as a *vicus* and *portus* with a large population of merchants and craftsmen, as well as Carolingian royal officials and a certain class of *primores vici* notable for their firm adoption of Christianity. At the same time, however, this emporium clearly was the center of an active slave trade.[48]

Other notable visitors to Haithabu include the Norwegian trader Ottar, whose travel tales apparently made quite a stir at King Alfred's court, the ninth-century English adventurer Wulfstan, and the intriguing tenth-century Cordoban merchant Al-Tartushi, who described the settlement's large size and bustling activity, its abundant freshwater wells, and the heterogeneous religious practices of its inhabitants.[49]   The written and archaeological evidence thus indicates that Haithabu, by virtue of its non-agrarian trade and production, permanent settlement, mint, churches and administrative role, was a major urban place in the Carolingian empire with far-reaching commercial ties. Haithabu's later decline may well be related to disruptions brought about as it became a pawn between Danish and German rulers. In the early tenth century, for example, Haithabu reportedly passed under the dominion of the Saxon emperor Henry the Fowler, who installed a resident margrave and a "colony of Saxons" in the emporium. A century later it was ceded back to Denmark by the Salian emperor Conrad II. Finally, the destructive fire attested by site excavations can most likely be attributed to the recorded burning of Haithabu c.1050 by Harald Hardrada of Norway in his conflict with the Danish king Svein.[50]

The Scandinavian emporia followed a generally similar developmental pattern, though with occasional significant variations. Many of these sites, previously known only from limited written references, have become more clearly identified by archaeological investigations of the past several decades. Ribe in western Denmark and Kaupang in south coastal Norway are good examples. Excavations at Ribe (Fig. 6.2.A) revealed a substantial trade and production center occupied intensively from the early eighth to the eleventh century.[51] Initial farming and perhaps market sites were succeeded by such urban features as metal and glass-working shops and permanent tenements. At first unfortified, Ribe was walled in the tenth century and later became a suburb of the larger, high medieval town with castle and cathedral immediately across the river.

In Norway, Kaupang and its early urban role also has received attention. The merchant Ottar reported to King Alfred that before landing at Haithabu, he had been under sail for five days from the port called "Sciringes-heal," evidently in east coastal Norway.[52] The site of Ottar's ninth-century emporium remained quite unknown, despite antiquarian efforts, until the modern excavation campaign at Kaupang, today a small farming hamlet in the Tjølling district of the archaeologically-rich Vestfold province.[53] Indeed, attention first had been directed to this area in the early nineteenth century, when it was noted that title-deeds of the fifteenth century designated the Tjølling area as Skiringssal (<Sciringes-heal). The suggestive etymology of the name Kaupang itself also was recognized (Old Swedish *koping*, Old English *ceaping*, Old Norse *Kaupangr* = "trading place, market").[54]

Recent excavations at Kaupang have revealed a small settlement of rect-angular and boat-shaped timber structures arranged along cobbled roads running parallel to the bay and fronted by several stone jetties (Fig. 6.2.B). A mid- to-late ninth century dating was established by coin finds (Anglo-Saxon, Carolingian, Arabic), ceramic analysis, and carbon-14 tests. Evidence of trade included numerous Anglo-Irish brooches, Rhenish, Frisian, and Slavic pottery, and remains of "Frisian" cloth, probably from the Dorestad or Haithabu areas.[55] Metalworking of all types evidently was conducted at Kaupang; indeed, the quantities of slag, ingots, crucibles, and tools identify several structures as workshops. Moreover, there appears to have been a prominent soapstone industry at the site, producing a range of finished articles for export such as domestic utensils, cauldrons, and fishing gear.[56]

Like many other emporia, Kaupang had no fortifications. It was provided with natural protection, however, by steep cliffs to landward and a series of skerries sheltering the harbor area from open sea. Thus it is somewhat curious that occupation within the emporium seems not to have extended much beyond c.900. It has been suggested that progressive harbor silting eventually shifted Kaupang's trade and craft functions to nearby Tønsberg.[57] On the other hand, the immediate area remained densely settled, judging by the continued use of cemeteries containing rich cremation and boat burials.[58] Still, the overall impression of this site is that of a semirural settlement that had a brief but intensive floruit of commercial and industrial activity as part of the emerging ninth-century network of North Sea *wics*. Indeed, Kaupang, like Ribe, may have been more a small-scale, even seasonal, gathering site for merchants and craftsmen than a large, permanent emporium comparable to those of northern Germany or England.[59] But Kaupang's concentration of traders and craftsmen as well as its planned layout does suggest the kind of central, probably royal, direction encountered at other emporium-type towns. In this regard, one perhaps may note the presence of a nearby royal vill (Husby), and the fact that the Vestfold area was the ancestral home of Harald Fairhair's clan, who united Norway c.872.[60]

The overseas trade routes and emporia that bound together England, northern France, Frisia, Germany, Denmark, and Norway into a large commercial network extended well into the Baltic area. Two Swedish emporia, Helgö and Birka, played particularly prominent roles in this eastern trade zone. Helgö, located on the small island of Lillön in Lake Mälar on the east coast of central Sweden some twenty miles west of Stockholm, seems to have been an important entrepôt and production center from a very early date (Fig. 6.3.A). The modern excavations, led by Wilhelm Holmqvist, have produced quite significant and sometimes startling results.[61]

The settlement at Helgö was comprised of groups of tightly packed timber-frame houses, some with entrance ramps, porches, and stone foundations, all arranged on artificial terraces along a sloping hillside leading down to the harbor area. There appears to have been a succession of at least three settlement foci from the fifth to the ninth centuries A.D. In particular, an unusually large and varied amount of material evidence indicates that Helgö had been a substantial metalworking center as early as the fifth and sixth centuries A.D. Thousands of mold fragments for iron and bronze buckles and brooches have been uncovered, along with many smithies' tools, balance weights, keys and padlocks, spearheads, and knives. This industrial production evidently continued, though on a diminishing scale, through the eighth century.[62]

Long-distance trade also had a significant role at Helgö. The earliest evidence includes two large hoards of late Roman and Byzantine gold coins (c.425–525), along with a large "Coptic" bronze ladle and a late Roman-type silver bowl, both of sixth- or early seventh-century provenance. Groups of Roman provincial glassware and small bronze domestic items from the Slavic Baltic (c.300–700) also emerged at the Helgö excavations. In addition, a variety of imported gold objects were found, including rings, bracelets, and several dozen "Nordic" bracteates probably used in Germanic religious cults.[63]   But the two most sensational finds that demonstrate Helgö's overseas contacts are the magnificent "Celtic" crozier and more remarkable Buddha statuette. The bronze crozier crook, decorated with colored glass, enamel, and millefiori inlay, is thought to have been brought from eighth-century Ireland as Viking plunder for sale or trade at the Helgö emporium.[64] The bronze Buddha figure, most likely produced in northern India c.600, presents quite a puzzle. It is usually regarded as further evidence of the Vikings' new trade connections with Byzantium, the Caliphate, and the Far East opened during the early ninth century. More significant was the subsequent trade network established by the Varangian Rus from their military-commercial towns (gorods) along the great waterways of eastern Europe. Due to the Varangians' conquests and commercial activities, the furs, hides, and slaves of the North and Slavic lands could be exchanged for commodities sought in western Europe, such as Islamic silver and exotic items like silks and spices (Map 6.3).[65]

The early date at which Helgö flourished as a commercial and production center, and its particular concentration of industrial activities, are the most notable aspects of this emporium. Indeed, its peak period of prosperity coincides with the reestablishment of Mediterranean trade routes to northern Europe in the age of Justinian.[66] Helgö was then already a specialized settlement of traders and craftsmen clearly "emancipated" from the countryside. As Herbert Jankuhn reminds us, this spatial and functional separation is one of the primary characteristics of early medieval urbanism.[67] The lack of an identifiable agrarian component at Helgö makes it somewhat unlikely that this was a settlement of part-time farmer-traders, while the succession of settlement clusters over a long period rules out the possibility of a temporary or seasonal market. Rather, Helgö's primary economic function was evidently industrial, that is, it was a site where raw materials (especially iron) extracted from the north were worked and distributed.[68] In this regard, one can reasonably speculate that the town had been established by the Vendel or Svea kings, whose great wealth was based mainly on control of this iron trade between the Mälar valley and northern Sweden. Many of the artifacts uncovered in the early medieval Swedish royal graves are nearly identical to those found recently in Helgö.[69] Although an Iron Age hill fort stood on the southern side of Helgö, the exposed emporium site itself was never fortified. By the early ninth century, at any rate, most of Helgö's industrial and commercial functions appear to have been supplanted by nearby Birka, an emporium more clearly under Swedish royal aegis.[70]

Birka was located on another island (Björkö) in Lake Mälar, about five miles northwest of Helgö. Excavations begun in the late nineteenth century and renewed more recently by Björn Ambrosiani have disclosed important details of what was apparently the primary Scandinavian emporium of the ninth and tenth centuries.[71] The site consisted of a central occupation zone of some 30 acres with timber-frame houses and workshops, an extensive series of cremation and inhumation graves, and four harbor areas. A later defensive wall enclosed the central emporium zone and its adjacent hill fort (Fig. 6.3.B). Long-distance trade evidently was the mainstay of Birka's prosperity. Indeed, this emporium's better port facilities may account in part for its supplanting of Helgö. Three of Birka's four harbors were natural, including one for shallow-draught vessels and a main harbor area on the town's west side; all have yielded evidence of jetties and docks. An intriguing artificial harbor also lay just east of Birka (Salviksgropen), where vessels entered through a tunnel-like gate to set anchor in a dredged, square cove.[72] Birka was clearly more than a seasonal trading site.

Specific material evidence of Birka's trade derives from its 2,000 burials, beginning c.780–800, and numerous coin deposits. Glassware and ceramic from the Carolingian Rhineland, Slavic pottery, Rhenish and Anglo-Saxon brooches, hides and furs from the north, along with remains of Byzantine and Chinese silks, have all been found at Birka.[73] Nearly two hundred coins, predominantly of the ninth and early tenth centuries, thus far have been recovered. Significantly, two-thirds of these are Arabic silver issues; the remainder include Frankish, Anglo-Saxon, Byzantine, and local Scandinavian varieties. In addition to this coinage, over one hundred balance-weights of the type used by merchants and three complete sets of scales emerged from the Birka burials.[74]

Archaeological and numismatic evidence thus has demonstrated that a large part of Birka's overseas trade was oriented eastward, along the Viking routes to Byzantium and the Islamic world. Birka hence operated in the same trading sphere as Helgö but at a later date, in the quickened economic milieu of the ninth and tenth centuries.[75] Indeed, this emporium owed its dominant position largely to the fact that it was the eastern terminus of North Sea commerce and the staging point for "far east" trade (Map 6.3).[76] At the same time, recent excavations have shown that Birka was also the center of a more regional economy. Although its specialized economic functions, distinct house forms, rich graves, and burial customs clearly mark it off from surrounding agrarian settlements, these local villages and the steadily growing rural population of Mälar evidently represented major markets for Birka's craft products.[77]

In the case of Birka, unlike Kaupang and Helgö, substantial historical evidence permits further insight into the social and political dimensions of this prosperous northern emporium. Our two main sources are the *Life of St. Anskar*, written c.880, and the late eleventh-century ecclesiastical history of Adam of Bremen. Birka appears in both works primarily by virtue of its important role in the Scandinavian missions sponsored by Frankish rulers.

Anskar first came to Birka c.830, on invitation of a certain King Björn, who was responsive to the Carolingian missionary campaign and on good terms with Louis the Pious.[78] The bishop's efforts apparently resulted in only a few conversions, however, and his distress over this unsatisfactory situation eventually prompted a second visit c.850. With royal support and the help of his previous converts, Anskar then was able to erect churches and begin forming the core of a Christian community based on Birka.[79] But upon his death in 865, the kings of Sweden with many of their followers apostacized and drove out this fledgling mission.[80] The evangelization of Sweden had to be taken up again and brought to fruition by Bishop Unni, who, according to Adam of Bremen, began his work again from Birka in 935.[81]

In the *Vita Anskarii*, Birka is called an emporium (*vicus*) and port (*portus*), inhabited by both ordinary folk (*populi*) and many rich merchants (*negotiatores*), where there was "an abundance of all goods and much treasure."[82] Next to the *wic* stood a place of temporary refuge, called a *civitas/urbs*, which is described as being "not very strong" (*non multum firma*).[83] This is presumably the old hill fort which later was enclosed within Birka's earthen wall. It was to this refuge that the inhabitants fled, under the direction of Herigar, the "prefect of the *vicus*" and "king's counselor," when Birka suddenly was raided by Danes (c.830).[84] There are also several references to a general assembly (*conventum populi publicum*) of this ninth-century emporium, which determined major issues such as the adoption of Christianity. At these meetings, the king, or prefect or leading men, appear to have had the right of first address.[85] Adam of Bremen's later description of Birka portrays a still-prosperous port, where merchant ships from a host of northern peoples met for trade.[86] But some hints are also given of worsened conditions, such as frequent pirate attacks and the deliberate obstruction of harbor access.[87]

Indeed, historical and archaeological evidence combines to indicate that Birka was lapsing into decline from the mid-tenth century. When Bishop Adalward of Sigtuna paused there on a journey (c.1060), he found only desertion and waste.[88] No Anglo-Saxon coins of Aethelred II, used to pay the last major Danegeld, have been found at Birka, though they are numerous elsewhere in Sweden. In fact, a small hoard of late-tenth-century coins is the last evidence of site occupation.[89] A series of defensive works also belongs to this later period. For example, Birka's rampart was erected apparently rather hastily c.950, after the emporium had been without fortifications for over a century. The old hill fort, now enclosed along with the *wic*, seems to have been more densely occupied at this time. Indeed, paleobotanical studies have shown that this late tenth-century intramural area was considerably smaller than the extent of the ninth-century emporium.[90]

Several possible reasons for Birka's decline can be suggested. The fortification campaign may have been a response to periodic raids mentioned in the historical sources or to events surrounding the tradition that Birka finally was destroyed by Danish forces at the close of the tenth century.[91] But since there is no firm archaeological evidence of widespread destruction, larger economic factors more likely were responsible for this emporium's declining fortunes. Thus, Birka's important long-distance commerce probably suffered from such events as the interruption of the Volga route after c.950 by Turkic invasion, along with the subsequent growth of Russian towns and the reopening of Mediterranean-Northern trade by the Italian cities.[92]

Finally, one must mention briefly the case of Sigtuna, an important late emporium north of Birka, with its excellent natural harbor and more favorable position on the iron-trade route between Mälar and northern Sweden.[93] Indeed, it is generally believed that much of Birka's population gradually shifted to this nearby site during the late tenth and early eleventh centuries. Whatever the explanation may be for Birka's decline (and a combination of factors is more probable), Sigtuna does appear to have been the prime beneficiary.[94] Such a settlement shift has been observed at a number of other emporia discussed in this chapter and underscores how dependent these early towns were on fluctuating patterns of commerce, as well as adequate defense and royal protection.

It is quite likely that these North Sea and Scandinavian emporia, like Anglo-Saxon *wics*, had been royal creations. King Godfred's foundation of the main *wic* at Haithabu is attested explicitly. The case of Kaupang is less clear, though its planned layout and industrial concentration can be regarded as signs of direct royal involvement. Such important emporia as Helgö and Birka are unlikely to have been born and flourished independently of those Swedish kings whose power and influence are commemorated in the great burial mounds of Vendel and Old Uppsala. Royal authority over Birka may well have been represented by the *praefectus vici*, an official whom we have seen before in the Anglo-Saxon *wic*-reeve. The fact that the Swedish king could give property in Birka to missionaries lends support to the view that this emporium had a royal foundation. In addition, the proximity of Swedish royal vills to both Helgö and Birka may have been a source of needed protection and economic support.[95] At any rate, the predominantly eastern trade of the Scandinavian emporia, built to some extent on the previous experiences of Dorestad and Haithabu, clearly had a major impact on the early stages of western Europe's economic revival.[96]

The concentration of commercial and/or industrial activities, dense populations, spatial separation from the countryside, and in some cases mints and multiple churches all distinguish these sites as towns. The first steps in their creation were taken by early Frankish kings, and their fellow Anglo-Saxon rulers did not lag far behind. For that matter, it is very likely that *wics* were founded either to strengthen established royal authority, as in Francia, or to support claims to unitary kingship, as in England and Scandinavia. By establishing fixed centers for trade and production, aspiring royal families could control resources that otherwise might have gone to competing noble clans. Tolls collected on trade at these *wics* provided a lucrative income for the further growth and consolidation of royal authority. It is no coincidence that most emporia can be closely associated with particular royal lines and stood near royal capitals or royal estates that could provide security and markets for their products.[97] Early Anglo-Saxon emporia prospered by virtue of common interests between Frankish and English rulers and the brisk cross-Channel commerce they promoted. From the late sixth to the early ninth centuries, such Anglo-Saxon emporia as Hamwic, Sarre, Fordwich, Ipswich, Lundenwic, and Eorforwic actively participated in this mutually beneficial trade with their continental counterparts of Quentovic, Dorestad, and Haithabu. This commercial network later expanded to include the Scandinavian emporia as well, though the evidence for these Baltic-English connections is admittedly less full.

The Viking onslaughts of the ninth and tenth centuries brought significant changes to *wics* in England and on the Continent. Before this time, emporia probably received what little protection they needed from nearby royal capitals and royal vills. Faced now with sudden and frequently repeated attacks, a number of unfortified *wics* were destroyed outright, and others gradually were abandoned in favor of neighboring walled sites. Certain prominent emporia such as Haithabu and Birka did receive fortifications, which prolonged their lives for a time, but they too were to fall victim to fluctuations in the wider economic currents of tenth-century Europe.

NOTES

1. An essential starting point for the study of these continental *wics* is F. Petri, "Die Anfänge des mittelalterlichen Städtewesens in den Niederlanden und dem angrenzenden Frankreich," in *Studien zu den Anfängen des europäischen Stadtewesens*, ed. T. Mayer (Constance: J. Thorbecke, 1958), pp. 227–95, esp. 248–67. See also E. Ennen, "Das Städtewesen Nordwestdeutschlands von der frankischen bis zur salischen Zeit," in C. Haase, ed., *Die Stadt des Mittelalters*, Wege der Forschung, 243–45 (3 vols., Darmstadt: Wissenschaftliche Buchgesellschaft, 1969–1973), I, pp. 163–75; H. Jankuhn, "Frühe Städte in Nord und Ostseeraum," in *Topografia urbana e vita cittadina nell'alto medioevo in occidente* (2 vols., Spoleto: Centro Italiano di Studi Sull'Alto Medioevo, 1974), I, pp. 153–201; L. Schütte, *Wik: eine Siedlungsbezeichnung in historischen and sprachlichen Bezügen* (Cologne: Böhlau, 1976), esp. pp. 93–121; also now: H. Clarke and A. Simms, eds., *The Comparative History of Urban Origins in Non-Roman Europe*, 2 vols., British Archaeological Reports (hereafter B.A.R.) International Series, 255 (Oxford, 1985); H. Clarke and B. Ambrosiani, *Towns in the Viking Age* (NY: St. Martin's Press, 1991), pp. 46–89.

2. M. P. Charlesworth, *Trade-Routes and Commerce of the Roman Empire* (2d ed. rev., Cambridge: University Press, 1926), pp. 170–89, 208–214; T. Frank, *An Economic Survey of Ancient Rome*, Vol. 4, *Rome and Italy of the Empire* (Baltimore: Johns Hopkins Press, 1940), pp. 287–92; R. Rémondon, *La crise de l'empire romain de Marc-Aurèle à Anastase* (Paris: Presses Universitaires de France, 1964), p. 332, Map 8.

3. E. Demougeot, "Les invasions germaniques et la rupture des relations entre la Bretagne et la Gaule," *Le Moyen Age* 68 (1962), 1–50; R. Hodges, *Dark-Age Economics: The Origins of Towns and Trade A.D. 600–1000* (NY: St. Martin's Press, 1982), pp. 29–30.

4. See J. Werner's fundamental study: "Fernhandel und Naturalwirtschaft im östlichen Merovingerreich nach archäologischen und numismatischen Zeugnissen," in *Moneta e scambi nell'alto medioevo* (Spoleto: Centro Italiano di Studi sull'Alto Medioevo, 1961), pp. 557–618, esp. pp. 563–94. Also: H. Adelson, "Early Medieval

Trade Routes," *American Historical Review* 65 (1959–60), 271–87; A. R. Lewis, *The Northern Seas: Shipping and Commerce in Northern Europe A.D. 300–1100* (Princeton: Princeton University Press, 1958), pp. 129–30; Hodges, *Dark-Age Economics*, p. 31.

5. M. Biddle, "Development of the Anglo-Saxon Town," in *Topografia urbana e vita cittadina*, I, pp. 206–12; E. Ennen, *Die europäische Stadt des Mittelalters* (Göttingen: Vandenhoeck & Ruprecht, 1972), pp. 34–45; J. Hubert, "Evolution de la topographie et de l'aspect des villes de Gaules du V\u1d49 au X\u1d49 siècle," in *La città nell'alto medioevo* (Spoleto: Centro Italiano di Studi Sull'alto Medioevo, 1959), pp. 529–58; D. M. Nicholas, "Medieval Urban Origins in Northern Continental Europe," *Studies in Medieval and Renaissance History* 6 (1969), pp. 69–79. Also: Jankuhn, "Vor- und frühformen der Stadt in archäologischer Sicht," in *Geschichtswissenschaft und Archaologie: Untersuchungen zur Siedlungs-Wirtschafts-und Kirchengeschichte*, eds. Jankuhn and R. Wenskus (Sigmaringen: Jan Thorbecke Verlag, 1979), pp. 246–50; E. James, *The Origins of France: From Clovis to the Capetians* (NY: St. Martin's Press, 1982), pp. 43–63; Hodges and D. Whitehouse, *Mohammed, Charlemagne, and the Origins of Europe* (Ithaca: Cornell University Press, 1983), pp. 82–88.

6. P. Grierson, "Commerce in the Dark Ages: A Critique of the Evidence," *Transactions of the Royal Historical Society* 9 (1959), pp. 123–40; G. Duby, *Guerriers et paysans, VII\u1d49–XII\u1d49 siècle: premier essor de l'économie européenne* (Paris: Gallimard, 1973), pp. 60–83; P. H. Sawyer, "Kings and Merchants," in *Early Medieval Kingship*, eds. Sawyer and I. Wood (Leeds: University Press, 1977), pp. 140–41, 144–45; Hodges, *The Anglo-Saxon Achievement: Archaeology and the Beginnings of English Society* (Ithaca: Cornell University Press, 1989), pp. 41–42; C. J. Arnold, *An Archaeology of the Early Anglo-Saxon Kingdoms* (London: Routledge, 1988), pp. 50–51, 59–61. J. Callmer, "Three Fundamental Perspectives for the Study of Trade and Exchange in Northern Europe in the Second Half of the First Millennium A.D.," in *Trade and Exchange in Prehistory*, eds. B. Hardh, et al. (Lund: Bloms Boktryckeri, 1988), pp. 261–70, esp. 264–66.

7. The evidence has been well reviewed by R. Latouche, *Les origines de l'économie occidentale* (Paris: A. Michel, 1956), pp. 141–46. See further, Lewis, *Northern Seas*, pp. 143–47, 220–26; Sawyer, "Kings and Merchants," pp. 149–51; P. Geary, *Before France and Germany: The Creation and Transformation of the Merovingian World* (NY: Oxford University Press, 1988), pp. 101–3, 177–78. Again, slaves, furs, salt, and wool were among the main North European exports, as they were to be in Carolingian times.

8. Other factors include the establishment of the anti-Frankish Lombard kingdom in northern Italy and the Justinianic plague. Mediterranean trade by nearly all accounts did fall to low levels in the late seventh century yet never ceased entirely, and the Alpine route would be reopened in the eighth century. See G. Hodgett, *A Social and Economic History of Medieval Europe* (London: Methuen, 1972), pp. 43–47; Hodges, *Dark-Age Economics*, pp. 33–34; A. Cameron, *The Mediterranean World in Late Antiquity A.D. 395–600* (London: Routledge, 1993), pp. 101–23.

9. Paris and Cologne, for example, were primary Merovingian royal residences. See Latouche, *Les origines*, pp. 118–20; Lewis, *Northern Seas*, pp. 157–58, 173–74; Geary, *Before France and Germany*, pp. 97–99; Hodges, *Dark-Age Economics*, pp. 39, 48–49. See further on trade routes, Nicholas, "Medieval Urban Origins," pp. 80–81.

10. P. Grierson and M. Blackburn, *Medieval European Coinage I: The Early Middle Ages* (Cambridge: University Press, 1986), pp. 122–24. See also: Chap. 4, above.

11. For discussions of early Frankish fairs, see R. Doehaerd, *Le haut moyen âge occidentale: économie et sociétés* (Paris: Presses Universitaires de France, 1971), pp. 223–25; A. Lombard-Jourdan, "Les foires aux origines des villes," *Francia* 10 (1982), pp. 429–48, and on the Neustrian-Kentish marriage, see Chap. 4, above.

12. As do I. N. Wood, "The Merovingian North Sea,"*Alingas Occasional Papers on Medieval Topics* 1 (1983), 1–26, and "The Franks and Sutton Hoo," in *People and Places in Northern Europe*, eds. Wood and N. Lund (Woodbridge, Suffolk: Boydell Press, 1991), pp. 12–14; J. M. Wallace-Hadrill, *Bede's "Ecclesiastical History of the English People": A Historical Commentary* (Oxford: Clarendon Press, 1988), pp. 32–33; J. Campbell, "The Lost Centuries: 400–600," in *The Anglo-Saxons*, ed. Campbell (London: Penguin, 1982), p. 38.

13. For Quentovic ("the *wic* on the river Canche"), see J. Dhondt, "Les problèmes de Quentovic," in *Studi in onore di Amintore Fanfani* (6 vols., Milan: Giuffre, 1962), I, pp. 185–248; M. Rouche, "Les Saxons et les origines de Quentovic," *Revue du Nord* 59 (1977), 457–78; D. Hill, et al., "Quentovic Defined," *Antiquity* 64 (1990), 51–58.

14. Grierson and Blackburn, *Medieval European Coinage*, pp. 134–35. Coins from the Quentovic mint are well represented in the Crondall hoard [Hampshire, c.650] (Map 3.1); ibid., pp. 126–27. For Continental *wic* coinage, see further, W. Jesse, "Wik-Orte und Münzprägung," *Hansische Geschichtsblätter* 73 (1955), 106–16.

15. Hodges, *Dark-Age Economics*, p. 36. The first Anglo-Saxon *thrymsas* and *sceattas* were apparently struck to accommodate this Frankish trade: ibid., pp. 108–11, and see Chaps. 4 and 5, above.

16. Bede, *Historia Ecclesiastica* (hereafter *Hist. Eccl.*), iv.1; ed. C. Plummer (2 vols., Oxford: Clarendon Press, 1896); Eddius Stephanus, *Vita S. Wilfridi*, xxv, ed. B. Colgrave (Cambridge: University Press, 1927); Willibald, *Vita S. Bonifatii*, v, ed. W. Levison, *Monumenta Germaniae Historica* (hereafter *MGH*), *Scriptores Rerum Germanicarum* (hereafter *SS RG*), XLVIII (Hanover, 1905).

17. For reviews of these Frankish sources, see Latouche, *Les origines de l'économie occidentale*, pp. 158, 197–98; Petri, "Anfänge des mittelalterlichen Stadtewesens," pp. 248–49, 265–66; Ennen, "Stadtewesen Nordwestdeutschlands," pp. 167–68. It has indeed been suggested that the models for Frankish emporia were late Roman-Byzantine border toll stations: Duby, *Premier essor*, p. 121. See further, A. H. M. Jones, *The Later Roman Empire, 284–602* (2 vols., Norman: University of Oklahoma Press, 1964), II, pp. 825–27; H. W. Haussig, *A History of Byzantine Civilization*, trans. J. M. Hussey (NY: Praeger, 1971), pp. 62–64, 171–73.

18. *Two of the Saxon Chronicles Parallel* (hereafter *ASC*), eds. J. Earle and C. Plummer (2 vols., Oxford: Clarendon Press, 1892–99), s.a. 839[842]A; Nithard, *Histoire des fils de Louis le Pieux*, iv.3.

19. Doehaerd, *Le haut moyen âge*, p. 285; Hodges, *Dark-Age Economics*, pp. 98, 174.

20. For excavations at Dorestad, see: W. A. van Es and W. Verwers, "Dorestad, III: Archäologisches," in *Reallexikon der germanischen Altertumskunde*, ed. J. Hoops (2d ed., Berlin: De Gruyter, 1968–), VI (1985), pp. 65–76; Verwers, "Dorestad: A

Carolingian Town?" in *The Rebirth of Towns in the West*, eds. R. Hodges and R. Hobley, Council for British Archaeology (hereafter *C.B.A.*) Research Reports, 68 (London, 1988), pp. 52–56; Hodges, *Dark-Age Economics*, pp. 74–76; Clarke and Ambrosiani, *Towns in the Viking Age*, pp. 18, 19, 25–29. There are several useful, though older, summaries, e.g.: Jankuhn, "Nord und Ostseeraum," pp. 162–70; H. van Regteren Altena, "The Origin and Development of Dutch Towns," *World Archaeology* 2 (1970), 128–40 esp. 130–31.

21. Ennen, "Städtewesens Nordwestdeutschlands," p. 166; Hodges, "Ports of Trade in Early Medieval Europe," *Norwegian Archaeological Review* 11 (1978), 97–98.

22. Grierson and Blackburn, *Medieval European Coinage*, pp. 137–38, 149–54.

23. The very earliest occupation evidence at Dorestad (c.625–50) comes from a nearby area across the Rhine, close to the probable site of the old Roman fort of Levefanum. It has been suggested plausibly that the Merovingian kings resettled this and other ruinous forts of the Rhine *limes* as they extended their hegemony northward: Verwers, "Dorestad," p. 52; Ennen, *Europäische Stadt des Mittelalters*, pp. 47, 50; Hodges, *Dark-Age Economics*, pp. 87–94.

24. *Vita S. Wilfridi*, xxvi; Bede, *Hist. Eccl.*, v. 19.

25. Verwers, "Dorestad," p. 54; Hodges, *Dark-Age Economics*, p. 88.

26. Alcuin, *Vita S. Willibrordi*, v, ed. Levison, in *MGH SS RM*, VII (Hanover, 1919); Willibald, *Vita S. Bonifatii*, iv.

27. See Jankuhn, "Nord-und Ostseeraum," p. 168, and Hodges, *Dark-Age Economics*, p. 41, for "histograms" of Dorestad coinage.

28. The Frankish documentary evidence is examined by Ennen, "Städtewesens Nordwestdeutschlands," pp. 165–67; H. Planitz, *Die deutsche Stadt im Mittelalter* (Cologne: Böhlau, 1954), pp. 48–49, 58–59. A Carolingian fort stood on the western fringe of the town.

29. Alcuin, *Carmina*, iv, lix, ed. E. Dümmler, in *MGH Poetae*, I (Berlin, 1881).

30. A. Verhulst, "Les origines urbaines dans le Nord-Ouest de l'Europe: essai de synthèse," *Francia* 14 (1986), pp. 69–70; Hodges, *Dark-Age Economics*, pp. 40–42.

31. Doehaerd, *Le haut moyen âge occidentale*, pp. 285–87.

32. Ibid., p. 286; Hodges, *Dark-Age Economics*, p. 174.

33. For this site-group, see: Ennen, *Europäische Stadt des Mittelalters*, pp. 47–54; Jankuhn, "Nord- und Ostseeraum," pp. 171–95, and "The Interdisciplinary Approach to the Study of the Early History of Medieval Towns," in *Comparative History of Urban Origins*, I, pp. 15–42; U. Lobbedey, "Northern Germany," in *European Towns: Their Archaeology and Early History*, ed. M. W. Barley (London: Academic Press, 1977), pp. 127–57; Hodges, *Dark-Age Economics*, pp. 74–86; Clarke and Ambrosiani, *Towns in the Viking Age*, pp. 29–31, 50–89.

34. Jankuhn, "Nord- und Ostseeraum," p. 171, and Map 7, and "Vor-und frühformen der Stadt," pp. 264-66; Lewis, *Northern Seas*, pp. 210–20; Doehaerd, *Le haut moyen âge occidentale*, pp. 287–89; Hodges, *Dark-Age Economics*, pp. 42–43; Hodges and Whitehouse, *Mohammed, Charlemagne, and the Origins of Europe*, pp. 111–22. For some important recent collections of archaeological and historical studies on commerce, transport, and emporia in early northern, central, and eastern Europe, see Jankuhn, et al., eds. *Archäologische und naturwissenschaftliche Untersuchungen an ländlichen und frühstadtischen Siedlungen im deutschen Küstengebiet vom 5. Jahrhundert v. Chr. bis zum 11. Jahrhundert n. Chr* (Weinheim:

Acta Humaniora, 1984), Vol. 2, *Handelsplätze des frühen und hohen Mittelalters;* K. Düwel, et al., eds. *Untersuchungen zu Handel und Verkehr der Vor- und Frühgeschichtlichen Zeit in Mittel-und Nordeuropa* (4 vols., Göttingen: Vandenhoeck & Ruprecht, 1985–87), esp. Pt. III, *Der Handel des frühen Mittelalters* (1985) and Pt. IV, *Der Handel der Karolinger- und Wikingerzeit* (1987); M. Müller-Wille, ed., *Oldenburg-Wolin-Staraja Ladoga-Novgorod-Kiev: Handel und Handelsverbindungen im südlichen und östlichen Ostseeraum während des frühen Mittelalters* (Mainz: Römisch-Germanischen Kommission, 1989).

35. For the Haithabu excavations, see: Jankuhn, "Nord- und Ostseeraum," pp. 176–86; Lobbedey, "Northern Germany," pp. 136–142; K. Schietzel, "Haithabu: A Study on the Development of Early Urban Settlements in Northern Europe," in *Comparative History of Urban Origins*, I, pp. 147–181; K. Randsborg, *The Viking Age in Denmark: The Formation of a State* (NY: St. Martin's Press, 1980), pp. 85–90; and J. Stark, *Haithabu-Schleswig-Danewerk: Aspekte eines Forschungsgeschichte mittelalterlicher Anlagen in Schleswig-Holstein,* B.A.R. Internat. Ser. 432 (Oxford, 1988); Clarke and Ambrosiani, *Towns in the Viking Age*, pp. 56-63.

36. Jankuhn, "Nord- und Ostseeraum," p. 177; Lobbedey, "Northern Germany," p. 139; Stark, *Haithabu*, pp. 50–53, 157–59.

37. Jankuhn, "Nord- und Ostseeraum," pp. 180, 183–84; Ennen, *Europäische Stadt des Mittelalters,* pp. 48–49; Randsborg, *Viking Age,* pp. 89–90; Stark, *Haithabu,* pp. 150–57.

38. For the street pattern, buildings, and tenements, see Schietzel, "Haithabu," pp. 150–61 and Figs. 6.2–6.11; Jankuhn, "Nord- und Ostseeraum," pp. 180–83; Stark, *Haithabu,* pp. 37–48, 54–61, and Figs. 13, 24. Remains of several Viking age ships have been found just off the harbor jetty.

39. Schietzel, "Haithabu," pp. 161–72.

40. Randsborg, *Viking Age,* pp. 80–81; Clarke and Ambrosiani, *Towns in the Viking Age*, p. 157. For the temporary decline of Haithabu c.830 and its possible causes, see Hodges and Whitehouse, *Mohammed, Charlemagne, and the Origins of Europe,* pp. 158–64. But for the enduring ties between this town and its surrounding countryside, see: Müller-Wille, "Hedeby und sein Umland," in *Trade and Exchange in Prehistory*, eds. Hardh, et al., pp. 271–78.

41. Stark, *Haithabu,* pp. 76–87. There now appears to have been some connection between the nearby Danevirke fortifications and the earliest unwalled settlement at Haithabu (ibid., pp. 117–21, 157–68). Also, an old hill fort to the north of the initial settlements may have served as a temporary refuge.

42. Randsborg, *Viking Age,* pp. 149–51, and Fig. 41; Grierson and Blackburn, *Medieval European Coinage,* p. 154.

43. Jankuhn, "Nord- und Ostseeraum," p. 184; Lobbedey, "Northern Germany," pp. 138–39. The elaborate system of timber-lined town wells is also a tenth-century feature: Schietzel, "Haithabu," p. 172.

44. The fortified town of Schleswig (Sliaswich), across the Schlei, seems to have received most of Haithabu's population, though there may have been some settlement overlap: Stark, *Haithabu*, pp. 160–68; Randsborg, *Viking Age,* pp. 86, 90; Schietzel, "Haithabu," p. 175, and see, Hodges, *Dark Age Economics,* pp. 72–84 for possible wider implications.

45. *Annales Regni Francorum*, s.a. 772, 777, ed. F. Kurze, in *MGH SS RG*, VI (Hanover, 1895). The Saxon warlord Widukind, leading a fierce anti-Frankish revolt, had taken refuge with the Danes.

46. Ibid., s.a. 782. See further, Hodges and Whitehouse, *Mohammed, Charlemagne, and the Origins of Europe*, pp. 115–17.

47. *Annales Regni Francorum*, s.a. 808. For this identification, see: Schietzel, "Haithabu," p. 178; Randsborg, *Viking Age*, p. 15; Hodges, *Dark-Age Economics*, p. 78. On Reric, see also, W. Hensel, *Anfänge der Städte bei den Ost- und Westslawen* (Bautzen: Domowina Verlag, 1967), pp. 58–59; and G. Fehring, "The Archaeology of Early Lübeck: The Relation between the Slavic and German Settlement Sites," in *Comparative History of Urban Origins*, eds. Clarke and Simms, I, pp. 269–75; cf. J. Herrmann, "Hinterland, Trade, and Craftworking in the Early Trading Stations of the North-Western Slavs," in *Comparative History of Urban Origins*, I, pp. 251–53.

48. Rimbert, *Vita S. Anskarii*, xxiv, xxxi, ed. C. Dahlmann, in *MGH Scriptores* (hereafter *SS*), II (Hanover, 1829); *Vita S. Rimberti*, xviii, ed. Pertz, in *MGH SS*, II.

49. On the journeys of Ottar (Old English Ohthere) and Wulfstan, see *Alfred's Anglo-Saxon Version of Orosius*, ed. B. Thorpe, in R. Pauli, *The Life of Alfred the Great* (London: H. Bohn, 1853), pp. 249–57. Extracts from Al-Tartushi's journals are assembled by J. Brøndsted, *The Vikings*, trans. K. Skov (Harmondsworth: Penguin Books, 1965), pp. 42–43. See further, H. Steuer, "Zur ethnischen Gliederung der Bevölkerung von Haithabu anhand der Gräberfelder," *Offa* 41 (1984), 189–212.

50. Adam of Bremen, *Gesta Hammaburgensis Ecclesiae Pontificum*, i.57, ii.56, ed. B. Schmeidler, in *MGH SS RG*, II (3d ed., Hanover, 1917); Snorri Sturluson, *Heimskringla*, s.v. *Haralds Saga Sigurdarsonar*, xxxiv, trans. L. M. Hollander (Austin: University of Texas Press, 1964). Adam of Bremen mentions a second burning of the site by Slavs in 1066: *Gesta Hammaburgensis Ecclesiae Pontificum*, iii.51.

51. H. Jansen, "Early Urbanization in Denmark," in *Comparative History of Urban Origins*, I, pp. 191-94; M. Bencard and L. Jorgensen, "The Foundation of Ribe," *Antiquity* 64 (1990), 576-83; Clarke and Ambrosiani, *Towns in the Viking Age*, pp. 52-54, 163-64. For Anskar's construction of a church at Ribe and the involvement of Danish kings, see: Rimbert, *Vita S. Anskarii*, xxxii, and overviews by Randsborg, *Viking Age in Denmark*, pp. 12-23.

52. *Alfred's Anglo-Saxon Version of Orosius*, p. 253.

53. The principal excavator (1950–) has been Charlotte Blindheim: "Kaupang in Skiringssal: A Norwegian Port of Trade from the Viking Age," in *Vor- und Frühformen der europäischen Stadt im Mittelalter*, eds. H. Jankuhn, et al. (2 vols., Göttingen: Vandenhoeck & Ruprecht, 1973-74), II, pp. 40–57. See also Jankuhn, "New Beginnings in Northern Europe and Scandinavia," in *European Towns*, pp. 363–65; Clarke and Ambrosiani, *Towns in the Viking Age*, pp. 65-67.

54. Blindheim, "Kaupang," pp. 41–45, discusses previous research.

55. Ibid., pp. 46–53. A small amount of finds suggests eighth-century and even earlier occupation. North Sea/Baltic emporia, however, apparently did not have as regular a street grid as did many Anglo-Saxon *wics*: Clarke and Ambrosiani, *Towns in the Viking Age*, pp. 139–41.

56. Blindheim, "Kaupang," pp. 50–55. Remains of a Viking cargo ship (carbon-14 dated as c.800 A.D.) carrying honestones was found in 1970 at the mouth of the

(Oslo) fjord leading up to Kaupang (ibid., p. 55). See further, Jankuhn, "Northern Europe and Scandinavia," p. 368; Hodges, *Dark-Age Economics*, pp. 125–26.

57. Blindheim, "Kaupang," pp. 52, 55, 57; Hodges, *Dark-Age Economics*, p. 98. See also H.-E. Lidén, "Urban Archaeology in Norway," in *European Towns*, ed. Barley, pp. 85–86.

58. Blindheim, "Kaupang," pp. 43–47.

59. Ibid., pp. 56–57; S. Cohen, "The Earliest Scandinavian Towns," in *The Medieval City*, eds. H. Miskimin, et al. (New Haven: Yale University Press, 1977), pp. 320–21; Hodges, *Dark-Age Economics*, pp. 50–51, 81. But Kaupang was certainly more permanent than those summer rendezvous of medieval Scandinavia where goods were regularly exchanged between ships at sea: Hodges, *Dark-Age Economics*, p. 51; H. Thorlaksson, "Comments on Ports of Trade in Early Medieval Europe," *Norwegian Archaeological Review* 11 (1978), 112–14.

60. Blindheim, "Kaupang," p. 56; I. Skovgaard-Petersen, "The Historical Context of the First Towns in Northern and Eastern Europe," in *Proceedings of the Eighth Viking Congress*, eds. H. Bekker-Nielsen, et al. (Odense: University Press, 1981), pp. 13–14.

61. King Gustavus VI of Sweden took personal interest in this modern effort. On the excavations, see W. Holmqvist, "Helgö, eine Vorform der Stadt?" in *Vor- und Frühformen der europäischen Stadt*, II, pp. 21–29, and, more fully, "Helgö, An Early Trading Settlement in Central Sweden," in R. Bruce-Mitford, ed., *Recent Archaeological Excavations in Europe* (London: Routledge & Kegan Paul, 1975), pp. 111–32. See also Jankuhn, "Northern Europe and Scandinavia," pp. 362–68; B. Ambrosiani, "Urban Archaeology in Sweden," in *European Towns*, pp. 103–14; Hodges, *Dark-Age Economics*, pp. 83–85; Clarke and Ambrosiani, *Towns in the Viking Age*, pp. 69-71.

62. Holmqvist, "Helgö," pp. 115–18, 127–29; Ambrosiani, "Urban Archaeology in Sweden," pp. 109–10; Hodges, *Dark-Age Economics*, p. 83, and Fig. 20, for a photo of an excavated Helgö workshop. Occupation appears to have shifted from east to west on the site over time.

63. Holmqvist, "Helgö," pp. 120–127 and Pl. 25. For the pictorial gold plaques, see further, E. Bakka, "Methodological Problems in the Study of Gold Brakteates," *Norwegian Archeological Review* 1 (1968), 5–35; K. Hauck, "Bilddenkmäler: Zur Religion," in *Reallexikon der germanischen Altertumskunde*, ed. Hoops, II (1976), pp. 577–90, and D. G. Russo, "Sacral Kingship in Early Medieval Europe: The Germanic Tradition" (M.A. thesis, University of New Hampshire, 1978), pp. 29–31, 70–71.

64. Holmqvist, "Helgö," pp. 118–20 and Pl. 23b.

65. Ibid., pp. 121–22 and Pl. 23a; Hodges, *Dark-Age Economics*, p. 85. For the larger issue of Baltic-Varangian-Far Eastern trade, see Lewis, *Northern Seas*, pp. 308–17; H. Davidson, *Viking Road to Byzantium* (London: Allen & Unwin, 1976), pp. 52–56, 64–67; Sawyer, *Kings and Vikings: Scandinavia and Europe A.D. 700–1100* (London: Methuen, 1982), pp. 123–25; Duby, *Premier essor*, pp. 139–41, 148–50; Randsborg, *Viking Age*, pp. 152–66. The early Russian-Slavic *gorod* presents some interesting functional parallels to those here proposed for eighth- and ninth-century Anglo-Saxon burghs. See M. Tikhomirov, *The Towns of Ancient Rus*, trans. Y. Sdobnikov (2d ed., Moscow: Foreign Languages Publishing House, 1959), pp. 7–30; L. N. Langer, "The Medieval Russian Town," in *The City in Russian History*, ed. M. Hamm (Lexington, KY: University Press of Kentucky, 1976), pp. 11–33, esp. 11–13;

W. Hensel, "The Origins of Western and Eastern European Slav Towns," in *European Towns*, ed. Barley, pp. 373–90, esp. 375–85; H. Birnbaum, "Kiev, Novgorod, Moscow: Three Varieties of Urban Society in East Slavic Territory," in *Urban Society of Eastern Europe in Premodern Times*, ed. B. Krekić (Berkeley: University of California Press, 1987), pp. 1–59; Clarke and Ambrosiani, *Towns in the Viking Age*, pp. 107–27. For site-plans of the major Slavic emporia of Menzlin and Wollin (Wolin), see Fig. 6.4A, B.)

66. See n.4, above; Hodges, *Dark-Age Economics*, pp. 32–33, 37–40. This early floruit also may explain the absence of written references to the town.

67. Jankuhn, "Interdisciplinary Approach," p. 40.

68. Holmqvist, "Helgö," pp. 130–31; Jankuhn, "Northern Europe and Scandinavia," pp. 367–68; Hodges, *Dark-Age Economics*, pp. 144–46, and Fig. 27, for a Baltic distribution map of cast dress ornaments from Helgö's workshops. This is an interesting precursor to the later trade in North European iron products with the East: Lewis, *Northern Seas*, pp. 116, 195–97. For a denial of Helgö's urban status, based largely on cemetery evidence, see Clarke and Ambrosiani, *Towns in the Viking Age*, p. 71.

69. Holmqvist, "Helgö," pp. 132; Jankuhn, "Northern Europe and Scandinavia," p. 367; Ambrosiani, "Urban Archaeology in Sweden," p. 112. The possible connection of the Vendel royal clan with East Anglia and its main emporium at Ipswich should be recalled as well: R. Bruce-Mitford, "The Sutton Hoo Ship-Burial: Comments on General Interpretation," in Bruce-Mitford, *Aspects of Anglo-Saxon Archaeology* (New York: Harper & Row, 1974), pp. 47–60, and Chap. 5, above.

70. Ambrosiani, "Urban Archaeology in Sweden," p. 108. Indeed, it has been suggested that such ultimate transfers of urban populations and functions to nearby sites were characteristic features of early Scandinavian town development: Clarke and Ambrosiani, *Towns in the Viking Age*, p. 138; R. S. Lopez, "Of Towns and Trade," in *Life and Thought in the Early Middle Ages*, ed. R. Hoyt (Minneapolis: University of Minnesota Press, 1967), pp. 34, 41.

71. On the Birka excavations, see Ambrosiani, "Neue Ausgrabungen in Birka," in *Vor- und Frühformen der europäischen Stadt*, II, pp. 58–63, and "Urban Archaeology in Sweden," pp. 105–7, 109, 112–14; Clarke and Ambrosiani, *Towns in the Viking Age*, pp. 71-76, 157; Jankuhn, "Nord- und Ostseeraum," pp. 186–90; Cohen, "Earliest Scandinavian Towns," pp. 317–320; Hodges, *Dark-Age Economics*, pp. 85–86. Its foundation has been placed c.750; average annual population is estimated at about 1,000 individuals.

72. Ambrosiani, "Neue Ausgrabungen," pp. 58–59; Cohen, "Earliest Scandinavian Towns," p. 320, properly noting that the artificial, fortified harbor is reminiscent of descriptions of the harbor at Jomsborg (Wollin?), base of the Jomsvikings. See further, Brøndsted, *Vikings*, pp. 155-58, 161-62.

73. Jankuhn, "Nord- und Ostseeraum," p. 190. Portions of a Frisian cargo vessel also were discovered: Jankuhn, "Northern Europe and Scandinavia," p. 360. See further: H. Clarke, "English and Baltic Trade in the Middle Ages: An Evaluation of the Evidence," in *Society and Trade in the Baltic during the Viking Age*, ed. S. O. Lindquist (Visby: University Press, 1985), pp. 113–20; V. I. Evison, "Some Vendel, Viking, and Saxon Glass," in *Trade and Exchange in Prehistory*, eds. B. Hardh, et al., pp. 237–45.

74. Hodges, *Dark-Age Economics*, p. 85; Davidson, *Viking Road to Byzantium*, pp. 69–70. Birka evidently had an important ninth- and tenth-century mint, striking copies of Anglo-Saxon and Frisian *sceattas*: Jankuhn, "Northern Europe and Scandinavia," pp. 361, 366; cf. K. Skaare, "Mints in Viking Age Scandinavia," in *Eighth Viking Congress*, eds. Bekker-Nielsen, et al., p. 38; Cohen, "Earliest Scandinavian Towns," pp. 318–19.

75. Holmqvist, "Helgö," pp. 25–27.

76. Jankuhn, "Nord- und Ostseeraum," pp. 189–90; Hodges and Whitehouse, *Mohammed, Charlemagne, and the Origins of Europe*, p. 125.

77. Ambrosiani, "Neue Ausgrabungen," pp. 62–63, and "Birka–A Planted Town Serving an Increasing Agricultural Population," in *Eighth Viking Congress*, eds. Bekker-Nielson, et al., pp. 19–22. Clarke and Ambrosiani, among others, emphasize nowadays that the development of early medieval towns was closely connected to the economic prosperity and growing population densities of their immediate rural hinterlands, which created demand for specialized urban products; defense and long-distance trade were secondary factors: *Towns in the Viking Age*, pp. 87–89, 128–30. They also conclude that most, though not all, early Scandinavian towns appear to have been deliberate foundations by high-status individuals and formed part of the infrastructure of royal or aristocratic estates (Ibid., p. 137). See further: Jankuhn, "Vor-und frühformen der Stadt," p. 263; G. Astill, "Towns and Town Hierarchies in Saxon England," *Oxford Journal of Archaeology* 10 (1991), pp. 101-3.

78. Rimbert, *Vita S. Anskarii*, ix–xi, ed. Dahlmann.

79. Ibid., ix, xxv–xxviii. The Danish king Horic I, whom Anskar knew from Haithabu, also supported the Swedish mission.

80. Ibid., xxxiii.

81. Adam of Bremen, *Gesta Hammaburgensis Ecclesiae Pontificum*, i.62–63, ed. Schmeidler. Unni died and was buried in Birka, though his head was brought back to Bremen (ibid., i.64).

82. Rimbert, *Vita S. Anskarii*, xi, xix. Archaeological evidence does suggest that Birka's ninth-century merchants comprised a class distinct from the rural population: Clarke and Ambrosiani, *Towns in the Viking Age*, p. 175.

83. Rimbert, *Vita S. Anskarii*, xix.

84. Ibid., xi, xix. The attack was led by King Björn's exiled brother, Anoundus (also styled *rex*), who offered to lift the assault for a payment of 100 pounds of silver. The use of hill forts or royal forts near *wics* as refuges is a recurrent phenomenon: Planitz, *Die deutsche Stadt*, pp. 48–50; Jankuhn, "Vor-und frühformen der Stadt," pp. 266-67.

85. Rimbert, *Vita S. Anskarii*, xix, xxvii. These gatherings represent a notable reappearance of the early Germanic Assembly or *Thing* in an urban setting, similar no doubt to the still-obscure folkmoot of Anglo-Saxon London.

86. Such as Danes, Swedes, "Sembi" (Prussians?), Slavs, and "Scythians" (Sarmatians?): Adam of Bremen, *Gesta*, i.62.

87. Ibid.: "For the people of Birka, very often assailed by the inroads of pirates... have blocked that bight of the restless sea for a hundred or more stadia by masses of hidden rocks."

88. Ibid., iv.29.

89. Brøndsted, *The Vikings*, p. 163.

90. Ambrosiani, "Neue Ausgrabungen," p. 62, and Pl. 2; Jankuhn, "Nord- und Ostseeraum," p. 189.

91. Brøndsted, *The Vikings*, p. 163.

92. Ambrosiani, "Urban Archaeology in Sweden," p. 105; Davidson, *Viking Road to Byzantium*, pp. 54–56, 70; B. Fritz, "Die Vor-und Frühgeschichte der skandinavischen Stadt," in *Topografia urbana*, I, p. 146. See further: Lewis, *Northern Seas*, pp. 370–78; Hodgett, *Social and Economic History*, pp. 49–55; Haussig, *Byzantine Civilization*, p. 308. The Swedish emporia of Västergarn, Paviken, and Visby on Gotland (Map 6.2) appear to have had their peak growth at this time: Hodges, *Dark-Age Economics*, p. 82; and in more detail, see: P. Lundström, "Paviken I bei Västergarn – Hafen, Handelsplatz, und Werft," in *Vor- und Frühformen der europäischen Stadt*, eds. Jankuhn, et al., II, pp. 82–93; Clarke and Ambrosiani, *Towns in the Viking Age*, pp. 80-87 and Figs. 4.28, 4.29.

93. Ambrosiani, "Urban Archaeology in Sweden," pp. 105, 108, and Fig. 6; Fritz, "Vor- und Frühgeschichte der skandinavischen Stadt," p. 145; Hodges, *Dark-Age Economics*, p. 98; Sawyer, *Kings and Vikings*, p. 130. For valuable discussions of eleventh-century Sigtuna, with its royal mint, regular street plan, numerous churches, and merchant guilds, see: Cohen, "Earliest Scandinavian Towns," pp. 321–22; Clarke and Ambrosiani, *Towns in the Viking Age*, pp. 76-79.

94. Ambrosiani, "Urban Archaeology in Sweden," p. 105, noting such other factors in Birka's decline as falling sea-levels that excluded heavy-draught vessels and the proliferation of small towns in the region.

95. Ambrosiani, "Birka–A Planted Town," pp. 22–23. Holmqvist, "Helgö," p. 131; Skovgaard-Petersen, "First Towns in Northern and Eastern Europe," pp. 14–16; Jankuhn, "Northern Europe and Scandinavia," p. 368.

96. Fritz, "Die Vor-und Frühgeschichte der skandinavischen Stadt," pp. 142–43; Lewis, *Northern Seas*, pp. 308–17; Jankuhn, "Northern Europe and Scandinavia," pp. 359–60; Hodges and Whitehouse, *Mohammed, Charlemagne, and the Origins of Europe*, pp. 102–22.

97. Biddle, "Towns," pp. 114–16; Hodges, *Anglo-Saxon Achievement*, pp. 85–86, 99–100; cf. Clarke and Ambrosiani, *Towns in the Viking Age*, pp. 89, 175, 177; Astill, "Archaeology, Economics and Early Medieval Europe," *Oxford Journal of Archaeology* 4 (1985), pp 227-29.

Chapter 7

Anglo-Saxon Burghs: Mercia and Wessex (c.750–950 A.D.)

By the middle of the ninth century, the initial contours of an Anglo-Saxon urban landscape were in place. First, many of the former Roman *colonia*, *municipia*, and *civitas*-capitals had been resettled, primarily by Anglo-Saxon kings and churchmen during the late fifth to early seventh centuries as administrative and ecclesiastical capitals of incipient Heptarchic realms. Second, one can point to a number of trading and production centers, the emporia or *wics*, founded primarily during the seventh and eighth centuries, most often by royal initiative and as conduits for the accumulation of state-building wealth and prestige. These Anglo-Saxon emporia, sited as a rule near their respective territorial capitals, were not only centers of local commerce and industry but also were frequently linked with overseas emporia and trading networks encompassing northern France, Frisia, Germany, Scandinavia, and the Baltic.

Ninth-century events significantly altered the configuration of this early townscape. Under the impact of shifting trade patterns and Viking attacks, many prominent Anglo-Saxon emporia declined and soon disappeared. The main beneficiaries of these changed circumstances were the older Roman centers that had emerged as Anglo-Saxon royal capitals, such as Canterbury, Winchester, London, and York. Archeological and written sources reveal that these sites assumed expanded urban functions and had increasingly dense permanent populations late in the ninth century. Attention has been drawn to their new commercial and industrial districts with planned road networks as well as tightly packed tenements that sprang up within the protective confines of reinforced walls and fortifications. By incorporating the population and at times the area of their associated *wics*, these older royal and ecclesiastical administrative centers (some now called burghs [O.E. *burga*]) emerged as places with more numerous and intensive urban functions.

In addition to these older sites with expanded town functions, another group of places, many on new sites, appear in Alfredian sources as burghs. The establishment and growth of the Anglo-Saxon burghs or boroughs certainly is a significant aspect of early English urban history. Modern interpretations of their essential nature and functions have varied greatly, however. One need only recall in this regard the major debate over the boroughs waged by Carl Stephenson in America and James Tait in England, as described in the first chapter. The interchange between these two accomplished medieval urban historians served to focus scholarly attention on several key issues of early burghal development, although it did not entirely resolve them. Moreover, the prolonged and at times acrimonious tone of the controversy tended to repress research for an entire generation. The subject of the Alfredian burghs may be addressed more productively today by posing a new set of questions concerning the evidence and by refraining from overly exclusive or dogmatic interpretations. The towns of Anglo-Saxon England, like those of the ancient world and the high middle ages, were complex, fluid entities. In addition, one now can take into account the significant body of archaeological evidence relating to the Anglo-Saxon burgh which has been accumulating in recent years.

It generally has been assumed that the roots of the English borough are to be found in the burghs of Wessex established by King Alfred (871-899) during the Viking wars.[1] There is little doubt that these West Saxon burghs are the best-known examples, largely because of their recorded prominence in the stirring events of these years and the subsequent reconquest from the Danes. It must be borne in mind, however, that most surviving Anglo-Saxon written sources derive from West Saxon court circles and naturally promulgate their particular views. Certainly the role played by Alfred and his successors in the development of the burghal system was critical. But the possibility must be raised that the weight and provenance of our sources may have obscured a wider, rather more complex background to the Anglo-Saxon burgh. There is, in fact, a range of evidence that strongly suggests that the Anglo-Saxon burgh actually predated Alfred's time and appeared first not in Wessex but rather in inland Mercia.

This evidence of pre-Alfredian, Mercian burghs has significant implications and merits closer scrutiny than it has received. Among written sources, the first document to be noted is a charter issued in 749 at the Synod of Gumley (Leicestershire), whereby King Aethelbald specified immunities granted to the churches and monasteries of Mercia. The authenticity of this particular charter, attested by the bishops of Litchfield and Leicester, seems assured.[2] Aethelbald declares that the religious houses and churches of his realm "shall remain free from public exactions (*vectigalia*)" and "from all works (*opera*) and burdens (*onera*), except alone those which are to be done in common and which all people are ordered to do by edict of the king, that is, the building (*instructio*) of bridges and the necessary defenses (*defensiones*) of fortresses (*arces*) against enemies." These two services are not at all to be remitted, since they are "agreed to be necessary for the houses of God." Aethelbald then proceeds to forbid forced offerings demanded from churches for the provisioning of kings and leading men, though such donatives may be given freely, and he commands in general that all *tribulationes* by royal officials that can harm or impede the Church shall cease. As Aethelbald piously admonishes, the dignity of his realm promotes prosperity on earth and the ripening of merits in heaven.

This Mercian charter, though concerned primarily with ecclesiastical immunities, contains what may be the earliest reference to the presence of pre-Alfredian, non West Saxon fortified sites in Anglo-Saxon England. Although the nature of these *arces* is not more clearly set forth, several important points may be noted. First, the duties of fortress-defense and bridgebuilding are grouped together as the two burdens from which no one in Mercia, including churchmen, was to be exempt. Moreover, both activities and obligations are associated directly with the king: they are cited specifically as duties imposed by royal edict. The reservation of these two common burdens in this Mercian grant of immunity must bring to mind the threefold reservations, the so-called *trim(n)oda necessitas*, of bridge building, fortress defense, and army service—that appear prominently in later Anglo-Saxon charters.

Further close reading of this Mercian text can disclose some significant details regarding the eighth-century fortresses under consideration. For example, it will be noted that the diploma speaks of fortress defense, not fortress construction, implying that distinctive fortified centers were already in place within Mercia by 749. Indeed, the precise wording suggests that the obligation regarding fortresses amounted to required garrison duty at these sites. Furthermore, mention of the empowering royal edict implies that the two common burdens were being imposed at that time under some unspecified pressing circumstances. The additional statement that they were agreed necessary for the churches of Mercia also suggests recent imposition in the face of immediate threat.

Although the early appearance of these fortified sites and their Mercian context are somewhat surprising, the fact that they apparently arose during Aethelbald's reign does make sense. Aethelbald had become king of Mercia in 716 upon the death of his kinsman Coelred. Following the demise of King Wihtred of Kent (725) and the abdication of Ine in Wessex (726), he embarked on a course of Mercia expansion that soon made him the most powerful king in southern England. Indeed, Bede, writing c.730, observed that Aethelbald was then overlord of all English provinces south of the Humber.[3] This overlordship, reflected in Aethelbald's charter-style *Rex Britanniae*, is most likely equivalent to the position of *Bretwalda* later noted in the *Anglo-Saxon Chronicle*.[4] The evidence suggests that Aethelbald's position as head of this confederacy was founded on his effective military leadership. In fact, Aethelbald had spent a good part of his youth in exile with his war band, and he remained very much the warrior-king.[5] It is worthwhile attempting to identify Aethelbald's opponents, for this can shed some light on those "enemies" cited in his charter of 749 relating to necessary fortress defense.

The objects of Athelbald's aggression appear to have been the kingdom of Wessex and the Welsh. The *Anglo-Saxon Chronicle* records that in 733, after a campaign of unknown duration, Aethelbald took Somerton and incorporated this large frontier area of Wessex into "greater" Mercia (Map 7.1.A).[6] In 741 he engaged and probably defeated the new West Saxon king, Cuthred, for we see the latter accompanying Aethelbald three years later on a campaign against the Welsh.[7] There had been repeated Welsh incursions into Mercian territory during the early eighth century; indeed, the construction of Wat's Dyke along the River Dee (Map 7.2.A) has been attributed to Aethelbald.[8] It is therefore along the two disputed borders with Wessex and Wales that one would best expect to find the burghs of pre-Alfredian Mercia.

Additional light is cast on this evidence by the correspondence of the Anglo-Saxon missionary bishop, Boniface. In 745, Boniface and seven other bishops of the Frankish Church sent a letter upbraiding Aethelbald for his lax personal morals, as well as for the theft of church revenues, and complained that his officials had imposed "greater violence and servitude on monks and priests than any other Christian king before."[9] These complaints were made somewhat more specific three years later in a letter from Boniface to Archbishop Cuthbert of Canterbury. There, Boniface criticizes "the violence and servitude of monks with royal works and buildings (*operibus et aedificiis regalibus*) which is not heard of in the entire Christian world except so much [as it is] among the English people."[10] It would appear that Aethelbald had been compelling religious subjects to perform or provide corvée labor on royal building projects that may well have included fortified sites. This violation of traditional ecclesiastical freedom from secular works is what the above-mentioned Synod of Gumley apparently sought to redress. If so, Mercian churchmen or workers on ecclesiastical estates would no longer have been under compulsion to participate directly in bridge building and fortress construction, as they seem to have been before 749.

The reservations of bridge building and fortress defense are not specifically mentioned again in extant Mercian charters until the reign of Aethelbald's renowned successor, Offa (755-796). Two grants are of particular interest, each issued by Uhtred, subking (*regulus*) of the Hwicce, with confirmation by Offa, his Mercian overlord. Both charters concern the bestowal of an estate at Eastun, near Worcester, to the "faithful thegn" (*fidelis minister*) Aethelmund, son of a certain Ingeld who had been *dux* and *praefectus* under King Aethelbald. The first diploma is dated 767; the subsequent, confirmatory charter was issued in 770. The two diplomas state that in return for a "fitting price," this land is to be free from all public tribute, small or great, and from all works by king or noble, except for the building of bridges or the necessary defenses of fortresses against enemies.[11] The wording of the reservation clauses here is essentially the same as that employed in Aethelbald's charter of Gumley twenty years before. The presence of fortresses and the need for their defense thus continue to be attested in late eighth-century Mercia.

Indeed, these Mercian *arces* appear more frequently in Offa's charters. Moreover, they are now encompassed within a threefold reservation clause that has expanded to include universal army service in Mercia proper and its subject realms. For example, in a record of a synod held at Clovesho (792), Offa grants wide immunities to the churches of Kent, "except for campaign (*expeditio*) if necessary within Kent or Sussex against pagan seamen with transgressing fleets, and the building (*constructio*) of bridges and the strengthening (*munitio*) of fortresses against pagans also within the borders of Kent."[12] The subsequent phrase, "by his [Offa's] petition and instruction," suggests that these three obligations were being imposed on the Kentish churches for the first time in 792.[13] In another charter of more secular nature (793 X 796 A.D.), Offa bestowed on Aethelmund an estate in Gloucestershire free from all services and fiscal obligations, reserving only the duties of campaign service, bridge building, and fortress defense. Indeed, this charter contains the first clear statement that the three burdens are obligatory for all people subject to Mercian rule, none being excused.[14]

If the construction of mid eighth-century Mercian burghs had been occasioned as suggested here by hostilities with the West Saxons and Welsh, many of Offa's burghs also appear to have been a defensive reaction to early Viking attacks against dependent Mercian realms to the east and south. Offa's charter of 792 expressly refers to seaborne raids in Kent and Sussex and the necessity of defending Kentish fortresses against such assaults. The *Anglo-Saxon Chronicle* records the first Danish raids on England as taking place sometime during the reign of King Beorhtric of Wessex (786-802), Offa's son-in-law and subordinate.[15] That Danish attacks also had been directed against Mercian-controlled Kent during this last decade of the eighth century is supported further by the fact that Kentish charters refer to common burdens first being imposed *contra paganos*.[16] Also, it may be no coincidence that at this time Charlemagne, who had important diplomatic and trade relations with Offa, was building a series of defensive fortifications against the "Northmen" along the North Sea and Channel coasts.[17]

Place-name evidence contained within Offa's charters provides some additional insights into these elusive early burghs. First, however, some general remarks must be made about the uses and meanings of the term burgh (*burh*) itself in Anglo-Saxon sources. *Burh/burg* appears both as a single (simplex) form and in various compounds, especially as place-names. All have the primary meaning "fortification, fortified place, refuge"—(*burh, burg, byrig, buri, beorh, beorg*).[18] Specific instances of its use in pre-Alfredian sources bear connotations ranging from a fortified private dwelling of king or noble, to a defensible center of popular refuge, to a more expansive, densely-settled site built and fortified under royal aegis. This does not rule out functions other than defense, such as administration and commerce. The earliest appearance of *burh* in Anglo-Saxon legal documents is in the *Laws of King Ine* (Wessex), compiled c.688–694. In Cap.45 of this law code (O.E. *dōm*, "doom") a graduated scale of compensations is imposed for the offense of *burhbryce*— breaking into the fortifications or fortified premises of the king or his bishop, an ealdorman, a royal thegn, or a landholding *gesith*. The implication appears to be that a *burh/burg* was a peculiarly aristocratic site.[19] From the mid-eighth century there is the famous story of the West Saxon King Cynewulf's murder inside the *burh* (fortified with gates) at his royal vill of Merantun.[20]   As we have seen, mid-eighth-century Canterbury is designated as *Cantwara burh*, "the fortified place of the Kentish people," which probably indicates a center of local refuge akin to the continental *Volksburgen*.[21] A very early entry in the *Anglo-Saxon Chronicle* also mentions that King Ida of Northumbria (547–559) built *Bebban burh* (Bamburgh/Bamborough), "which was first enclosed by a fence/stockade (*hege*) and thereafter by a wall (*weall*)."[22]   These fortifications were apparently all timber-built, for Bede relates the story of how in the seventh century Penda's army had attempted to set fire to Bamborough's wall and gates during a Mercian invasion of Northumbria.[23]

The form of many *burh* place-names in early Anglo-Saxon sources suggests that they had been private strongholds founded by or belonging to locally important leaders (e.g., Wihtgarasburh, Posentesburh, Cnebbanburg, Fledanburg).[24] Others indicate the *burh*'s location or composition (West-burg, Stanbeorh), while some imply an abandoned or overgrown condition (Haeslburg, Ulenbeorge).[25] In Anglo-Saxon literary sources written in Latin, *burh* is generally rendered *arx*, although if a larger site was implied, it could be presented as *urbs, castrum*, or *civitas*. There was, however, a decided preference for reserving *castrum/ceaster* names for sites with known Roman backgrounds.[26]

With this overview of *burh* usage in mind, we can return to Mercian charter evidence. Focusing on only those Offan diplomas regarded as certainly or likely genuine, one encounters references to some eight burghs within territories under Offa's control. In Gloucestershire, there are Coccanburh (Cockbury), Sulmonnesburg (Salmonsbury), Westburg (Westbury), and Heanburh (Henbury), along with Herrihtesbeorh, Imman-beorg, Inwinesburg (all unidentified), and, in Kent, Eohingaburh (unidenti-fied).[27] The personal name prefixes suggest again that many of these burghs were strongholds initially belonging to prominent local nobles. Two of them, however (Westburg, Heanburh), appear to have been under direct royal control at the time of bestowal. Their geographic concentration is, in fact, near the troubled Welsh border and Offa's Dyke.[28] Given the chance survival of Mercian documents of any kind, these early burghs could very well represent only a fraction of the fortified sites in Offa's realm.

Indeed, a range of evidence suggests that quite a few sites in the Midlands and southern England were developed by Mercian overlords into fortified centers for trade from the mid-eighth century (Map 7.2.A). The old Roman towns of Canterbury, Rochester, and London represent good examples of one aspect of this process. It will be recalled that Canterbury, after a short period of virtual abandonment, had been resettled c.450–600 as the royal and ecclesiastical capital of the Kentish kingdom. Before the seventh century, however, intramural occupation appears to have been quite meager and restricted to two areas: around a presumed royal palace adjacent to the old Roman amphitheater (southeast quadrant) and also around the cathedral (northeast quadrant). Excavations have revealed quite clearly that intramural settlement intensified during the late seventh century, a period that saw the establishment of Canterbury's famous school under Theodore of Tarsus, the growth of nearby emporia such as Fordwich and Sandwich, and the extension of Mercian suzerainty over Kent. It is only during the reigns of Aethelbald and Offa, however, that Canterbury emerges as a fortified site with heightened economic life. Offa in particular appears to have exercised an effective overlordship over Kent from the 760s, when he began to confirm charters of various Kentish subkings.[29] Mid-eighth-century Canterbury we recall, is called *Cantwara burh*. Indeed, site excavations have shown that most of its Roman gates were then in use and possibly strengthened. The main east-west axial street, where houses were already tightly packed by the early ninth century, was known as *burhstraet* and passed from the cathedral district through Burgate to the extramural St. Augustine's. Also noteworthy is the fact that Canterbury in ninth-century documents is designated not only *burh* but *port*—a trading center. Indeed, references such as *ingan burgware* suggest that locational or perhaps social distinctions had emerged among Canterbury's townspeople. Ninth-century

Canterbury also has the distinction of being the site of England's earliest recorded town guild.[30]

Mercian charters provide additional information about fortification, trade, and administration within eighth-century Canterbury. For example, in a private charter of 762, a certain Dunwald, thegn of the former Kentish ruler Aethelberht II, conveys to St. Augustine's Abbey his intramural residence (*villa*), "at Queen's Gate (*Quenegatum*) in the market-place (*forum*) of the town (*urbs*)." The boundary clauses indicate that the holding extended northward to a "walled enclosure" (*maceria*) inside and adjoining the old Roman circuit. Dunwald specifically declares that he had received this and other properties along with their tribute from Aethelberht.[31] In a somewhat later diploma (786), Offa himself granted property (interestingly described as a *vicus*) within Canterbury, "in the northern part of the selling-place" (*locus venalis*), to his thegn Ealdberht and the latter's sister.[32] Indeed, there are indications that such tenements, whose general designation *tun* may imply some degree of fortification, were being established at this time both within Canterbury and just outside its walls.[33] It will also be recalled that Offa's influential new silver coins (pennies) were struck in Canterbury from the 760s, and the town housed Mercia's primary mint into the ninth century.[34] Indeed, trade and its resultant tolls must have attained significant levels and been under royal purview, for one finds a reeve (*praefectus*) named Aldhun who is said to reside at the king's vill in Canterbury during this period.[35] Thus a variety of evidence indicates that Canterbury under eighth-century Mercian control had become a refortified, defended place and a center of royal and ecclesiastical administration called a *burh*, housing an intramural market, dense occupation with distinct tenements, a mint, and multiple churches. Already a town by our definition since the seventh century, it had clearly acquired a greater range and intensity of urban functions during the succeeding century.

Rochester in Kent, like Canterbury, had been resettled as a royal and episcopal center in the early seventh century. Written and archaeological evidence indicates, however, a very small population before the late seventh century. Indeed, King Aethelberht I's initial charter conveying property to the cathedral (604) implies large areas of vacant land within the old Roman walls.[36] Yet there are signs of quickening activity at Rochester from the late seventh century as Mercia extended its sway over Kent. The site was sufficiently important, for instance, to be sacked by an invading Mercian army in 676.[37] Bishop Tobias (692–726) undertook an expansion of the cathedral, and there is evidence of a new, larger lay cemetery established just to the cathedral's east.[38] Several eighth-century charters also demonstrate that the church was augmenting its holdings within Rochester, and they include incidental references to a number of gates and streets in use.[39] Moreover, it has been suggested that Rochester's strategic bridge across the upper Medway was restored as part of Offa's apparent program of defensive works.[40]   Evidence of seventh- and eighth-century commercial and craft activity is slight but does include recent finds of a bronze metalworker's die, pottery, and *sceatta* coinage.[41]   Therefore, although Rochester is not explicitly called a burgh, it does appear to have become a refortified center with increased commercial activity within the period of Mercian supremacy and especially during Offa's reign. In the ninth century, Rochester was a fortified place (*burh*) and a market (*port*) with a royal mint established c.810.[42] Despite fortifications, it was also a target of repeated Viking attacks beginning in 842. The most renowned episode was the year-long siege of Rochester (884–885) when half the Danish host was held off by its townspeople behind their walls until King Alfred arrived with a relief force.[43]

The development of Anglo-Saxon London from a thinly populated royal and ecclesiastical town into a burgh with additional defensive and commercial functions has been outlined, and it was suggested that this Lundenburh of Alfredian sources had emerged primarily from an incorporation of extramural Lundenwic and its commercial life into the refortified old Roman walled town during the late ninth century. Although the main burghal program at London was Alfredian, certain of its features may well have appeared earlier, during the Mercian overlordships of Aethelbald and Offa. Several of these aspects already have been mentioned, among them, the refortification of a proposed palace precinct and high-status *hagas* in the Cripplegate-Aldermanbury area, and the involvement of eighth-century Mercian kings in the growth of London's mint. In addition, recent excavations suggest that the redevelopment of the town's intramural eastern waterfront into a dense residential and commercial area with planned streets and tenement alignments likely had commenced several decades before Danish occupation began (871).[44] Also, West Smithfield market beyond Cripplegate has been identified as a planned and controlled commercial site created initially by Offa.[45] Thus as at Canterbury and Rochester, there are indications that London under Mercian control had undergone selective refortification of intramural sites accompanied by planned settlement and new commercial activity prior to the larger-scale, more comprehensive burghal program of Alfred.

These three proposed cases of eighth-century Mercian burghs are all on former Roman sites where existing materials or structures could be reused. Other probable places in this category are Cambridge, Leicester, and Lincoln.[46] In addition to this group, there is a second series of likely eighth-century burghs with military and commercial functions developed on non-Roman sites under Mercian direction. Among these, Hereford, Tamworth, and Northampton can serve as representative cases for closer examination.

Hereford ("Army-Ford") occupied a strategic position at a crossing of the River Wye along the approaches to central Wales. It appears to have been a central place or capital of the obscure early Anglo-Saxon kingdom of the Magonsaete (Map 3.1), which was incorporated into an expanding Mercia in the mid-eighth century.[47] There was chronic Mercian and Welsh conflict in this border area from the seventh century, and the line of Offa's Dyke ran just to the west (Map 7.3). Indeed, the two most prominent eighth-century Mercian rulers, Aethelbald and Offa, both played a role in early Hereford tradition: Aethelbald as founder of the first minster (St. Guthlac's) and Offa as its lavish benefactor.[48]

Recent archaeological findings now point to significant Mercian royal activity at Hereford. In particular, excavations have revealed here the most complex and best-preserved sequence of Anglo-Saxon defense works yet known (Fig. 7.1.B).[49] The earliest phase, dated to the late eighth-century Offan period, consisted of a banked ditch succeeded soon after on the same lines by a gravel and clay rampart. This formed a rectangular *enceinte* of some 50 acres along the north bank of the Wye, including the cathedral, the early ford, and a series of intersecting roads whose regularity strongly suggests deliberate planning. A number of such primary street and place names (e.g., King Street, King's Ditch, Offa Street) could indicate that Mercian royal holdings within Hereford lay adjacent to a central ecclesiastical precinct. The construction date of this proposed Offan burgh is undetermined, though it likely took place in the early years of the reign, which saw repeated battles with the Welsh, including an apparently decisive Mercian victory at or near Hereford c.760.[50] This dating also would accord with charter evidence, which implies a Mercian policy of fortifying or refortifying strategic sites, beginning in central Mercia c.750. Although there is some evidence of pre-ninth-century commercial and craft activity at Mercian Hereford,[51] on the whole it is the military function of the burgh that is most evident here, especially its role as a border stronghold.[52]

Another non-Roman site likely to have been developed as an eighth-century Mercian burgh is Tamworth in the central Midlands (Fig. 7.1.C). Its line of tenth-century stone walls has now been found to be underlain by an earlier, probably Offan-period defense. The enclosed area is slightly larger than that at Hereford and again includes an early minster site and river crossing.[53] Tamworth perhaps is best known, along with Repton, as the site of a major Mercian royal manor from the seventh to tenth centuries. The Mercian assembly (*witan*) met here frequently, several times under the personal direction of Offa.[54] It is thus possible that the eighth-century fortification of Tamworth was intended to protect a preferred royal residence or palace complex. This suggestion is supported by the discovery at Tamworth of a two-story watermill dated c.750–800 with horizontal overshot wheel and millstones imported from the Rhineland. The sophisticated technique of this mill and its potential grain output imply that it was meant to serve a significant site such as a royal estate.[55] The tenth-century stone circuits of Hereford and Tamworth bear testimony to these places' important rank in the later Mercian burghal system. Their recently disclosed lowest foundations suggest, however, that the Aethelflaedan system had an earlier, Offan-period model.[56]

Finally, a similar case for the development of an early Mercian burgh can be made for Northampton, located on the River Nene in the east Midlands. The first substantial written evidence regarding Northampton appears only in the tenth century, when the site was a military base for the Danish host that had invaded and settled this area after 877. Indeed, it would appear that Northampton was then the "capital" of a Danish jarldom extending north to the River Welland.[57] When Mercia was incorporated into Wessex and divided into shires during the tenth century, its chief shire towns generally remained those centers that had been fortified by either the Danes or Aethelflaed and Edward the Elder. This at least must raise the possibility that these sites had been chosen as army bases because they had once been defensive and possibly administrative centers of pre-Viking age Mercia.[58] Such now seems to have been the case at Hereford and Tamworth. The discovery at Northampton of elaborate eighth-century buildings regarded as a palace complex, along with other defensive features, lends further weight to this contention.

The Northampton proposed palace complex consisted of a rectangular stone hall of substantial size (130 feet by 35 feet), set on cut-stone foundations with finely graveled floors southeast of the later Norman castle. Immediately to the west was found another, contemporary stone structure, underlying the medieval St. Peter's Church, which is considered part of the original Old Minster (Fig. 7.1.D). Both of these substantial buildings have been dated to the late eighth or very early ninth century.[59] Moreover, next to these stone structures were the remains of five large, mechanical mortar mixers–very rare finds in Anglo-Saxon England but not uncommon on high-status Carolingian sites.[60] Excavations further revealed that the impressive stone hall had been preceded by a slightly smaller timber long-hall first erected perhaps in the later seventh century. Indeed, this southwest quadrant of Northampton has yielded sunken huts, pottery, ornaments, and burials, which indicate continuous Anglo-Saxon occupation from the late fifth century.[61] But the construction of the timber and then stone halls seems to mark a real change in the site's status, a change contemporaneous with the forging of Mercian supremacy under Aethelbald and Offa. In view of these discoveries, it is surprising that documentary evidence is virtually silent on Northampton before the tenth century. Early Mercian royal authority is suggested, however, by a late seventh-century charter granting royal property there to Peterborough Abbey.[62] It also is considered likely, though not yet certain, that late Anglo-Saxon defenses that enclosed the western area of primary settlement were set up along the lines of older, Offan works and that the site's southern bridgehead had been fortified during the late eighth century.[63] While there is as yet only slight evidence of pre-tenth-century trade or industry, a pre-Viking market area has been tentatively identified in the eastern zone near All Saints Church.[64] Northampton thus appears to have been an early Mercian royal and ecclesiastical center on a non-Roman site, which saw significant development during the century of Mercian supremacy in central and southern England. Whether it in fact was provided with defenses and some accompanying commerce is a probable, though somewhat more speculative, assumption than is the case with Hereford and Tamworth.

These proposed eighth-century Mercian burghs, established on both former Roman and non-Roman sites, represent important developments in early English urban history. Unfortunately, they have received far less attention than have the earlier *wics* and the later Alfredian burghs. Unlike the open coastal emporia, these Mercian burghs formed a network of newly fortified inland sites with associated markets. The stimulus for their development appears to have been Mercia's expansionist policy, its growing international trade, and the need to meet early Viking assaults. These sites' internal street patterns, however, generally do not show the degree of central planning exhibited by Alfred's burghs, nor do they seem to have had dense intramural permanent occupation apart from their enclosed royal and ecclesiastical compounds. Rather, their primary focus of settlement and commercial activity, especially on the non-Roman sites, was immediately extramural, much as in contemporary continental towns.[65] Nonetheless, in a wider sense, these suggested early Mercian burghs do appear to attest a concerted royal program of creating defended administrative and military centers that would promote inland trade. Their royal and ecclesiastical administrative roles, probable defenses, and markets are sufficient criteria for them to be regarded as urban places. When these towns received new fortifications in the late ninth to early tenth centuries, by either Danish jarls or West Saxon rulers, they exhibit more significant populations of traders and craftsmen along with mints and regular street plans.[66]

Fortified places akin to the proposed Mercian burghs are not attested in West Saxon sources until the mid-ninth century. As we have seen, there is some written evidence for West Saxon private strongholds called burghs from the seventh century, but on the whole it does not suggest any general policy of creating fortified centers or refortifying the central places of the realm. Authentic West Saxon charters first speak of fortresses and fortifications only during the reigns of Kings Aethelwulf (839–858) and Aethelbald (858–860) in connection with the imposition of military obligations on bookland tenure (landholding by charter) in Wessex.

The earliest reference is especially significant, for it relates directly to the burgh of Canterbury. In a charter of 839, King Aethelwulf grants to a certain

Ithda an estate (*villa*) from his royal holdings within Canterbury and two parcels of appurtenant fields, which "I will free from the yoke of all secular burdens small and great, known and unknown except for these two conditions, that is, army-service *(expeditio)* and the strengthening *(munitio)* of the fortress *(arx)*."[67]   This shows, first, that Canterbury then was considered a fortified place or *burh (arx)* and that its general protection was a royal responsibility even after Canterbury had passed from Mercian to West Saxon control. The actual maintenance of its defenses, however, was being charged to inhabitants of the *burh* itself as a condition of bookland tenure. Subsequent West Saxon charters mention the obligation to strengthen and build fortresses as part of the threefold common burdens *(trim(n)oda necessitas)* that the kings of Wessex then were imposing on bookland.[68]

For example, in a charter of 842, Aethelwulf granted to his earldorman *(princeps)* Eanulf two estates in Somerset to be free from all royal tribute, lordly control, and forced works, "except army-service, the construction *(structura)* of bridges, and the strengthenings *(munitiones)* of fortresses *(arces)* which is universal *(communis)* for all people."[69]   Two additional extant charters of Aethelwulf conveyed Kentish property to royal thegns *(ministri)* with similar reservation clauses,[70] as do several diplomas (including one to the Church) of his son and successor, Aethelbald.[71] A series of West Saxon charters (862–863) issued by the joint kings Aethelbert and Aethelred I to their earldormen in Berkshire, Wiltshire, and Kent bear the *trimoda necessitas* clause, including one which specifically cites the duties of fort and bridge *constructio*.[72] It must be pointed out that the obligations of army service and bridgework are attested in West Saxon charters before fortress work was added.[73] Indeed, it appears that West Saxon rulers gradually were attempting to procure effective defensive measures for their realms by tying the three services to those hereditary bookland tenures they were so generously granting away.[74]

Archaeological evidence supports the written sources that indicate that burghal fortification and construction came rather late to Wessex. As we shall soon see, excavations of those burghs listed in the important tenth-century text, the *Burghal Hidage*, have shown that their initial fortifications date mainly from the reigns of Alfred, Edward the Elder, and Aethelstan. There are, however, a number of probable exceptions. For example, preliminary investigations suggest that the Anglo-Saxon defenses of such later burghs as Wallingford, Wareham, Malmesbury, Lydford, and Oxford may indeed have been begun by Alfred's predecessors.[75] When the Danes captured Canterbury and London in 851, they are said to have "broken through *(abraecan)*," that is, presumably through substantial fortifications, and there is further documentary evidence of defensive bridge work begun at Winchester in 859.[76] Asser also intimates that fortified sites were already established in Wessex before Alfred began his concentrated program of burghal construction.[77] Thus there is a range of evidence not only for pre-Alfredian burghs in Mercia but also in Wessex itself. Still, it is a striking fact that West Saxon burghs, like the imposition of fortress building itself, appear nearly a century later than similar developments in Mercia.

This rather late appearance is puzzling since there was certainly a need for defensible centers in Wessex against the Danes for example, during the first half of the ninth century. It has been contended that late eighth-century Viking raids on Mercian-controlled areas of England were countered by a program of refortifying older administrative centers and creating new fortified places, both of which could serve as foci for trade. Charlemagne, as we have seen, also embarked on a program of fortress building in northern and western Francia. There are several possible explanations for this apparent West Saxon tardiness. First, although the historical evidence is sketchy, there do not seem to have been large-scale, concerted Viking assaults on Wessex until the mid-830s. Second, the nature of the attacks that followed was sufficiently different to call forth new defensive measures. Both of these circumstances formed the background for the appearance of West Saxon burghs and must be considered in some detail.

Even though there is annalistic and charter evidence for early Viking raids in southeast England, especially Kent and Sussex, from the initial two decades of the ninth century, the first assault recorded of any magnitude took place in 835 when Sheppey (Kent) near the mouth of the Thames was sacked.[78] At this time England south of the Thames and East Anglia was subject to King Egbert of Wessex (802–839), Alfred's grandfather, who is also the last recorded *Bretwalda* or overlord of all English peoples south of the Humber (Map 7.1.B). Moreover, Ebert maintained close relations with the Carolingian court where he had previously lived in exile.[79] Indeed, the unleashing of major Viking assaults on southern England during his reign was most likely related to dynastic strife among Charlemagne's successors, a strife that undermined the unity of Carolingian defensive policy against the Danes and the diplomacy that also had contained this restless people.[80]

Although it is possible that Egbert instituted some important military innovations he had learned personally from Charlemagne, his efforts against the Danish Vikings were not always successful.[81] Upon his death, Danish attacks became more frequent and were directed against important towns such as Hamwic/Southampton (840, 842), London (842, 851), Rochester (842), Sandwich (850), and Canterbury (851) (Map 7.3).[82] By the 850s, Viking armies descending on Wessex evidently were considerably larger than raiding parties and had begun to winter-over in England.[83] Wessex and its defensive policies clearly were beleaguered, and it is just at this time that the duty of fortress work appears in Wessex charters.

Indeed, it may be no coincidence that Charles the Bald had responded to a serious Viking threat (855–856) by issuing a series of capitularies that called for the construction of new fortresses and bridges along with guard duty in his Frankish realm. One of these acts pointedly states that such work is to be done "according to ancient custom and that of other peoples."[84] West Saxon and Carolingian ties had been close since the reign of Egbert, and both kingdoms lived under a common Viking threat. Egbert lived in Francia for some time, as noted, and his son Aethelwulf married Charles the Bald's daughter, Judith, at Verberie in 855.[85] Charles also is known to have sent and maintained a diplomatic mission headed by Griffo, port-reeve of Quentovic, probably at the West Saxon court (858–866).[86] Given such contacts, one can assume at least a mutual awareness of defensive innovations as well. Whether Charles the Bald's fortification program was inspired by existing West Saxon practice may never be known conclusively, but it clearly proved successful enough to turn the Viking "Great Army" upon England.[87] The early burghs and fortifications that were likely established in Wessex c.840–860 failed to provide adequate protection, however. What appears to have been most lacking was an effective plan for manning burghal defenses to counteract sudden Viking attacks. Only Alfred's dramatic burghal program was to solve this immediate problem and promote economic and social developments already underway in West Saxon fortified towns.

Written evidence indicates that pre-Alfredian burghs overall were not only military strongholds or refuges but also centers of substantial permanent populations and trading activity. Indeed, a sense of common identity and purpose on the part of *burh*-dwellers begins to emerge in the charters of this time. The collective designation *burhware/burgware* becomes common enough for burghal inhabitants in ninth-century diplomas. As we have seen, settlement density increases, and there are suggestions of further divisions within the burghal population based perhaps on residence, occupation, or class. Commercial life at some of the larger burghs is attested by their designations as *ports*, a term initially designating trading centers or market towns, both inland and coastal, which acquired in the tenth century the technical meaning of shire boroughs under royal authority with mints and markets.[88] Direct references to traders and commerce in these pre-Alfredian burghs are somewhat rare, but one does encounter a *merk(c)ator*, for example, on intramural royal property granted to a Canterbury thegn (839).[89] Indeed, according to late Anglo-Saxon law, a merchant who had made three journeys overseas by his own means was entitled to noble or thegnly rank and rights.[90] In a charter of 857, the bishop of Worcester received the property (*haga*) of Coelmund, the king's reeve (*praefectus*) in London for a fixed price and yearly rent, along with the liberty of "measure, weight, and size, as is the custom in the port."[91] Along with this evidence of heightened communal and commercial activity, these same burghs also included large agricultural areas as well as intramural tenements with attached arable just outside the walls.[92]

Such indications of intensified commerce and more concentrated settlement must warn us against regarding even these pre-Alfredian burghs as exclusively military strongholds. The written record does suggest, however, that this quickened intramural life was attained only after some concerted efforts at fortification had been made. Most of the evidence for both fortification and trade concerns older Roman walled sites such as Canterbury, Rochester, Winchester, and London. Indeed, as has been noted, many of these same places appear to have become fortified burghs with significant commercial life while under Mercian control during the later eighth century. Initial West Saxon fortress work apparently involved the strengthening of existing defenses at primary centers of administrative, military, and commercial importance rather than *burghal* construction on new sites. These refurbished West Saxon defenses, though ultimately proving inadequate, provided incentive for that increased intramural settlement and intensified economy disclosed by charter evidence of the 850s and 860s. Also, population-shifts from nearby unwalled *wics* into these refortified centers may well have been a major factor in the latters' revitalization. The West Saxon burghs of Alfred and his successors, which now must be considered, continue to display both these defensive and commercial facets.

The pivotal text for the study of late ninth-century Anglo-Saxon burghs is an untitled vernacular document that has become known as the *Burghal Hidage*. There are a number of extant versions. The text primarily employed here ("A") is from a transcript of the oldest-known manuscript (c.1025), of Wessex provenance, destroyed in the Cotton Library fire of 1731.[93] Six post-Conquest manuscripts ("B") survive, each containing some textual variations, but all apparently derived as well from a lost late Anglo-Saxon archetype.[94]

The *Burghal Hidage* begins with a list of thirty-three burghs accompanied by statements of how many hides (*hida*) of land "belong" (*hyrdh*) to each, with numbers ranging from 100 to 2,400 hides (Fig. 7.2.B). After this, a concluding section explains with mathematical precision that if each hide (c.40 acres) is "represented" (*gemannod*) by one man, and sixteen hides (c.640 acres) are required for the maintenance and defense of an acre's breadth of wall (66 feet), then every pole of wall (5.5 yards/16.5 feet) can be manned (*gesettan*) by four men. Extrapolations for incrementally larger circuits are then made, using the basic equation of four men per pole. Each defender would thus be positioned about four feet apart along the wall.

The program of burghal defense described in this document is clearly large-scale. A total of over 28,000 men would be required for all listed burghs.[95] Moreover, the fortified places cited form an orderly circuit of Wessex, beginning in the southeast and proceeding clockwise west to north until returning to the southeast (Figs. 7.2.D and 7.2.A).[96] The scope and precision of this text likely identify it as an official memorandum outlining an intended royal program of burghal defense. Indeed, the *Burghal Hidage* properly has been called "the earliest unquestionably administrative document in English history."[97]   Behind its apparent simplicity lie many difficulties, however.

The first problem confronting interpretation of the *Burghal Hidage* concerns the textual usage of hides and hidation. Bede, writing c.730, tells us somewhat indirectly that the Anglo-Saxon hide was the amount of land regarded as sufficient to support one family.[98] This varied considerably in size according to region, but in Wessex a "small hide" of about 40 acres seems to have prevailed.[99] Other sources reveal that in addition to this social sense, the hide was also an important fiscal unit for the assessment of royal tribute and services. For example, the early Anglo-Saxon document known as the *Tribal Hidage* clearly gives assessments for whole regions and peoples in hidage units. It was probably a Mercian tribute list begun in the late seventh century and updated during the Offan age.[100] This text indicates that Mercian kings at least had set certain renders, expressed in hides, for regions based on their size and resources. The same practice evidently was employed on a wider scale in regard to individual estates. Anglo-Saxon charters from nearly their first appearance measure land grants in hidage units as expressions of the degrees of assessments due for royal tribute and services.[101]

More to the point for our discussion is the evidence that the hide likely was used from early times as a unit of assessing specifically military service. Unfortunately, the customary quota remains uncertain, although a Mercian charter of 801 details that the holder's obligation to the host was limited to sending five men for his thirty hides.[102] As noted, however, the *Burghal Hidage* clearly states the requirement of one man's service per hide for burghal defense. Whether responsibility for this quota fell on holders of intramural properties alone or also on those with surrounding estates, comparison of hidation figures may at least provide an approximation of these burghs' relative size and importance (Fig. 7.2.C).

Another major problem associated with the *Burghal Hidage* is its date and what this may tell us about burghal developments in Wessex. Internal evidence provides a number of important clues. First, most listed burghs are exclusively West Saxon, occur first in order of citation, and can be regarded as a core group. Oxford, however, was a Mercian site, which according to the *Anglo-Saxon Chronicle* only came under the control of King Edward the Elder of Wessex (899-924) in 911, while Mercian Buckingham was not fortified as a West Saxon burgh until 914.[103] Moreover, the bulk of Mercian burghs that were built c.910–914 under the direction of that realm's famous coruler, the Lady Aethelflaed (Edward the Elder's sister), are not included at all, and these presumably would have passed to King Edward on Aethelflaed's death in 918.[104]   These facts thus would place the "A" document's compilation between 911 and 914. The presence of Mercian Worcester and Warwick in the "B" group and their absence from "A" would suggest that the final *Burghal Hidage* text as we have it represents an updated version compiled by Alfred's successor, Edward, after 918.

An alternate chronological scheme is possible, however. The *Anglo-Saxon Chronicle*, we recall, dramatically records that Alfred recaptured London from the Danes in 886 and entrusted it to the Mercian ealdorman Aethelred, Aethelflaed's husband.[105]   According to the *Treaty of Alfred and Guthrum* (c.886–890), Oxford and Buckingham along with London also were in Alfred's hands.[106]   If Alfred's bestowal also included nearby Oxford and Buckingham, the *Burghal Hidage* "A" text could have been compiled just before 886. This would imply a significant Danish recovery of English territory between the Thames and the Lea, about which there are several hints in charters and annals.[107]   The written evidence therefore suggests that the *Burghal Hidage* in its full "B" form is most likely a revised and expanded early tenth-century compilation of a core burghal list "A" first drawn up by Alfred's command c.885.

There is clear textual evidence that Alfred did create a series of fortified places for his realm by strengthening the defenses of established sites and building entirely new fortresses. Asser, writing c.893, speaks, albeit in general terms, of "the cities (*civitates*) and towns (*urbes*) he [Alfred] restored, and the others he constructed anew where there had been none before."[108]   The biographer also remarks that Alfred's work in this regard was not yet complete, an observation supported by the *Anglo-Saxon Chronicle*'s reference (892) to a half-built fort (*faesten/geweorc*) stormed by the Vikings along the Kentish fens (perhaps Eorpeburnan of the *Burghal Hidage*).[109]   Asser does mention that Alfred had built "a well-fortified *arx* with elegant workmanship" near Athelney (probably Lyng, Dorset, of the *Burghal Hidage*) but does not indicate when it was constructed.[110]   He also describes Wareham (Dorset) as a fortified site that had been secure from a Danish attack in 876 and implies that Shaftesbury (Dorset) was fortified as well by his time.[111]   Though the precise chronology of Alfred's burghal work remains rather obscure, one may suggest that it had begun in earnest with his dramatic emergence from the swamps of Athelney (878) where he had successfully rallied his forces around a temporary fortification.[112]

It thus is fair to assume that the thirty specifically West Saxon burghs of the *Burghal Hidage*, which constitute the nucleus of the text, belonged to Alfred's kingdom-wide fortification program. This does not preclude the possibility that some of the listed sites, notably Winchester, may well have received earlier defensive strengthening. And again, the list should not be considered a comprehensive table of all burghs existing in Alfred's Wessex.[113]

Still, it is an invaluable and revealing source, especially when employed along with archaeological evidence. For example, there is a striking correspondence between tabulated *Burghal Hidage* wall lengths (Fig. 7.2.B) and the actual extents of remaining medieval circuits. Thus, Wareham's quota of 1,600 men, at four men per pole of wall, gives a total mural length of 2,200 yards/6,600 feet; its three bank-and-ditch defenses actually measure 2,180 yards/6,540 feet. For Cricklade, the *Burghal Hidage* defenses would measure 2,062 yards/6,186 feet, while the actual circuit stands at 2,300 yards/6,900 feet; and for Winchester, 3,300 yards/9,900 feet compared to 3,318 yards/9,954 feet.[114]

It is also possible to identify several different types of sites. The largest listed burghs, judging by hidation and corresponding mural lengths, are predominantly old Roman walled towns (Winchester, Chichester, Bath, Exeter). Excavations on these sites have shown that Alfredian-period fortification consisted primarily in the strengthening of Roman stone circuits. The defenses of other burghs that were new foundations, both on large, open sites (Wallingford, Wareham, Cricklade, Oxford) and a few on promontory positions (such as Wilton, Lewes, Malmesbury), were done with earthen banks and sometimes timber revetments.[115]

Moreover, the larger burghs have yielded significant evidence of regular, internal planning. This pattern includes, a central or spinal east-west street (High Street) often used as a market; one or two adjacent back-streets parallel to High Street; and an intramural or wall-street running just inside the circuits and linking all internal streets (Fig. 7.3.A). The result was a skillfully designed, defensible enclosure whose internal space was logically divided into blocks for a range of uses. The prominent medieval urban archaeologist Martin Biddle first observed these features during his intensive Winchester excavations, which began three decades ago.[116] Since then, the "Winchester pattern" has been identified at most of the larger Alfredian burghs of the *Burghal Hidage*, including the above-cited old Roman towns, new large burghs on open sites, and probably (as suggested above) at certain important non-listed burghs such as London, Canterbury, and Rochester. It was apparently also adopted in a modified form for several of the new, small, promontory burghs (Watchet, Axebridge, Lydford) (Figs. 7.3.B-F).[117] The smallest burghs of the *Burghal Hidage* are generally sites that were reused Iron Age and Roman hill-forts (Chisbury, Hastings, Portchester, Pilton, Halwell, Southampton) or somewhat larger forts (Burpham and Eashing) on new sites. These smaller burghs average only 515 hides each and show no sign of internal planning.[118]

Such differences in size and planning suggest that the *Burghal Hidage* was recording several types or categories of burghs, which might be called burghal towns and burghal forts. Such a distinction is in fact implied by the words of Asser, King Alfred's biographer. Indeed, this possibility is strengthened by a closer look at the tabulated sizes of listed burghs and their subsequent development. For example, the fifteen largest sites, with evidence of internal planning and a wall length of more than 1,000 yards/3,000 feet all went on to become prosperous eleventh-century boroughs.[119] It is also these larger burghs that furnish most of our evidence for coin production, markets, courts, and substantial, active populations c.775–925.[120] In contrast, six listed sites with no internal planning and less than 1,000 yards of wall (primarily hill forts) had all but disappeared by 1086.[121] The written and archaeological evidence thus supports a distinction between *Burghal Hidage* sites that were being founded and used for multifunctional purposes (burghal towns), and other places created as military enclosures only (burghal forts) (Fig. 7.2.B).

A number of other historical texts allow further insight into the internal activities of these late ninth- and early tenth-century burghs. One good example is a vernacular charter (c.889–899) regarding the fortification of Worcester, issued by the Mercian rulers Aethelred and Aethelflaed, with King Alfred standing witness.[122] It states that at the urging of Bishop Waerferth of Worcester, Aethelred and Aethelflaed "ordered the *burh* at Worcester to be built for the protection of the people" and the security of the cathedral church. The bishop and his church are to receive half the revenue (*gerihta*, "rights/dues") "in the market (*ceapstow*) or in the street, both within the fortification (*byrg*) and without." These public assessments include a land rent on burghal tenements, a tax for the upkeep of the *burh*-wall, and fines for fighting, theft, and market offenses. The other half of such profits was retained by Aethelred and Aethelflaed. Outside the marketplace, however, the bishop, as largest landowner, was to have his full customary revenues.[123] The charter also specifies that tolls on salt cartage from nearby Droitwich now were to go to King Alfred.[124]

This document discloses a number of significant points. First, it strongly implies that Worcester's fortification was accompanied at the same moment by the establishment of a burghal market, a street-grid, and individual tenements. The site was meant to be more than a military stronghold.[125] Those responsible for the building of the burgh were secular lords, in this case Mercian rulers, but with the significant approval and oversight of the West Saxon king. The burgh at Worcester appears unusual, however, in not being founded on royal domain land.[126] In addition, the inhabitants' personal duty of maintaining the *burh*-wall, as set forth in the *Burghal Hidage*, is acquitted here by a money payment. There is also more than a suggestion of a local court, though whether this was a specifically burghal court or one encompassing a wider area is unclear.

Bishop Waerferth has been encountered before, receiving several grants in London, one for a marketplace (889) and another for a holding with appurtenant mooring rights (898/899). It is very likely that these properties were the same and lay within the Alfredian Thames-side redevelopment area west of Wallbrook. Asser, in his biography of King Alfred, does observe that the king "restored" (*restauravit*) London honorably (*honorifice*) following its recapture (886) and made it habitable again.[127] It also has been observed that the second grant to Waerferth is said to have been conferred consequent to a conference at Chelsea between Alfred, Aethelred, Waerferth, and Plegmund where the "rebuilding" or "renewal" (*instauracio*) of London had been the chief topic.[128] Hereafter, London, referred to in the sources as a *burh*, clearly was also being revived as a commercial place, with large-scale permanent settlement and trading activities that would complement its traditional administrative and ceremonial functions.[129] The defensive-commercial reconstruction at the burgh of Worcester is a significant parallel development.

As noted, this multiplicity of urban functions within a planned layout appears characteristic of the larger Alfredian burghs. Indeed, the Alfredian burghal town, even if inspired by eighth-century Mercian burghs, was a very significant creation. The scale and recurrence of this plan strongly points to central, royal direction concerned with providing effective defense, economic growth, and stable administration.[130] The same concerted royal initiative can be seen in the detailed regulations of the *Burghal Hidage*. This full program of burghal towns and forts bears striking testimony to Alfred's authority, command of resources, and bold vision.

Alfred's ambitious program of burghal work must be seen as part of the imposition of "common burdens" on bookland holdings in Wessex, which began during the mid-ninth century. Asser speaks directly of King Alfred's orders concerning "the building of fortresses and other things for the common good of the while realm."[131] Reservations of the three common burdens is a standard feature of Alfredian land grants.[132] There is evidence, however, of considerable initial resistance. For example, Asser recalls the "great trouble and vexation... he [Alfred] had with his own people who would undertake of their own accord little or no work for the common needs of the kingdom."[133] As a result, the royal biographer says, fortresses commanded to be built were often delayed or not even begun. Only Alfred's persistent urging and ultimately chastisement, along with disastrous Viking raids, brought obedience to the king's will and orders.[134] Asser makes it quite clear that the recalcitrant people he has in mind here are the West Saxon nobles upon whom the duties of the common burdens, including burghal construction, fell by charter.

Once again, both the Alfredian burghal forts and the more multifunctional burghal towns were intended to have military roles, though this tactical aspect has been misunderstood at times. In particular, the distribution and siting of the burghs can give the erroneous impression that they were merely static, defensive strongholds. Thus, it is true that the Alfredian burghs as a whole were well distributed throughout Wessex in such a way that no place was more than about twenty miles distance, or a day's march, from such a fortified site. They were also as a rule strategically located to command navigable rivers, inlets, and roadways.[135] But textual evidence indicates that the Alfredian burghs were not only static, defensible places but also garrisoned staging points for offensive actions taken in conjunction with a reformed West Saxon army.

The *Anglo-Saxon Chronicle* refers to this program when it recounts that Alfred "had divided his army (*fyrd*) into two, so that half of its men were at home, half on service, apart from the men who guarded the burghs."[136] This division of the *fyrd* into rotating forces ensured there would always be troops in the field rather than levies called for an emergency and then disbanded. Moreover, permanent burghal garrisons would join campaigns with the *fyrd* or with those warriors remaining at home to defend and administer their lands. In 893, for example, the *fyrd* of the western shires was joined by an army comprising local burghal garrisons and "the king's thegns who were at home near the fortifications" in an attack on Viking-held Buttington.[137] Similar coordinated action between burghal forces, fyrds, and local nobles can be seen in the West Saxon offensive against Hertford north of London in 895.[138]

This mutual support between garrisoned and fortified burghs, a mobile and regular *fyrd*, and local thegnly forces proved most effective. It deprived the Vikings of their chief tactical advantages—freedom of movement and surprise attack—while also permitting concerted offensive operations. Fortified burghs presented major obstacles to Viking advances and, if besieged, could be relieved by the *fyrd* or neighboring forces. Burghal troops could pursue a raiding party, and the *fyrd* might lead a variety of operations without endangering the security of the localities. Indeed, the Vikings' initial successes against Wessex were reversed dramatically in the 890s due largely to these military reforms centered around the burghs.[139]

Thus, although some major towns in Mercia and Wessex were apparently fortified and economically stimulated before Alfred's time, it was only under Alfred that these selective, tentative developments were more clearly systematized and extended throughout Wessex. Older Roman towns were refortified and redesigned with planned areas for economic development and population expansion. Entirely new towns were built for similar multifunctional purposes, complemented by a series of strategic military forts. The Alfredian burghal system stemmed the Viking threat and reinvigorated English urban life.

When King Alfred of Wessex lay dying in 899, he could look back with satisfaction on a successful and momentous reign. His burghal system had helped to secure the kingdom from what seemed to be certain defeat, while the threat of a common enemy had served to unite English resistance around the banner of the valiant West Saxon king. Indeed, Alfred's reoccupation of London had been a high-water mark of the Danish wars, and he continued to implement his burghal program through the remainder of his reign.

After Alfred's death, Aethelred, ealdorman of Mercia and his wife, Aethelflaed, built their famous series of Mercian burghs. Lady Aethelflaed alone is credited specifically with five such sites (Map 7.2.A).[140] Excavations suggest that, like the Alfredian burghs, they were intended as either simple forts or fortified multifunctional towns.[141] It was these Mercian burghs that were used by Aethelflaed's brother, King Edward the Elder of Wessex as bases for his celebrated "reconquest" of England south of the Humber (912–921). In the course of these campaigns, Edward constructed or refortified over a dozen additional sites. (Map 7.2.B).[142] Five of them were built on riverbanks across from previous Danish forts to which they now were linked by bridges. This created a system of double burghs controlling passage and trade along important rivers, as seems to have been done earlier in Carolingian Francia and probably by Alfred as well.[143]

Moreover, at this time Edward was reorganizing the administration of central England around the newly created burghs which had passed under his control at Aethelflaed's death (918). Each of the new shires in western Mercia now had a burgh or borough that served as its administrative center and gave its name to the shire. These new divisions deliberately disregarded ancient Mercian tribal regions and appear to have been patterned after the pre-Viking age shire system of Wessex.[144] In eastern Mercia, the existing Danish burghs and their settlement areas generally were incorporated intact under Edward's authority.[145]

The Edwardian burghs were very definitely royal creations. As the kings of Wessex consolidated their political control over all England in the course of the tenth century, so too did they attempt to elevate the economic role of their royal burghs or boroughs. This process is evident in the late Anglo-Saxon dooms. For example, Edward the Elder's first law code commands that "no one shall buy or sell except in a burgh (called *port*)" and with the witness of the king's *port*-reeve.[146] This demonstrates that these places, apart from their military role, had commercial functions as markets and that the king was trying to restrict all trade and its profits at these royal towns. As it turned out, Edward's son, King Aethelstan (924–939) later had to make allowance for some non-burghal trade, but only that of low value.[147] In this same code, Aethelstan refers to the burgh specifically as both a fortress (*burh*) and a place of trade (*port*)[148]

This second code of Aethelstan is also significant because of its decrees concerning moneying and mints. It declares that "there shall be one coinage throughout the king's realm, and no man shall mint money except in a town (*port*)."[149] If a moneyer is found guilty of issuing base or substandard coins, his working hand shall be cut off and fastened up on the mint.[150] The following clause stipulates how many moneyers there shall be in what are apparently the king's major burghs, and concludes with the important statement, "and one in [each of] the other burghs."[151] Clearly the late Anglo-Saxon burgh was systematically and officially acquiring added urban functions. The provision of royal mints underscores both its heightened economic and royal administrative roles. Indeed, Aethelstan is credited with the installation of new mints in a total of twenty-two identified sites, all of which in the tenth century were royal burghs or boroughs.[152] Also, during his reign, many of the older single-function burghal forts appear to have been replaced locally by new multifunctional burghal towns.[153] Such places with their mints and markets thus acquired several more defining urban functions with royal backing.

After Aethelstan's death (939), the pace of royal town foundation in Wessex slowed but did not cease entirely.[154] One major trend in the development of established late Anglo-Saxon towns, especially larger sites, was the growth of suburban settlement along with a proliferation of suburban (and urban) churches.[155] Another notable urban development of the mid tenth century involved the great expansion of industrial operations such as pottery production and metalworking in many towns, apparently to meet mounting rural demand.[156] Indeed, it has been estimated that the number of urban places in Anglo-Saxon England increased from about ten sites in 880 to about fifty in 930; by 1066 the total number was to reach perhaps one hundred, thus closely approaching the number of towns of all types in Roman Britain.[157] Much of this late Anglo-Saxon urban growth can be attributed to the royal policy of establishing small market towns, many furnished with mints, on royal estates near existing burghs to augment royal revenues, especially during the reigns of Edgar (959-975) and Aethelred II (978-1016).[158] In late Anglo-Saxon times, urban life was an important aspect of English society and the complexities of this urbanism become increasingly more apparent in the sources. Its structure was established, however, over the course of nearly four hundred years.

NOTES

1. See E. A. Gukind's curious sketch of Anglo-Saxon towns: *International History of City Development* (8 vols., NY: Free Press, 1964–72), vol. VI, *Urban Development in Western Europe: The Netherlands and Great Britain* (1971), pp. 152–57, 182–83, and the literature cited in Chap. 1, above.

2. *Cartularium Saxonicum* (hereafter *Cart. Sax.*), ed. W. de Gray Birch (4 vols., London: Whiting & Co., 1885–99), No. 178. On its authenticity, see: P. H. Sawyer, *Anglo-Saxon Charters* (London: Royal Historical Society, 1968), No. 92, p. 95; E. John, *Land Tenure in Early England* (Leicester: University Press, 1960), pp. 66–70.

3. Bede, *Historia Ecclesiastica* (hereafter *Hist. Eccl.*), v. 23, ed. Plummer (2 vols., Clarendon Press, 1896).

4. *Cart. Sax.* No. 154, and cf. also Nos. 157, 162; *Two of the Saxon Chronicles Parallel* (hereafter *ASC*), eds. J. Earle and C. Plummer (2 vols., Oxford Clarendon Press, 1892–1899), s.a. 827A. See further, John, *Orbis Britanniae and Other Studies* (Leicester: University Press, 1966), pp. 7–8, 17–19; P. Wormald, "Bede, the *Bretwaldas*, and the Origins of the *Gens Anglorum*," in *Ideal and Reality in Frankish and Anglo-Saxon Society*, ed. Wormald (Oxford: Clarendon Press, 1983), pp. 104–11; and S. Fanning, "Bede, *Imperium*, and the *Bretwaldas*," *Speculum* 66 (1991), 1–26.

5. Felix, *Vita Sancti Guthlaci*, xlix, ed. B. Colgrave (Cambridge: University Press, 1956). See F. M. Stenton, *Anglo-Saxon England* (hereafter *ASE*) (3d ed., Oxford Clarendon Press, 1971), pp. 203–205, for a sound assessment of Aethelbald's career. This Mercian ruler's predecessor, King Wulfhere (659-675) likely had enjoyed a similar overlordship: Ibid., pp. 34, 84-85. He is credited with the foundation or completion of various minsters, such as those of St. Peter's, Gloucester (Chap. 3, above), and Peterborough (*ASC* 656E).

6. *ASC* 733A.

7. Ibid., 741, 743A.

8. Like Aethelbald, the future St. Guthlac (then also a young war band leader of noble (royal? Mercian stock) took part in these raids and was himself held captive by the Welsh: *Vita S. Guthlaci*, xvi–xviii, xxxv. The *Welsh Annals* record Mercian and Welsh warfare in this area from Penda to Offa's reigns: *Annales Cambriae*, s.a. 644–797, ed. Morris (Chichester: Phillimore, 1980). For Wat's Dyke and Aethelbald, see C. Fox, *Offa's Dyke* (London: British Academy, 1955), pp. 271–73; H. P. R. Finberg, *The Formation of England 550-1042* (St. Albans: Paladin, 1976), pp. 96-98; D. H. Hill, *An Atlas of Anglo-Saxon England* (Toronto: Toronto Press, 1981), p. 75. The inscription on "Eliseg's Pillar" from the upper Dee commemorates a Welsh recovery of territory taken from the English c.750. See W. Davies, *Wales in the Early Middle Ages* (Leicester: University Press, 1982), p. 203.

9. *S. Bonifatii et Lulli Epistolae*, lxxiii, ed. E. Dümmler, in *Monumenta Germaniae Historica* (hereafter *MGH*), *Epistolae* (hereafter *EE*), III (2d ed., Berlin, 1957).

10. Ibid., lxxviii.

11. *Cart. Sax.*, Nos. 202, 203. This Aethelmund later received property from Offa at Westburg, Glouc. (see n.14, below) and died in battle against the West Saxons (*ASC* 800A).

12. *Cart. Sax.*, No. 848.

13. Ibid. See further, N. Brooks, "The Development of Military Obligations in Eighth and Ninth-Century England," in *England before the Conquest*, eds. P. Clemoes and K. Hughes (Cambridge: University Press, 1971), p. 79; R. Abels, *Lordship and Military Obligation in Anglo-Saxon England* (Berkeley: University of California Press, 1988), p. 54.

14. *Cart. Sax.*, No. 274. See Brooks, "Military Obligations," p. 78.

15. *ASC*, 787A[789].

16. *Cart. Sax.*, Nos. 335 (811 A.D.), 348 (814 A.D.).

17. *Annales Regni Francorum*, s.a. 800, ed. F. Kurze, in *MGH Scriptores Rerum Germanicarum* (hereafter *SS RG*), VI (Hanover, 1895); Einhard, *V. Karoli Magni*,

xvii, ed. O. Holder-Egger, in *MGH SS RG, XXV* (Hanover, 1911). See P. H. Sawyer, *Kings and Vikings: Scandinavia and Europe A.D. 700–1100* (London: Methuen, 1982), pp. 78–81. On Charlemagne and Offa, see also: *ASE*, pp. 215–24; J. M. Wallace-Hadrill, *Early Germanic Kingship in England and on the Continent* (Oxford: Clarendon Press, 1971), pp. 109–23. For Charlemagne and Egbert, Alfred's grandfather, see nn. 79-81, below.

18. J. Bosworth, T. Toller, and A. Campbell, *An Anglo-Saxon Dictionary* (2 vols., Oxford: University Press, 1898–1972), s.v. *burh/burg, beorh* (cf. Old Saxon *burg* "fort," Gothic *baurgs* "fort, town"); A. H. Smith, *English Place-Name Elements* (2 vols., Cambridge: University Press, 1956), I, pp. 58–62, and in a wider, continental perspective: W. Schlesinger, "Stadt and Burg im Lichte der Wortgeschichte," *Studium Generale* 16 (1963), 433–44; D. M. Nicholas, "Medieval Urban Origins," in *Studies in Medieval and Renaissance History* 6 (1969), pp. 100–101.

19. *Laws of Ine*, xlv, ed. F. A. Attenborough, in Attenborough, *The Laws of the Earliest English Kings* (Cambridge: University Press, 1922), and cf. *Laws of Alfred*, xl, ed. Attenborough, *Laws of the Earliest English Kings*, where the fine for *cyninges burgbryce* remains the same but is reduced for all other noble classes. See further, F. Liebermann, *Die Gesetze der Angelsachsen* (3 vols., Halle: M. Niemeyer, 1903–16), II, pp. 330–31, III, p. 76. For these ranks of Anglo-Saxon nobility, see: H. M. Chadwick, *Studies on Anglo-Saxon Institutions* (Cambridge: Cambridge University Press, 1905), pp. 318-27, 378-83; *ASE*, pp. 305-6; H. R. Loyn, *The Governance of Anglo-Saxon England* (Stanford: Stanford University Press, 1984), pp. 47-50.

20. *ASC* 755A. It is generally believed that pre-Alfredian material in this earliest manuscript ("Parker Chronicle") was derived in part from a mid eighth-century series of West Saxon annals and regnal lists. See *ASE*, pp. 15–16.

21. *ASC* 754A. See also: *Cart. Sax.*, No. 248 (786 A.D.), where the people of Canterbury are called *burhwara*, "the *burh* dwellers." In 804 kings Cenwulf of Mercia and Cuthred of Kent granted property within the walls of Canterbury to the convent of Limming "ad necessitatis refugium" (ibid., No. 317).

22. *ASC* 547A.

23. Bede, *Hist. Eccl.*, iii.16. The account implies concentrated settlement. He calls Bamborough *urbs regia* and observes that it was named after Bebba, a former queen.

24. *ASC* 530A, 661A; *Cart. Sax.*, Nos. 71, 76. Several important early monastic foundations also are described as *burga*, etc., among them, Malmesbury (Meldumesburg), and Glastonbury (Glastingebirig): Ibid., Nos. 103, 285.

25. Ibid., Nos. 130, 164, 216, 274; *Codex Diplomaticus Aevi Saxonici*, ed. J. M. Kemble (6 vols., London: British Historical Society, 1839–48), No. 64 ("Hazelburg," "Stoneburg," "Westburg," "Owlburg").

26. Bosworth-Toller-Campbell, *Anglo-Saxon Dictionary*, s.v. *burh/burg*; J. Campbell, "Bede's Words for Places," in *Places, Names, and Graves*, ed. P. H. Sawyer (Leeds: Leeds University Press, 1979), pp. 34-53; Schlesinger, "Stadt und Burg," pp. 439–40.

27. *Cart. Sax.*, Nos. 213, 230, 246, 272, 274. Note that Salmonsbury also is described as *urbs* (town) and Cockbury as equipped with a *geat* (gate).

28. In Aethelbald's genuine charters, only three possible burghs appear: two are in Gloucestershire: Ibid., Nos. 137, 164, and 165. See further: Finberg, *Formation of England*, pp. 99-100.

29. *Cart. Sax.*, Nos. 195, 196; see also his wide distribution of lands to the Church: ibid., Nos. 213, 214, 219, 234, 246, 257, 275. Offa's suzerainty over Kent suffered an apparent setback c.775 but was reestablished in the final decade of his reign: *ASC* 773A [776]: *Cart. Sax.*, Nos. 247, 248, 254, 255, 263, 265, 293. See further, *ASE*, pp. 206–208; Loyn, *Governance*, pp. 25–28; Wormald, "The Age of Offa and Alcuin," in *The Anglo-Saxons*, ed. J. Campbell (Hammondsworth: Penguin Books, 1982), pp. 110–14; and D. P. Kirby, *The Earliest English Kings* (London: Unwin Hyman, 1991), pp. 163–84.

30. T. Tatton-Brown, "The Towns of Kent," in *Anglo-Saxon Towns in Southern England*, ed. J. Haslam (Chichester: Phillimore, 1984), pp. 7-9; N. Brooks, *The Early History of the Church of Canterbury* (Leicester: University Press, 1984), pp. 24–25; J. Haslam, "Market and Fortress in England in the Reign of Offa," *World Archaeology* 19 (1987), 81–82; M. Houliston, "Recent Excavations: Canterbury," *Medieval Archaeology* 33 (1989), 198; Haslam, "Market and Fortress," 81–82. For settlement density, see *Cart. Sax.* Nos. 373, 426, 519. There was also a spate of new intramural church constructions c. 740–60, presumably in response to a growing population: N. Brooks, *Church of Canterbury*, p. 51, and Chap. 4, above. For references to Canterbury's functions as fortified place and market, as well as to possible social gradations and its enigmatic *cnihtengild*, see *Cart. Sax.*, nos. 248, 378, 426, 492, 497, 515. Note there were still large areas of arable within the walls. Mid-tenth-century Canterbury charters speak of three "fraternities" (*geferscipas*): *innan burhware, utan burhware, micle gemettan* (ibid., nos. 1010, 1212). For useful discussions of these groupings, see J. Tait, *The English Medieval Borough* (Manchester: University Press, 1936), p. 9; *ASE*, pp. 526–28, and N. Brooks, *Canterbury*, pp. 18–30 with comments on ultraviolet enhancement of fragmentary charter No. 515.

31. *Cart. Sax.*, No. 192.

32. Ibid., No. 248. The tenement's name was Curringtun, and it was part of a larger grant including a Kentish rural estate.

33. Ibid., Nos. 373, 407.

34. R. Dolley, "The Coins," in *The Archaeology of Anglo-Saxon England*, ed. D. M. Wilson (London: Methuen, 1976), pp. 353–54; P. Grierson and M. Blackburn, *Medieval European Coinage I: The Middle Ages* (Cambridge: University Press, 1986), pp. 279–81; Tatton-Brown, "Towns of Kent," p. 7.

35. *Cart. Sax.*, No. 319. Aldhun attests Kentish royal charters of 765 and 778, the former with Offa's confirmation (ibid., Nos. 192, 227). He perhaps was involved with Canterbury's trade, for he is described as "strenuus et predives" and as having traveled overseas (ibid., Nos. 293, 320). Aldhun had received a Kentish rural estate from King Egbert and then bestowed it on Christ's Church (Canterbury) where his relative, Jaenberht, was archbishop. Offa, however, seized the property because it had been granted without his consent as overlord (ibid., Nos. 293, 319, 332).

36. Ibid., No. 3 (604 A.D.). The grant confers some two-thirds of the entire intramural area but is not without suspicion: Sawyer, *Anglo-Saxon Charters*, No. 1, p. 69; A. Campbell, ed., *Charters of Rochester* (London: British Academy, 1973), p. xxii. For the early archaeological evidence, see Tatton-Brown, "Towns of Kent," pp.

12–16; P. Drewett, et al., *The South-East to A.D. 1000* (London: Longman, 1988), pp. 306–309.

37. Bede, *Hist. Eccl.*, iv.12.

38. Ibid., v.23. See Tatton-Brown, "Towns of Kent," p. 14, for the material evidence.

39. *Cart. Sax.*, Nos. 193, 196, 242, 255. The inhabitants of Rochester are called simply Ceastruwara, "the *ceaster* dwellers," and apparently had customary swine-pastures just outside. Ibid., No. 175 (762 A.D.). The same charter also mentions the presence of a royal *procurator* at Rochester.

40. Tatton-Brown, "Towns of Kent," p. 15.

41. Ibid., pp. 12, 14; Drewett, et al., *South-East*, p. 307; Grierson and Blackburn, *Medieval European Coinage*, p. 281. See *Cart. Sax.*, No. 242 (781 A.D.), whose boundary clauses suggest a central street market in Rochester.

42. *ASC* 885A [884]; *Cart. Sax.*, No. 518. See Tatton-Brown, "Towns of Kent," p. 15; Grierson and Blackburn, *Medieval European Coinage*, pp. 272–75.

43. *ASC* 839A [842], 885A [884]; cf. Aethelweard, *Chronicon*, ed. A. Campbell (London: Thomas Nelson, 1962), p. 44.

44. T. Dyson and J. Schofield, "Saxon London," in *Anglo-Saxon Towns in Southern England*, p. 293 and Figs. 98, 99 for Alfredian structural evidence and finds of Ipswich ware. See also, Chaps. 4 and 5, above.

45. Haslam, "Market and Fortress," 83; Tatton-Brown, "The Topography of Anglo-Saxon London," *Antiquity* (1986), 23.

46. Haslam, "Market and Fortress," 80–81 and Table 1. For Cambridge, also see M. Lobel, "Cambridge," in *Atlas of Historic Towns* II, ed. Lobel (London: Lovell Johns Ltd., 1975), pp. 1–5. The case of Lincoln, the former Roman *colonia*, is especially interesting (Fig. 7.1.A). Preliminary excavations revealed evidence of significant late Roman occupation, followed by fifth-century urban decline and virtual abandonment, then Anglo-Saxon resettlement (early seventh century). The old walled fortress and *colonia* were evidently occupied in Mercian times, and signs of a pre-Viking age extramural *wic* (Wigford) also have been found: C. J. Arnold, *Roman Britain to Saxon England* (Bloomington: Indiana University Press, 1984), pp. 38, 46; M. J. Jones, "New Streets for Old: The Topography of Roman Lincoln," in *Roman Urban Topography in Britain and the Western Empire*, eds. F. Grew and B. Hobley, Council for British Archaeology (hereafter C.B.A.) Research Reports 59 (London, 1985), pp. 86–93; B. Gilmour, "The Anglo-Saxon Church of St. Paul-in-the-Bail," *Medieval Archaeology* 23 (1979), 214–18; Haslam, Market and Fortress," pp. 96-99; H. Clarke and B. Ambrosiani, *Towns in the Viking Age* (NY: St. Martin's Press, 1991), pp. 10–11, 96–99.

47. Theodore of Tarsus had established a diocese for the Magonsaettan centered at Hereford before 680, and the celebrated Cuthbert transferred from there to Canterbury c.740: A. Haddan and W. Stubbs, eds., *Councils and Ecclesiastical Documents Relating to Britain and Ireland*, (3 vols., Oxford: Clarendon Press, 1869–71), III, pp. 126, 130, 340. See further, *ASE*, pp. 46–48; H. P. R. Finberg, "The Princes of the Magonsaete," in *The Early Charters of the West Midlands*, ed. Finberg (Leicester: University Press, 1961), pp. 217–24, and K. Pretty, "Defining the Magonsaete," in *The Origins of Anglo-Saxon Kingdoms*, ed. S. Bassett (Leicester:

University Press, 1989), pp. 171–83. The people of Herefordshire were still called Magonsaetan in the early eleventh century: *ASC* 1016D.

48. *The Victoria History of the Counties of England* (hereafter *VCH*) Herefordshire, I (London, 1908), pp. 348–49; *ASE*, p. 210; M. R. James, "Two Lives of St. Ethelbert, King and Martyr," *English Historical Review* 32 (1917), 214–44; D. W. Rollason, "The Cults of Murdered Royal Saints,"*Anglo-Saxon England* 11 (1983), pp. 9, 21. Offa supposedly was expiating for his treacherous decapitation of King Aethelbert (Ethelbert) of East Anglia at Sutton Walls, a Mercian estate some four miles north of town: *ASC* 792A[794]. Aethelbert was buried in Hereford and became its patron saint.

49. For what follows, see: R. Shoesmith, *Hereford City Excavations 2, Excavations on or Close to the Defences*, C.B.A. 46 (London, 1982); also see Lobel, "Hereford," in *Atlas of Historic Towns I*, ed. Lobel (London: Lovell Johns, 1969), pp. 1–4 and corresponding topographical maps; M. Biddle, "The Towns," in *Archaeology of Anglo-Saxon England*, ed. Wilson, pp. 120–22; J. Steane, *The Archaeology of Medieval England and Wales* (Athens, GA: University of Georgia Press, 1984), p. 35; Clarke and Ambrosiani, *Towns in the Viking Age*, pp. 44–45, and Fig. 3.7.

50. *Annales Cambriae*, s.a. 760.

51. Lobel, "Hereford," p. 2. Remains of several eighth-century corn dryers packed with reused Roman stone may have been part of the intramural royal estate in the western zone: P. Rahtz, "Gazetteer of Anglo-Saxon Domestic Settlement Sites," in *Archaeology of Anglo-Saxon England*, ed. Wilson, p. 423, and "Buildings and Rural Settlement," Ibid., pp. 86, 91.

52. Hereford was one of the Mercian burghs utilized by Edward the Elder and Aethelflaed in their reconquest of the southern Danelaw, and most of its Anglo-Saxon stone circuits are of tenth-century provenance. It appears to have been strongly refortified along with a Norman-style castle by Edward the Confessor's nephew, Ralph of Vexin, and then Harold Godwinson as a forward base confronting Wales. See Lobel, "Hereford," pp. 2–5.

53. Biddle, "Towns," p. 121; Rahtz, Gazetteer," p. 442; Haslam, "Market and Fortress," 83, 90; Clarke and Ambrosiani, *Towns in the Viking Age*, pp. 39-40.

54. *Cart. Sax.*, Nos. 34, 39, 239, 259. See further, F. Liebermann, *The National Assembly in the Anglo-Saxon Period* (Halle: M. Niemeyer, 1913), pp. 43–46.

55. Wilson, "Craft and Industry," in *Archaeology of Anglo-Saxon England*, ed. Wilson, p. 276 and Pl. 12A, noting that the only other comparable Middle Saxon mill is that found on the royal estate of Old Windsor. See also, R. Hodges, *The Anglo-Saxon Achievement* (Ithaca: Cornell University Press, 1989), pp. 112–13, and Fig. 44; Steane, *Archaeology of England and Wales*, p. 169.

56. Haslam, "Market and Fortress," 83-84, and see also, *ASC* 913C, 913, and 914D for possible earlier fortifications at Tamworth and Hereford.

57. Frequent raids were launched from Northampton against the armies of Edward the Elder (*ASC* 917[916], 921[920]A), until the surrender of Jarl Thurferth and "the entire host which owed obedience to Northampton." (Ibid.).

58. Haslam, "Market and Fortress," 78–81; Loyn, *Governance of Anglo-Saxon England*, pp. 133–40; P. Stafford, *The East Midlands in the Early Middle Ages* (Leicester: University Press, 1985), pp. 46–47, 135–43.

59. For results of the Northampton excavations, see J. H. Williams, "From 'Palace to Town': Northampton and Urban Origins," *Anglo-Saxon England* 13 (1984), pp. 113–36, and Figs. 7-10. Also see Haslam, "Market and Fortress," 84; Hodges, *Anglo-Saxon Achievement*, pp. 129–32; Clarke and Ambrosiani, *Towns in the Viking Age*, pp. 37-39, and Fig. 3.4.

60. Williams, "Northampton," pp. 135–36; Steane, *Archaeology of England and Wales*, pp. 228–29 and Pl.7.3.

61. Williams, "Northampton," pp. 116–20. Northampton's timber hall is most similar to the royal Northumbrian palace excavated at Yeavering; the secular(?) stone hall is regarded as "totally without parallel" in England: Ibid., p. 123. They are much more elaborate than the contemporary "thegnly" long halls found at nearby Raunds: Hodges, *Anglo-Saxon Achievement*, pp. 110–12.

62. *Cart. Sax.*, No. 22 (664 A.D.). There are mixed opinions on this charter's authenticy, however. See Sawyer, *Anglo-Saxon Charters*, No. 68, p. 88.

63. Haslam, "Market and Fortress," 84.

64. Ibid. For opinions that Northampton and Tamworth were only proto-urban high-status estates until the tenth century, see Clarke and Ambrosiani, *Towns in the Viking Age*, pp. 37–39. The proposed commercial component of Offan burghs also has been questioned: G. Astill, "Towns and Town Hierarchies in Saxon England," *Oxford Journal of Archaeology* 10 (1991), p. 103.

65. Haslam, "Market and Fortress,", 86–88. For Frankish parallels, see in general, Ennen, *Stadt des Mittelalters*, pp. 38–45; M. Fixot, "Une image idéale, une réalité difficile: les villes du VIIe au IXe siècles," in *Histoire de la France urbaine*, ed. G. Duby (5 vols., Paris: Editions du Seuil, 1980–85), I, pp. 514–16; and two case studies: Lobbedey, "Northern Germany: Hamburg," in *European Towns*, ed. Barley, pp. 130–34; H. Galinié, "Reflections on Early Medieval Tours," in *Rebirth of Towns*, pp. 57–62.

66. Biddle, "Towns," pp. 120–22; Haslam, "Market and Fortress," 83–89.

67. *Cart. Sax.*, No. 426.

68. The essential starting point for study of this topic remains that of W. H. Stevenson, "Trinoda Necessitas," *English Historical Review* 29 (1914), 689–702, to be supplemented by *ASE*, 289–92; John, *Land Tenure in Early England*, pp. 64–79; N. Brooks, "Development of Military Obligations," pp. 80–84; Abels, *Lordship and Military Obligation*, pp. 52–66; G. Dempsey, "Legal Terminology in Anglo-Saxon England: *The Trinoda Necessitas* Charter," *Speculum* 57 (1982), 843–49.

69. *Cart. Sax.*, No. 438. See also, H. P. R. Finberg, ed., *The Early Charters of Wessex* (Leicester: University Press, 1966), No. 405. Again, *munitio* seems to imply fortifying or strengthening rather than wholesale new construction.

70. *Cart. Sax.*, Nos. 442 (843 A.D.), 467 (855 A.D.).

71. Ibid., No. 495 (858 A.D.), to Winchester Cathedral and No. 500 (860 A.D.) to his thegn Osmund for a Wiltshire estate.

72. Ibid., Nos. 504, 506 (Kent: "exceptis tribus necessariis causis expeditione et arcis pontisque constructione"), 507, 508. Upon Aethelbald's death (860), Aethelberht succeeded to central and western Wessex, and his brother, Aethelred I, continued to rule Kent, Essex, Surrey, and Sussex (*ASC* 860A). For a clarification of this involved succession, see: Kirby, *Earliest English Kings*, pp. 200–201.

73. *Cart. Sax.*, No. 451 (847 A.D.) reserves army service and bridge work. Several earlier charters have similar reservations but their authenticity is suspect. See Sawyer, *Anglo-Saxon Charters*, Nos. 268, 271, 273. A diploma (794) of King Beohtric, in whose reign took place the first recorded Danish raid on Wessex, reserved army service alone as incumbent on all *comites*: *Early Charters of Wessex*, ed. Finberg, No. 398. See further, Abels, *Lordship and Military Obligation*, pp. 54–56.

74. Aethelwulf had even "booked" a tenth of all his lands to the Church and his nobles before departing on pilgrimage to Rome: *ASC* 855A; *Cart. Sax.*, No. 486; Asser, *De rebus gestis Aelfredi, [Life of King Alfred]*, xi, ed. W. H. Stephenson (Oxford: Clarendon Press, 1904). See further, Finberg, "King Aethelwulf's Decimations," in *Early Charters of Wessex*, pp. 187–213; Abels, *Lordship and Military Obligation*, pp. 60–61; and nn. 2, 11, and 12, above, for earlier Mercian practice.

75. Astill, "The Towns of Berkshire," in *Anglo-Saxon Towns in Southern England*, pp. 73–76; Haslam, "The Towns of Wiltshire," Ibid., pp. 115–17; D. A. Hinton, *Alfred's Kingdom: Wessex and the South 800–1500* (London: Dent, 1979), pp. 34–39; N. Brooks, "England in the Ninth Century: The Crucible of Defeat," *Transactions of the Royal Historical Society*, 5th ser. 29 (1979), pp. 9–10, 17–18. Oxford's defenses may even have been a Mercian construction: Haslam, "Market and Fortress," 83–84.

76. For Canterbury and London, see *ASC* 851A. On the Winchester evidence, note the short tenth-century poem attributing construction of the upstream bridge to Bishop Swithun in 859: A. A. Locke, *In Praise of Winchester: An Anthology in Prose and Verse* (London: Constable, 1912), p. 129, quoted and discussed with additional evidence by Biddle, in *Winchester Studies* I (Oxford: Clarendon Press, 1976), pp. 271–72.

77. Asser, *Life of King Alfred*, xlix, liv.

78. *ASC* 832A [835]. The Danes had built their own fortresses in Kent while the area was under Mercian control, that is, before Egbert's annexation (825); *Cart. Sax.*, No. 370 (822), states the obligation to destroy pagan *arces*.

79. *ASC* 823A [825], 827A [829]; *Annales Bertiniani*, ed. Waitz, *MGH SS RG*, V (Hanover, 1883), s.a. 839. See further, Kirby, *Earliest English Kings*, pp. 189–93. Egbert had been forced to flee Wessex after Beorhtric, scion of a rival royal family, became king (786). He apparently stayed for a time with Offa in Mercia, but again was obliged to leave (probably when Beorhtric married Offa's daughter in 789) and evidently spent his remaining years of exile with Charlemagne: *ASC* 836A[839].

80. R. McKitterick, *The Frankish Kingdoms under the Carolingians, 757–987* (London: Longman, 1983), pp. 170–76; *ASE*, pp. 240–41.

81. *ASC* 833A[836]. Possible innovations include the use of sturdier war horses and the long-distance expedition led by local nobles in his name. In its entries for Egbert's reign, the *Anglo-Saxon Chronicle* begins to report rather regularly of distant campaigns by local (shire) forces (*fyrds*) led by the king or his ealdormen, first against rival realms, and then against the Welsh and Danes as far afield as Devon and Cornwall: *ASC* 800[802], 823[825], 827[829], 833[836], 835A[838]. See further: R. Whitlock, *The Warrior Kings of Saxon England* (NY: Dorset Press, 1991), pp. 39–42, 92–93, and in greater depth: Abels, *Lordship and Military Obligation*, pp. 11–37, 58–78. Offa may have taught him some similar lessons.

82. *ASC* 837A [840], 839A [842], 851A [850–51].

83. Ibid., 851A [850], 855A. On this Viking tactical change, see Kirby, *Earliest English Kings*, pp. 210–11; Hill, *Atlas of Anglo-Saxon England*, p. 36; Wormald, "The Ninth Century," in *The Anglo-Saxons*, ed. J. Campbell, pp. 144–45.

84. *Edictum Pistense* [Pîtres], xxvii, eds. A. Boretius and V. Krause, *MGH Legum*, II: 1 (Hanover, 1890), No. 173 [864 A.D.]. See further, McKitterick, *Frankish Kingdoms*, pp. 233–35; Fixot, "Les villes," pp. 516–21; Abels, *Lordship and Military Obligation*, pp. 68–69, 72–73.

85. *ASC* 836A [839], 855A; *Annales Bertiniani*, s.a. 856. On these connections, see also, P. Stafford, "Charles the Bald, Judith, and England," in *Charles the Bald: Court and Kingdom*, eds. M. Gibson and J. Nelson, British Archaeological Reports (hereafter B.A.R.), 101 (London, 1981), pp. 137–40; Kirby, *Earliest English Kings*, pp. 192–93, 198–200.

86. *Ex Miraculis S. Wandregisili*, xv, ed. O. Holder-Egger, *MGH SS*, XV; 1 (Hanover, 1887).

87. Kirby, *Earliest English Kings*, pp. 199, 212–13, 217; Hill, *Atlas*, p. 38. N. Brooks, "Crucible of Defeat," pp. 7–11 argues for the truly large scale of this Viking enterprise.

88. *Cart. Sax.*, Nos. 426 (Canterbury), 492 (London), and cf. the shipping channels at Rochester (ibid., No. 518 [868 A.D.]. For the later meaning: *I Edward*, i; *II Aethelstan*, xii–xiv, ed. Attenborough, in Attenborough, *Laws*. See also C. Stephenson, *Borough and Town* (Cambridge, MA: Mediaeval Academy of America, 1933), pp. 65–67; P. H. Sawyer, "Kings and Merchants," in *Early Medieval Kingship*, eds. Sawyer and I. Wood (Leeds: University Press, 1979), p. 153, and n. 30, above.

89. *Cart. Sax.*, No. 426: "unum merkatorem quem lingua nostra mangere nominamus."

90. *Be Gethyncdhum*, vi, ed. Liebermann, *Gesetze*, I, p. 459, III, p. 259.

91. *Cart. Sax.*, No. 492. "Habeat intus liberaliter modium et pondera et mensura sicut in portu mos est." This Coelmundingchaga is also described as a "wealthy little estate" (*gazifer agellulus*) not far from the west gate. It may have stood at the eastern edge of the *wic*: A. Vince, *Saxon London: An Archaeological Investigation* (London: Seaby, 1990), p. 20.

92. *Cart. Sax.*, Nos. 335, 373, 402, 426, 449, 486, 497, 502. Intramural plots and those with appurtenant fields had much higher values than rural properties. See N. Brooks, *Church of Canterbury*, p. 27.

93. A. J. Robertson, ed., *Anglo-Saxon Charters* (Cambridge: University Press, 1939), pp. 246–49, and commentary, pp. 494–96.

94. These have been collated and discussed with a proposed restored version by David Hill, "The Burghal Hidage: The Establishment of a Text," *Medieval Archaeology* 13 (1969), 84–92. See also S. Keynes and M. Lapidge, trans., "The Burghal Hidage," in *Alfred the Great* (Harmondsworth: Penguin, 1983), pp. 193–94 and commentary, pp. 339–41.

95. The "B" texts have an appendix that states: "That is all 27,000 hides and seventy [27,070] which belong to it and thirty to Wessex," that is, thirty burghs belong to Wessex. This is followed by the inclusion of two Mercian burghs, Worcester and Warwick. In Hill's restored text, hidage totals amount to 27,071, omitting Buckingham, Worcester, and Warwick north of the Thames which are likely tenth-

century additions: "Burghal Hidage," 87. For the Anglo-Saxon hide, see nn. 98-102, below.

96. This burghal list is quite selective. For example, London is not mentioned, nor are the burghs of Kent, Cornwall, and most of the Midlands. Those that are included, however, clearly identify the text as a Wessex document. For the chronological implications, see nn. 103–7, below.

97. Wormald, "Ninth Century," p. 154.

98. Bede, *Hist. Eccl.*. iii.4, 24, iv.16. Also see Eddius Stephanus, *V. Wilfridi*, viii, xli, ed. B. Colgrave (Cambridge: University Press, 1927), for other early references to hides. See further, T. Charles-Edwards, "Kinship, Status, and the Origins of the Hide," *Past and Present* 56 (1972), 3–33.

99. Usually not linear acres but an aggregate of various strips from separate estates. In especially prosperous areas of rich soils like much of Wessex a hide of 30 or 40 acres likely was customary; elsewhere, 120 acres. The classic studies are F. W. Maitland, *Domesday Book and Beyond* (Cambridge: University Press, 1897), pp. 357–99, 476–83 and J. Tait, "Large Hides and Small Hides," *English Historical Review* 17 (1902), 280–82.

100. *Cart. Sax.*, No. 297. See further, *ASE*, pp. 295-97; C. R. Hart, "The *Tribal Hidage*," *Transactions of the Royal Historical Society* 21 (1971), pp. 133-57; Hill, *Atlas*, pp. 76-77; Loyn, *Governance*, pp. 34-37. It has been attributed initially to King Wulfhere; see. e.g., Hodges, *Dark-Age Economics*, p. 189, but cf. Hart, "*Tribal Hidage*," p. 157, and N. Brooks, "The Formation of the Mercian Kingdom," in *Origins of Anglo-Saxon Kingdoms*, ed. Bassett, pp. 159-60.

101. For example, *Cart. Sax.*, Nos. 42 (690 A.D.), 72 (688), 154 (736), 230 (779), 438 (842). 550 (882), using Lat. *manentes, cassati* for hides. On royal food rents levied by hidage, see ibid., No. 273 (791 X 796) and *Law of Ine*, lxx.1, ed. Attenborough.

102. *Cart. Sax.*, No. 201. This ratio of five or six men per hide becomes more evident but was probably not universal even in late Anglo-Saxon times. See further, Abels, *Lordship and Military Obligation*, pp. 97–115.

103. *ASC* 912A [911], 915D [914].

104. Ibid., 910C, 912–15C, 918C.

105. Ibid., 886A.

106. *Alfred and Guthrum*, i, ed. Attenborough.

107. *Cart. Sax.*, No. 659; *ASC* 894A [893], 895A [894], 896A [895], 905A [904]. See further on this revised chronology: R. H. C. Davis, "Alfred and Guthrum's Frontier," *English Historical Review* 97 (1982), 803–10. The absence of most former Mercian burghs is still rather puzzling.

108. Asser, *Life of King Alfred*, xci, ed. Stevenson.

109. Ibid.; *ASC* 893A[892]. See B. K. Davison, "The Burghal Hidage Fort of Eorpeburnan: A Suggested Identification," *Medieval Archaeology* 16 (1972), 123–27; but cf. F. Kitchen, The *Burghal Hidage*: Towards the Identification of Eorpeburnan," *Medieval Archaeology* 28 (1984), 175–78.

110. Asser, *Life of King Alfred*, xcii.

111. Ibid., xlix, xcviii. William of Malmesbury reported an inscription he had seen in Shaftesbury recording, "In the year of the Lord's Incarnation 880 King Alfred made this town (*urbs*) in the eighth year of his reign." *De Gestis Pontificum*

Anglorum, ed. N. Hamilton, Rolls Series 52 (London, 1870), p. 186. A fragment of this actually was found and a rubbing made: Keynes and Lapidge, "Burghal Hidage," p. 340. The absence of Shaftesbury from the "A" text of the *Burghal Hidage* is most likely a scribal error (ibid.).

112. *ASC* 878A; Asser, *Life of King Alfred*, lv; also, Ibid., liv (878) for the unfinished fort (*arx*) at Cynuit (Dorset).

113. The exclusion of Kentish burghs such as Canterbury and Rochester is particularly glaring and may be due to that region's distinctive use of *sulungs* rather than hides as measurement units. See n. 96, above and Map 7.2.B for non-listed West Saxon burghs.

114. See Hill, "Burghal Hidage," 91, and *Atlas of Anglo-Saxon England*, p. 85, Table 149; Hinton, *Alfred's Kingdom*, pp. 35, 37.

115. The archaeological evidence is outlined by Biddle, "Towns," pp. 129–31; Hinton, *Alfred's Kingdom*, pp. 31–39; C. Platt, *The English Medieval Town* (NY: David McKay Co., 1976), pp. 19–20; H. Turner, *Town Defences in England and Wales 900–1500* (Hamden, CT: Archon Books, 1971), pp. 53–53, 147–200 ("Gazetteer").

116. Biddle, "Archaeology and the History of British Towns," *Antiquity* 42 (1968), 109–16, and "Towns," pp. 130–33; Biddle and Hill, "Late Saxon Planned Towns, *Antiquaries Journal* 51 (1971), 70–85. Each block appears initially to have been fairly large (1.25 acres at Winchester) and under lordly jurisdiction, with subsequent division into smaller, narrow tenements. Streets apparently were laid out on the basis of a regular four-pole unit (66 feet=1 rod): Biddle, "The Study of Winchester: Archaeology and History in a British Town, 1961–1983," *Proceedings of the British Academy* 69 (1983), pp. 125–26.

117. L. Ralegh Radford, "The Pre-Conquest Boroughs of England, Ninth to Eleventh Centuries," *Proceedings of the British Academy* 64 (1978), pp. 133–42; Biddle, "Towns," p. 131. Certain historians and archaeologists have suggested, contra Biddle (and Haslam), that most large Anglo-Saxon burghs or "burghal towns," whether Mercian or West Saxon, were but sparsely occupied military sites prior to the late tenth century when they did begin to evidence significant commercial activity and intramural resettlement. The cases of Winchester, Canterbury, and London are too exceptional, they contend, to serve as models for the military and commercial-industrial nature of "burghal towns" overall. See: Hinton, *Alfred's Kingdom*, pp. 40-41, 59-67; Astill, "Town Hierarchies," pp. 101-109. This curious reappearance of the Pirenne and Stephenson position is not yet fully substantiated.

118. Biddle, "Towns," p. 126.

119. Winchester (*Domesday Book* [hereafter *DB*] London: Record Commission, 1783–1816), I, 39bc; Cricklade (*DB*, I, 67bc); Chichester (*DB* I, 23ab); Bath (*DB* I, 87b); Exeter (*DB* I, 100a); Wallingford (*DB* I, 56a); Wareham (*DB* I, 75d); Bridport (*DB* I, 75a); Oxford (*DB* I, 154a); Wilton (*DB* I, 64c); Lewes (*DB* I, 26a); Malmesbury (*DB* I, 64c); plus Buckingham, Worcester, and Warwick (*DB* I, 143a, 172a, 238a). See further, Hill, *Atlas*, pp. 143–44 and Tables 235, 236. Five smaller sites with internal planning also became successful post-Conquest boroughs (Shaftesbury, Langport, Christchurch, Axbridge, and Lydford): *DB* I, 75a, 86b, 38d, 86b, 100b, while Lyng, a very small burgh with planning, did not.

120. Alfredian mints were located in Winchester, London, Canterbury, Exeter, and Gloucester: Grierson and Blackburn, *Medieval European Coinage*, pp. 309–15.

For economic, judicial, and social activity, see, nn. 122–26, below, nn. 29–35, above, and the individual discussions of major unlisted burghs in this chapter.

121. Chisbury, Portchester, Pilton, Halwell, Eashing, Eorpeburnan, and Burpham. See further, Hill, "Towns as Structures and Functioning Communities through Time: The Development of Central-Places from 600 to 1066," in *Anglo-Saxon Settlements*, ed. D. Hooke (London: Blackwell, 1988), pp. 200–203. Two places in the group of burghal forts (Hastings, Southwark?) did continue on to become post-Conquest boroughs (*DB* I, 17b, 32a). Other exceptions include Sashes, a large site lost by 1086, and Southampton, where the position of the burgh is unclear. See Biddle, "Towns," p. 127; Astill, "Towns of Berkshire," pp. 63–64; P. Holdsworth, "Saxon Southampton," in *Anglo-Saxon Towns in Southern England*, pp. 337–40.

122. *Cart. Sax.*, No. 579. See also the improved edition by Florence Harmer: *Select English Historical Documents of the Ninth and Tenth Centuries* (Cambridge: University Press, 1914), No. 13, pp. 106–107.

123. For discussions of these burghal rights, see: Tait, *English Medieval Borough*, pp. 19–24; *ASE*, pp. 528–29, and esp. Harmer, "Chipping and Market: A Lexicographical Investigation," in *The Early Cultures of North-West Europe*, eds. C. Fox and B. Dickens. H. M. Chadwick Memorial Studies (Cambridge: University Press, 1950), pp. 343–44. Bishop Waerferth was one of four Mercian scholars invited by King Alfred to better educate his court and kingdom. The two men's close personal relationship is reflected in Alfred's will. See Asser, *Life of King Alfred*, lxxvii; *Cart. Sax.*, No. 553.

124. Control of salt trading was one of the earliest and most lucrative of Mercian royal rights: ibid., Nos. 137, 138, 552; Finberg, ed., *Early Charters of the West Midlands*, No. 212. See further: Sawyer, "Kings and Merchants," pp. 147–48.

125. Worcester had been an important ecclesiastical administrative center from c.680 and enjoyed significant trading privileges during the eighth century: Haddan and Stubbs, eds., *Councils*, III, pp. 127–28; *Cart. Sax.*, Nos. 98, 102. It has been suggested that the *ceapstow* of this Alfredian-period text may even refer to a preexisting market associated with the cathedral church that was now being brought partly under lordly control: Sawyer, *From Roman Britain to Norman England* (London: Methuen, 1976), pp. 229–30; S. Reynolds, *An Introduction to the History of English Medieval Towns* (Oxford: Clarendon Press, 1977), p. 30.

126. Most new burghs of the late ninth and early tenth centuries were founded on the king's holdings. See, Tait, *Medieval English Borough*, pp. 17, 21; *ASE*, p. 529. Waerferth continued to grant land in Worcester to Aethelred and Aethelflaed: *Cart. Sax.*, No. 608 (904 A.D.). See further, N. Baker, et al., "From Roman to Medieval Worcester: Development and Planning in the Anglo-Saxon City," *Antiquity* 66 (1992), 72–73, and Fig. 5.

127. Asser, *Life of King Alfred*, lxxxiii. The *Anglo-Saxon Chronicle* (886A [885]) states merely that Alfred "occupied" (*gesette*) London, but Aethelweard reports that Alfred "besieged" it and then strengthened the ranks of the garrison guarding the fortress (*arx*): *Chron.*, ed. Campbell, p. 46. Old English *gesettan* is regrettably rather ambiguous.

128. *Cart. Sax.*, No. 577. Notice *instauracio* rather than *restauracio*, and the appearance of new streets. See also, Chap. 5, above.

129. *ASC* 886A [885], 894A [893]. Aethelweard again refers to London as an *arx* (i.e., *burh*) s.a. 900: *Chron.*, p. 52.

130. The effort and coordination involved in constructing Alfred's entire burghal system has been compared to that needed for the building of Offa's Dyke or the Edwardian castles of Wales: Abels, *Lordship and Military Obligation*, p. 77; Ralegh Radford, "Pre-Conquest Boroughs," p. 152. But cf. Astill, "Town Hierarchies," pp. 100-101.

131. Asser, *Life of King Alfred*, xci.

132. *Cart. Sax.*, Nos. 550, 567, 568, and 581 (with the significant phrase: "excepting... common expedition, rebuilding of travel bridge, [and] construction of royal fortress").

133. Asser, *Life of King Alfred*, xci.

134. Ibid.

135. Hinton, *Alfred's Kingdom*, pp. 30–31; Abels, *Lordship and Military Obligation*, p. 70, Map 2.

136. *ASC* 894A[893]. For useful discussions of this important passage, see: Keynes and Lapidge, *Alfred the Great*, pp. 285–86; Abels, *Lordship and Military Obligation*, pp. 63–68.

137. *ASC* 894A [893]

138. Ibid., 896A [895]; cf. ibid., 894A [893] for earlier military action by the London *burhwaran* against the Viking base at Benfleet.

139. See further, Keynes and Lapidge, *Alfred the Great*, pp. 42–43; Loyn, *Governance of Anglo-Saxon England*, pp. 70–71; Abels, *Lordship and Military Obligation*, pp. 68–74, observing that this integrated system is what military strategists now refer to as "defense in depth."

140. *ASC*, s.a. 907C (Chester); 910C (Bremesburh); 912C (Scergeat, Bridgnorth); 913C (Tamworth, Stafford); 914C (Eddisbury, Warwick); 915C (Chirbury, Weardburh, Runcorn). Aethelflaed's burghs were Bremesburh, Scergeat, Bridgnorth, Tamworth, and Stafford. See further, F. T. Wainwright, "Aethelflaed, Lady of the Mercians," in *The Anglo-Saxons*, ed. P. Clemoes (London: Bowes & Bowes, 1959), pp. 53–70; *ASE*, pp. 324-29.

141. Biddle, "Towns," pp. 134–35; Hill, "Development of Central Places," p. 203; Ralegh Radford, "Pre-Conquest Boroughs," pp. 148, 150–52; cf. Astill, "Town Hierarchies," p. 108.

142. *ASC* 913A [912] Hertford; 918A [917] Buckingham; 919A [918] Bedford; 920A [919] Maldon; 921C Cledemutha; 921A [920] Towcester, Wigingamere, Huntingdon, Colchester; 922A [921] Stamford, Nottingham; 923A [922] Thelwall, Manchester; 924A [923], Bakewell, Nottingham. See further: *ASE*, pp. 327-31; Whitlock, *Warrior Kings*, pp. 100–108; cf. Haslam, who contends that new Edwardian burghs had both military and commercial functions (among others) from the outset but exhibit less regular internal planning (single axial streets) than Alfredian burghs, were generally smaller, and sited to control river and inland routes: "The Towns of Devon," in *Anglo-Saxon Towns in Southern England*, ed. Haslam, pp. 262-64.

143. Double burghs were at Hertford, Buckingham, Bedford, Stamford, and Nottingham (n. 142, above). Edward built both burghs at Buckingham. See further, Biddle, "Towns," pp. 136–37; Abels, *Lordship and Military Obligation*, pp. 72–73, noting Alfredian examples. For a valuable case study, see C. Mahany and D. Roffe,

"Stamford: The Development of an Anglo-Scandinavian Borough," *Anglo-Norman Studies* 5 (1982), pp. 197–219.

144. *ASE*, pp. 336–39; D. J. V. Fisher, *The Anglo-Saxon Age* (London: Longman, 1973), pp. 255–57.

145. *ASE*, pp. 336–37; Loyn, *Governance of Anglo-Saxon England*, pp. 133–36.

146. *I Edward*, i, ed. Attenborough. For further implications, see Sawyer, *Roman Britain to Norman England*, pp 230–31; Stafford, *Unification and Conquest* (London: Edward Arnold, 1989), pp. 141–42.

147. Less than 20 pence: *II Aethelstan*, xii, ed. Attenborough. This concession forces us to bear in mind the strength of non-urban trade and the limitations of the king's monetary policy: Stafford, *Unification and Conquest*, pp. 213–14; Astill "Town Hierarchies," pp. 109-10.

148. *II Aethelstan*, xiii, xiii.1.

149. Ibid., xiv. See Loyn, "Boroughs and Mints A.D. 900–1066," in *Anglo-Saxon Coins*, ed. R. Dolley (London: Methuen, 1961), pp. 122–35.

150. *II Aethelstan*, xiv.1.

151. Ibid., xiv.2. London was to have eight mints, Canterbury seven, Winchester six, Rochester three, Southampton, Lewes, Wareham, Exeter, Shaftesbury two each, and Hastings one. See further on this ordering: Loyn, "Boroughs and Mints"; D. M. Metcalf, "Anglo-Saxon Coins 2: Alfred to Edgar," in *Anglo-Saxons*, ed. J. Campbell, p. 131.

152. Hill, *Atlas of Anglo-Saxon England*, Figs. 215, 224–25; Loyn, "Towns in Late Anglo-Saxon England," in *England Before the Conquest*, eds. Clemoes and Hughes, pp. 118–19.

153. Biddle, "Towns," pp. 137–138; D. Hill, "Development of Central-Places," p. 208; but cf. Haslam, "Towns of Devon," pp. 264-66.

154. Hill, *Atlas of Anglo-Saxon England*, Fig. 235.

155. See Biddle, "Towns," p. 140; J. Campbell, "The Church in Anglo-Saxon Towns," in *The Church in Town and Countryside*, ed. D. Baker, Studies in Church History 16 (Oxford: Blackwell, 1979), pp. 119–35, esp. 122-35.

156. J. G. Hurst, "The Pottery," in *Archaeology of Anglo-Saxon England*, ed. Wilson, pp. 314–39; J. Campbell, "Norwich and Winchester," in *Anglo-Saxons*, ed. Campbell, p. 175.

157. Biddle, "Towns," pp. 137, 141.

158. Loyn, "Towns in Late Anglo-Saxon England," pp. 126–27; Ralegh Radford, "Pre-Conquest Boroughs," pp. 146–47; Haslam, "Introduction," in *Anglo-Saxon Towns in Southern England*, ed. Haslam, pp. xiv–xvi; Hill, *Atlas of Anglo-Saxon England*, pp. 133, 143, and Fig. 187; Stafford, *Unification and Conquest*, pp. 214–15.

Chapter 8

Conclusion

Romano-British urbanism at its height had constituted a vibrant complex of functions. Written sources agree with archaeological evidence that this urban vitality endured in most towns until the mid-fourth century. Thereafter, the complex began to dissolve under the combined impact of political, economic, and social pressures. As curial leadership was undermined, the Romano-British urban economy faltered, town-country ties were severed, and urban trade and industry slackened. This devolution is visible in the archaeological evidence of urban structural decay, loss of amenities, and settlement contraction that began in the mid-fourth century and steadily intensified. By the early fifth century, Romano-British urban functions had become few and feeble, and most towns were but thinly populated shells that lapsed into dereliction and virtual abandonment by the mid-fifth century. At that time, Romano-British urbanism can be said to have effectively expired. An occasional squatter among the ruins cannot be used as an argument for urban settlement prolongation or of ongoing urban functions.

The case studies presented in this book have revealed that one must be wary of apocalyptic portraits of widespread town destruction by Anglo-Saxon invaders that have followed Gildas's model. Indeed, the overall archaeological evidence indicates that most Romano-British towns were essentially abandoned by the time of the Anglo-Saxons' arrival. Their end had come not by Germanic fire and sword but by slow decay and desertion. Gildas thus appears to have been more accurate in his picture of continuing town dereliction than in its causes. Moreover, the material evidence, if handled prudently, can be of great assistance in evaluating the much-debated issue of continuities from late Roman to early Anglo-Saxon times. Initial discoveries of early Anglo-Saxon town occupation were accompanied by overly bold interpretations. The finds of sunken huts, pottery, and metalwork do not in fact prove conclusively that Anglo-Saxon town settlement began while late or sub-Roman towns were still occupied. Rather, the weight of recent archaeological evidence is in favor of significant periods of settlement lapse and abandonment between the last Roman and first Anglo-Saxon occupation within specific towns. And no case at all can be made for continuity of urbanism; by c.450 A.D. at the latest, Romano-British town life was moribund. The record of towns from late Roman Britain to early Anglo-Saxon England is thus an account of discontinuity in regard to both urban settlement and urbanism.

The theory of the assumption of town control by early Anglo-Saxon mercenaries in a sub-Roman context is also tenuous. Although some textual evidence for such a process does exist, it is vague at best, and there are as yet no firm archaeological findings of a significant Anglo-Saxon presence within former Roman towns before the late fifth century. Indeed, the bulk of written and material evidence indicates that initial Anglo-Saxon settlement in these old Roman towns was a limited royal and then ecclesiastical reoccupation of abandoned sites that occurred from the late fifth to the early seventh centuries. These places, though they fall far short of possessing the full range of Romano-British urban functions, can be considered the first Anglo-Saxon towns by virtue of their walls, their royal and ecclesiastical activity with likely low-level supporting trade and crafts, and their spatial differentiation from the surrounding countryside.

Kings and bishops thus played pivotal roles in this rebirth of towns in the early Anglo-Saxon period. Indeed, the growth of Anglo-Saxon royal authority in the seventh century likely had much to do with the foundation of the second major type of town in Anglo-Saxon England: the emporium or *wic*. Recent excavations have demonstrated that these sites were important regional trade and production centers in many early English kingdoms and were very likely centrally planned and organized. The somewhat more limited written evidence points in the same direction, namely, that these emporia were created by kings of competing, incipient Anglo-Saxon realms as sources of state-building wealth and resources. Moreover, archaeological and written evidence indicate mutual economic and political relationships between these emporia and the nearby early capitals of Anglo-Saxon kings and bishops already established within former Roman towns. In themselves, the Anglo-Saxon emporia of the seventh to ninth centuries ranked as towns because of their large permanent populations engaged in intensive nonagricultural activities, their planned street networks, dense housing, and sometimes mints and multiple churches. Their important continental counterparts and trading partners around the North Sea and Baltic littorals appear to evidence high-status foundation and control as well.

The destruction of many Anglo-Saxon emporia by ninth-century Viking assaults is attested by both textual and archaeological evidence. Indeed, in a number of cases there are signs of decline on the eve of these attacks. Yet it is probable that the increasing documentary references to expanded urban functions at many of the older walled towns from the ninth century reflect in part an absorption of commercial and industrial populations from their razed or abandoned emporia. In any event, many ninth-century Anglo-Saxon burghs were not only walled administrative centers but now important places of trade and production with dense planned settlement, mints, and numerous churches. Though they often maintained substantial intramural areas for cultivation (as did Romano-British towns), they were clearly entities distinct in function and structure from rural settlements .

Finally, the origin and growth of these Anglo-Saxon burghs were examined by reevaluations of relevant textual evidence and considerations of recent archaeological findings. There are significant indications that the better-known Alfredian burghs were modeled upon Mercian burghs of the eighth century. The evidence of charters and archaeology reveals that these earlier Mercian burghs had been designed as both fortified places and centers of commerce. Study of the *Burghal Hidage* and recent burghal excavations has shown that the burghs of Alfred and his successors were also more complex than heretofore generally recognized. In some cases, they were simple forts with single military function, but the majority evidently were intended to be both strongholds and trading places. These latter sites were multifunctional towns with an expanded range of urban functions. Alfred's successors continued to create such burghal towns in conjunction with their political unification of England in the tenth century. The late Anglo-Saxon burgh as seen in the laws, annals, and material evidence can be classified as a town by virtue of a full dozen features and functions identified in the first chapter as distinctively urban. They equaled and even surpassed in number the urban features that can be used to characterize Romano-British towns as towns. Indeed, one may say that the record of town development in early England is an account of the cumulative spatial concentration of previously limited and disparate functions that together added up to urbanization. England's urban landscape took shape anew after the Roman departure and, having undergone a series of significant changes amid nearly five hundred years of political and economic fluctuations, was essentially in place by the mid-tenth century.

Selected Bibliography

PRIMARY SOURCES

Adam of Bremen. *Gesta Hammaburgensis Ecclesiae Pontificum*. Edited by B. Schmeidler. 3d ed. *MGH SS RG*, II. Hanover, 1917.

Aethelweard. *Chronicon*. Edited by A. Campbell. London: Thomas Nelson, 1962.

———. *Versus De Patribus Regibus et Sanctis Eboracensis Ecclesiae*. Edited by E. Dümmler. *MGH Poetae*, I; 1. Berlin, 1881.

Alcuin. *Epistolae*. Edited by E. Dümmler. *MGH EE*, IV. Berlin, 1895.

———. *Vita S. Willibrordi*. Edited by W. Levison. *MGH SS RM*, VII. Hanover, 1919.

Alfred's Anglo-Saxon Version of Orosius. Edited by B. Thorpe. *The Life of Alfred the Great*, by R. Pauli. London: H. Bohn, 1853.

Altfrid. *Vita S. Liudgeri*. Edited by G. Pertz. *MGH SS*, II. Hanover, 1829.

Ammianus Marcellinus. *Res gestae*. Edited by J. Rolfe. 3 vols. London: W. Heinemann, 1963.

Anglo-Saxon Charters. Edited by A. J. Robertson. Cambridge: University Press, 1939.

Annales Bertiniani. Edited by G. Waitz. *MGH SS RG*, V. Hanover, 1883.

Annales Regni Francorum. Edited by F. Kurze. *MGH SS RG*, VI. Hanover, 1895.

Aristotle. *Politics*. Translated by E. Barker. Oxford: Clarendon Press, 1946.

Asser. *De rebus gestis Aelfredi. [Life of King Alfred]*. Edited by W. H. Stephenson. Oxford: Clarendon Press, 1904.

Bede. *Historia Ecclesiastica*. Edited by C. Plummer. 2 vols. Oxford: Clarendon Press, 1896.

S. Bonifatii et Lulli Epistolae. Edited by E. Dümmler. 2d ed. *MGH EE*, III. Berlin, 1957.

Cartularium Saxonicum. Edited by W. de Gray Birch. 4 vols. London: Whiting & Co., 1885–1899.

Chronica Gallica. Edited by T. Mommsen. *MGH AA. Chronica Minora, I*. Hanover, 1892.

———. *De Officiis*. Edited by W. Miller. London: Heinemann, 1913.

Cicero. *De Inventione*. Edited by H. Hubbell. London: Heinemann, 1949.

Codex Diplomaticus Aevi Saxonici. 6 vols. Edited by J. M. Kemble. London: British Historical Society, 1839–1848.

Constantius. *Vita S. Germani*. Edited by W. Levison. *MGH SS RM*, VII. Hanover, 1919.

Corpus Inscriptionum Latinarum. 16 vols. Berlin: G. Reimer, 1862–

Councils and Ecclesiastical Documents Relating to Britain and Ireland. Edited by A. Haddan and W. Stubbs. 3 vols. Oxford: Clarendon Press, 1869–1871.

Domesday Book. 4 vols. London: Record Commission, 1783–1816.

Early Charters of the Cathedral Church of St. Paul, London. Edited by M. Gibbs. Camden Third Series, 58. London: Royal Historical Society, 1939.

Eddius Stephanus. *Vita S. Wilfridi.* Edited by B. Colgrave. Cambridge: University Press, 1927.

Edictum Pistense. Edited by A. Boretius and V. Krause. *MGH Legum. Capitularia Regum Francorum,* II; 1. Hanover, 1890.

Ex Miraculis S. Wandregisili. Edited by O. Holder-Egger. *MGH SS,* XV;1. Hanover, 1887.

Felix. *Vita S. Guthlaci.* Edited by B. Colgrave. Cambridge: University Press, 1956.

Gildas. *De excidio Britonum.* Edited by M. Winterbottom. Chichester: Phillimore, 1978.

Historia et Cartularium Monasterii Sancti Petri Gloucestriae. Edited by W. H. Hart. 3 vols. Rolls Series, 33. London, 1863–1867.

The Laws of the Earliest English Kings. Edited by F. A. Attenborough. Cambridge: University Press, 1922.

Monasticon Anglicanum. Edited by W. Dugdale. Rev. ed. 6 vols. London: Bohn, 1846.

Nennius. *Historia Brittonum.* Edited by J. Morris. Chichester: Phillimore, 1980.

Nithard. *Histoire des fils de Louis le Pieux.* Edited by P. Lauer. 2d ed. Paris: Société d'Edition Les Belles Lettres, 1964.

Orosius. *Historia adversus paganos.* Edited by C. Zangemeister. Bonn: C. Gerold, 1882.

S. Patricius. *Confessio.* Edited by A. B. E. Hood. Chichester: Phillimore, 1978.

Rimbert. *Vita S. Anskarii.* Edited by C. Dahlmann. *MGH SS,* II. Hanover, 1829.

The Roman Inscriptions of Britain. Edited by R. G. Collingwood and R. P. Wright. Oxford: Clarendon Press, 1965.

The Ruin. Edited by R. F. Leslie. *Three Old English Elegies.* Manchester: University Press, 1961.

Simeon of Durham. *Symeonis Monachi Opera Omnia.* Edited by T. Arnold. 2 vols. Rolls Series 75. London, 1882–1885.

Sulpicius Severus. *Dialogi.* Edited by C. Halm. *Corpus Scriptorum Ecclesiasticorum Latinorum,* I. Bonn, 1866.

Tacitus. *Annales.* Edited by R. Ogilvie and I. A. Richmond. Oxford: Clarendon Press, 1967.

Two of the Saxon Chronicles Parallel [Anglo-Saxon Chronicle]. Edited by J. Earle and C. Plummer. 2 vols. Oxford: Clarendon Press, 1892–1899.

Vita Willibaldi Episcopi Eichstetensis. Edited by O. Holder-Egger. *MGH SS,* XV;1. Hanover, 1887.

Vita S. Rimberti. Edited by G. Pertz. *MGH SS,* II. Hanover, 1829.

Willibald. *Vita S. Bonifatii.* Edited by W. Levison. *SS RG,* XLVIII. Hanover, 1905.

Zosimus. *Historia Nova: The Decline of Rome.* Translated by J. Buchanan and H. Davis. San Antonio, Texas: Trinity University Press, 1967.

SECONDARY WORKS

Abbott, Frank, and Johnson, A. *Municipal Administration in the Roman Empire*. Princeton: Princeton University Press, 1926.

Abels, Richard. *Lordship and Military Obligation in Anglo-Saxon England.* Berkeley: University of California Press, 1988.

Aberg, Nils. *The Anglo-Saxons in England during the Early Centuries after the Invasion*. Translated by S. Charleston. Uppsala: Almquist & Wiksells, 1926.

Abrams, P., and Wrigley, E. A., eds. *Towns in Societies: Essays in Economic History and Historical Sociology*. Cambridge: University Press, 1978.

Adams, Eleanor N. *Old English Scholarship in England from 1566–1800*. New Haven: Yale University Press, 1917.

Addyman, P. V. "Saxon Southampton: A Town and International Port of the 8th to the 10th Century." *Vor- und Frühformen der europäischen Stadt*, eds. Jankuhn, et al., I, 1973, pp. 218–28.

————. "York and Canterbury as Ecclesiastical Centres." *European Towns*, ed. Barley, 1977, pp. 499–509.

Adelson, H. "Early Medieval Trade Routes." *American Historical Review* 65 (1959–1960), 271–87.

Alcock, Leslie. *Arthur's Britain: History and Archaeology A.D. 367–634*. Harmondsworth: Penguin Books, 1971.

————. *Economy, Society, and Warfare among the Britons and Saxons*. Cardiff: University of Wales Press, 1987.

Alexander, J. "The Beginnings of Urban Life in Europe." *Man, Settlement, and Urbanism*, eds. Ucko, et al., 1972, pp. 843–50.

Allan, J., et al. "Saxon Exeter," *Anglo-Saxon Towns*, ed. Haslam, 1984, pp. 385–414.

Ambrosiani, Bjorn. "Urban Archaeology in Sweden." *European Towns*, ed. Barley, 1977, pp. 103–26.

Andersson, H. *Urbanisierte Ortschaften und lateinische Terminologie. Studien zur Geschichte des nordeuropäischen Städtewesens vor 1350*. Göteborg: Kunglig Vetenskaps-och Vitterhets-Samhället, 1971.

Arnold, C. J. "Wealth and Social Structure: A Matter of Life and Death." *Anglo-Saxon Cemeteries 1979*, eds. Rahtz, et al., 1980, pp. 81–142.

————. "Stress as a Stimulus for Socio-Economic Change: Anglo-Saxon England in the Seventh Century." *Ranking, Resource, and Exchange*, eds. Renfrew and Shennan, 1982, pp. 124–31.

————. *Roman Britain to Saxon England*. Bloomington: Indiana University Press, 1984.

————. *An Archaeology of the Early Anglo-Saxon Kingdoms*. London: Routledge, 1988.

Ashley, William. "The Beginnings of Town Life in the Middle Ages." *Quarterly Journal of Economics* 10 (1896), 359–406.

Astill, Grenville. "The Towns of Berkshire." *Anglo-Saxon Towns*, ed. Haslam, 1984, pp. 53–86.

————. "Archaeology Economics, and Early Medieval Europe." *Oxford Journal of Archaeology* 4 (1985), pp. 215-31.

————. "Towns and Town Hierarchies in Saxon England." *Oxford Journal of Archaeology* 10 (1991), pp. 95-117.

Aston, Michael, and Bond, James. *The Landscape of Towns*. London: J. M. Dent, 1976.

Bailey, K. "The Middle Saxons." *Origins of Anglo-Saxon Kingdoms*, ed. Bassett, 1989, pp. 108–22.

Baker, N., et al. "From Roman to Medieval Worcester: Development and Planning in the Anglo-Saxon City." *Antiquity* 66 (1992), 65–74.

Baldwin, R. "Intrusive Burial Groups in the Late Roman Cemetery at Lankhills, Winchester—A Reassessment of the Evidence." *Oxford Journal of Archaeology* 4 (1985), pp. 93-104.

Ballard, Adolphus. *Domesday Boroughs*. Oxford: Clarendon Press, 1904.

Balzaretti, R. "Debate: Trade, Industry, and the Wealth of King Alfred, I." *Past and Present* 135 (1992), 142–50.

Barber, R., et al. "Recent Excavations of a Cemetery in Londinium." *Britannia* 21 (1990), 1–12.

Barker, P. "The Latest Occupation of the Site of the Baths Basilica at Wroxeter. "*End of Roman Britain*, ed. Casey, 1979, pp. 175–81.

Barley, M. W., ed. *European Towns: Their Archaeology and Early History*. London: Academic Press, 1977.

Barnish, S. J. B. "The Transformation of Classical Cities and the Pirenne Debate." *Journal of Roman Archaeology* 2 (1989), 385–400.

Bartholomew, Philip. "Fifth-Century Facts." *Britannia* 13 (1982), 261–70.

Bassett, Steven, ed. *The Origins of Anglo-Saxon Kingdoms*. Leicester: University Press, 1989.

Bateson, Mary. "The Burgesses of Domesday and the Malmesbury Wall." *English Historical View* 21 (1906), 709–23.

Bekker-Nielsen, H., et al., eds. *Proceedings of the Eighth Viking Congress*. Odense: University Press, 1981.

Bencard, M., and Jorgensen, L. "The Foundation of Ribe."*Antiquity* 64 (1990), 576-83.

Benevolo, L. *The European City*. Translated by C. Ipsen. Oxford: Blackwell, 1993.

Benton, John F., ed. *Town Origins: The Evidence from Medieval England*. Lexington, MA: D. C. Heath, 1968.

Beresford, Maurice, and Finberg, H. P. R. *English Medieval Boroughs: A Hand-List*. Totowa, NJ: Rowman & Littlefield, 1973.

Berghaus, P. "Die frühmittelalterliche Numismatik als Quelle der Wirtschaftsgeschichte." *Geschichtswissenschaft und Archäologie*, eds. Jankuhn and Wenskus, 1979, pp. 411-29.

Berkhout, C., and Gatch, M., eds.*Anglo-Saxon Scholarship: The First Three Centuries*. Boston: G. K. Hall, 1982.

Biddle, Martin. "Archaeology and the History of British Towns."*Antiquity* 42 (1968), 109–16.

————. "Archaeology and the Beginnings of English Society." *England before the Conquest*, eds. Clemoes and Hughes, 1971, pp. 391–408.

————. "The Development of the Anglo-Saxon Town." *Topografia urbana*, 1, 1974, pp. 203–30.

———. "The Towns." *Archaeology of Anglo-Saxon England*, ed. Wilson, 1976, pp. 99–150.

———, et al., eds. *Winchester Studies*. Oxford: Clarendon Press, 1976–   .

———. "The Study of Winchester: Archaeology and History in a British Town, 1961–1983." *Proceedings of the British Academy* 69 (1983), pp. 93–135.

———. "A City in Transition: 400–800." *Atlas of Historic Towns: London*, ed. Lobel, 1989, pp. 20–29.

———, and Hill, David H. "Late Saxon Planned Towns." *Antiquaries Journal* 51 (1971), 70–85.

Birnbaum, H. "Kiev, Novgorod, Moscow: Three Varieties of Urban Society in East Slavic Territory." *Urban Society of Eastern Europe in Premodern Times*. Edited by B. Krekić. Berkeley: University of California Press, 1987, pp. 1–59.

Blindheim, Charlotte, "Kaupang in Skiringssal: A Norwegian Port of Trade from the Viking Age." *Vor- und Frühformen der europäischen Stadt*, eds. Jankuhn, et al., II, 1974, pp. 40–57.

Boon, George C. *Silchester: The Roman Town of Calleva*. Rev. ed. London: David & Charles, 1974.

Brady, Robert. *An Historical Treatise of Cities and Burghs or Boroughs*. London: S. Lowndes, 1690.

Braudel, Fernand. *Civilisation matérielle et capitalisme, XV*⁻*–XVIII*ᵉ *siècles*. Paris: Librairie Armand Colin, 1967.

Brisbane, Mark. "Hamwic (Saxon Southampton): An 8th Century Port and Production Centre." *Rebirth of Towns*, eds. Hodges and Hobley, 1988, pp. 101–8.

Brøndsted, J. *The Vikings*. Translated by K. Skov. Harmondsworth: Penguin Books, 1965.

Brooks, Dodie A. "A Review of the Evidence for Continuity in British Towns in the 5th and 6th Centuries." *Oxford Journal of Archaeology* 5 (1986), pp. 77–102.

———. "The Case for Continuity in Fifth-Century Canterbury Re-Examined." *Oxford Journal of Archaeology* 7 (1988), pp. 99–114.

Brooks, Nicholas P. "The Development of Military Obligations in Eighth and Ninth-Century England." *England before the Conquest*, eds. Clemoes and Hughes, 1971, pp. 69–84.

———. "England in the Ninth Century: The Crucible of Defeat." *Transactions of the Royal Historical Society*, 5th Series 29 (1979), pp. 1–20.

———. *The Early History of the Church of Canterbury*. Leicester: University Press, 1984.

———. "The Creation and Early Structure of the Kingdom of Kent." *Origins of Anglo-Saxon Kingdoms*, ed. Bassett, 1989, pp. 55–74.

———. "The Formation of the Mercian Kingdom." *Origins of Anglo-Saxon Kingdoms*, ed. Bassett, 1989, pp. 159-70.

Brown, Peter. *The Making of Late Antiquity*. Cambridge, MA: Harvard University Press, 1978.

Bruce-Mitford, Rupert, ed. *Aspects of Anglo-Saxon Archaeology*. New York: Harper & Row, 1974.

———, ed. *The Sutton Hoo Ship-Burial*. 3 vols. London: British Museum Publications, 1975–1983.

Brühl, C.-R. *Fodrum, Gistum, Servitium Regis*. Kölner Historische Abhandlungen, 14. Cologne: Böhlau, 1968.

Bullough, Donald. "Social and Economic Structure and Topography in the Early Medieval City." *Topografia urbana*, 1, 1974, pp. 351–99.

Burnham, B. C., and Wacher, J. S. *The Small Towns of Roman Britain*. Berkeley: University of California Press, 1990.

Butler, R. M., ed. *Soldier and Civilian in Roman Yorkshire*. Leicester: University Press, 1971.

Butlin, R. A. "Urban and Proto-Urban Settlements in Pre-Norman Ireland." *The Development of the Irish Town*. Edited by R. A. Butlin. London: Croom Helm, Ltd., 1977, pp. 11-27.

Cam, H. M. *England before Elizabeth*. 3d ed. London: Hutchinson University Library, 1967.

Camden, William. *Britannia, or a Chorographical Description of Great Britain and Ireland*. Translated and edited by E. Gibson. 2d ed. rev. 2 vols. London: M. Matthews, 1722.

Cameron, A. "Late Antiquity—The Total View." *Past and Present* 88 (1980), 129–35.

Cameron, K. "The Significance of English Place-Names." *Proceedings of the British Academy* 62 (1976), pp. 135-55.

———, ed. *Place-Name Evidence for the Anglo-Saxon Invasion and Scandinavian Settlements*. Nottingham: English Place-Name Society, 1977.

Campbell, James, ed. *The Anglo-Saxons*. London: Penguin, 1982.

Carter, Alan. "The Anglo-Saxon Origins of Norwich: The Problems and Approaches." *Anglo-Saxon England* 7 (1979), pp. 175–204.

Carver, Martin. "Kingship and Material Culture in Early Anglo-Saxon East Anglia." *Origins of Anglo-Saxon Kingdoms*, ed. Bassett, 1989, pp. 141–58.

———. *Arguments in Stone: Archaeological Research and the European Town in the First Millennium*. London: Oxbow Books, 1993.

Casey, Peter, ed. *The End of Roman Britain*. B.A.R. 71. Oxford, 1979.

Chadwick, H. M. *Studies on Anglo-Saxon Institutions*. Cambridge: University Press, 1905.

Chambers, R. A. "The Late- and Sub-Roman Cemetery at Queenford Farm, Dorchester-on-Thames, Oxon." *Oxoniensia* 52 (1988), 35–69.

Charles-Edwards, T. "Kinship, Status, and the Origins of the Hide." *Past and Present* 56 (1972), 3–33.

Cherry, Bridget. "Ecclesiastical Architecture." *Archaeology of Anglo-Saxon England*, ed. Wilson, 1976, pp. 151–200.

La città nell'alto medioevo. Centro Italiano di Studi sull'alto medioevo. Settimane 6. Spoleto, 1959.

Clarke, G. N. *The Roman Cemetery at Lankhills*. Oxford: University Press, 1979.

Clarke, H., and Simms, A., eds. *The Comparative History of Urban Origins in Non-Roman Europe*. B.A.R. International Series 255. 2 vols. Oxford, 1985.

———, and Ambrosiani, Bjorn. *Towns in the Viking Age*. New York: St. Martin's Press, 1991.

Clemoes, Peter, and Hughes, Katherine, eds. *England before the Conquest*. Cambridge: University Press, 1971.

Cohen, Sidney. "The Earliest Scandinavian Towns." *The Medieval City*. Edited by H. Miskimin, et al. New Haven: Yale University Press, 1977, pp. 313–25.

Collingwood, R. G., and Myres, J. N. L. *Roman Britain and the English Settlements*. 2d ed. Oxford: Clarendon Press, 1937.

Colvin, H. M. "Domestic Architecture and Town-Planning." *Medieval England*. Edited by A. L. Poole. Rev. ed. 2 vols. Oxford: Clarendon Press, 1958, I, pp. 37–97.

Conzen, M. "The Use of Town Plans in the Study of Urban History." *The Study of Urban History*. Edited by H. Dyos. Leicester: University Press, 1968, pp. 113–30.

Coote, Henry C. *A Neglected Fact in English History*. London: Bell & Daldy, 1864.

Copley, Gordon. *Archaeology and Place-Names in the Fifth and Sixth Centuries*. B.A.R. 147. Oxford, 1986.

Cowie, R., and Whytehead, R. "Lundenwic: The Archaeological Evidence for Middle Saxon London." *Antiquity* 63 (1989), 706–18.

Cramp, Rosemary. "Northumbria: The Archaeological Evidence." *Power and Politics in Early Medieval Britain and Ireland*. Edited by S. Driscoll and M. Nieke. Edinburgh: University Press, 1988, pp. 69–78.

Crummy, P. "The Origins of Some Major Romano-British Towns." *Britannia* 13 (1982), 125–34.

Cunliffe, Barry. *Roman Bath*. Reports of the Research Committee of the Society of Antiquaries of London 24. Oxford: University Press, 1969.

———. *Iron-Age Communities in Britain*. London: Routledge & Kegan Paul, 1974.

———. "Saxon Bath." *Anglo-Saxon Towns*, ed. Haslam, 1984, pp. 345–57.

———. *The City of Bath*. New Haven: Yale University Press, 1987.

———. *Wessex to A.D. 1000*. London: Longmans, 1993.

Daniell, C. "York and the Whitby Author's *Anonymous Life of Gregory the Great*." *Northern History* 29 (1993), 197–99.

Darby, H. C. *Domesday England*. Cambridge: University Press, 1977.

Darling, M. J. "The Caistor-by-Norwich Massacre Reconsidered." *Britannia* 18 (1987), 263–72.

Darlington, Reginald R. "The Early History of English Towns." *History* 23 (1938), 141–50.

Davidson, Hilda. *The Viking Road to Byzantium*. London: Allen & Unwin, 1976.

Davies, Wendy. *Wales in the Early Middle Ages*. Leicester: University Press, 1982.

Davis, R. H. C. "Alfred the Great: Propaganda and Truth." *History* 56 (1971), 69–82.

———. "Alfred and Guthrum's Frontier." *English Historical Review* 97 (1982), 803-10.

Dempsey, G. "Legal Terminology in Anglo-Saxon England: The Trinoda Necessitas Charter." *Speculum* 57 (1982), 843–49.

Detsicas, A. *The Cantiaci*. Gloucester: Alan Sutton, 1983.

Dickinson, R. E. *The West European City: A Geographical Interpretation*. London: Routledge & Kegan Paul, 1951.

Dickinson, Tania. *Cuddesdon and Dorchester-on-Thames: Two Early Saxon "Princely" Sites in Wessex*. B.A.R. 1. Oxford, 1974.

Dixon, P. "The Cities Are Not Populated as Once They Were." *City in Late Antiquity*, ed. Rich, 1992, pp. 145–60.

Dodgshon, R. A.,and Butlin, R. A., eds. *An Historical Geography of England and Wales*. 2d ed. London: Academic Press, 1990.

Dopsch, Alfons. *Wirtschaftliche und soziale Grundlagen der europäischen Kulturentwicklung*. 2d ed. rev. 2 vols. Vienna: Verlag Von L. W. Seidel & Sohn, 1923–1924.

Down, A., and Rule, M. *Chichester Excavations I*. Chichester: Chichester Civic Society, 1971.

Drewett, Peter, et al. *The South-East to A.D. 1000*. London: Longman, 1988.

Duby, Georges. *Guerriers et paysans, VIIᵉ–XIIᵉ siècle: premier essor de l'économie européene*. Paris: Gallimard, 1973.

———, ed. *Histoire de la France urbaine*. 5 vols. Paris: Seuil, 1980–1985.

Dugdale, William. *The Antiquities of Warwickshire Illustrated; From Records, Leiger-Books, Manuscripts, Charters, Evidences, Tombes, and Armes*. London: Thomas Warren, 1656.

Dumville, David N. "The Anglian Collection of Royal Genealogies and Regnal Lists." *Anglo-Saxon England* 5 (1976), pp. 23–50.

———. "Sub-Roman Britain: History and Legend." *History* 62 (1977), 173–92.

———. "The Origins of Northumbria: Some Aspects of the British Background." *Origins of Anglo-Saxon Kingdoms*, ed. Bassett, 1989, pp. 213-22.

———. "The *Tribal Hidage*: An Introduction to Its Texts and Their History." *Origins of Anglo-Saxon Kingdoms*, ed. Bassett, 1989, pp. 225–30.

Dunnett, R. *The Trinovantes*. London: Duckworth, 1974.

Düwel, K., et al., eds. *Untersuchungen zu Handel und Verkehr der Vor- und frühgeschichtlichen Zeit in Mittel- und Nordeuropa*. 4 vols. Göttingen: Vandenhoeck & Ruprecht, 1985–1987.

Dyer, Christopher. "Recent Developments in Early Medieval Urban History and Archaeology in England." *Urban Historical Geography: Recent Progress in Britain and Germany*. Edited by D. Denecke and G. Shaw. Cambridge: University Press, 1988, pp. 69–80.

Dyson, Tony, and Schofield, John. "Saxon London." *Anglo-Saxon Towns*, ed. Haslam, 1984, pp. 285–313.

Ekwall, E. *Old English Wic in Place-Names*. Uppsala: Lundequista Bokhandeln, 1964.

Ennen, Edith. *Die europäische Stadt des Mittelalters*. Göttingen: Vandenhoeck & Ruprecht, 1972.

———. "The Early History of the European Town: A Retrospective View." *Comparative History of Urban Origins*, eds. Clarke and Simms, I, 1985, pp. 3–14.

Esmonde Cleary, A. S. *Extra-Mural Areas of Romano-British Towns*. B.A.R. 169. Oxford, 1987.

———. *The Ending of Roman Britain*. Savage, MD: Barnes & Noble, 1990.

———. "Approaches to the Differences between Late Romano-British and Early Anglo-Saxon Archaeology." *Anglo-Saxon Studies in Archaeology and History*, 6. Edited by W. Filmer-Sankey. Oxford: Oxbow Books, 1993, pp. 57-63.

Evans, J. "From the End of Roman Britain to the 'Celtic West.'" *Oxford Journal of Archaeology* 19 (1990), pp. 91–103.

Evans, J. G. *The Environment of Early Man in the British Isles*. Berkeley: University of California Press, 1975.

Evison, Vera. *The Fifth-Century Invasions South of the Thames*. London: Thames & Hudson, 1965.

——, ed. *Angles, Saxons, and Jutes*. Oxford: Clarendon Press, 1981.

Fanning, Stephen. "Bede, *Imperium*, and the *Bretwaldas*." *Speculum* 66 (1991), 1–26.

Faull, M. L. "Roman and Anglian Settlement Patterns in Yorkshire." *Northern History* 9 (1974), 1–25.

Fellows-Jensen, G. "The Vikings in England: A Review." *Anglo-Saxon England* 14 (1975), pp. 181–206.

Finberg, H. P. R. *The Formation of England 550-1042*. St. Albans: Paladin, 1976.

——, ed. *Gloucestershire Studies*. Leicester: University Press, 1957.

Finley, Moses. "The Ancient City: From Fustel de Coulanges to Max Weber and Beyond." *Economy and Society in Ancient Greece* by M. Finley. New York: Viking Press, 1982, pp. 3–23.

Fisher, D. J. V. *The Anglo-Saxon Age*. London: Longman, 1973.

Fox, Levi, ed. *English Historical Scholarship in the Sixteenth and Seventeenth Centuries*. London: Oxford University Press, 1956.

Freeman, Edward A. "The Alleged Permanence of Roman Civilization in England." *Macmillan's Magazine*, 22 (1870), 211–28.

——, *The History of the Norman Conquest of England*. 3d ed. rev. 6 vols. Oxford: Clarendon Press, 1877–1879.

——. *English Towns and Districts: A Series of Addresses and Sketches*. London: Macmillan, 1883.

Frend, W. H. C. "*Ecclesia Britannica*: Prelude or Dead End?" *Journal of Ecclesiastical History* 30 (1979), 129–44.

Frere, Sheppard. *Roman Canterbury: The City of Durovernum*. Canterbury: J. A. Jennings, 1962.

——. "The End of Towns in Roman Britain." *Civitas Capitals of Roman Britain*, ed. Wacher, 1966, pp. 87–100.

——. *Verulamium Excavations*. 3 vols. Oxford: Oxford University Committee for Archaeology, 1972–1984.

——. *Britannia: A History of Roman Britain*. 3d ed. London: Routledge & Kegan Paul, 1987.

——, et al. "Roman Britain in 1989: Canterbury." *Britannia* 21 (1990), 360-62.

Fulford, M. G. *Silchester: Excavations on the Defenses*. Gloucester: Alan Sutton, 1984.

——. "Excavations on the Sites of the Amphitheatre and Forum-Basilica at Silchester, Hampshire: An Interim Report." *Antiquaries Journal* 65 (1985), 39–81.

——. "The Economy of Roman Britain." *Research on Roman Britain*, ed. Todd. 1989, pp. 175–201.

Fussner, F. *The Historical Revolution: English Historical Writing and Thought 1580–1640*. New York: Columbia University Press, 1962.

Fustel de Coulanges, Numa D. *La cité antique*. 2d ed. Paris: Hachette, 1866.

——. Le problème des origines de la propriété foncière." *Revue des Questions Historiques* 45 (1889), 349–439.

Galinié, H. "Reflections on Early Medieval Tours." *Rebirth of Towns*, eds. Hodges and Hobley, 1988, pp. 57-62.

Garnsey, Peter. "Aspects of the Decline of the Urban Aristocracy in the Empire." Aufstieg und Niedergang der Römischen Welt. Edited by H. Temporini. Berlin: W. de Gruyter, I, 1974, pp. 229-52.

————, and Saller, R. The Roman Empire: Economy, Society, and Culture. Berkeley: University of California Press, 1987.

Garwood, P. "Social Transformation and Relations of Power in Britain in the Late Fourth to the Sixth Century." Scottish Archaeological Review 6 (1989), 90–106.

Geary, P. Before France and Germany: The Creation and Transformation of the Merovingian World. New York: Oxford University Press, 1988.

Gelling, Margaret. Signposts to the Past: Place-Names and the History of England. London: J. M. Dent, 1978.

Gillam, John. "Romano-Saxon Pottery: An Alternative Interpretation." End of Roman Britain, ed. Casey, 1979, pp. 103–18.

Gransden, Antonia. Historical Writing in England I. Ithaca: Cornell University Press, 1974.

————. "Antiquarian Studies in Fifteenth-Century England." Antiquaries Journal 60 (1980), 75–97,

————. Historical Writing in England II. Ithaca: Cornell University Press, 1982.

Gras, N. S. B. An Introduction to Economic History. New York: Harper & Bros., 1922.

Green, Alice S. Town Life in the Fifteenth Century. 2 vols. London: Macmillan, 1894.

Grew, F., and Hobley, B., eds. Roman Urban Topography in Britain and the Western Empire. C.B.A. 59. London, 1985.

Grew, R., and Steneck, N., eds. Society and History: Essays by Sylvia L. Thrupp. Ann Arbor: University of Michigan Press, 1977.

Grierson, Philip. "Commerce in the Dark Ages: A Critique of the Evidence." Transactions of the Royal Historical Society. 5th Series 9 (1959), pp. 123–40.

————, and Blackburn, M. Medieval European Coinage I: The Early Middle Ages. Cambridge: University Press, 1986.

Grimes, W. F. The Excavation of Roman and Mediaeval London. New York: Praeger, 1968.

Gross, Charles. The Gild Merchant. Oxford: Clarendon Press, 1890.

————. A Bibliography of British Municipal History. New York: Longmans, Green & Co., 1897.

Gutkind, E. A. International History of City Development. 8 vols. New York: Free Press, 1964–1972.

Gutnova, E. Review of Towns and Urban Handicraft in England in the Tenth to Thirteenth Centuries [in Russian] by Yakov Levitsky. Srednie Veka 20 (1961), 240–46. Translated by I. Rudnytsky, Town Origins, ed. Benton, 1968, pp. 37–41.

Hall, R. A., ed. Viking Age York and the North. C.B.A. 27. London, 1978.

————. "York 700–1050." Rebirth of Towns, eds. Hodges and Hobley, 1988, pp. 125–32.

————. "Sources for Pre-Conquest York." People and Places in Northern Europe, eds. Wood and Lund, 1991, pp. 83–94.

Hall, T. Mittelalterliche Stadtgrundrisse. Stockholm: Almquist & Wiksell, 1978.

Hammond, Mason. The City in the Ancient World. Cambridge, MA: Harvard University Press, 1972.

Hanning, Robert W. *The Vision of History in Early Britain*. New York: Columbia University Press, 1966.

Hanson, R. P. C. *Saint Patrick: His Origins and Career*. Oxford: University Press, 1968.

Harden, Donald B., ed. *Dark Age Britain*. London: Methuen, 1956.

Hardh, B., et al., eds. *Trade and Exchange in Prehistory*. Lund: Bloms Boktryckeri, 1988.

Harmer, Florence. "Chipping and Market: A Lexicographical Investigation." *Early Cultures of North-West Europe*. H. M. Chadwick Memorial Studies. Edited by C. Fox and B. Dickens. Cambridge: University Press, 1950, pp. 335–57.

Hart, C. R. "The *Tribal Hidage*." *Transactions of the Royal Historical Society*. 5th Series 21 (1971), pp. 133–58.

Haselgrove, C. "The Later Iron Age in Southern Britain and Beyond." *Research on Roman Britain*, ed. Todd, 1989, pp. 3-18.

Haslam, Jeremy. "Introduction." *Anglo-Saxon Towns*, ed. Haslam, 1984, xi-xviii.

———. "The Towns of Devon." *Anglo-Saxon Towns*, ed. Haslam, 1984, pp. 249-83.

———. "The Towns of Wiltshire." *Anglo-Saxon Towns*, ed. Haslam, 1984,pp. 87-147.

———. "Market and Fortress in England in the Reign of Offa." *World Archaeology* 19 (1987), 76-93.

———, ed. *Anglo-Saxon Towns in Southern England*. Chichester: Phillimore 1984.

Hassall, M. W. C. "Roman Urbanization in Western Europe." *Man, Settlement and Urbanism*, eds. Ucko, et al., 1972, pp. 857–61.

Haussig, H. W. *A History of Byzantine Civilization*. Translated by J. M. Hussey. New York: Praeger, 1971.

Haverfield, F. *The Romanization of Roman Britain*. 4th ed. rev. Oxford: Clarendon Press, 1923.

Havinghurst, A. F., ed. *The Pirenne Thesis: Analysis, Criticism, and Revision*. Lexington, MA: D. C. Heath, 1969.

Hawkes, Sonia L., et al., eds. *Anglo-Saxon Studies in Archaeology and History I*. B.A.R. 72. Oxford, 1979.

——— and Dunning, G. "Soldiers and Settlers in Britain, Fourth to Fifth Century." *Medieval Archaeology* 5 (1961), 1–70.

Hedeager, L. *Iron-Age Societies: From Tribe to State in Northern Europe, 500 B.C.–A.D. 700*. Oxford: Blackwell, 1992.

Heighway, Carolyn M., ed. *The Erosion of History: Archaeology and Planning in Towns*. London: Council for British Archaeology, 1972.

———. *Anglo-Saxon Gloucestershire*. Gloucester: Alan Sutton, 1987.

Hemmeon, Morley de Wolf. *Burgage Tenure in Medieval England*. Cambridge, MA: Harvard University Press, 1914.

Henig, M. *The Religion of Roman Britain*. London: Batsford, 1984.

Hensel. W. *Anfänge der Städte bei den Ost- und Westslawen*. Bautzen: Domowina Verlag, 1967.

Herrmann, J. "Hinterland, Trade, and Craftworking of the Early Trading Stations of the North-Western Slavs." *Comparative Study of Urban Origins*, eds. Clarke and Simms, I, 1985, pp. 249-66.

Higham, N. *The Northern Counties to A.D. 1000*. London: Longmans, 1986.

Hill, David H. "The Burghal Hidage: The Establishment of a Text." *Medieval Archaeology* 13 (1969), 84–92.
———. "The Relationship of Offa's and Wat's Dykes."*Antiquity* 48 (1974), 309–12.
———. "Continuity from Roman to Medieval: Britain." *European Towns*, ed. Barley, 1977, pp. 293–302.
———. *An Atlas of Anglo-Saxon England*. Toronto: University of Toronto Press, 1981.
———. "Towns as Structures and Functioning Communities through Time: The Development of Central Places from 600 to 1066."*Anglo-Saxon Settlements*,ed. Hooke, 1988, pp. 197–212.
———, et al. "Quentovic Defined." *Antiquity* 64 (1990), 51–58.
Hills, Catherine. "The Archaeology of Anglo-Saxon England in the Pagan Period: A Review." *Anglo-Saxon England* 8 (1979), pp. 297–329.
———. "The Anglo-Saxon Settlement of England." *The Northern World*. Edited by D. M. Wilson. London: Thames & Hudson, 1980, pp. 71–94.
Hingley, R. "Towns, Trade, and Social Organization in Later Roman Britain." *Scottish Archaeological Review* 3 (1984), 87–91.
Hinton, David A. *Alfred's Kingdom: Wessex and the South 800–1500*. London: J. M. Dent, 1979.
———. "The Towns of Hampshire." *Anglo-Saxon Towns*, ed. Haslam, 1984, pp. 149–65.
Hobley, B. "Lundenwic and Lundenburh: Two Cities Rediscovered." *Rebirth of Towns*, eds. Hodges and Hobley, 1988, pp. 69–82.
Hodder, I., and Orton, C. *Spatial Analysis in Archaeology*. Cambridge: University Press, 1976.
Hodges, Richard. "Ports of Trade in Early Medieval Europe." *Norwegian Archaeological Review* 11 (1978), 97–117.
———. *Dark-Age Economics: The Origins of Towns and Trade A.D. 600–1000*. New York: St. Martin's Press, 1982.
———. "The Evolution of Gateway Communities: Their Socio-Economic Implications." *Ranking, Resource, and Exchange*, eds. Renfrew and Shennan, 1982, pp. 117-23.
———. *The Anglo-Saxon Achievement: Archaeology and the Beginnings of English Society*. Ithaca: Cornell University Press, 1989
———. "Emporia, Monasteries and the Economic Foundation of Medieval Europe." *MedievalArchaelogy*, edited by C. L. Redman. Binghamton: State University of New York Press, 1989, pp. 57–72.
———, and Hobley B., eds. *The Rebirth of Towns in the West, A.D. 700–1050*. C.B.A. 68. London, 1988.
———, and Whitehouse, D. *Mohammed, Charlemagne, and the Origins of Europe*. Ithaca: Cornell University Press, 1983.
Hodgett, G. *A Social and Economic History of Medieval Europe*. London: Methuen, 1972.
Hodgkin, R. H. *A History of the Anglo-Saxons*. 3d ed. 2 vols. Oxford: Clarendon Press, 1952.
Holmqvist, Wilhelm. "Helgö, eine Vorform der Stadt?" *Vor- und Frühformen der europäischen Stadt*, eds. Jankuhn, et al., II, 1974, pp. 21–29.

Hooke, Della, ed. *Anglo-Saxon Settlements*. London: Blackwell, 1988.

Hoops, J., ed. *Reallexikon der Germanischen Altertumskunde*. 4 vols. Strasbourg: K. Trubner, 1911-1919.

Hopkins, I. "Economic Growth and Towns in Classical Antiquity." *Towns in Societies*, eds. Abrams and Wrigley, 1978, pp. 35–77.

Hoskins, W. G. *Local History in England*. London: Longmans, 1959.

Howe, N. *Migration and Mythmaking in Anglo-Saxon England*. New Haven: Yale University Press, 1989.

Hubert, Jean. "Evolution de la topographie et de l'aspect des villes de Gaule du Ve au Xe siècles." *La citta nell'alto medioevo*, 1959, pp. 529–58.

Huggett, J. W. "Imported Grave Goods and the Early Anglo-Saxon Economy." *Medieval Archaeology* 32 (1988), 63-96.

Hunter, M. "Germanic and Roman Antiquity and the Sense of the Past in Anglo-Saxon England." *Anglo-Saxon England* 3 (1974), pp. 29–50.

Hunter Blair, P. *Northumbria in the Days of Bede*. New York: St. Martin's Press, 1976.

———. *An Introduction to Anglo-Saxon England*. 2d ed. Cambridge: University Press, 1977.

James, E. "The Origins of Barbarian Kingdoms: The Continental Evidence." *Origins of Anglo-Saxon Kingdoms*, ed. Bassett, 1989, pp. 40–52.

Jankuhn, Herbert. "Die frühmittelalterlichen Seehandelsplätze im Nord-und Ostseeraum." *Studien zu den Anfängen des europäischen Stadtewesens*, ed. Mayer, 1958, pp. 451–98.

———. "Frühe Stadte im Nord- und Ostseeraum." *Topografia urbana*, 1, 1974, pp. 153–201.

———. "Vor-und Frühformen der Stadt in archäologischer Sicht." *Gesichtswissenschaft und Archäologie*, eds. Jankuhn and Wenskus, 1979, pp. 241-68.

———. "The Interdisciplinary Approach to the Study of the Early History of Medieval Towns." *Comparative History of Urban Origins*, eds. Clarke and Simms, I, 1985, pp. 15–42.

———, et al., eds. *Vor-und Frühformen der europäischen Stadt im Mittelalter*. 2 vols. Göttingen: Vandenhoeck & Ruprecht, 1973-1974.

———, and Wenskus, eds. *Geschichtswissenschaft und Archäologie: Untersuchungen zur Siedlungs-Wirtschafts-und Kirchengeschichte*. Sigmaringen: Jan Thorbecke Verlag, 1979.

Jansen, H. "Early Urbanization in Denmark." *Comparative History of Urban Origins*, eds. Clarke and Simms, I, 1985, pp. 183-216.

Janssen, W. "The Origins of the Non-Roman Town in Germany." *Comparative History of Urban Origins*, eds. Clarke and Simms, I, 1985, pp. 217–35.

Jäschke, K.-U. "Frühes Christentum in Britannien." *Archiv für Kulturgeschichte* 56 (1974), 91–123.

Jenkins, F. "St. Martin's Church at Canterbury: A Survey of the Earliest Structural Features." *Medieval Archaeology* 9 (1965), 11–15.

John, Eric. *Land Tenure in Early England*. Leicester: University Press, 1960.

———. *Orbis Britanniae and Other Studies*. Leicester: University Press, 1966.

Johns, C. M., and Potter, T. W. "The Canterbury Late Roman Treasure." *Antiquaries Journal* 55 (1985), 313–52.

Johnson, Stephen. *The Roman Forts of the Saxon Shore.* New York: St. Martin's Press, 1976.

———. *Later Roman Britain.* London: Collins, 1980.

Jones, A. H. M. *The Later Roman Empire, 284–602.* 2 vols. Norman, OK: University of Oklahoma Press, 1964.

Jones, B., and Mattingly, D. *An Atlas of Roman Britain.* Oxford: Blackwell, 1990.

Jones, M. E. "Climate, Nutrition, and Disease: An Hypothesis of Romano-British Population." *End of Roman Britain,* ed. Casey, 1979, pp. 231–51.

———, and Casey, P. "The *Gallic Chronicle* Restored: A Chronology for the Anglo-Saxon Invasions and the End of Roman Britain." *Britannia* 19 (1988), 367–98.

Keen, L. "The Towns of Dorset." *Anglo-Saxon Towns,* ed. Haslam, 1984, pp. 203–47.

Kemble, John M. *The Saxons in England: A History of the English Commonwealth till the Period of the Norman Conquest.* 2 vols. London: Longman, 1849.

Kendrick, Thomas D. *British Antiquity.* London: Metheun, 1950.

Kent, J. P. C. "The End of Roman Britain: Literary and Numismatic Evidence Reviewed." *End of Roman Britain,* ed. Casey, 1979, pp. 15–27.

Keynes, S., and Lapidge, M. *Alfred the Great.* Harmondsworth: Penguin Books, 1983.

Kingsford, C. L. *English Historical Literature in the Fifteenth Century.* Oxford: Clarendon Press, 1913.

Kirby, D. P. "Problems of Early West Saxon History." *English Historical Review* 80 (1965), 10–29.

———. *The Earliest English Kings.* London: Unwin Hyman, 1991.

Köbler, G. "*Civitas* und *vicus, burg, stat, dorf* und *wik.*" *Vor- und Frühformen der europäischen Stadt,* eds. Jankuhn, et al., I, 1973, pp. 61–76.

Lambarde, William. *A Perambulation of Kent: Conteining the Description, Hystorie and Customes of that Shyre.* London: Ralph Newberie, 1576.

Langer, L. N. "The Medieval Russian Town." *The City in Russian History.* Edited by M. Hamm. Lexington, KY: University Press of Kentucky, 1976, pp. 11–33.

Lappenberg, J. M. *A History of England under the Anglo-Saxon Kings.* Translated and revised by B. Thorpe. 2 vols. London: John Murray, 1845.

Larson, L. M. *The King's Household in England Before the Norman Conquest.* Madison: University of Wisconsin Press, 1904.

Latouche, Robert. *Les origines de l'économie occidentale.* Paris: A. Michel, 1956.

Leach, P., ed. *Archaeology in Kent to A.D. 1500.* C.B.A. 48. London, 1982.

Leland, John. *The Itinerary of John Leland.* Edited by L. Toulmin-Smith. 5 vols. London: G. Bell, 1907–1910.

Leveau, P. "La ville antique et l'organisation de l'espace rural: villa, ville, village." *Annales. E.S.C.* 37 (1983), 920–42.

Levine, J. M. *Humanism and History: Origins of Modern English Historiography.* Ithaca: Cornell University Press, 1987.

Levison, Wilhelm. "St. Alban and St. Albans." *Antiquity* 15 (1941), 337–59.

———. *England and the Continent in the Eighth Century.* Oxford: Clarendon Press, 1946.

Lewis, A. R. *The Northern Seas: Shipping and Commerce in Northern Europe A.D. 300–1100.* Princeton: Princeton University Press, 1958.

Lieberman, Felix. *Die Gesetze der Angelsachsen.* 3 vols. Halle: M. Niemeyer, 1903–1916.

———. *The National Assembly in the Anglo-Saxon Period.* Halle: M. Niemeyer, 1913.

Liebeschütz, W. "The End of the Ancient City." *City in Late Antiquity,* ed. Rich, 1992, pp. 1–49.

Lingard, John. *The History of England from the First Invasion by the Romans to the Accession of William and Mary in 1688.* 6th ed. 10 vols. London: Charles Dolman, 1855.

Lobel, Mary D., et al., eds. *The Atlas of Historic Towns.* London: Lovel Johns, 1969– .

———. "Some Reflections on the Topographical Development of the Pre-Industrial Town in England." *Tribute to an Antiquary.* Edited by F. Emmison and R. Stephens. London: Leopard's Head Press, 1976, pp. 141–63.

Lohaus, A. *Die Merowinger und England.* Munich: Arbeo-Gesellschaft, 1974.

Lombard-Jourdan, A. "Les foires aux origines des villes." *Francia* 10 (1982), pp. 429–48.

Lopez, R. S. "Of Towns and Trade." *Life and Thought in the Early Middle Ages.* Edited by R. S. Hoyt. Minneapolis: University of Minnesota Press, 1967, pp. 30–50.

Loyn, H. R. "Towns in Late Anglo-Saxon England: The Evidence and Some Possible Lines of Enquiry." *England before the Conquest,* eds. Clemoes and Hughes, 1971, pp. 115–28.

———. *The Governance of Anglo-Saxon England.* Stanford: Stanford University Press, 1984.

Lyon, Bryce. *The Origins of the Middle Ages: Pirenne's Challenge to Gibbon.* New York: W. W. Norton, 1972.

———. *Henry Pirenne: A Biographical and Intellectual Study.* Preface by F. L. Ganshof. Ghent: E. Story-Scientia, 1974.

McKisack, May. *Medieval History in the Tudor Age.* Oxford: Clarendon Press, 1971.

McKitterick, R. *The Frankish Kingdoms under the Carolingians, 751-987.* London: Longmans, 1983.

Maddicott, J. R. "Trade, Industry and the Wealth of King Alfred." *Past and Present* 123 (1989), 3–51.

Madox, Thomas. *Firma Burgi, or an Historical Essay Concerning the Cities, Towns, and Buroughs of England Taken from Records.* London: R. Gosling, 1726.

Maine, H. S. *Ancient Law.* 3d ed. New York: Henry Holt & Co., 1883.

Maitland, Frederick W. *Domesday Book and Beyond: Three Essays in the Early History of England.* Cambridge: University Press, 1897.

———. *Township and Borough.* Cambridge: University Press, 1898.

Maloney, J., and Hobley, B., eds. *Roman Urban Defences in the West.* C.B.A. 57. London, 1983.

Manley, J. "Cledemutha: A Late Saxon *Burh* in North Wales." *Medieval Archaeology* 31 (1987), 13-46.

Mann, J. "The Administration of Roman Britain." *Antiquity* 35 (1961), 316–20.

Marchese, R., ed. *Aspects of Graeco-Roman Urbanism: Essays on the Classical City.* B.A.R., International Series 188. Oxford, 1984.

Margary, I. *Roman Roads in Britain*. 3d ed. rev. London: John Baker Publishers, Ltd., 1967.

Marsden, P., and West, B. "Population Change in Roman London." *Britannia* 23 (1992), 133–40.

Martin, G. H. "The Town as Palimpsest." *The Study of Urban History*. Edited by H. Dyos. New York: St. Martin's Press, 1968, pp. 155–69.

————. "New Beginnings in North-West Europe." *European Towns*, ed. Barley, 1977, pp. 405–15.

————. "Domesday Book and the Boroughs." *Domesday Book: A Reassessment*. Edited by P. H. Sawyer. London: Edward Arnold, 1985, pp. 143–63.

————, and McIntyre, S. *A Bibliography of British and Irish Municipal History*. Leicester: University Press, 1972.

Mayer, Theodor, ed. *Studien zu den Anfängen des europäischen Städtewesens*. Constance: J. Thorbecke, 1958.

Mayr-Harting, H. *The Coming of Christianity to England*. New York: Schocken Books, 1972.

Mazzolani, L. S. *The Idea of the City in Roman Thought*. Translated by S. O'Donnell. Bloomington: Indiana University Press, 1970.

Mendyk, Stan. *"Speculum Britanniae": Regional Study, Antiquarianism and Science in Britain to 1700*. Toronto: University of Toronto Press, 1989.

Merewether, H. A., and Stephens, A. J. *The History of the Boroughs and Municipal Corporations of the United Kingdom, from the Earliest to the Present Time; With an Examination of Records, Charters and Other Documents, Illustrative of Their Constitution and Powers*. 3 vols. London: Stevens & Sons, 1835.

Merrifield, R. *London: City of the Romans*. Berkeley: University of California Press, 1983.

————. "Roman London." *Atlas of Historic Towns: London*, ed. Lobel, 1989, pp. 10–19.

Metcalf, D. M. "The Prosperity of Northwestern Europe in the Eighth and Ninth Centuries." *Economic History Review* 20 (1967), 344–57.

Meyer, G. "Bardowick." *Reallexikon der Germanischen Altertumskunde*, ed. Hoops. 2d ed., II, 1976, pp. 53-54.

Miller, Molly. "Bede's Use of Gildas." *English Historical Review* 90 (1975), 241–61.

————. "The Dates of Deira." *Anglo-Saxon England* 8 (1979), pp. 35–61.

Millet, M. *The Romanization of Britain: An Essay in Archaeological Interpretation*. Cambridge: University Press, 1990.

Milne, G., and Goodburn, D. "The Early Medieval Port of London A.D. 700–1200." *Antiquity* 64 (1990), 629–36.

Mumford, Lewis. *The City in History: Its Origins, Its Transformations, and Its Prospects*. New York: Harcourt, Brace & World, Inc., 1961.

Munby, Julian. "Saxon Chichester and Its Predecessors." *Anglo-Saxon Towns*, ed. Haslam, 1984, pp. 315–30.

Mundy, John H. "Medieval Urbanism." *The Medieval Town*. Edited by J. H. Mundy and P. Riesenberg. Princeton: D. Van Nostrand Co., Inc., 1958, pp. 9–94.

Myres, J. N. L. *Anglo-Saxon Pottery and the Settlement of England*. Oxford: Clarendon Press, 1969.

————. *The English Settlements*. Oxford: Clarendon Press, 1981.

————, and Green, B. *The Anglo-Saxon Cemeteries of Caistor-by-Norwich and Markshall, Norfolk.* London: Society of Antiquaries, 1973.

Nelson, J. L. "A King Across the Sea: Alfred in Continental Perspective." *Transactions of the Royal Historical Society.* 5th Series 36 (1986), pp. 45–68.

Nicholas, D. "Medieval Urban Origins in Northern Continental Europe: State of Research and Some Tentative Conclusions." *Studies in Medieval and Renaissance History* 6 (1969), pp. 53–114.

Noonan, T. "The Vikings in Russia: Some New Directions and Approaches to an Old Problem." *Social Approaches to Viking Studies.* Edited by R. Samson. Glasgow. Cruithne Press, 1991, pp. 201–206.

Oberman, H., and Brady, T., Jr., eds. *Itinerarium Italicum.* Leiden: E. J. Brill, 1975.

Oman, Charles. *England before the Norman Conquest.* 8th ed. rev. London: Methuen, 1938.

Pearce, S. *The Kingdom of Dumnonia: Studies in History and Tradition in South-Western Britain A.D. 350-1150.* Padstow, Cornwall: Lodenek Press 1978.

Pearson, Charles H. *History of England during the Early and Middle Ages.* 2 vols. London: Bell & Daldy, 1867.

Pelteret, D. "Slave-Raiding and Slave-Trading in Early England." *Anglo-Saxon England* 9 (1981), pp. 99–114.

————. "Slavery in the Danelaw." *Social Approaches to Viking Studies,* ed. Samson, 1991, pp. 179–88.

Petit-Dutaillis, Charles. *Studies and Notes Supplementary to Stubbs' "Constitutional History."* Translated by W. E. Rhodes. Manchester: University Press, 1908.

Petri, F. "Die Anfänge des mittelalterliche Städewesens in den Niederlanden und dem angrenzenden Frankreich." *Studien zu den Anfängen des europäischen Städtewesens,* ed. Mayer, 1958, pp. 227–95.

Piggott, S. "Antiquarian Thought in the Sixteenth and Seventeenth Centuries." *English Historical Scholarship,* ed. Fox, 1956, pp. 93-114.

Pirenne, Henri. "L'Origine des constitutions urbaines au moyen âge." *Revue Historique* 53 (1893), 52–83.

————. "L'Origine des constitutions urbaines au moyen âge II." *Revue Historique* 57 (1895), 57–98.

————. "Villes, marchés et marchands au moyen âge." *Revue Historique* 67 (1898), 59–70.

————. *Social and Economic History of Medieval Europe.* New York: Harcourt, Brace & Co., 1937.

————. *Medieval Cities.* Princeton: Princeton University Press, 1925; Rev. ed. New York: Doubleday, 1956.

Planitz, Hans. *Die deutsche Stadt im Mittelalter.* Cologne: Böhlau, 1954.

Platt, Colin. *The English Medieval Town.* New York: David McKay Co., 1976.

Pollack, F., and Maitland, F. W. *The History of English Law Before the Time of Edward I.* 2d ed. 2 vols. Cambridge: University Press, 1898.

Pörtner, R. *The Vikings.* Translated by S. Wilkins. New York: St. Martin's Press, 1975.

Potter, T. M., and Johns, C. *Roman Britain.* Berkeley: University of California Press, 1992.

Pounds, N. *An Economic History of Medieval Europe.* London: Longmans, 1974.

Pretty, Kate. "Defining the Magonsaete." *Origins of Anglo-Saxon Kingdoms*, ed. Bassett, 1989, pp. 171–83.

Price, J., et al., eds. *Recent Research in Roman Yorkshire*. B.A.R. 193. Oxford, 1988.

Pythian-Adams, Charles. "Jolly Cities, Goodly Towns: The Current Search for England's Urban Roots." *Urban History Yearbook* 1 (1977), pp. 30–39.

Radley, J. "Economic Aspects of Anglo-Danish York." *Medieval Archaeology* 15 (1971), 37–57.

Rahtz, Philip. "Gazetteer of Anglo-Saxon Domestic Settlement Sites." *Archaeology of Anglo-Saxon England*, ed. Wilson, 1976, pp. 405–52.

———, et al., eds. *Anglo-Saxon Cemeteries 1979*. B.A.R. 82. Oxford, 1980.

Ralegh Radford, C. A. "The Pre-Conquest Boroughs of England, Ninth to Eleventh Centuries." *Proceedings of the British Academy* 64 (1978), pp. 131–53.

Randsborg, Klaus. *The Viking Age in Denmark: The Formation of a State*. New York: St. Martin's Press, 1980.

Redman, C. L. *The Rise of Civilization: From Early Farmers to Urban Society in the Ancient Near East*. San Francisco: W. H. Freeman & Co., 1978.

Reece, Richard. "Town and Country: The End of Roman Britain." *World Archaeology* 12 (1980), 77–92.

———. "Models of Continuity." *Oxford Journal of Archaeology* 8 (1989), pp. 231-36.

———. "The End of the City in Roman Britain." *City in Late Antiquity*, ed. Rich, 1992, pp. 136–44.

Renfrew, C., and Shennan, S. eds. *Ranking, Resource, and Exchange*. Cambridge: University Press, 1982.

Reynolds, Robert L. "Town Origins." *Great Problems in European Civilization*. Edited by K. Setton and H. Winkler. New York: Prentice-Hall, Inc., 1954, pp. 173–205.

Reynolds, Susan. *An Introduction to the History of English Medieval Towns*. Oxford: Clarendon Press, 1977.

Rich, J., ed. *The City in Late Antiquity*. London: Routledge, 1992.

———, and Wallace-Hadrill, A., eds. *City and Country in the Ancient World*. London: Routledge, 1991.

Rigold, S. "The Two Primary Series of *Sceattas*." *British Numismatic Journal* 30 (1960), 6–53; 35 (1966), 1–6.

Rivet, A. L. F. *Town and Country in Roman Britain*. London: Hutchinson University Library, 1958.

———, ed. *The Roman Villa in Britain*. London: Routledge & Kegan Paul, 1969.

Rodwell, W., and Rowley, T., eds. *The 'Small Towns' of Roman Britain*. B.A.R. 15. Oxford, 1975.

Russell, J. C. "Demographic Aspects of the Norman Conquest." *Seven Studies in Medieval English History*. Edited by R. Bowers. Jackson: University Press of Mississippi, 1983, pp. 3-20.

Russo, Daniel G. "Sacral Kingship in Early Medieval Europe: The Germanic Tradition." M.A. thesis, University of New Hampshire, 1978.

Salway, Peter. *Roman Britain*. Oxford: Clarendon Press, 1981.

———. *The Oxford Illustrated History of Roman Britain*. Oxford: Oxford University Press, 1993.

Samson, R. "Rethinking Trading, Raiding, and Hoarding." *Social Approaches to Viking Studies*, ed. Samson, 1991, pp. 123–33.

——, ed. *Social Approaches to Viking Studies*. Glasgow: Cruithne Press, 1991.

Sawyer, P. H. *Anglo-Saxon Charters*. London: Royal Historical Society, 1968.

——. *From Roman Britain to Norman England*. London: Methuen, 1976.

——. *Kings and Vikings: Scandinavia and Europe A.D. 700–1100*. London: Methuen, 1982.

——. "The Royal *Tun* in Pre-Conquest England." *Ideal and Reality*, ed. Wormald, 1983, pp. 273–99.

——, ed. *Domesday Book: A Reassessment*. London: Edward Arnold, 1985.

——, and Wood, I., eds. *Early Medieval Kingship*. Leeds: University Press, 1977.

Schietzel, K. "Haithabu: A Study on the Development of Early Urban Settlements in Northern Europe." *Comparative Study of Urban Origins*, eds. Clarke and Simms, I, 1985, pp. 15–42.

Schledermann, Helmuth. "The Idea of the Town: Typology, Definitions and Approaches to the Study of the Medieval Town in Northern Europe." *World Archaeology* 2 (1970), 115–27.

Schlesinger, Walter. "Stadt und Burg im Lichte der Wortgeschichte." *Studium Generale* 16 (1963), 433–44.

Schofield, J., et al., eds. *Recent Archaeological Research in English Towns*. London: Council for British Archaeology, 1981.

——, and Leech, R., eds. *Urban Archaeology in Britain*. C.B.A. 61. London, 1987.

Schütte, L. *Wik: eine Siedlungsbezeichnung in historischen und sprachlichen Bezügen*. Cologne: Böhlau, 1976.

Seeliger, G. "Stadtverfassung." *Reallexikon der Germanischen Altertumskunde*, ed. Hoops, IV, 1919, pp. 244–59.

Shoesmith, R. *Hereford City Excavations 2, Excavations on or Close to the Defences*. C.B.A. 46. London, 1982.

Sjoberg, Gideon. *The Pre-Industrial City: Past and Present*. New York: Free Press, 1960.

Skovgaard-Petersen, I. "The Historical Context of the First Towns in Northern and Eastern Europe." *Eighth Viking Congress*, eds. Bekker-Nielsen et al., 1981, pp. 9–18.

Smith, A. H. *English Place-Name Elements*. 2 vols. Cambridge: University Press, 1956.

Southern, R. M. "Aspects of the European Tradition of Historical Writing: 4. The Sense of the Past." *Transactions of the Royal Historical Society*, 5th Series 23 (1973), pp. 246–56.

Stafford, Pauline. *The East Midlands in the Early Middle Ages*. Leicester: University Press, 1985.

Stark, J. *Haithabu*. B.A.R. International Series 432. Oxford, 1988.

Steane, John. *The Archaeology of Medieval England and Wales*. Athens, GA: University of Georgia Press, 1984.

Stenton, Frank M. *Latin Charters of the Anglo-Saxon Period*. Oxford: Clarendon Press, 1955.

——. *Anglo-Saxon England*. 3d ed. Oxford: Clarendon Press, 1971.

Stephenson, Carl. *Borough and Town: A Study of Urban Origins in England.*
    Cambridge, MA: Mediaeval Academy of America, 1933.
————. "The Problem of the Common Man in Early Medieval Europe." *American
    Historical Review* 51 (1946), 419–38.
Stevens, C. E. "Gildas and the *Civitates* of Britain." *English Historical Review* 52
    (1937), 193–201.
Stevenson, W. H. "Dr. Guest and the English Conquest of South Britain." *English
    Historical Review* 17 (1902), 625–42.
————. "Trinoda Necessitas." *English Historical Review* 29 (1914), 689–702.
Stewart, I. "Anglo-Saxon Gold Coins." *Scripta Nummaria Romana: Essays Presented
    to Humphrey Sutherland.* Edited by R. Carson and C. Kraay. London: Spink
    & Son, 1978, pp. 143–72.
Stow, John. *A Survay of London. Contayning the Originall, Antiquity, Increase, Modern
    Estate, and Description of that Citie.* London: John Wolfe, 1598.
Stubbs, William. *The Constitutional History of England in Its Origin and Development.*
    5th ed. 3 vols. Oxford: Clarendon Press, 1891–1895.
Sutherland, C. H. V. *English Coinage 600–1900.* London: Batsford, 1973.
————. *Roman Coins.* New York: Putnam's, 1974.
Tait, James. "The Study of Early Municipal History in England." *Proceedings of the
    British Academy* 10 (1921–1923), pp. 201–17.
————. *The English Medieval Borough: Studies on Its Origins and Constitutional
    History.* Manchester: University Press, 1936.
Tatton-Brown, T. "Towns of Kent." *Anglo-Saxon Towns,* ed. Haslam, 1984, pp. 1–35.
————. "The Topography of Anglo-Saxon London." *Antiquity* 60 (1986), 21–28.
Thomas, Charles. *Christianity in Roman Britain to A.D. 500.* Berkeley: University of
    California Press, 1981.
Thompson, E. A. "Gildas and the History of Britain." *Britannia* 10 (1979), 203–26.
————. *St. Germanus of Auxerre and the End of Roman Britain.* Woodbridge, Suffolk:
    Boydell Press, 1984.
————. "Ammianus Marcellinus and Britain." *Nottingham Medieval Studies* 34 (1990),
    1–15.
Thompson, James W. *A History of Historical Writing.* 2 vols. New York: Macmillan,
    1942.
Tikhomirov, M. *The Towns of Ancient Rus.* Translated by Y. Sdobnikov. 2d ed.
    Moscow: Foreign Languages Publishing House, 1959.
Todd, M., ed. *Research on Roman Britain 1960–1989.* Britannia Monograph Series,
    2. London: Society for the Promotion of Roman Studies, 1989.
Topografia urbana e vita cittadina nell'alto medioevo in occidente. 2 vols. Centro
    Italiano di Studi Sull'Alto Medioevo. Settimane 21, 22. Spoleto, 1974.
Turner, Hilary. *Town Defenses in England and Wales, 900–1500.* Hamden, CT:
    Archon Books, 1971.
Turner, Sharon. *The History of the Anglo-Saxons.* 2d ed. 2 vols. London: Longman,
    1807.
Ucko, P. J., et al., eds. *Man, Settlement, and Urbanism.* London: Duckworth, 1972.
Unwin, George. *Studies in Economic History.* London: Macmillan, 1927.
van Regteren Altena, H. "The Origin and Development of Dutch Towns." *World
    Archaeology* 2 (1970), 128–40.

van Werveke, H. "The Rise of the Towns." *The Cambridge Economic History of Europe*. Vol. III: *Economic Organization and Policies in the Middle Ages*. Edited by M. M. Postan, et al. Cambridge: University Press, 1963, pp. 3-41.

Vercauteren, F. "La circulation des marchands en Europe occidentale du VIe - Xe siècle: aspects économiques et culturels." *Centri e vie di irradiazione della civiltà nell'alto medioevo*. Centro Italiano di Studi Sull'Alto Medioevo. Settimane 11. Spoleto, 1964, pp. 393–411.

————. "Conceptions et méthods de l'histoire des villes médiévales au cours du dernier demi-siècle." *XIIe Congrès International des Sciences Historiques*. Vienna, 1967, V, pp. 649-66.

Verhulst, Adriaan. "Les origines urbaines dans le Nord- Ouest de l'Europe: essai de synthèse." *Francia* 14 (1986), pp. 57–81.

Verlinden, C. "Markets and Fairs." *The Cambridge Economic History of Europe*. Vol. III: *Economic Organization and Policies in the Middle Ages*. Edited by M. M. Postan, et al. Cambridge: University Press, 1963, pp. 119-53.

Verwers, W. "Dorestad: A Carolingian Town?" *Rebirth of Towns*, eds. Hodges and Hobley, 1988, pp. 52–56.

The Victoria History of the Counties of England. Edited by H. A. Doubleday, et al., London, 1900–   .

Vince, Alan. *Saxon London: An Archaeological Investigation*. London: Seaby, 1990.

Wacher, John S., ed. *The Civitas Capitals of Roman Britain*. Leicester: University Press, 1966.

————. *The Towns of Roman Britain*. Berkeley: University of California Press, 1974.

————. "Cities from the Second to Fourth Centuries." *Research on Roman Britain 1960–1989*, ed. Todd, 1989, pp. 75–90.

Wade, Keith. "Ipswich." *Rebirth of Towns*, eds. Hodges and Hobley, 1988, pp. 93–100.

Wainwright, F. T. "Aethelflaed, Lady of the Mercians." *The Anglo-Saxons*. Edited by P. Clemoes. London: Bowes & Bowes, 1959, pp. 53–70.

Waitz, G. *Deutsche Verfassungsgeschichte*. 9 vols. Berlin: Weidmann, 1874–1885.

Wallace-Hadrill, John M. *Early Germanic Kingship in England and on the Continent*. Oxford: Clarendon Press, 1971.

————. *Bede's "Ecclesiastical History of the English People": A Historical Commentary*. Oxford: Clarendon Press, 1988.

Weber, Max. "Die Stadt." *Archiv für Sozialwissenschaft und Sozialpolitik* 47 (1920–1921), 621–772.

Webster, Graham. *The Cornovii*. London: Duckworth, 1975.

————, ed. *Fortress into City*. Totowa, NJ: Barnes & Noble, 1988.

Welch, Martin. *Discovering Anglo-Saxon England*. University Park, PA: Pennsylvania State University Press, 1993.

Wells, P. S. *Farms, Villages, and Cities: Commerce and Urban Origins in Late Prehistoric Europe*. Ithaca: Cornell University Press, 1984.

Welsby, D. *The Roman Military Defense of the British Provinces in its Later Phases*. B.A.R. 101. Oxford, 1982.

Welsford, Jean. *Cirencester*. Gloucester: Alan Sutton, 1987.

Wenskus, R. "Randbemerkungen zum Verhältnis von Historie und Archäologie, insbesondere mittelalterliche Geschichte und Mittelalterarchäologie."

Geschichtswisenschaft und Archäologie, eds. Jankuhn and Wenskus, 1979, pp. 637-57.

Werner, Joachim. "Fernhandel und Naturalwirtschaft im östlichen Merovingerreich nach archäologischen und numismatischen Zeugnissen." *Moneta e scambi nell'alto medioevo.* Centro Italiano di Studi Sull'Alto Medioevo. Settimane 8. Spoleto, 1961, pp. 557–618.

Wheatley, P. "The Concept of Urbanism." *Man, Settlement and Urbanism*, eds. Ucko, et al., 1972, pp. 601–37.

Wheeler, R. E. M. "The Topography of Saxon London." *Antiquity* 8 (1934), 290–302.

White, D. A. "Changing Views of the *Adventus Saxonum* in Nineteenth and Twentieth Century English Scholarship." *Journal of the History of Ideas* 32 (1971), 585–94.

Whitehouse, D. "Archaeology." *Medieval Studies: An Introduction.* Edited by J. M. Powell. 2d ed. Syracuse: Syracuse University Press, 1992, pp. 162-84.

Whitelock, Dorothy. *The Beginnings of English Society.* Harmondsworth: Penguin Books, 1952.

Whitlock, R. *The Warrior Kings of Saxon England.* New York: Dorset Press, 1991.

Whittaker, C. R. "The Consumer City Revisited: The *Vicus* and the City." *Journal of Roman Archaeology* 3 (1990), 110–18.

Whittock, M. J. *The Origins of England 410–600.* Totowa, NJ: Barnes & Noble, 1986.

Wightman, Edith M. *Gallia Belgica.* Berkeley: Univesity of California Press, 1985.

Williams, J. H. "From 'Palace' to 'Town': Northampton and Urban Origins." *Anglo-Saxon England* 13 (1984), pp. 113–36.

Williamson, T. *The Origins of Norfolk.* Manchester: University Press, 1993.

Wilson, D. M., ed. *The Archaeology of Anglo-Saxon England.* London: Methuen, 1976.

———, ed. *The Northern World.* London: Thames & Hudson, 1980.

Wolff, P., ed. *Guide international d'histoire urbaine.* Vol. 1, *Europe.* Paris: Klincksieck, 1977.

Wood, Ian. "The Fall of the Western Empire and the End of Roman Britain." *Britannia* 18 (1987), 251–62.

———. "The Franks and Sutton Hoo." *People and Places in Northern Europe*, eds. Wood and Lund, 1991, pp. 1–14.

———, and Lund, N., eds. *People and Places in Northern Europe.* Woodbridge, Suffolk: The Boydell Press, 1991.

Wormald, Patrick, ed. *Ideal and Reality in Frankish and Anglo-Saxon Society.* Oxford: Clarendon Press, 1983.

———. "The Emergence of Anglo-Saxon Kingdoms." *The Making of Britain: The Dark Ages.* Edited by L. M. Smith. London: Macmillan, 1984, pp. 49–62.

Wright, Thomas. "On the Existence of Municipal Privileges under the Anglo-Saxons." *Archaeologia* 32 (1847), 298–311.

Yorke, Barbara. "Joint Kingship in Kent c.570–785." *Archaeologia Cantiana* 99 (1983), 1–20.

———. "The Jutes of Hampshire and Wight and the Origins of Wessex." *Origins of Anglo-Saxon Kingdoms*, ed. Bassett, 1989, pp. 84-96.

———. *Kings and Kingdoms of Early Anglo-Saxon England.* London: Seaby, 1990.

———. "Fact or Fiction? The Written Evidence for the Fifth and Sixth Centuries A.D." *Anglo-Saxon Studies in Archaeology and History*, 6. Edited by W. Filmer-Sankey. Oxford: Oxbow Books, 1993, pp. 45–50.

Yule, Brian. "The Dark Earth and Late Roman London." *Antiquity* 64 (1990), 620–28.

Maps and Figures

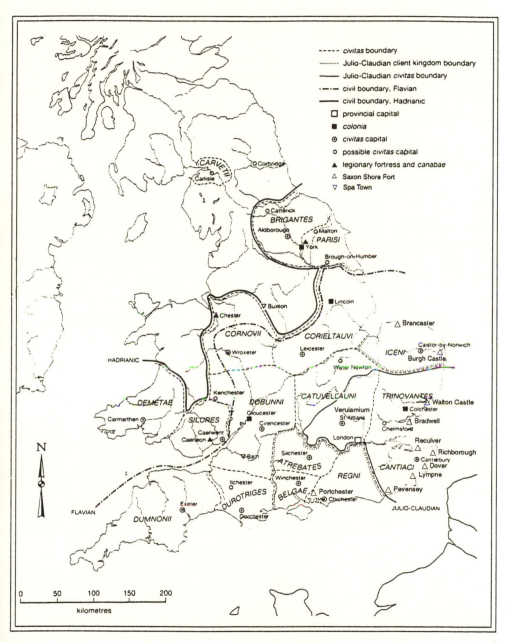

Map 2.1. Romano-British Towns and Cantons. (Adapted from Jones and Mattingly, *Atlas of Roman Britain,* 1990; Johnson, *Later Roman Britain*, 1980)

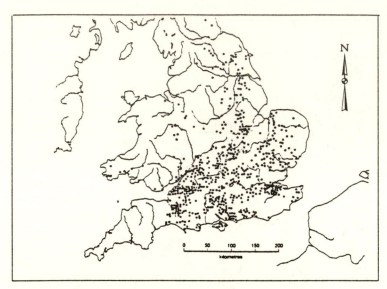

A. Romano-British Villas. (Adapted from Jones and Mattingly, *Atlas of Roman Britain*, 1990; Rivet, ed., *Roman Villa in Britain*, 1969)

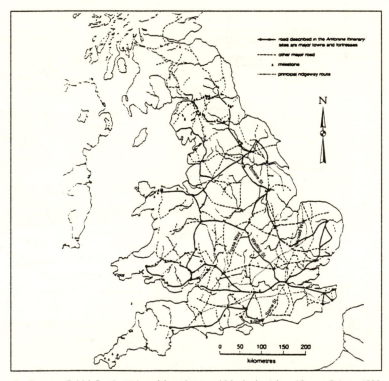

B. Romano-British Roads. (Adapted from Jones and Mattingly, *Atlas of Roman Britain*, 1990; Margary, *Roman Roads in Britain*, 1967)

Map 2.2.A,B. Romano-British Villas and Roads

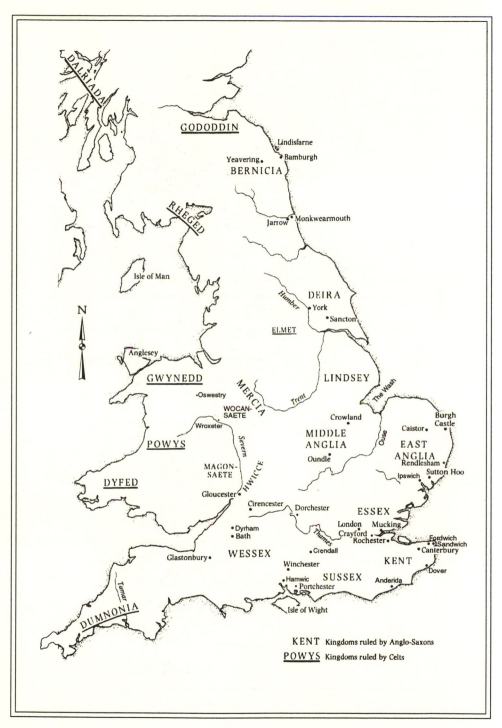

Map 3.1. England c. 675 A.D. (Adapted from Campbell, ed., *Anglo-Saxons,* 1982)

263

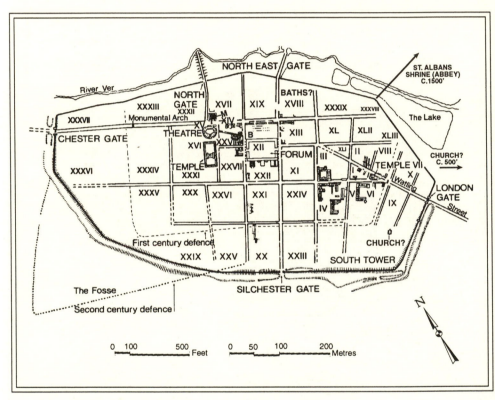

Figure 3.1. Plan of Romano-British Verulamium. (Adapted from Wacher, *Towns of Roman Britain*, 1974; Jones and Mattingly, *Atlas of Roman Britain*, 1990, Salway, *History of Roman Britain*, 1993)

264

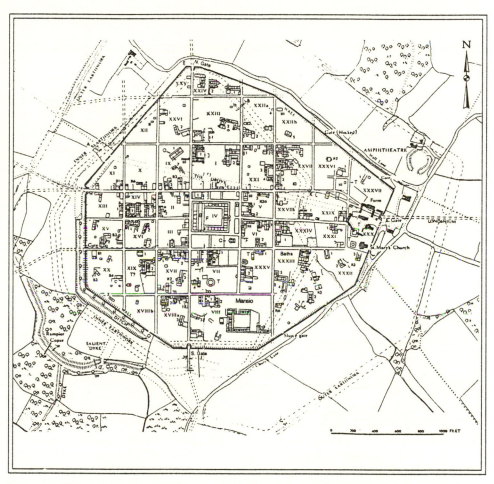

Figure 3.2. Plan of Romano-British Silchester [Calleva Atrebatum]. (Adapted from Wacher, *Towns of Roman Britain*, 1974; Boon, *Silchester*, 1974; Fulford, *Silchester Excavations*, 1984)

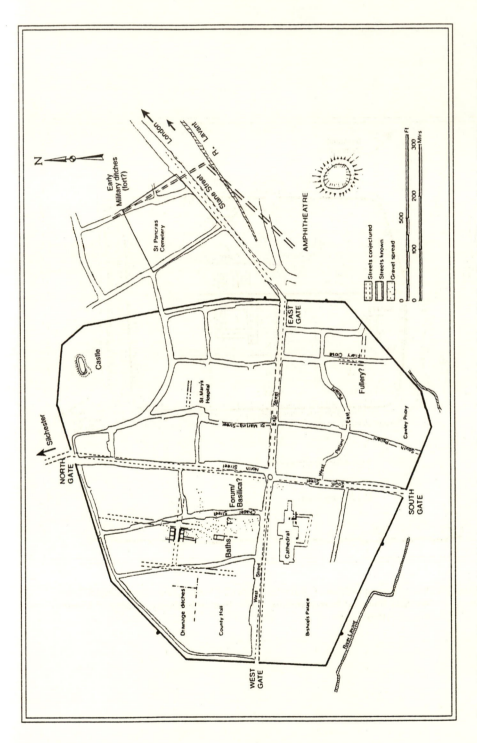

Figure 3.3 Plan of Romano-British Chichester [Noviomagus Regnensium]. (Adapted from Wacher, *Towns of Roman Britain*, 1974; Esmonde Cleary, *Extra-Mural Areas of Romano-British Towns*, 1987)

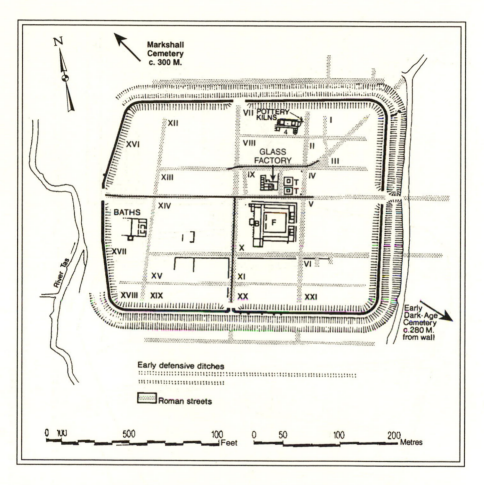

Figure 3.4. Plan of Romano-British Caistor-by-Norwich [Venta Icenorum]. (Adapted from Wacher, *Towns of Roman Britain*, 1974; Esmonde Cleary, *Ending of Roman Britain*, 1990)

267

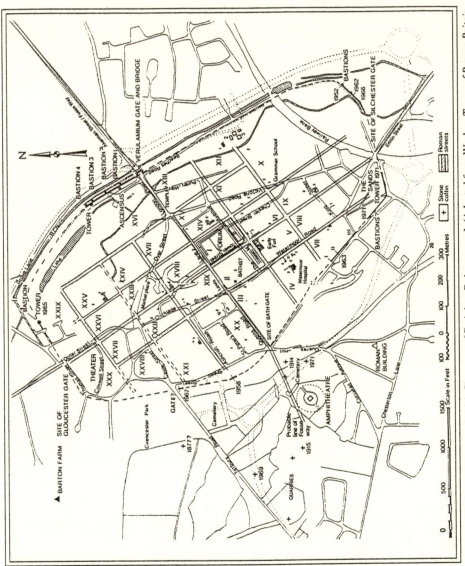

Figure 3.5. Plan of Romano-British Cirencester [Corinium Dubunnorum]. (Adapted from Wacher, *Towns of Roman Britain*, 1974; McWhirr, "Cirencester," in Webster, ed., *Fortress into City*, 1988)

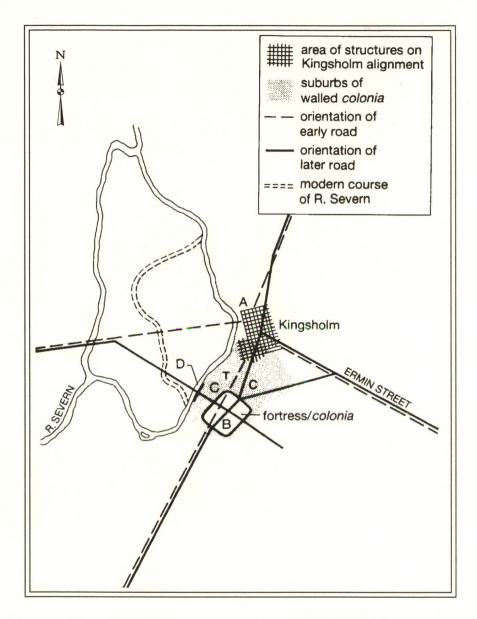

Figure 3.6. Development Plan of Romano-British Gloucester [Glevum] and its Region. A – Kingsholm vexillation fortress; B – Gloucester legionary fortress/walled *colonia*; C – main suburbs of Roman Town; D – Roman Quay; T – Roman Tilery. (Adapted from Jones and Mattingly, *Atlas of Roman Britain,* 1990; Hurst, "Gloucester," in Webster, ed., *Fortress into City,* 1988)

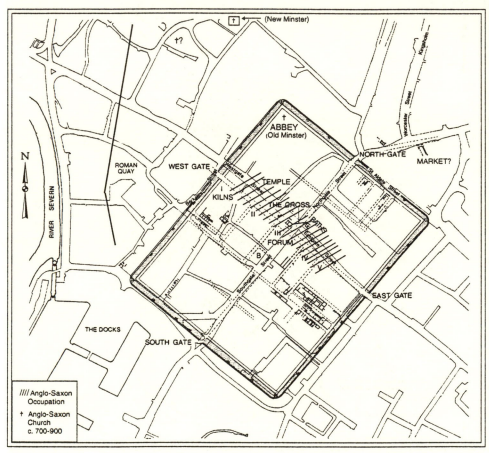

Figure 3.7. Plan of Gloucester. (Adapted from Wacher, *Towns of Roman Britain,* 1974; Hurst, "Gloucester," in Webster, ed., *Fortress into City,* 1988; Heighway, "Saxon Gloucester," 1984)

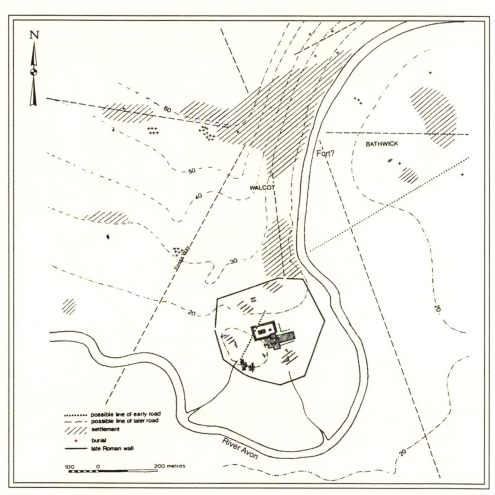

Figure 3.8. Development Plan of Romano-British Bath [Aquae Sulis] and its Region. (Adapted from Cunliffe, *City of Bath*, 1987; Esmonde Cleary, *Extra-Mural Areas of Romano-British Towns*, 1987)

271

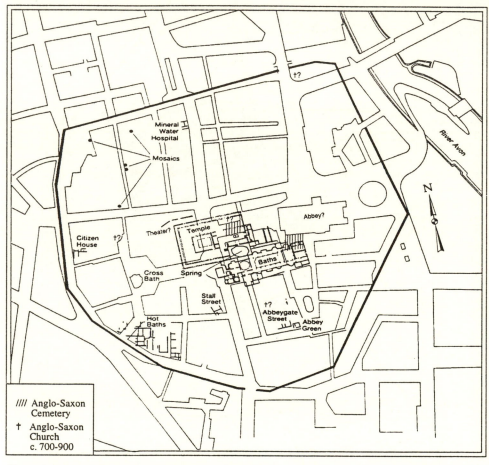

Figure 3.9. Plan of Bath. (Adapted from Burnham and Wacher, *Small Towns of Roman Britain*, 1990; Cunliffe, *City of Bath*, 1987).

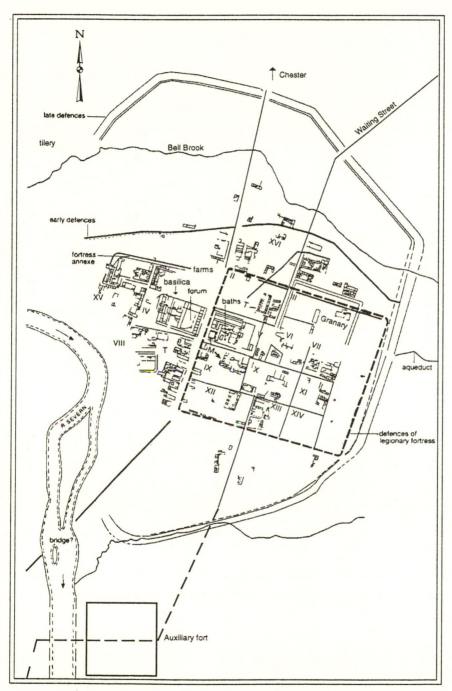

Figure 3.10. Plan of Romano-British Wroxeter [Viroconium]. (Adapted from Jones and Mattingly, *Atlas of Roman Britain*, 1990; Webster, "Wroxeter," in Webster, ed., *Fortress into City*, 1988; Wacher, *Towns of Roman Britain*, 1974)

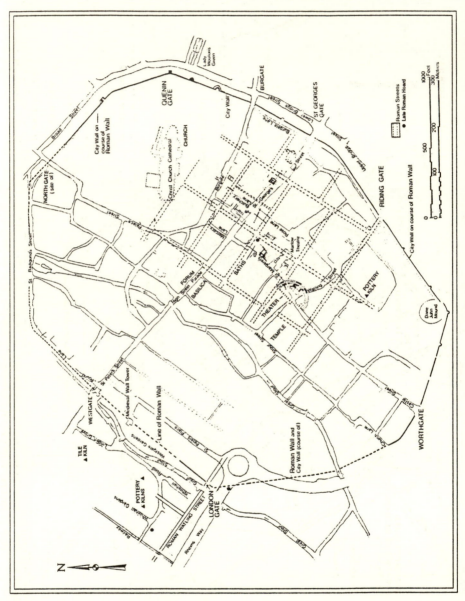

Figure 4.1. Plan of Romano-British Canterbury (*Durovernum Cantiacorum*). (Adapted from Wacher, *Towns of Roman Britain*, 1974; Frere et al., "Roman Britain: Canterbury," 1990)

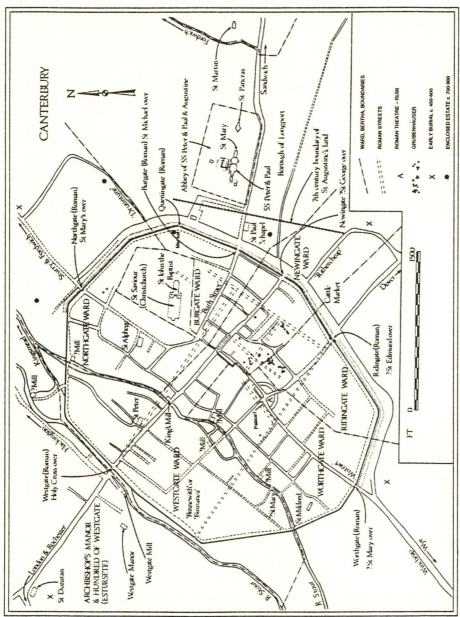

Figure 4.2. Plan of Anglo-Saxon Canterbury. (Adapted from Tatton-Brown, "Towns of Kent," 1984; N. Brooks, *Church of Canterbury*, 1984; D. Brooks, "Fifth-Century Canterbury," 1988)

275

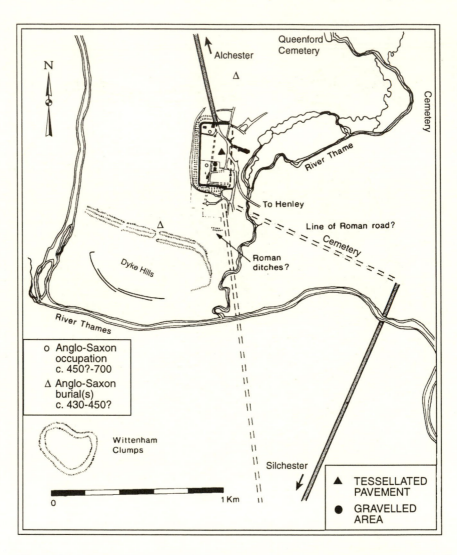

Within the figure:

N

Alchester

Queenford
Cemetery

Δ

Cemetery

River Thame

To Henley

Line of Roman road?

Δ

Cemetery

Dyke Hills

Roman
ditches?

River Thames

o Anglo-Saxon
  occupation
  c. 450?-700

Δ Anglo-Saxon
  burial(s)
  c. 430-450?

Wittenham
Clumps

Silchester

0   1 Km

▲ TESSELLATED
   PAVEMENT

● GRAVELLED
   AREA

Figure 4.3. Plan of Dorchester-on-Thames. (Adapted from Burnham and Wacher, *Small Towns of Roman Britain,* 1990; Esmonde Cleary, *Ending of Roman Britain,* 1990).

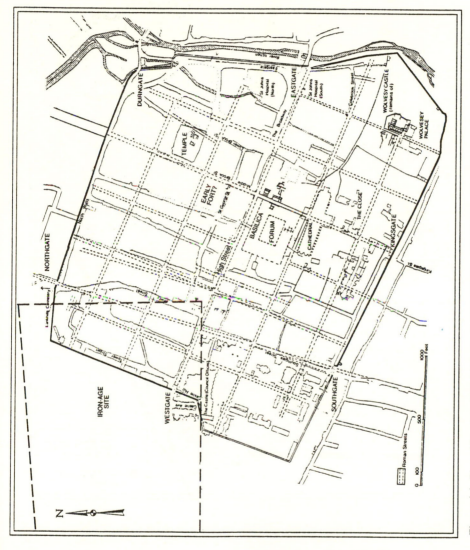

Figure 4.4. Plan of Romano-British Winchester [Venta Belgarum]. (Adapted from Wacher, *Towns of Roman Britain*, 1974; Biddle, "Study of Winchester," 1983)

277

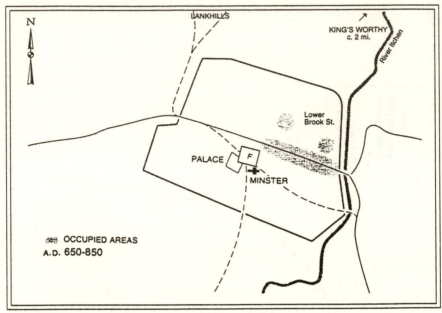

A. Winchester, c. 650-850 A.D. (Adapted from Biddle, "Study of Winchester," 1983; Hinton, "Towns of Hampshire," 1984)

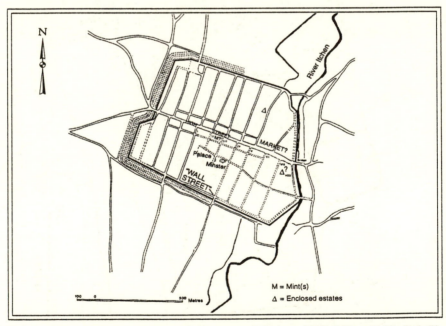

B. Winchester, c. 880-886 A.D. (Adapted from Biddle, "Study of Winchester," 1983; P. Wormald, "The Burhs," in Campbell, ed., *Anglo-Saxons*, 1982)

Figure 4.5.A,B. Plans of Anglo-Saxon Winchester

278

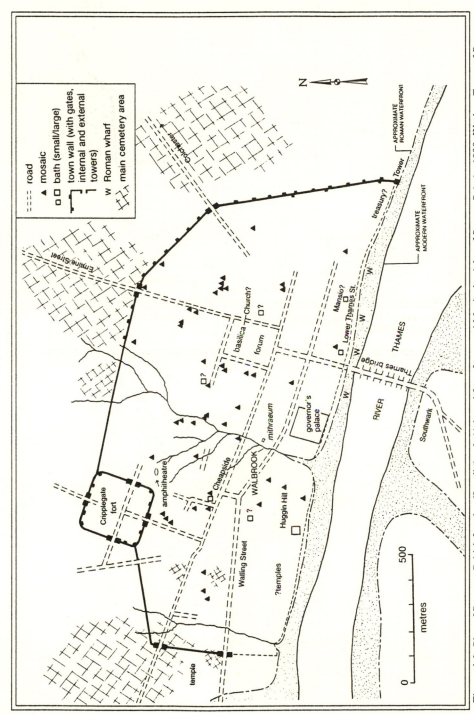

Figure 4.6. Plan of Romano-British London [Londinium]. (Adapted from Jones and Mattingly, *Atlas of Roman Britain*, 1990; Wacher, *Towns of Roman Britain*, 1974; Merrifield, *London*, 1983)

279

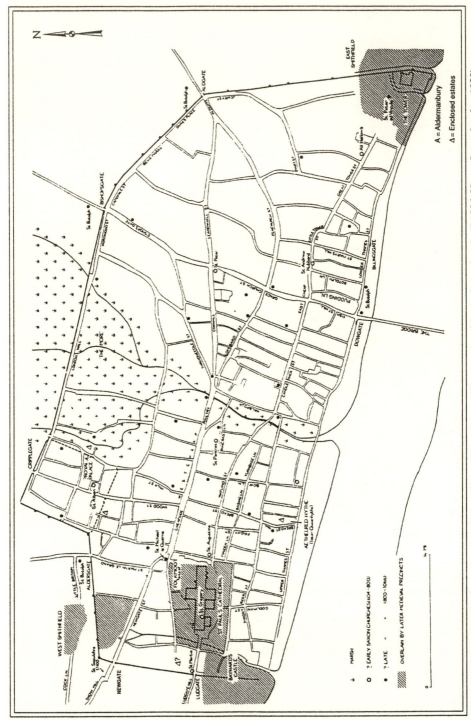

Figure 4.7. Plan of Anglo-Saxon London. (Adapted from Tatton-Brown, "Topography of Anglo-Saxon London," 1986; Vince, *Saxon London*, 1990)

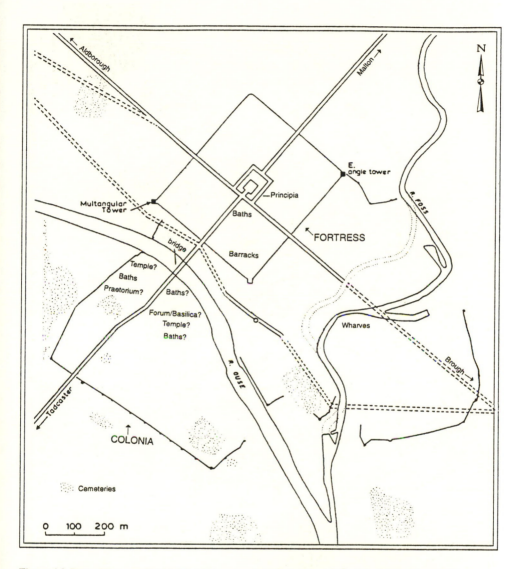

Figure 4.8 Plan of Romano-British York [Eboracum]. (Adapted from P. Buckland, "The Stones of York," in Price et al., eds., *Recent Research in Roman Yorkshire*, 1988; Wacher, *Towns of Roman Britain*, 1974; Ramm, "End of Roman York," 1971)

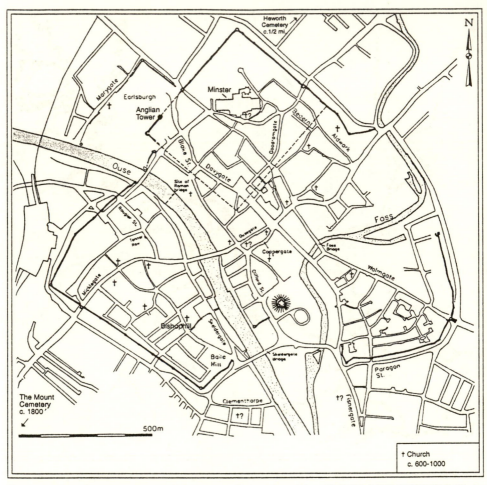

Figure 4.9 Plan of Anglian and Anglo-Scandinavian York. (Adapted from Hall, "York 700-1050," 1988; Clarke and Ambrosiani, *Towns in the Viking Age*, 1991)

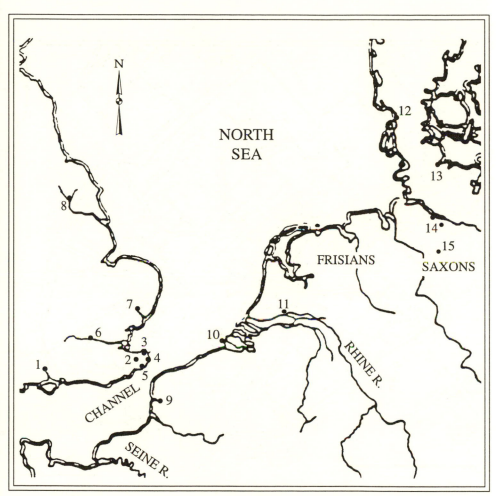

Map 5.1. Anglo-Saxon, Channel, and North Sea *wics*, c. 500-850 A.D. 1. Hamwic. 2. Fordwich. 3. Sarre. 4. Sandwich. 5. Dover. 6. London. 7. Ipswich. 8. York. 9. Quentovic. 10. Domburg. 11. Dorestad. 12. Ribe. 13. Hedeby (Haithabu). 14. Bardowic. 15. Brunswick. (Adapted from Biddle, "Development of the Anglo-Saxon Town," 1974; Clarke and Simms, eds., *Comparative History of Urban Origins,* 1985)

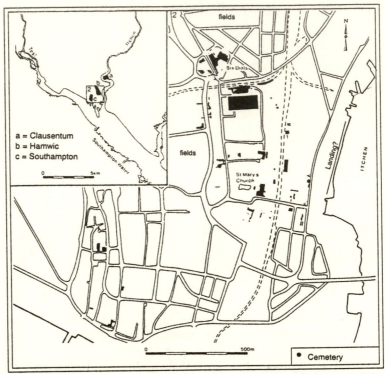

a = Clausentum
b = Hamwic
c = Southampton

A. Hamwic. (Adapted from Brisbane, "Hamwic," 1988; Clarke and Ambrosiani, *Towns in the Viking Age*, 1991)

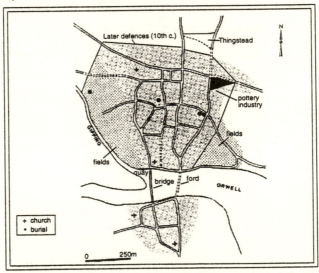

B. Ipswich. (Adapted from Wade, "Ipswich," 1988; Clarke and Ambrosiani, *Towns in the Viking Age*, 1991)

Figure 5.1.A,B. Plans of Anglo-Saxon *wics*: Hamwic and Ipswich

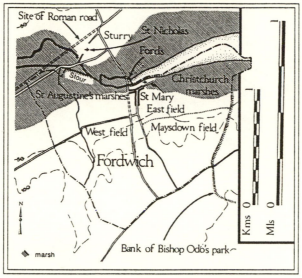

A. Fordwich. (Adapted from Tatton-Brown, "Towns of Kent," 1984)

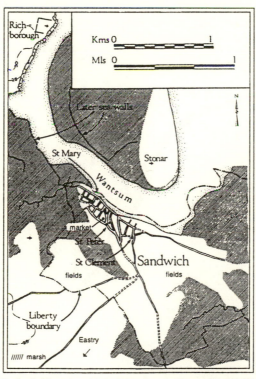

B. Sandwich. (Adapted from Tatton-Brown, "Towns of Kent," 1984)

Figure 5.2.A, B. Plans of Anglo-Saxon *wics*: Fordwich and Sandwich

285

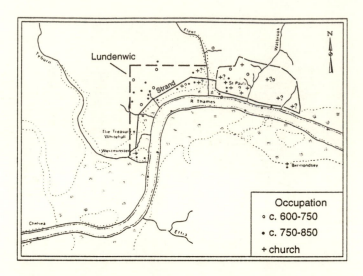

A. Lundenwic, on the Strand. (Adapted from Vince, *Saxon London*, 1990; Cowie and Whytehead, "Lundenwic," 1989)

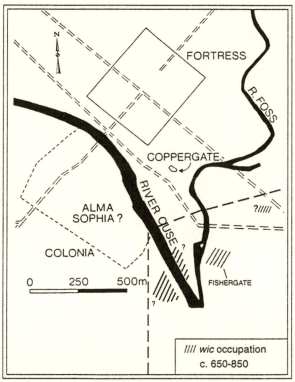

B. Eoforwic, by Fishergate. (Adapted from Hall, "York 700-1050," 1988; Hodges, *Anglo-Saxon Achievement*, 1989)

Figure 5.3.A,B. Plans of Anglo-Saxon *wics*: Lundenwic and Eoforwic

286

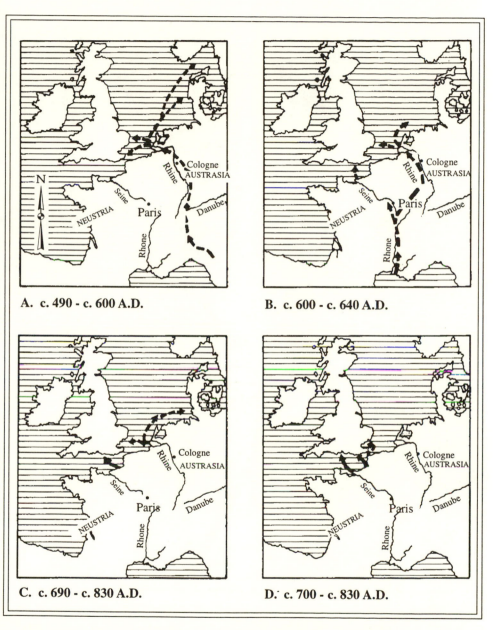

A. c. 490 - c. 600 A.D.

B. c. 600 - c. 640 A.D.

C. c. 690 - c. 830 A.D.

D. c. 700 - c. 830 A.D.

Map 6.1.A-D. Trade Routes in Western Europe, c.500-850 A.D. (Adapted from Hodges and Whitehouse, *Mohammed, Charlemagne, and the Origins of Europe*, 1983)

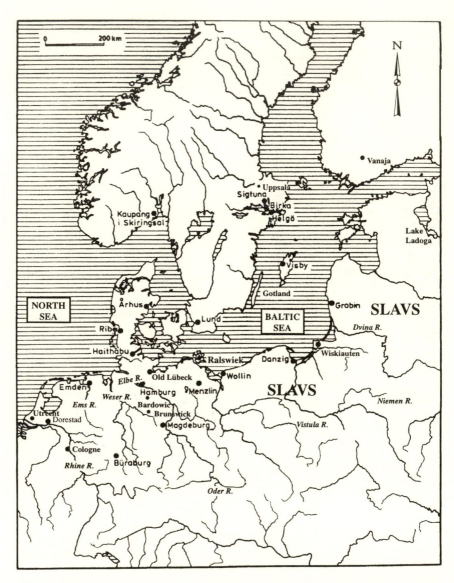

Map 6.2. Continental *wics* in Northern and Eastern Europe, c.700-1000 A.D. (Adapted from Clarke and Simms, eds., *Comparative History of Urban Origins*, 1985)

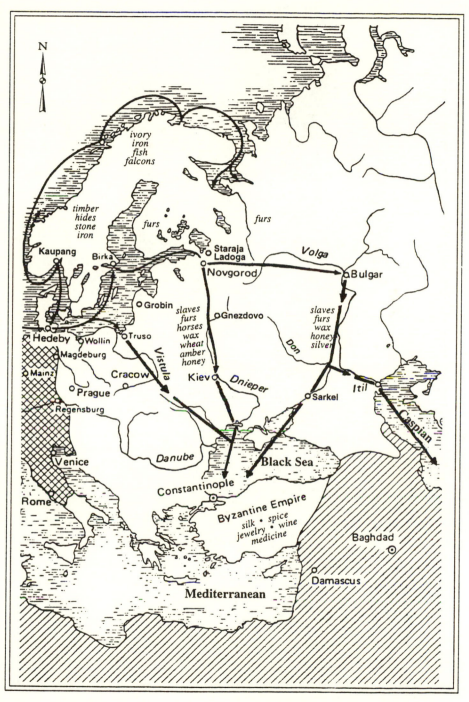

Map 6.3. Viking Trade Routes in Eastern Europe, c.750-1000 A.D. (adapted from R. Pörtner, *The Vikings,* 1975; Clarke and Simms, eds. *Comparative History of Urban Origins,* 1985)

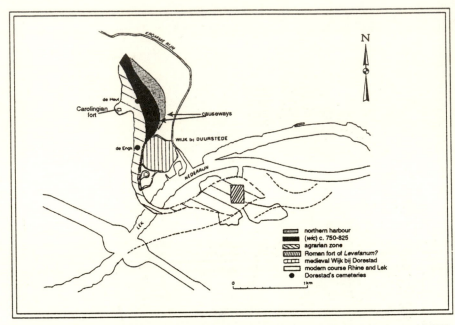

A. Dorestad. (Adapted from Clarke and Ambrosiani, *Towns in the Viking Age*, 1991; Verwers, "Dorestad," 1988).

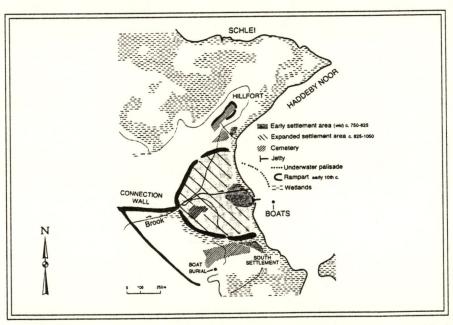

B. Haithabu [Hedeby]. (Adapted from Clarke and Ambrosiani, *Towns in the Viking Age*, 1991; Schietzel, "Haithabu," 1988)

Figure 6.1 A,B. Site Plans of North Sea *wics*: Dorestad and Haithabu

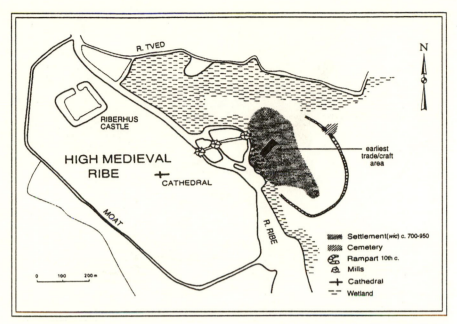

A. Ribe. (Adapted from Clarke and Ambrosiani, *Towns in the Viking Age*, 1991; Bencard and Jorgensen, "Foundation of Ribe," 1990)

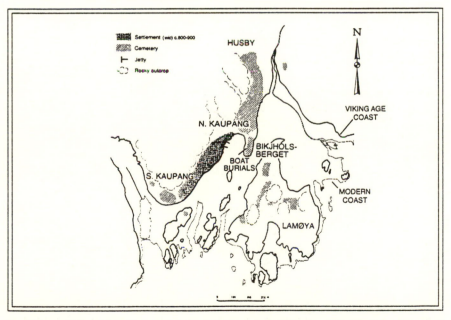

B. Kaupang. (Adapted from Clarke and Ambrosiani, *Towns in the Viking Age*, 1991; Blindheim, "Kaupang," 1974)

Figure 6.2 A,B. Site Plans of North Sea *wics*: Ribe and Kaupang

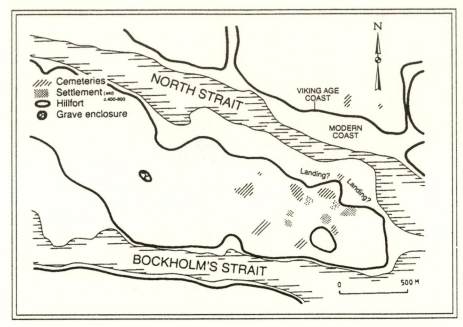

A. Helgö. (Adapted from Clarke and Ambrosiani, *Towns in the Viking Age*, 1991; Holmqvist, "Helgö," 1974)

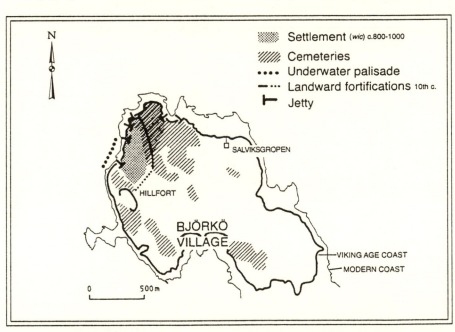

B. Birka. (Adapted from Clarke and Ambrosiani, *Towns in the Viking Age*, 1991; Ambrosiani, "Urban Archaeology in Sweden," 1977)

Figure 6.3 A,B. Site Plans of Scandinavian-Baltic *wics*: Helgö and Birka

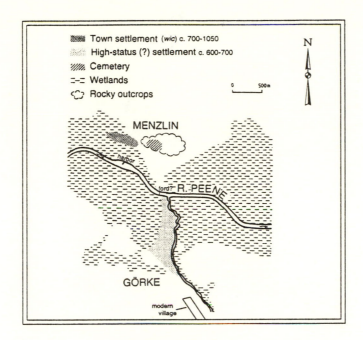

A. Menzlin. (Adapted from Clarke and Ambrosiani, *Towns in the Viking Age*, 1991; Herrmann, "North-Western Slavs," 1985)

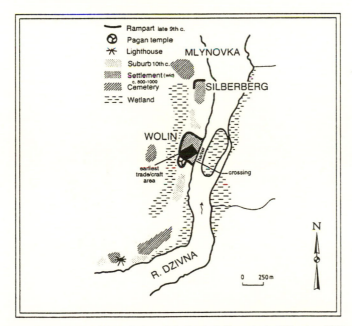

B. Wollin. (Adapted from Clarke and Ambrosiani, *Towns in the Viking Age*, 1991; Filipowiak, "Wolin," 1974)

Figure 6.4 A,B. Site Plans of Slavic-Baltic *wics*: Menzlin and Wollin

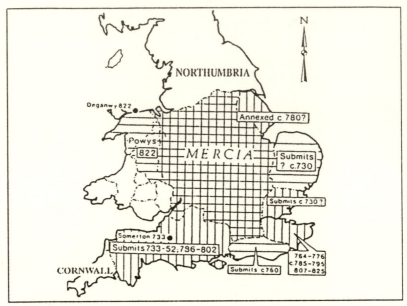

A. Mercia

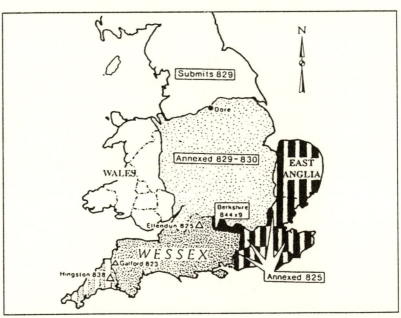

B. Wessex

Map 7.1.A,B. Growth of Mercia and Wessex (Adapted from Hill, *Atlas of Anglo-Saxon England*, 1981)

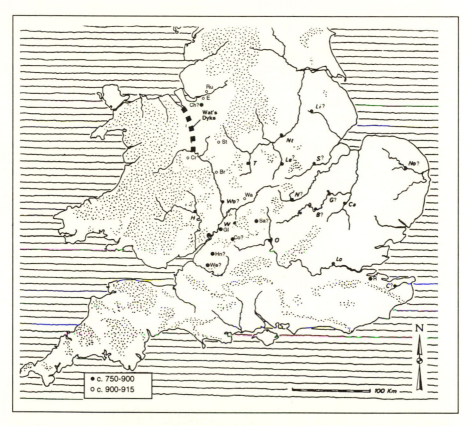

Map 7.2.A. Mercian Burghs. B – Bedford; Br – Bridgnorth; C – Canterbury; Ca – Cambridge; Ch – Chester; Co – Cockbury; Cr – Chirbury; E – Eddisbury; G – Godmanchester; Gl – Gloucester; H – Hereford; Hn – Henbury; Le – Leicester; Li – Lincoln;   Lo – London; N – Northampton; No – Norwich; Nt – Nottingham; O – Oxford;   R – Rochester; Ru – Runcorn; S – Stamford; Sa – Salmonsbury; St – Stafford;   T – Tamworth; W – Winchcombe; Wa – Warwick; We – Westbury; Wo – Worcester. (Adapted from Haslam "Market and Fortress in England in the Reign of Offa," 1987; Hill, *Atlas*, 1981)

Map 7.2.B. West Saxon Burghs. (Adapted from Hill, *Atlas*, 1981; Hinton, *Alfred's Kingdom*, 1979; Biddle, "Towns," 1976; Haslam, ed., *Anglo-Saxon Towns*, 1984)

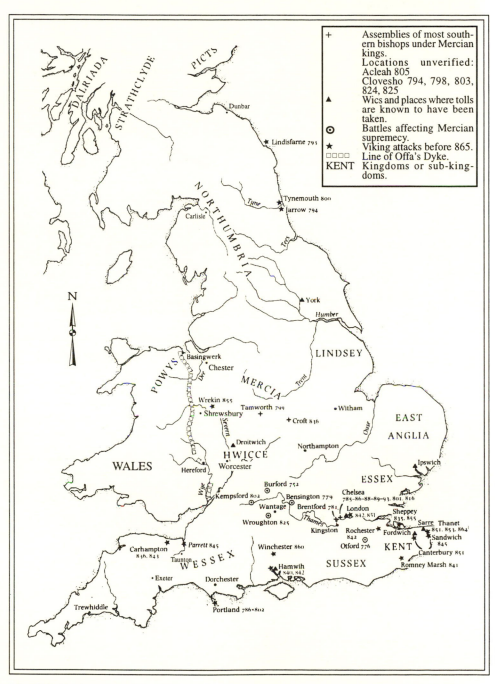

Map 7.3. England c.875 A.D. (Adapted from Campbell, ed., *Anglo-Saxons,* 1982)

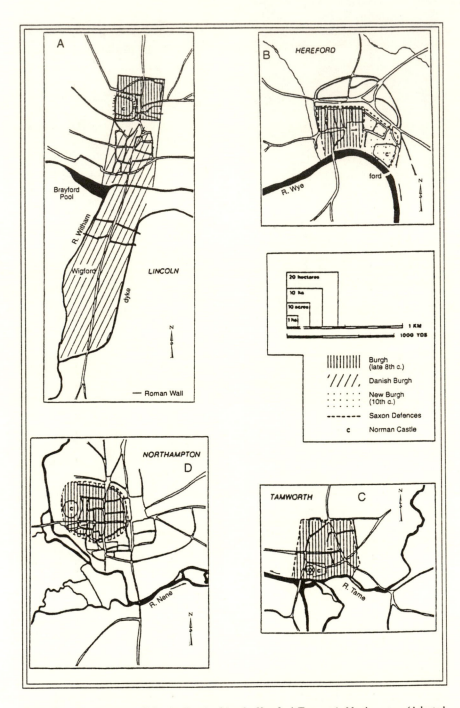

Figure 7.1 A-D. Site Plans of Mercian Burghs: Lincoln, Hereford, Tamworth, Northampton. (Adapted from Haslam, "Market and Fortress," 1987; Biddle, "Towns," 1976; Clarke and Ambrosiani, *Towns in the Viking Age*, 1991)

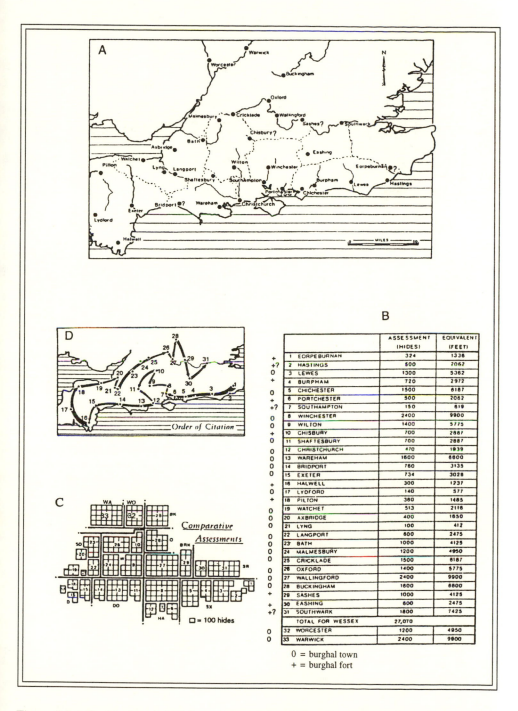

		ASSESSMENT (HIDES)	EQUIVALENT (FEET)
+	1 EORPEBURNAN	324	1338
+?	2 HASTINGS	500	2062
0	3 LEWES	1300	5362
+	4 BURPHAM	720	2972
0	5 CHICHESTER	1500	6187
+	6 PORTCHESTER	500	2062
+?	7 SOUTHAMPTON	150	619
0	8 WINCHESTER	2400	9900
0	9 WILTON	1400	5775
+	10 CHISBURY	700	2887
0	11 SHAFTESBURY	700	2887
0	12 CHRISTCHURCH	470	1939
0	13 WAREHAM	1600	6600
0	14 BRIDPORT	760	3135
0	15 EXETER	734	3028
+	16 HALWELL	300	1237
0	17 LYDFORD	140	577
+	18 PILTON	360	1485
0	19 WATCHET	513	2116
0	20 AXBRIDGE	400	1650
0	21 LYNG	100	412
0	22 LANGPORT	600	2475
0	23 BATH	1000	4125
0	24 MALMESBURY	1200	4950
0	25 CRICKLADE	1500	6187
0	26 OXFORD	1400	5775
0	27 WALLINGFORD	2400	9900
0	28 BUCKINGHAM	1600	6600
+	29 SASHES	1000	4125
+	30 EASHING	600	2475
+?	31 SOUTHWARK	1800	7425
	TOTAL FOR WESSEX	27,070	
0	32 WORCESTER	1200	4950
0	33 WARWICK	2400	9900

0 = burghal town
+ = burghal fort

Figure 7.2 A-D. The *Burghal Hidage*. (Adapted from Hill, *Atlas*, 1981; Biddle, "Towns," 1976; Keynes and Lapidge, *Alfred the Great*, 1983; Loyn,*Governance of Anglo-Saxon England*, 1984).

299

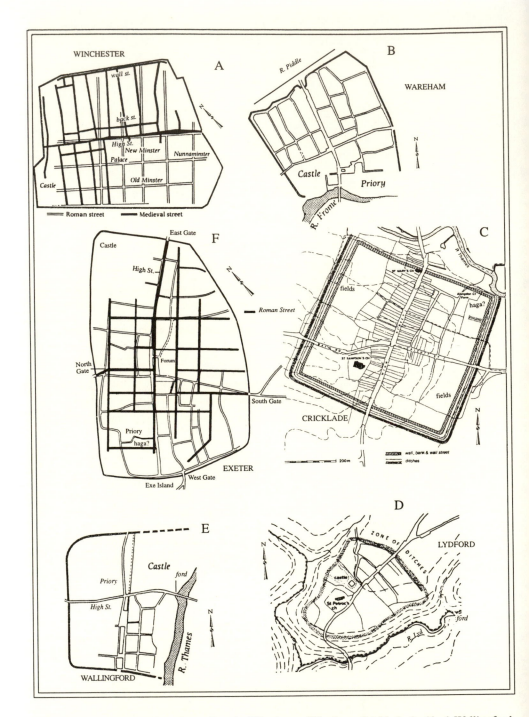

Figure 7.3 A-F. Plans of West Saxon Burghs: Winchester, Wareham, Cricklade, Lydford, Wallingford, Exeter. (Adapted from Wormald, "The Burhs," in Campbell, ed., *Anglo-Saxons*, 1982; Haslam, ed., *Anglo-Saxon Towns*, 1984; Biddle, "Towns," 1976; Ralegh-Radford, "Pre-Conquest Boroughs," 1978; Hinton, *Alfred's Kingdom*, 1979).

Index

About the Author

DANIEL G. RUSSO has taught in the fields of ancient and medieval history as adjunct assistant professor at St. Joseph College, and lecturer at the University of Connecticut, where he received his Ph.D. in history.

ISBN 0-313-30079-8

EAN

9 780313 300790

HARDCOVER BAR CODE